DENNIS SCHOLL

VALLEY MAP

Distances from Allentown

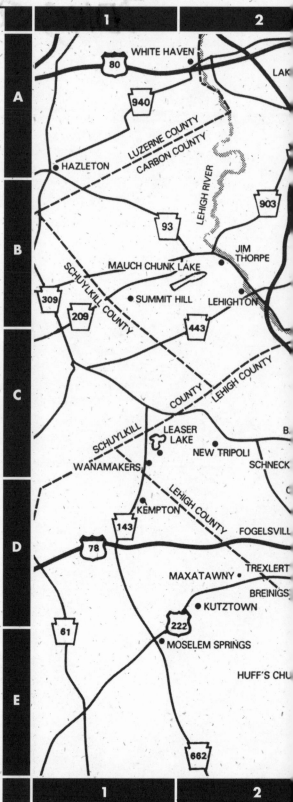

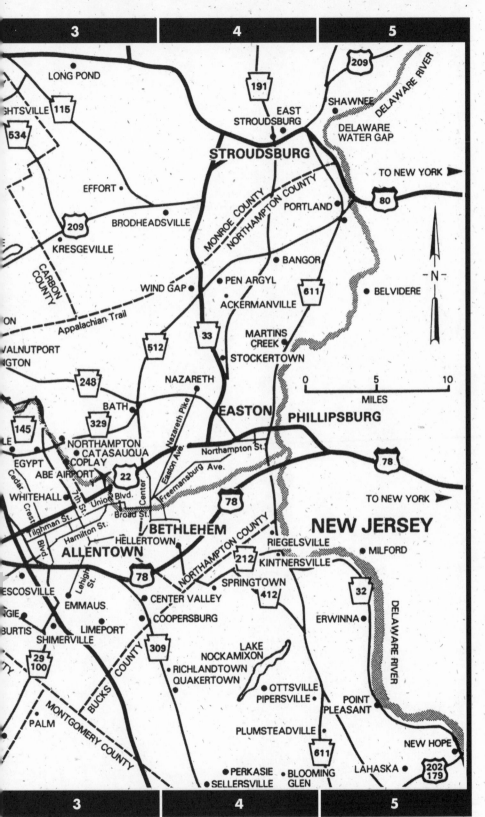

Map with permission of *The Morning Call* and *Valley Guide*

THE LEHIGH VALLEY

ROBERT HALMA
CARL S. OPLINGER

Illustrations by
Robert Halma and Lori Peters

THE LEHIGH VALLEY

A Natural and Environmental History

THE PENNSYLVANIA STATE UNIVERSITY PRESS
UNIVERSITY PARK, PENNSYLVANIA
A KEYSTONE BOOK

A Keystone Book is so designated to distinguish it from the typical scholarly monograph that a university press publishes. It is a book intended to serve the citizens of Pennsylvania by educating them and others, in an entertaining way, about aspects of the history, culture, society, and environment of the state as part of the Middle Atlantic region.

Library of Congress Cataloging-in-Publication Data

Halma, Robert, 1935–
    The Lehigh Valley : a natural and environmental history / Robert Halma,
        Carl S. Oplinger ; illustrations by Robert Halma and Lori Peters.
        p.   cm.
    Includes bibliographical references (p.   ).
    ISBN 0-271-02093-8 (alk. paper)—ISBN 0-271-02094-6 (pbk. : alk. paper)
    1. Natural history—Pennsylvania—Lehigh River Valley—Guidebooks.
        2. Lehigh River Valley (Pa.)—Guidebooks. I. Oplinger, Carl S., 1936–
        II. Title.
    QH105.P4 H35 2001
    508.748'22—dc21
    00-032673

It is the policy of The Pennsylvania State University Press to use acid-free paper for the first printing of all clothbound books. Publications on uncoated stock satisfy the minimum requirements of American National Standard for Information Sciences—Permanence of Paper for Printed Library Materials, ANSI Z39.48–1992.

C O N T E N T S

FIGURES

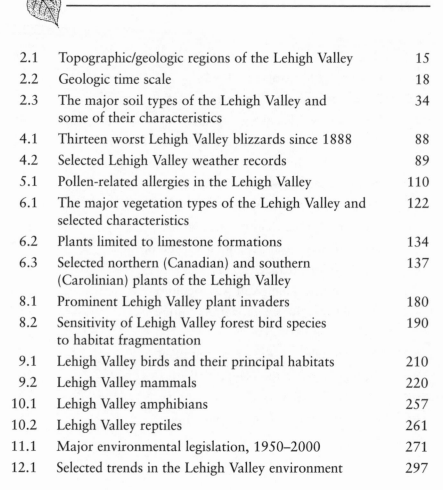

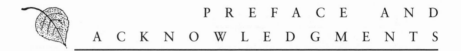

PREFACE AND ACKNOWLEDGMENTS

Mack Trucks, Bethlehem Steel, and Crayola Crayons are all widely recognized names, readily identified with the cities of Allentown, Bethlehem, and Easton, respectively. Much less widely recognized outside of the local area is the Lehigh Valley, a conspicuous physiographic valley that serves as the setting of these three major cities—a setting that is mostly ignored in conventional road maps. This delightful valley, with its fascinating natural history, is the focus of this book.

A growing interest in fitness, exercise, and outdoor activities has encouraged people of all ages to walk, hike, bicycle, canoe, and become involved in nature study. Each of these brings the participant closer to nature and raises a host of questions. "What is it? What's the name of this bug? Which tree is that? Why is it here?" Since there is no natural history guide for the Lehigh Valley, we have developed one to address the questions one might ask about the outdoors. The book is intended for the vacationer, walker, outdoorsperson, amateur naturalist, or resident—people curious about their natural environment.

The Lehigh Valley is located at about seventy-six degrees west longitude and forty degrees north latitude. It is situated close to the middle of the North Temperate Zone. The area comprised by Lehigh and Northampton Counties, covering about 730 square miles, forms the physical, cultural, and manufacturing core of the Lehigh Valley. (We do recognize that the valley is closely associated, in many natural history and other contexts, with adjacent counties. The area immediately north of the Lehigh Valley, the Poconos, is described in our book, *The Poconos: An Illustrated Natural History Guide* [New Brunswick: Rutgers University Press, 1988]. Similarly, *At The Crossroads: A Natural History of Southcentral Pennsylvania,* edited by David A. Zegers [Millersville, Pa.: Millersville University, 1994], introduces readers to the area to the southwest of the valley.)

Many contemporary natural history books with a general readership use the English system of measurement, and we use it here as well. However, we both recognize and appreciate the merits of the metric system in professional work. The following are useful conversions.

| 1 foot | 0.30 meters |
| 1 mile | 1.61 kilometers |

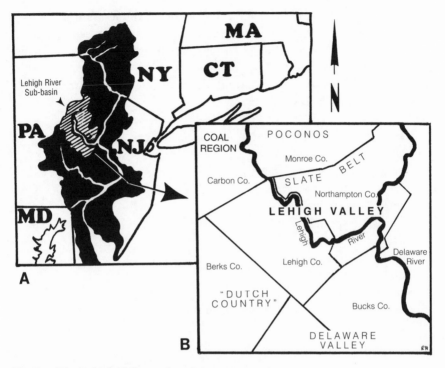

Fig. P.1 *The Lehigh Valley and environs*
A. The Lehigh Valley, seen in the context of the Delaware River basin and the Lehigh River sub-basin.
B. The Lehigh Valley (Lehigh and Northampton Counties), the Lehigh River, and the surrounding counties. The region is within three hundred miles, or a six-hour drive, of all of the large metropolitan areas of the eastern United States.

1 acre	0.41 hectares
1 square mile	259 hectares

Fahrenheit to Celsius: $°C = (°F - 32) \times \frac{5}{9}$
Celsius to Fahrenheit: $°F = °C \times \frac{9}{5} + 32$

Similarly, we use the common names of plants and animals. They are the names familiar to most of us; yet, as scientists, we recognize the value of the relatively stable technical name in comparison with the sometimes confusing common name (or names). The white potato, an important Lehigh Valley crop, may be called a potato, spud, white potato, Irish potato, Grumbiere, pomme de terre, or Kartoffel. Its scientific name, however, is only *Solanum tuberosum*.

For convenience, the common and scientific names for most species mentioned in this book are included in Appendix A. For reasons of space, we omit the technical names of some of the lesser organisms—such as invertebrates, grasses, sedges, and other nonflowering plants.

No bias is intended, but in the interest of simplicity we often use "he" to avoid the awkward he/she pronoun.

Abbreviations are largely standard in the field of natural history. Several are listed below:

xs	cross section
el.	elevation
mya	millions of years ago
fm.	formation
sp.	species
spp.	species (plural)
fls.	flowers
fr.	fruit
lvs.	leaves
cfs	cubic feet per second
mgd	millions of gallons per day

FROM THE TEXT TO THE TRAIL

This book is a hybrid of sorts. On the one hand, we have written a detailed account of the natural history of the Lehigh Valley; on the other hand, the book is both a field guide to help readers identify species, geologic formations, and the like, and a guide to inform readers about relevant attractions in the area. We see it as a text that encompasses the best features of the familiar field identification books, the more traditional "natural history/writings-about" books, and the traveler's directional guides.

There are numerous *Boxes* to help readers translate the textual material into the actual "let's see it" experience. We invite and encourage readers to extend the text into the environment of the living, dynamic Lehigh Valley. While the majority of the boxes direct the reader to the Lehigh Valley, several move into the continuing valley in Berks County and other neighboring counties. Some of the areas mentioned are public: parks, state game lands, preserves, and other easily accessible sites. For privately held areas, visitors must always secure permission from the owner first. Respect for property is important—as is respect for living organisms.

Be sure to prepare for any field excursion. The following are suggested: appropriate footgear and garments, a hand lens, a simple first-aid kit, binoculars, a notepad and pencil, a compass, a watch, a whistle (for emergencies), and a map. While some of these suggestions may be excessive, we prefer to err on the conservative side. Novices are often caught unawares in unfamiliar settings and environments.

Additionally, we recommend the following precautions.

HUNTING SEASON: During the season, it is best to stay out of known hunting areas such as state game lands. Hunting times are listed in local newspapers and posted in gun and tackle shops. Wear bright colors and proceed with caution.

INSECT PROBLEMS: Mosquitoes, deerflies, bees, blackflies, wasps, and hornets bite or sting. Insect repellent, combined with long-sleeved shirts and trousers, will give some measure of protection. Ticks may occur in moist brushlands, forest edges, and along trails. They readily attach themselves to the clothing or skin of passing hikers. Plain, light-colored clothing can help visitors spot these uninvited guests more easily. Ticks can transmit illnesses such as Lyme disease, and an attached tick should receive prompt attention. An application of alcohol or ammonia will usually cause the tick to release its hold after fifteen or twenty minutes. Call a medical center for more information on identifying and removing ticks.

POISONOUS SNAKES: The copperhead occurs uncommonly in the Lehigh Valley and, like most snakes, prefers rocky wooded areas (like those on the Blue or South Mountains). The timber rattlesnake is confined to the rocky ridges of the very northern edge of the valley. Both species are reclusive. They may bite if provoked or suddenly surprised by an invasion of their immediate space. Exercise caution and common sense.

RABIES: This is an acute, often fatal, viral disease of the central nervous system that occurs in a number of animals, but is transmissible to humans. Never approach or attempt to handle any strange-acting or unusually friendly wild animal. Similarly, never directly handle any dead animal, such as a "road kill."

POISONOUS PLANTS: The ubiquitous poison ivy can grow just about anywhere. It will climb trees, clamber over fences, sprawl out in the middle of a field, and invade the garden. It is easily identified by its three *shiny* leaflets (Fig. 6.6). Other plants to avoid or treat with respect include the stinging nettle (Fig. 8.6), poison sumac, and the numerous thorny or prickle-bearing plants, such as many of the brambles, some vines, and roses. Certain plants (or parts of plants) are poisonous if eaten, including some of the deadly Amanita mushrooms that are found in the Lehigh Valley. A useful book by Robert J. Hill and Donna Folland,

Poisonous Plants of Pennsylvania (Harrisburg, Pa.: Pennsylvania Department of Agriculture, Department of Plant Industry, 1986), lists about a hundred toxic species. Avoidance is the only safeguard. In the event of a suspected poisoning, identification is very important. The Delaware Valley Regional Poison Center number, serving the Lehigh Valley, is **1-800-722-7112.**

People Shaping the Environment

The counties of Lehigh and Northampton have a combined population of more than 550,000 persons who enjoy a relatively clean environment in a pleasant blend of city and country, manufacturing and farming, and traditional and modern architecture. Who helped shape and define this environment? Who are the present-day spokespersons for maintaining its quality? We can name several of the early settlers, such as the Moravians, who helped set the direction of the Lehigh Valley's development. But a few individuals have demonstrated (and, in some cases, continue to demonstrate) exceptionally keen environmental insight, support, awareness, and foresight. Here, we identify a number of those special people in mini-biographies (or *Cameos*) that are interspersed throughout the text. Usually they dovetail with a particularly relevant topic, but some people simply defy classification.

Continuing in the Field, Forest, or Garden

We hope that readers will find this guide enjoyable and instructive at home, in the yard, and in the field. The design and sequence of the book follows.

Chapter 1, "Lehigh Valley Patterns and Places," sketches an overview of the Lehigh Valley and provides a review of some fundamental principles of ecology.

Chapter 2, "The Geological History," leads the reader through the vast history of geologic time and explains how the valley was molded by both tectonic and geologic processes to its present physiography.

From the glacial episodes, we shift into Chapter 3, "Human History in the Lehigh Valley," in which we trace the influence of the native Americans and the early Moravian and German settlers on the development of deciduous forest land into an agricultural and urban environment.

Following the geologic and human histories, Chapter 4—"The Climate of the Valley"—deals briefly with those favorite conversation pieces, the climate and the weather. For the next several chapters, then, we invite the reader to look at a mostly biological environment: seasons, native vegetation, agricultural plants, roadside organisms and "islands," animals, and wetlands and watercourses.

Chapter 5, "The Natural History of the Seasons," walks with the reader through the months of the year in the valley with observations on the points of interest, change, anticipation, and reflection.

"Native Vegetation," the focus of Chapter 6, describes the general flora of the Lehigh Valley with detailed drawings to help visitors identify many common indigenous trees, shrubs, vines, and flowers.

In contrast to Chapter 6, Chapter 7, "The Agricultural Lehigh Valley," addresses more commercial plantings: grains, fruits, vegetables, lawns, and dairy farms. In addition, the chapter discusses regenerative agriculture.

Chapter 8, "Fragmented Forests, Edges, and Patches," takes up issues that have become increasingly important elements of our environment as development, farms, and various corridors continue to dissect our original forests. This chapter deals with the many edges and their effects—such as the invasion of weeds and numerous aliens that are becoming incorporated into our flora and fauna.

Throughout the various communities are an assortment of both native and introduced species of animals—the focus of Chapter 9, "Animals of the Lehigh Valley." The chapter moves from bats and butterflies to deer, bobcats, chipmunks, and shrews.

Water environments merit particular concern. Chapter 10, "Watercourse and Wetland Communities," deals with these special and protected areas, including river edges, swamps, marshes, ponds, creeks, and others. Water is the element connecting all these areas, and the community of plants and animals reflects this unique medium.

After reviewing the natural history of the Lehigh Valley, then, the book analyzes the quality of the environment and relevant laws. Chapter 11, "Environmental Legislation and the Valley," reviews the standards against which we evaluate our quality of life from an environmental perspective.

Following Chapter 11, we look to the future and ask difficult questions: "How will the preservation of land and natural areas balance out with the desire for development and recreation?" This is only one of several ongoing dilemmas discussed in Chapter 12, "Envisioning the Environmental Future of the Lehigh Valley." Central to that future is the continuing progress on the Delaware and Lehigh National Heritage Corridor, which will link the rich history of the valley to the experiences of citizens today and tomorrow.

THE NEXT STEP

The goal of this book is to present an overview of the natural history of the Lehigh Valley. Therefore, we have avoided extensive consideration of any one area—but we do recognize the need for additional information.

Appendix A provides a common-to-scientific and scientific-to-common name directory of most of the plants and animals in the book.

Appendix B helps direct the reader to selected websites in both a general and chapter-specific format. Far from exhaustive, it is nevertheless a reasonable guide for those who prefer to do web research.

Finally, there is a bibliography, arranged by chapter, for the entire book. In addition to the sources listed, there are many excellent identification manuals, field guides, and other audiovisual aids to field study. Bookstores often stock a wide range of guides for different levels of interest.

Assistance for a project such as this comes in many guises. We appreciate the careful reviews of certain chapter drafts provided by several local professionals: Bruce Rowell of Kutztown University; Anthony Verbalis of Cedar Crest College; Penn State Cooperative Extension Service Agent Bob Leiby; and the late Bill Dovico, meteorologist with the National Weather Service. Carolyn Nippert and Charlotte Fisler, both of the Cedar Crest College library staff, assembled the websites for Appendix B. Frederic Brock and Tom Kerr provided insightful comments about the future of the Lehigh Valley (see Chap. 12). We are also appreciative of the Penn State reviewers: Robert Brooks, for his careful reading of the manuscript and his equally thoughtful constructive remarks; E. W. Miller, for encouraging us to retain our focus on the Lehigh Valley; and Lee Stout, for help and guidance in a number of areas across many of the sub-disciplines. Students Karen Haase and Kathy Pearl were helpful in a variety of capacities. The book is better because of the hundreds of creative and inquiring minds that were part of our numerous field experiences—our students. Our families and college colleagues provided moral support and encouragement through a variety of book-writing delays. Foremost in coping with our interruptions, rewrites, and alterations was our superb typist, Linda Klosek.

Partway through this project, we engaged Lori Peters, a recent graduate of Cedar Crest (and award-winning art major) to "help" with some of the sketches. Her skills quickly led us to have her do about half of the artwork. Each illustration is identified by initials: L.P. signifies Lori Peters's work, and R.H., Robert Halma's. Sonja Schneider of Muhlenberg College did several sketches and is identified with those.

A number of the illustrations are based on other works, modified from them, or copied from them with permission. In particular, we wish to thank the *Morning Call,* Rutgers University Press, and the Pennsylvania Geological Survey.

The authors also wish to thank Sandy Thatcher, director of the Penn State Press, for the green light on the project when our work was still in its earliest stages. Last, we are most appreciative of the financial support from our respective institutions, Cedar Crest and Muhlenberg Colleges, granted through their faculty development committees.

Lehigh Valley Patterns and Places

Catasauqua, Cedar Creek, Zionsville, Iron Run, Slatedale,
Tatamy, Trexlertown, Chestnut Hill, Hokendauqua,
Siegfrieds Bridge, Mill Creek, Furnace Hill, Bethlehem,
Swabia Creek.

—BENJAMIN L. MILLER, "SELECTED TOPONYMY," 1939, 1941

More than four centuries ago, William Shakespeare asked the question,
"What's in a name?" The curious observer may ask the same question
about the Lehigh Valley. Many Lehigh Valley place names are based on
the family names of settlers, names of Indian origin, or settlers' occupa-
tions. Other place names honor the colonists' birthplaces or refer to bib-
lical names. And surprisingly often, valley place names are associated
with biological or geological features of the region. The early settlers had
an intimate association with the environment, and the place names they
used frequently marked the significance of natural settings. Names such
as Sandstone Ridge, Willow Run, Flint Hill, and others indicate that settlers used ecological markers before the word *ecology* was even coined.

What's in a name, indeed. What's in the name "Lehigh Valley"? "The
valley of the Lehigh River is *not* the Lehigh Valley." So wrote Richmond
E. Myers, longtime dweller in the valley (see Cameo 2.2). The Lehigh
Valley is a short section of the Great Valley region that runs from the
Saint Lawrence Valley to central Alabama. Our valley is bounded on the

north by the Blue (Kittatinny) Mountain ridge and on the south by the Lehigh Mountain range, known locally as South Mountain. For the purposes of this guidebook, we consider the Delaware River the eastern edge of the Lehigh Valley; the western edge fades into the drainage area of the Schuylkill River of neighboring Berks County. To know this fascinating area thoroughly, the naturalist or visitor must first consider the underlying environmental patterns that shape the valley—as they do elsewhere on the planet. This introductory chapter will present principal environmental patterns, and subsequent chapters will elaborate details of the more prominent patterns as they are seen in the Lehigh Valley.

GEOLOGIC PATTERNS

Geologists have identified physiographic provinces for our reference area (see Fig. 1.1). The Lehigh Valley is in the Great Appalachian Valley Section of the Ridge and Valley Province, bounded on the north by the even-crested, narrow-ridged Blue (Kittatinny) Mountain and on the south by South Mountain. Blue Mountain is a part of the Appalachian Mountain Section of the Ridge and Valley Province and extends in a southwest direction from the Delaware River to the Susquehanna River. The principal rock type of this mountain is quartzite of the Silurian era. South Mountain, composed mainly of Precambrian gneiss, represents a small portion of the New England Province, which enters Pennsylvania from New Jersey and continues to the southwest, terminating in isolated hills south of Robesonia, Berks County. (The Pennsylvania portion of the New England Province is called the Reading Prong.) The northern portions of the Great Valley are principally composed of shales, sandstones, and slate laid down in Ordovician times and designated the Martinsburg Formation. The southern half of the valley is composed of limestones and dolomites of Cambrian age. The impact of glacial movement on the valley, the intricacies of caves and sinkholes, and the geological history of the region are explored in Chapter 2.

DRAINAGE PATTERNS

The vast majority of streams in the study area flow into the Lehigh River, which enters the Delaware River at Easton. On the western edge of the

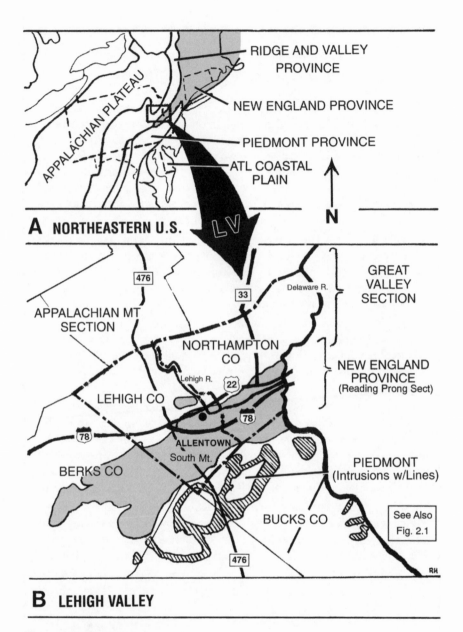

A NORTHEASTERN U.S.

RIDGE AND VALLEY PROVINCE

NEW ENGLAND PROVINCE

PIEDMONT PROVINCE

ATL COASTAL PLAIN

APPALACHIAN PLATEAU

LV

N

GREAT VALLEY SECTION

Delaware R.

APPALACHIAN MT SECTION

NORTHAMPTON CO

Lehigh R.

NEW ENGLAND PROVINCE (Reading Prong Sect)

LEHIGH CO

ALLENTOWN
South Mt.

BERKS CO

PIEDMONT (Intrusions w/Lines)

BUCKS CO

See Also Fig. 2.1

B LEHIGH VALLEY

Fig. 1.1 *Geologic map*
A. The northeastern United States.
B. The Lehigh Valley area.
The Lehigh Valley is bordered on the north by the Blue (Kittatinny) Mountain, which also includes the two-county northern line; on the south, by the southern downslope base of South Mountain; and on the east, by the Delaware River. The valley fades westward into Berks County.

BOX 1.1

Overlook Views of the Lehigh Valley

BAKE OVEN KNOB. The highest point in Lehigh County, this elevated dome presides over the valley at sixteen hundred feet—and resembles an old-fashioned "bake oven" on Blue Mountain. It may be reached by taking Route 309; just north of the Germansville area, turn east off of Route 309 onto Mountain Road, and then head north on Ulrich Road. This small road soon becomes a narrow, twisting gravel and dirt road. Proceed to the state game lands parking lot at the top of the ridge. Take the hiking trail to Bake Oven Knob.

HAWK MOUNTAIN. This world-renowned wildlife sanctuary in Berks County maintains two lookouts that provide a more distant view of the valley. At the Lenhartsville exit from Route I-78, proceed north for several miles and look for signs to Hawk Mountain. Open to members and others for a nominal daily trail pass fee.

PULPIT ROCK AND THE PINNACLE. Near Hawk Mountain, these Berks County promontories also offer views of the valley. They are located about three miles northwest of the Lenhartsville exit from Route I-78. From Pulpit Rock, one can hike northwest about two miles to the Pinnacle.

MOUNT PENN SCENIC LOOKOUT. Located on Mount Penn (a continuation of the Reading Prong, locally called South Mountain) at an elevation of about one thousand feet, this spot overlooks the Reading area and offers a long-distance view of the Great Valley. A pagoda and a lookout tower can be found on Skyline Drive, which can be accessed from a number of roads east of Reading.

SHIMERVILLE HILL. At the junction of Routes 29 and 100, south of Macungie, a popular light refreshment stand has parking, benches, and ice cream—all of which enhance the views of the western sections of the valley and of what colonial settlers called the "Macungie Plains."

MOUNTAINTOP CAMPUS OF LEHIGH UNIVERSITY. Visitors will find a panoramic view of the entire valley from an elevated enclosed observatory, Stabler Tower, in Iacocca Hall. The tower is generally open M–F, 9:00 A.M.–5:00 P.M. From Route 22, take I-378 south for five miles. On South Mountain, take a jughandle loop (east) onto Mountain Drive West. Follow the signs to campus and to Iacocca Hall.

APPALACHIAN TRAIL. Hikers may view parts of the valley from several sites on this scenic trail, which runs along the Blue Mountain ridge on the northern border of the valley.

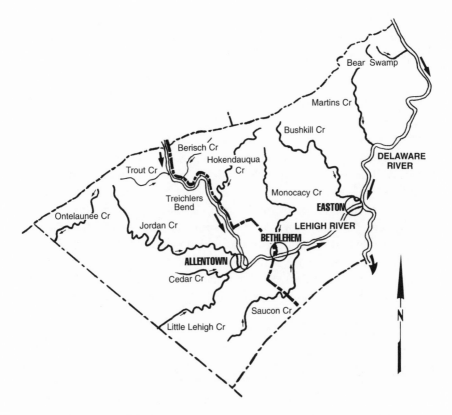

Fig. 1.2 *Major Lehigh Valley stream and river drainage*
Seven major streams drain the Lehigh Valley into the Lehigh River–Delaware
River systems. In the northwestern corner of Lehigh County, the Ontelaunee
Creek drains into the Schuylkill River.

valley, drainage is into the Schuylkill River, which itself drains into the
Delaware further south at Philadelphia. From its headwaters on the table-
like Pocono plateau, the Lehigh River drops about fifteen hundred feet
through the narrow band of resistant rocks of the Appalachian Mountains and emerges through the Blue Mountain at Palmerton. From
Palmerton to its mouth at the Delaware River, a distance of thirty-seven
miles, the Lehigh has dissected the softer shales, dolomites, and limestones
into an undulating, low-relief valley bounded on the north by the Blue
(Kittatinny) Mountain and on the south by the Lehigh Mountain range.
At Rockdale, the Lehigh River meets a ridge of hard sandstone and is
forced to turn east for about a mile. A major fault at Treichlers allows the
Lehigh to return to a southward flow. Thus, a great S-curve is formed, one
easily seen by travelers using Route 145 (which crosses the river by way

of Treichlers Bridge). When the Lehigh reaches Allentown, it encounters crystalline rocks, the gneisses of the Lehigh Mountain. The river is deflected to the east and moves on to its merger with the Delaware.

SOIL PATTERNS

The complex origins of soil are outlined in Chapter 2. But, in brief, soil has played a notable part in the region's history. German immigrants, who had landed in Penn's colony in the early 1700s, were drawn to settle in the Lehigh Valley partly by its rich soils—soils produced by the weathering of the limestones that constitute the southern half of the valley. The shale loams of the northern portion of the valley typically have good drainage, and with proper care, they have been productive for many generations of farmers. (The diverse crops grown in the Lehigh Valley include hay, field corn, wheat, soybeans, alfalfa, and potatoes.)

CLIMATE PATTERNS

Moderate might serve as a succinct description of climate patterns in the Lehigh Valley. Precipitation ranges from forty to forty-five inches. Rainfall occurs evenly throughout the summer months, and droughts of long duration are unusual. Severe thunderstorms and hurricane episodes are also rare events. Snowfall is variable; most storms produce fewer than ten inches, but blizzards have made their presence known in the valley, accompanied by winds that create drifts of several feet (see Table 4.1). Many veteran weather watchers argue that freezing rain is a more common occurrence in recent decades. The daily temperature range for a typical year (1992) is shown in Figure 4.1: the monthly range is generally fifteen to twenty degrees, and rare are the days with excessively low or high temperatures.

VEGETATION PATTERNS

The original deciduous forest that greeted the earliest European settlers to the valley has mostly been reduced to isolated woodlots or terrestrial "islands." These remnants are part of what was an oak chestnut forest until a blight in the early decades of the twentieth century almost eliminated chestnut trees from the region. Now a mixed oak forest with a wide variety of native and invasive tree species characterizes the remaining stands of trees. Other vegetation patterns include the floodplain and wetland communities, the flora of the slopes of Blue and South Mountains, and the wooded patches of varying size and shape—privately or publicly owned—that are squeezed among the urban and suburban communities, industrial zones, rural and agricultural lands, and transportation and utility corridors that crisscross the valley.

ENERGY FLOW PATTERNS

The most fundamental ecological pattern in the Lehigh Valley (and almost every other region on earth) is the pattern of energy flow. Though unusual places, such as deep-sea thermal vent communities, constitute exceptions to this rule, the one-way flow of energy from sunlight permits the varied life-forms on earth to flourish. Our sun, a middle-aged star ninety-three million miles from earth, is a "thermonuclear device" with temperature and composition such that it transforms hydrogen into helium with the release of tremendous amounts of energy. This energy, in the form of electromagnetic waves, travels through space; some of it—about one-billionth of the total output—reaches the outer atmosphere of the earth, a tiny, distant target in the vastness of space. Solar radiation is attenuated as it passes through the atmosphere, and half or more of the energy is absorbed, diffused, or diffracted as it travels toward the surface of the earth. Some of the solar energy that reaches the earth is reflected from the surface back into the atmosphere; some of this radiation, in turn, is trapped by "greenhouse gases," producing a natural greenhouse effect that allows Earth to avoid the temperature extremes typical of planets such as Mars and Venus.

Incredibly, less than 2 percent of the solar radiation reaching plants is used by them (and, ultimately, by the other life-forms on the planet). With the use of chlorophyll or other pigments, plants trap this elusive prey, light, and start the conversion of radiant energy into chemical energy in the intricate process of *photosynthesis*. Plants take in inorganic compounds (i.e., carbon dioxide and water) and combine them with the energy from sunlight to form organic compounds such as glucose, which is composed of carbon, hydrogen, and oxygen. The chemical energy stored in the bonds of these organic compounds is the source of energy for plants themselves and, directly or indirectly, for other life on earth. As plants engage in photosynthesis, they also produce oxygen. Plants must continually expend energy to stay alive even as they engage in photosynthesis. Therefore, they use a means of controlled breaking of bonds of fuel, such as glucose, in cellular respiration.

All energy transformations, including photosynthesis, obey the two laws of thermodynamics. With any transformation of energy from one form to another, energy is neither created nor destroyed (first law). The second law is readily seen in nature: when energy is transformed from one form to another, some of the energy is degraded into lower-quality, more dispersed energy. This degraded energy is usually in the form of heat energy.

The second law of thermodynamics is evident in the transformation of energy through the food chain. Plants serve as the base of the food chain. As *herbivores* (plant eaters) consume plants, the laws of energy dictate that with each energy transformation, some of the potential energy is transformed into heat. Thus there can never be as many plant eaters as plants. As *carnivores* (flesh eaters) eat herbivores, energy degradation dictates that fewer carnivores than herbivores will be found in a particular region. The inevitable heat losses with each transformation in a food chain, or more complex food web, means that top-level carnivores will always be rare.

While a continual one-way flow of energy from the sun makes life possible, the stuff of life—matter—is recycled. Bacteria and fungi, called "decomposers," are capable of degrading dead plants and animals as well as animal wastes. (Decomposers derive energy for their own functioning in this process, and some, called *anaerobes,* can do so even in the absence of oxygen.) So Nature has employed recycling for almost four billion years! (See Fig. 1.3.)

ECOSYSTEM PATTERNS AND CONCEPTS

The assemblage of plants and animals in a particular setting (for instance, a lake, forest, or meadow) and the interactions of those plants and animals result in an intricate, dynamic community termed an *ecosystem*. Intermeshed with the flow of energy among the various life-forms of an assemblage is the equally important cycling of matter between the nonliving and living components of such a community. One

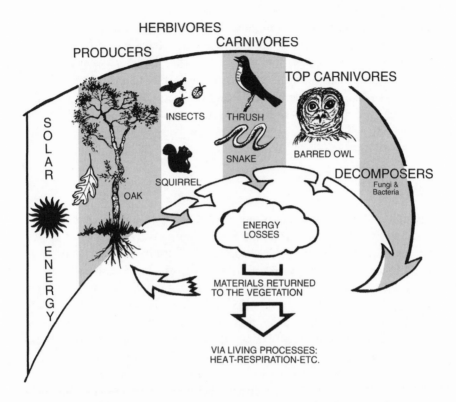

Fig. 1.3 *Energy flow and the cycling of matter in a generalized terrestrial community of the Lehigh Valley*

characteristic pattern is the cycling of *elements* between the living and nonliving components of an ecosystem. Such cycles are termed *biogeochemical cycles. Gaseous cycles,* those involving nitrogen, hydrogen, and oxygen, for example, have the earth's atmosphere or hydrosphere (the oceans) as the nonliving reservoir. The much slower *sedimentary cycles,* which involve elements such as phosphorus, sulfur, or iron, have the lithosphere (the earth's crust) as the reservoir.

The availability of vital elements, such as nitrogen or phosphorus, greatly influences the distribution and abundance of plants. An element, generally present as an inorganic compound, is picked up initially by green plants and incorporated into structural components such as sugars, lipids, and proteins. When plants are eaten by animals, the element may eventually find itself enmeshed in the structure of the animal. When plants and animals die, the element, often converted into complex organic compounds that form most of the structural features of plants and animals, must be pulled apart so that it can be taken up again by plants. Here is where those decomposers, the bacteria and fungi, play their vital role in biogeochemical cycles: they convert organic matter into inorganic compounds, the form available to plants. Since the amounts of individual elements present on the planet have not substantially changed since the earth's formation, it is clear that the matter of the planet has been recycled for billions of years.

Niche

The organisms that interact in an ecosystem carry out a particular role or function within the grand patterns of energy flow and matter cycles; that is, they fill a *niche* in the ecosystem. A useful analogy may be to think of the habitat in which an organism lives as its "address" and the niche as its "occupation." Some species have narrow niches; these "specialists" may live in only one microhabitat or set of conditions. Red-backed voles are small rodents that are found almost exclusively in two microhabitats—either in cool, shaded, rocky ravines where mossy rocks and decaying logs cover the forest floor, or along the edges of an adjacent sphagnum bog. American larch (tamarack), also typical of cool shady ravines, is a specialist plant. Other plants and animals, the "generalists," have broad niches. The white-footed mouse may be more common in wooded and semiwooded tracts, but it is not uncommon in brush land and along fencerows. In winter, it invades crop lands and, given the opportunity, settles into nearby cabins or homes. In contrast to tamarack, red maple may be viewed as a generalist plant species that tolerates a broad range of soil and climate conditions; it can be found on the dry slopes of a mountain ridge or in the swampy sections of a stream valley.

Life Histories

Members of an ecosystem exhibit distinctive differences in reproductive patterns or life histories. Certain species are said to be "opportunists," since they readily take advantage of random or unpredictable events that may occur in a region. These species can quickly locate a suitable place to settle and tend to have a broad tolerance of varied physical conditions in the environment. They are able to mature rapidly and produce large numbers of young that usually receive little or no assistance or care from the parents; individuals may only live to reproduce once. Opportunists also possess a variety of techniques to permit some members of the population, typically the young, to disperse to other suitable habitats even if adult mortality is high. Some biologists refer to opportunists as "r-strategists" (from the symbol r in the logistic equation): these are species whose population growth is on the "rising" part of a logistic growth curve.

The alternative life history pattern, found in species said to be "K-strategists," achieves a different kind of balance: organisms are able to maintain their population level at equilibrium or carrying capacity (the symbol K in the logistic equation). These "equilibrium species" are stable populations with long-lived individuals. The individuals mature more slowly, engage in delayed and repeated reproduction, produce few young and, in animal species, exhibit complex care and protection. In plant species, young are provided with stored food to assure them a good start in life. These species are able to sustain stable, persistent populations at carrying capacity, provided that there are no drastic alterations to the region. However, K-strategists lack the qualities of dispersal and broad tolerance to varied habitats that make the opportunists such good colonizers and pioneers of disturbed habitats. Obviously, both types of strategies have served organisms well in the long-term history of life on our planet.

SUCCESSION PATTERNS

In any land region on the earth, there are distinctive communities of plants and animals—such as those found in tropical rain forests, deserts, and tundra—that ecologists refer to as *biomes*. These biomes are the long-term results of climates typical of their regions of the world. The annual range in temperature and the amounts and patterns of precipitation are the principal factors that determine the formation of particular biomes. In our part of the world, the major biome is the temperate deciduous forest. Given time and freedom from disturbance, our region would mostly be covered with a forest composed of several types of oaks and hickories with a sprinkling of a few other hardwood species, such as ash, beech, birch, and maple.

During the early stages of life on the planet, bare rock served as the site for a succession of life-forms, starting with highly specialized organisms called lichens, a mutualistic association of algae and fungi. Over time, the activities of the lichens and the weathering processes, such as freezing and thawing, formed soil. Then mosses and ferns could take over, followed by annual plants, woody shrubs and, eventually, trees. Such *primary succession* is rarely witnessed, although cooled lava flows or rocks exposed by a retreating glacier can mimic the conditions of ancient times. A more common type of primary succession occurs in aquatic settings. Lakes may start with open water and a bottom barren of life; over time, numerous plants and animals will take their places in the succession of a lake into a shallow pond. Terrestrial *secondary succession*—that is, the sequence of vegetation that will develop if an abandoned farm field is left free of human intervention—is a phenomenon that most of us have witnessed. (Old field succession, a pattern frequently studied by ecologists in various regions of the country, is described in Chap. 8.)

ANIMAL PATTERNS

The types and distribution of plants are pivotal in determining what kinds of animals will be present in a region. Although well-established vegetation types such as mixed oak or beech-maple forest are recognized by authorities and genuinely useful in natural history study, animal patterns are not so evident. The mobility of animals and their adaptability to varying conditions have challenged the animal biologists who hoped to duplicate the work of their botanist colleagues. Between 1890 and 1910, C. Hart Merriam divided the North American continent into zones or regions to mark the northern and southern breeding limits of animals, especially mammals, amphibians, and reptiles. Merriam's scheme would place our area (and the rest of southeastern Pennsylvania) in the Carolinian Faunal Area. The south flank of the Blue Mountain would be the boundary of the zone to the north, the Alleghenian Faunal Area. (The merits and flaws of the life-zone system were reviewed by S. Charles Kendeigh in the mid-1950s.)

The intricate interplay of factors that have produced the patterns outlined here, combined with the universal flow of energy and the complex cycling of matter between living and nonliving components everywhere on the planet, make our Lehigh Valley a worthy (and handy) site for nature study.

The Geological History

[T]his theory [plate tectonics] by its conception, its nature, and its definition was applying for the job of Prime Mover. The name on the door changed. There was no alternative. The theory was panterrestrial, panoceanic. It was the past, the present and the future of the world, sixty miles deep. It was every scene that ever was on earth.

—JOHN MCPHEE, *In Suspect Terrain,* 1983

Running water, the greatest of all erosive forces on the earth's surface, has been cutting gradually (and, in a human lifetime, almost imperceptibly) into the shales and limestones of the Lehigh Valley. Headward erosion ever so slowly lengthens each tributary feeding the Lehigh and Delaware Rivers, while the abrasive downcutting processes lower the water channels. The channels, in turn, feed on the slopes that are infinitesimally retreating, widening the stream valleys. These forces have combined, for millions of years, to shape the valley into a gentle and low-relief topography. A casual visitor traversing the Lehigh Valley from east to west would hardly note any significant topographic change; by contrast, a north-south trip offers quite the opposite perspective.

A general map of the Lehigh Valley reveals distinct topographic regions (see Fig. 2.1 and Table 2.1). From the north, in order, they are the Blue (Kittatinny) Mountain, the shale/slate region, the limestone

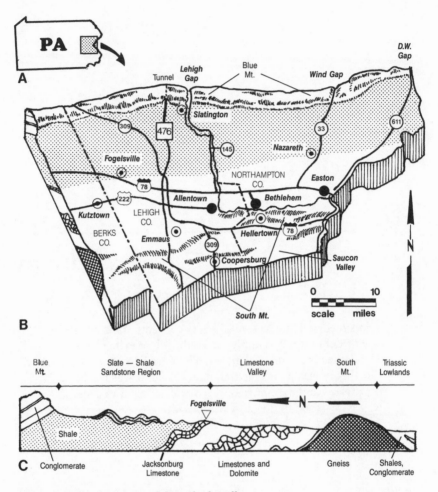

Fig. 2.1 *Bedrock geology of the Lehigh Valley*

A. The setting for the Lehigh Valley.

B. Bedrock. The five major geological regions are shown, along with reference roads, cities, and towns. Boundaries are general. (Rock ages are in Table 2.1.)

C. Generalized cross section. The cross section runs north to south through the Fogelsville area in Lehigh County. There is considerable vertical exaggeration. The Jacksonburg Formation, important in the manufacture of portland cement, has irregular outcroppings in Lehigh County but makes up a fairly well-defined band in Northampton County.

Table 2.1 *Topographic/geologic regions of the Lehigh Valley*

Characteristics	Blue Mountain	Shale (to Slate) Region	Limestone Valley	South Mountain
Location	Narrow northwest boundary of Lehigh Valley	Northern half of valley; north of line: Fogelsville-Nazareth-Belvidere, N.J.	Southern half of valley, from Fogelsville-Nazareth-Belvidere, N.J. to base of South Mountain	Southern boundary of Lehigh Valley
Topography	Even-crested linear mountain ridge, with gaps	Flat-topped stream divides; hillside slopes rounded; steep by streams; billowy	Broad; flat; little relief	Irregular mountains with offshoots; steeper on the north-facing slopes
Elevation (feet)	1,400–1,600 (at crest)	500–800	200–500	500–1,000
Formation	Tuscarora conglomerate and sandstone	Martinsburg shale/slate; sandstone	Jacksonburg, Beckmantown, Allentown, and Tomstown limestones	Pochuck gneiss of Reading Prong
Geological period and age (mya)	Silurian (408–438)	Ordovician (438–505)	Cambrian (505–570)	Precambrian (570–1,600?)
Principal rock type	Sedimentary to recrystallized-metamorphic quartzite	Sedimentary (shale and sandstone) to metamorphic (slate)	Sedimentary; largely recrystallized into low-grade marble	Metamorphic; crystalline
Other names	Kittatinny; Endless; First	Slate Belt (where suitable for that industry)	Cement Belt (the narrow belt of Jacksonburg limestone used for cement)	Durham Hills; Reading Hills; Lehigh Mountain

valley, and South Mountain. (A fifth region, the Brunswick conglomerate and mostly red shales of the Triassic, barely catches the very southern edge of the valley.) The first three regions belong to the Ridge and Valley Province, and the southern two of these are the "valley portion" of the Great Valley—a more or less continuous valley from Canada to Alabama. This Great Valley, predominantly composed of carbonate rocks, changes names according to local tradition: Shenandoah; Tennessee Valley; Champlain; for us, of course, the Lehigh Valley. To the west of this long sinuous valley lie the highly folded Appalachians, marked on their eastern border by the nearly continuous Blue Mountain. (The Lehigh Valley regions are summarized in Table 2.1.)

THE PRIME MOVER

The image of the continents slowly sliding about like lubricated pieces of a giant jigsaw puzzle must have stirred the imaginations of many before him, but it was geologist Alfred Wegener who, in 1924, formally proposed a theory of drifting continents. Largely due to Wegener's lack of a conceptual mechanism to move the continents, the theory fell out of favor until the 1960s, when new and creative elements of evidence—principally from the ocean floor—supported and expanded on the idea. It is widely accepted today under the title of *plate tectonics,* and it provides the framework for explaining the origins and geomorphology of the Lehigh Valley.

The mechanism that eluded Wegener was the slow, continual circulation of hot material from the earth's center upward through the mantle and the downward return of the same material, now cooled. The lithospheric plates slowly slide about on the asthenosphere (a soft, weak zone below the outer rigid lithosphere) and are driven by the convection currents.

Following the formation of the earth as a planet some 3.8–4.5 billion years ago (bya), a Laurentian block was created by the accretion of smaller plates. This single crustal block became the stable craton of North America. From its elevated central core, running water carried eroded sediments eastward into the shallow and warm Iapetus Ocean, which covered eastern North America. Parts of that deposition, which continued throughout the Cambrian period, are the carbonates, including the 500-million-year-old limestones that form the southern bedrock of the lower Lehigh Valley.

The somewhat quiescent, largely depositional Cambrian graded into the more restless and dramatic Ordovician, and during this early period

CAMEO 2.1
Three Early Geologists

In the first half of this century, geologist Alfred Wegener made a crucial contribution to scientific knowledge with his theory of drifting continents—and three other geologists advanced our knowledge of the Lehigh Valley. Benjamin LeRoy Miller, in addition to his research and numerous publications at Lehigh University, was the senior author of *Northampton County, Pennsylvania: Geology and Geography* (1939) and *Lehigh County, Pennsylvania: Geology and Geography* (1941). Combined, these two texts provide a thousand-page earth science framework for the valley. Edgar T. Wherry, from the University of Pennsylvania, wore many academic hats: in addition to geology, he also knew plant geography, ecology, botany, and chemistry. Although he published widely on the geology of the Triassic, the Lehigh Valley, and Pennsylvania, biologists may remember him for his books on flowers and ferns. Bradford Willard, an expert on the stratigraphy of the Paleozoic in Pennsylvania, chaired Lehigh University's Geology Department for many years. His *Pennsylvania Geology Summarized* (1962) introduced countless students and the general public to the exciting geology of the Commonwealth.

Three geologists; three areas of expertise; three contributors to the Lehigh Valley. And, probably, three geologists restlessly waiting for the revival of continental drift.

the first of three major Paleozoic-era *orogenic* (mountain-building) events occurred. In the Ordovician, a new volcanic landmass emerged east of North America. Its westward thrust onto the plate margin caused the Taconic Orogeny. Subsidence created the Appalachian basin, and for two hundred million years the basin received the sediments from the Taconic Mountains. Near the end of the Devonian period, a collision among Europe, Avalonia, and northeastern North America created the new Acadian Mountain range—an event called the Acadian Orogeny. As the basin filled and subsided, it became an alluvial plain; during the many advances (transgressions) and retreats (regressions) of the shoreline during the Carboniferous period, the vegetation of the swamps and peat bogs eventually became the extensive coal seams of Pennsylvania.

It was the third mountain-building episode near the close of Paleozoic era, however, that most significantly changed the Pennsylvanian

Table 2.2 *Geologic time scale*

YEARS AGO	ERA OR EON	PERIOD	ACTIVITY AFFECTING PENNSYLVANIA	MAIN ROCK TYPES OR DEPOSITS IN PENNSYLVANIA	DOMINANT LIFE FORMS IN PENNSYLVANIA
0 to 2 million	CENOZOIC ERA	QUATERNARY	Glaciation; periglacial erosion and deposition	Sand, silt, clay, gravel	Mammals, including humans
2 million to 67 million		TERTIARY	Weathering and erosion; creation of present landscape	Sand, silt, gravel	Mammals, grasses
67 million to 140 million	MESOZOIC ERA	CRETACEOUS	Erosion and weathering	Clay, sand	Dinosaurs, mammals, birds
140 million to 208 million		JURASSIC	Diabase intrusions; opening of Atlantic Ocean	Diabase	Dinosaurs, mammals, birds
208 million to 250 million		TRIASSIC	Separation of North America from Africa; sedimentation in rift valley	Shale, sandstone, diabase	Dinosaurs, early mammals and birds
250 million to 290 million	PALEOZOIC ERA	PERMIAN	ALLEGHANIAN OROGENY: Collision of Africa and North America; mountain building, thrust faulting, and folding; much erosion	Sandstone, shale	Insects, amphibians, reptiles
290 million to 365 million		PENNSYLVANIAN AND MISSISSIPPIAN (Carboniferous)	Alluvial deposition; eastward advance of shoreline followed by development of low, flat alluvial plain	Sandstone, siltstone, shale, coal, limestone	Trees, ferns, amphibians, air-breathing molluscs, insects
365 million to 405 million		DEVONIAN	ACADIAN OROGENY: Collision of Avalonia, Europe, and North America; formation of Catskill Delta	Conglomerate, sandstone, shale	Fish, amphibians, insects, land plants
405 million to 430 million		SILURIAN	Erosion of mountains; deposition of sand and mud	Conglomerate, sandstone, limestone	Corals, fish
430 million to 500 million		ORDOVICIAN	TACONIC OROGENY: Thrusting of volcanic arc; development of Appalachian basin	Shale, limestone, dolomite	Molluscs, bryozoa, graptolites
500 million to 570 million		CAMBRIAN	Transgression of the sea; carbonate deposition	Limestone, dolomite, quartzite	Trilobites, brachiopods
570 million to 2.5 billion	PROTEROZOIC EON		Accretion of microplates to form Laurentia	Schist, slate, marble	Blue-green algae, jellyfish, worms
2.5 billion to 3.8 billion	ARCHEAN EON		Bombardment by meteorites; creation of continental crust	None identified	Bacteria
3.8 billion to 4.5 billion	PRE-ARCHEAN EON		Formation of Earth and solar system	None identified	None identified

SOURCE: Barnes and Sevon 1996. With permission of the Commonwealth of Pennsylvania, Bureau of Topographic and Geologic Survey.

landscape: the Alleghanian Orogeny. The African and North American plates collided, which caused a deformation in the old Appalachian basin and raised an Alleghany mountain range about two and one-half miles high! The Piedmont Province has some of the remnants of that Permian range. The Appalachian Mountain section of eastern Pennsylvania was forced and compressed into numerous folds. At the end of the Permian, the major continents were joined together into a supercontinent called Pangaea. (Table 2.2 is a helpful synopsis and reference for those seeking more detail about the historical geology of Pennsylvania.)

The Mesozoic era, for Pennsylvania, was one of major change: the region was transformed from a depositional basin into an above-sea-level area, and it continued to experience erosion that subsequently sculpted the landscape features we see today. The resistant and folded ridges (such as the Blue Mountain) are reminders of a Silurian and Devonian past, and the valley itself is an expression of the Cambrian and Ordovician ages, more than five hundred million years ago—geologic features now significantly eroded into gentle relief.

Late in the Mesozoic, changing convection currents caused Pangaea, the supercontinent, to start to break apart. The African lithospheric plate moved southeastward relative to the North American plate, and as the separation (called "seafloor spreading") progressed, magma was forced upward to become "new rock" at the mid-Atlantic rift. (The spreading between Africa and North America continues at the rate of about two inches per year.) Continental separation during this era also formed long parallel troughs, bounded by faults, termed *rift basins*. One close to the Lehigh Valley, called the Gettysburg-Newark basin, partially falls between South Mountain and northern Philadelphia. The rift is mostly filled with Triassic-Jurassic red sandstone and shale, along with some igneous diabase intrusions.

The Cenozoic era was, for the most part, a continued period of erosion: much of our area was lowered by hundreds of feet, with the more resistant rocks becoming the higher ridge tops and the softer rocks—such as limestone and shale—becoming the valleys. Late in the Cenozoic era, during the Pleistocene epoch of about two million years ago, glaciers added another signature to the Lehigh Valley.

Rocks, Minerals, and Dollars

As suggested in Table 2.1 and implied from Figure 2.1, the Lehigh Valley has a modest variety of rock types for its size. A few of these, however, have especially helped shape the direction and economy of the valley. They are limestone, slate, iron, and (in the proximal Saucon Valley) zinc.

Limestone abounds in the southern half of the valley. The beds average nearly a mile in thickness. Being made largely from calcium carbonate ($CaCO_3$) and dolomite ($CaMg[CO_3]_2$), limestone is good, in powdered form, for "sweetening" the soil. Most of the farms throughout the valley at one time had their own "mini-quarries," from which the owners extracted the limestone, burned it in one of the numerous kilns, and spread it on the fields. Many of these residual quarry holes are now abandoned, filled with rubbish, and overgrown with weed trees such as aspen, sumac, and gray birch. The island-like tree clumps in the middle of fields are silent testimony to an earlier day, when liming was a do-it-yourself chore. Limestone continues to be used as flux for iron, for the manufacture of lime, and as crushed stone. Prior to the middle of the last century, limestone was used for construction stone; many local grand old hotels, taverns, and historic homes are readily recognized by their soft gray limestone walls, often featuring narrow white bands of calcium carbonate within the rocks.

The particular limestone that early on became valuable to the Lehigh Valley was an outcropping of the Jacksonburg Formation, a band about a mile wide, east to west, at the contact with the Martinsburg Shales (see Fig. 2.1). This particular carbonate rock type had the right mix for the manufacture of American portland cement—first made in the Lehigh Valley in 1871 by the Coplay Cement Company, founded by David O. Saylor, who also received a patent on the manufacturing process. By 1900, the Lehigh Valley was producing about 70 percent of the portland cement used in the United States. Names such as Coplay Cement, Lehigh Portland Cement Company, the Whitehall Cement Manufacturing Company, and others are familiar ones to longtime Lehigh Valley residents.

What limestone was to the southern Lehigh Valley, another rock type was to the northern communities: slate. Under the exceptional heat and pressure of lithospheric plate collisions, fine-grained rocks such as shale can metamorphose into slate. It is a particularly fine-grained rock, which (owing to the compressional stresses placed on it) develops fine lines of cleavage that yield durable and rigid sheets. Hence, it became useful for chalkboards, curbing stones, and billiard table tops, and it is still in evidence today locally in stately old buildings and in roofing slate. By World War II, the Lehigh Valley supplied nearly half of the slate produced in the United States. From its tentative start shortly after 1800, the slate industry became crucial to the northern communities of the valley, such as Slatington, Pen Argyl, and Slatedale, for well over one hundred years. In

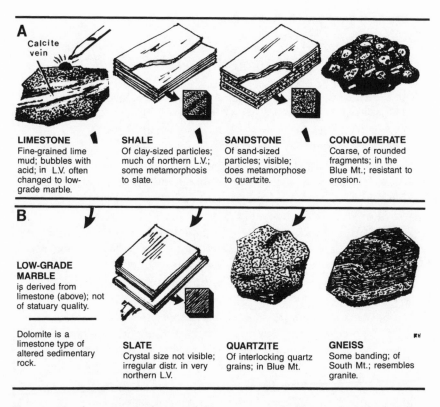

A

Calcite vein

LIMESTONE
Fine-grained lime mud; bubbles with acid; in L.V. often changed to low-grade marble.

SHALE
Of clay-sized particles; much of northern L.V.; some metamorphosis to slate.

SANDSTONE
Of sand-sized particles; visible; does metamorphose to quartzite.

CONGLOMERATE
Coarse, of rounded fragments; in the Blue Mt.; resistant to erosion.

B

LOW-GRADE MARBLE
is derived from limestone (above); not of statuary quality.

Dolomite is a limestone type of altered sedimentary rock.

SLATE
Crystal size not visible; irregular distr. in very northern L.V.

QUARTZITE
Of interlocking quartz grains; in Blue Mt.

GNEISS
Some banding; of South Mt.; resembles granite.

Fig. 2.2 *Hand specimens of some of the common rock types in the Lehigh Valley*
A. Sedimentary rocks. Limestone (or dolomite) is common in the southern Lehigh
   Valley.
B. Metamorphic rocks. These rock types comprise part of the Blue and South
   Mountains. South of South Mountain (in the Coopersburg-Hosensack area and
   on to Philadelphia), the bedrock is Brunswick conglomerate and red shale
   intruded by igneous diabase (trap rock). The whole area is part of the Juras-
   sic/Triassic Piedmont Physiographic Province, formed during the separation of
   North America and Africa.

the post–World War II period, synthetic materials cut substantially into
the slate market. A drive along such roads as Routes 33 and 476, just
south of Blue Mountain, reveals numerous piles of waste slate—remind-
ing the visitor of a Lehigh Valley geological resource.

  Iron ores are less regularly distributed than limestone or slate is
throughout the valley, yet these ores were also important to the valley's
early economy. In the late 1800s, surprisingly, Lehigh County led all of
the counties of Pennsylvania (and Pennsylvania, in turn, led the nation)
in iron ore production. With the opening of large steel mills in eastern

BOX 2.1

Exhibits of Minerals and Rocks

GILMAN MUSEUM. The museum has a display of worldwide minerals. It is situated at Lost River Caverns, just east of Route 412 in Hellertown. No charge for display only. Call (610) 838-8767 for tour information about limestone caverns.

LAFAYETTE COLLEGE. The Department of Geology, housed in Van Wickle Hall, maintains displays of minerals and rocks in the hallways. The college is just west of Sullivan Trail, about a mile north of Route 22 in Easton.

LEHIGH COUNTY MUSEUM. Located in the Old Courthouse at Fifth and Hamilton Streets, Allentown, the museum has a geology exhibit featuring rock samples of the county's geological column and a room of thirty-seven Lehigh Valley minerals. An adjacent geology garden features local rocks. Open to the public.

LEHIGH UNIVERSITY. Several large display cases with rocks and minerals are sponsored by the Department of Earth and Environmental Sciences, located in Williams Hall. The university is located in South Bethlehem, just east of Route 378.

MORAVIAN COLLEGE. The Collier Hall of Science (North Campus), at Main and Locust Streets in Bethlehem, has ten display cases of rocks, minerals, and fossils on the ground floor. The lobby features an active seismometer display.

THE READING PUBLIC MUSEUM. Located at 500 Museum Road, the museum boasts mineral, rock, fossil, and gem collections, including a display of Cambrian trilobites. There is a nominal admission charge. Take the West Reading Penn Avenue exit from Route 422; proceed for several blocks to Fifth Avenue (also called Museum Road); turn left (south) and travel about one-half mile to the museum on the right side of the road. Call (610) 371-5850 for museum hours.

Pennsylvania in the early twentieth century, local ore companies increased their own furnace capacities to try to meet the demand. Ultimately, as the steel industry continued to grow, it sought larger external ore sites and imported most of its ores. Local furnaces could not compete, and they slowly died out. Like the piles of waste slate, occasional slag heaps recall a once-thriving iron industry.

Like the special "cement" limestone of the Jacksonburg Formation, a distinctive zinc ore called "zincblende" was discovered near

Friedensville in Saucon Valley. A small section of this valley—a down-blocked section (called a "graben") of limestone, roughly 8 miles long by 2 miles wide, just south of South Mountain—contains the zinc deposits. Friedensville had the first entirely successful zinc furnace in the United States; the high-grade ore was used for zinc paints, brass, and the like. The operation was not without problems. Large pumps had to be installed in the deep mines to keep the groundwater from flooding the operation, and the functioning (and cessation) of the pumps moved the water table up and down, causing area supply problems. But water in any limestone bedrock can cause another set of problems: sinkholes.

SINKHOLES AND STALACTITES

Surface erosion is largely visible to the observer. But enormous erosion can result from a generally invisible source as well: groundwater. Groundwater dissolves soluble rocks; for the Lehigh Valley, that's limestone. In the precipitation process, carbon dioxide (CO_2) dissolves in the rain water, forming weak carbonic acid (H_2CO_3). As the acidified water permeates the land, it percolates through the fissures, fractures, and pore spaces in the rocks, slowly eating away at the calcium carbonate. (The process may be hastened a bit by the recent addition of anthropogenic acid rain.) Small cavities enlarge; large cavities become caves; caves go unnoticed—until the roof collapses, sometimes in a rather spectacular way! (See Fig. 2.3.) The resulting crater-like depression is called a sinkhole. One of the most highly publicized local sinkhole-related events was the slow collapse, in 1994, of the new Corporate Plaza Building in downtown Allentown. The building gradually lost its structural integrity as the foundation shifted, and a few weeks after the sinkhole-triggered process started, the building was demolished. At the time, Department of Environmental Resources geologist William Kochanov noted that Allentown was home to one of the state's worst sinkhole sites.

Sometimes the underground chambers become connected into a maze of sorts, forming an extensive cave system worthy of exploration. Lehigh County alone has more than twenty-five identified and mapped caves; almost all are on private property and not accessible. Three commercial caves with stalactites, stalagmites, and other exemplary cave features are noted in Box 2.2.

While we tend to think of limestone primarily in erosional terms, as in the case of sinkholes, calcite may also deposit itself as a household

Fig. 2.3 *A dump truck in a sinkhole in South Whitehall* The startled driver was, ironically, hauling a load of fill to plug another sinkhole. (Drawn from a Wayne Perry photograph in the *Morning Call,* 1979. With permission.)

impediment—in the form of bathtub rings, hard water, glassware stains, clogged water heaters, and the like. Water softener companies thrive, appropriately, in the Lehigh Valley.

GLACIERS IN THE VALLEY

In our review of the shaping of the North American plate and, in particular, of eastern Pennsylvania, we have come to appreciate the paradigmatic theory of plate tectonics—or, as writer John McPhee labels it, the Prime Mover. Running water has been the principal agent in reshaping those Prime Mover configurations by the relentless process of erosion. And so, perhaps one to two million or so years ago (a wink in geological time), the basic Lehigh Valley geology—and geography—was set: the granitic gneiss of South Mountain, the low-relief limestones, the northern hilly shales, and the sinuous and resistant Blue Mountain. But one last chapter was written by yet another force: ice.

As the climate of the earth cooled, the accumulating snow and ice mass built up to many thousands of feet in thickness in Canada, and it slowly advanced southward. Two episodes of cooling and subsequent glaciation left imprints on the Lehigh Valley. The first, or Illinoian— named after the state in which it was first mapped—receded about 150,000 years ago; the second, or Wisconsinan, barely reached the valley and then receded about 13,000 years ago.

Box 2.2

Places of Geological Interest

CAVES. Several dozen caves have been located and mapped throughout the limestone area—almost all on private property. Three commercial ones include:

CRYSTAL CAVE. In the Great Valley, take the Krumsville exit (Exit 5) from Route I-78 onto Route 737, and drive to the cave. Guided tours. The rock shop and museum are free of charge. Tours for a fee. Call (610) 683-6765 for more information.

LOST RIVER CAVERNS. (See Box 2.1, Gilman Museum.) Informative tours of the caverns—billed as "Nature's Underground Wonderland"—are available all year long. Call (610) 838-8767 for details.

ONYX CAVE. In the Great Valley, exit from Route I-78 at U.S. Highway 615; drive three miles to the stoplight, and turn left on Route 662. Follow the signs to the cave, which features tours and a natural rock museum.

CEMENT. The Jacksonburg Formation of limestone forms a narrow SW-NE band (see Fig. 2.1) in the Lehigh Valley—one easily identified by the alignment of smokestacks in the area—and outcrops along some of the roads. The historical Coplay Cement Kilns, which rise above the Saylor Park Cement Industry Museum, are worthy of a visit. The Atlas Cement Company Museum is adjacent to the Northampton Borough Municipal Building. Take MacArthur Road (Route 145) north to Route 329; go right (east) to the third light, and turn right onto Seigfried Street (which becomes Laubach Street). Look for the museum on the left. The museum has limited hours of operation, but offers tours by appointment. Call (610) 262-2576 for information. Donations are welcome.

CONGLOMERATE. The Shawangunk Formation is the principal formation of the Blue Mountain. Rounded quartz pebbles are cemented in silicaceous matrix; it is the hardest rock of the Lehigh Valley. There are excellent exposures at both the Lehigh Gap and the Delaware Water Gap. Several places of note along the Appalachian Trail that have good outcroppings *and* excellent views are Bears Rock, at the junction of Lehigh, Carbon, and Schuylkill Counties; Bake Oven Knob (see Box 1.1); and Wolf Rocks, described as the best view in eastern Pennsylvania along the Trail. Wolf Rocks is located one and one-half miles east of Fox Gap at Route 191.

BOX 2.2 (CONTINUED)

FOSSILS. Owing to rock flowage, shearing, and other tectonic forces, the Paleozoic rocks of the valley have poorly preserved fossils. Examples include bryozoans ("moss-animals"), stromatolites, graptolites, crinoids, and brachiopods. Please refer to Box 2.1 for information on fossil displays. A very few places are described in *Fossil Collecting in Pennsylvania*. Several dinosaur tracks in Triassic rock were discovered in 1978 along Route 309, just south of Coopersburg. This site, however, is not open to the public.

GNEISS. *Gneiss* is the granitic metamorphic rock of South Mountain, predominantly composed of quartz and feldspar. It outcrops at various places: some large exposed dark-colored boulders, combined with a spectacular view of Saucon Valley, can be seen at Bauer Rock (Big Rock), elevation 1,038 feet. From South Fourth Street (Allentown), go to the top of South Mountain, and proceed east on East Rock Road for about one-half mile; look for the radio tower and the astronomy society's observatory.

CAMEL'S HUMP. An impressive double-hill gneiss outcropping is located about one-quarter of a mile south of Route 22, near Route 512—and is a familiar landmark to motorists.

ELEPHANT ROCK. A weathered gneiss outcropping, roughly resembling an elephant in profile, can be found about one mile west of the intersection of Route 611 and Raubsville Road, Raubsville Village, along the Delaware River. Hexenkopf Rock (located at the top of Hexenkopf Hill, about three miles northwest of Riegelsville) is also a gneiss exposure.

IRON ORE. Historic Lock Ridge Furnace is a restored anthracite-fired iron furnace that was operational between 1867 and 1920 and is now open to the public. It is situated on the east side of Alburtis; look for signs to the park and museum. The Goetz Mine Sanctuary is a sixteen-acre abandoned open-pit iron ore mine in the center of the Pointe North residential development; it is located just west of Route 512, north of Route 22. The walking trail and meadow are part of a Wildlands Conservancy conservation easement.

LIMESTONE. Large cement plants, active quarries, and manufacturing are still important in the area. Inquire locally. Williams Quarry, located on Route 611—1.3 miles north of the junction of Routes 611 and 22—has excellent limestone and marble exposures. Visitors must obtain permission through the Department of Geology at Lafayette College in Easton.

BOX 2.2 (CONTINUED)

RIFT BASIN. Africa and North America, long fused together, started to separate about 220 million years ago, resulting in long troughs called *rift basins*. The Gettysburg-Newark basin, between Newark, N.J. and Gettysburg, Pa., lies between South Mountain and northern Philadelphia. It is an easy drive south along Routes 309, 313, 412, or 476; visitors will see mostly red sandstones and shales of the Triassic and Jurassic periods. The hills are an igneous diabase, somewhat neutral to gray in color, and blocky. Local areas of the rift basin just south of the Lehigh Valley include Center Valley and Saucon Valley.

RINGING ROCKS. A certain kind of igneous rock, called *trap rock,* can become broken into large pieces from periglacial action (regular freezing/thawing cycles). Some pieces respond to hammer taps with distinctive ringing sounds. The largest "ringing rock" boulder field in the East is located about one mile west of Upper Black Eddy (along the Delaware River) in a Bucks County park. Look for signs.

SANDSTONE. Both sandstone and shale form most of the bedrock of the northern half of the valley. (See Fig. 2.1.) State Game Land No. 205, immediately to the east of Route 100 and one mile north of Lyon Valley, has good shale outcroppings. Jacobsburg State Park, near the Belfast exit from Route 33, features sandstone exposures.

SINKHOLES. For the most part, developing sinkholes are quickly filled in by workers, since the sinkholes can pose a threat to public safety. Substantial sinkholes in residential areas usually make the front pages of local newspapers. Observe them with *caution*—sinkholes often grow. Occasional small "sinks" can be observed in fields and fallow land as large "dimples."

SLATE. Slate production is limited to the northern edge of the valley. Scores of excavations and mountains of waste slate can be observed around communities such as Pen Argyl, Bangor, and Slatington; good examples can also be found at Route 33, just west of Wind Gap, and at Route 476 just south of the turnpike tunnel. Any visit to a slate operation should be preceded by a telephone call. The Slate Belt Museum, on Route 611 near Route 512, Mt. Bethel, is open on summer weekends from 1:00–5:00 P.M. It features regional history, photos, tools, and displays, and a donation is suggested. Call (717) 897-6181 for details. The newly opened Slate Belt Heritage Center displays the traditions and accomplishments of the slate belt forefathers. Special exhibits emphasize Italian, Welsh, and Cornish cultures (among others) and the slate and textile industries. The museum is open on weekends,

---

BOX 2.2 (CONTINUED)

April through October, and at other times by appointment (call [610] 588-9985). For general information, call (610) 588-3434. Donations are appreciated. 30 N. First Street, Bangor.

WATER GAPS. The famous and highly scenic Delaware Water Gap can be observed from a comfortable rotunda on Route 611. There is a vertical exposure (about 1,200 feet) of the Blue Mountain conglomerate and sandstone cut by the Delaware River. The Lehigh Gap at Palmerton, cut by the Lehigh River through the Blue Mountain, marks the Lehigh-Northampton county line.

WIND GAPS. A wind gap is a water gap in which the water has been diverted or captured. (Route 33 passes through the geologic wind gap and just west of the town of Wind Gap.) Others on Blue Mountain include Little Gap, just north of Danielsville in Northampton County, and Lehigh Furnace Gap, about two miles southeast of Ashfield, in Carbon County.

The Illinoian glacier spread southward, but when it encountered those resistant and roughly parallel ridges of the South and Blue Mountains, it was forced to yield to their established barriers. Thus, the Illinoian flowed southeastward, filling most of the Lehigh Valley, and finally reached its terminus against much of South Mountain—as far west as Emmaus and thence northwestward along an irregular band west of the Lehigh River. (See Fig. 2.4.) While the ice advance stopped, the flowage continued; much debris in the form of sand, silt, clay, and miscellaneous boulders was deposited, forming a loosely defined band about a mile wide and, presently, twenty to thirty feet high, called a *terminal* (end) *moraine*. The band has the appearance of a subdued "swell and sag" topography—a kind of bumpy and knobby look—that one can best see in the few remaining woodlots (much of the rest of the surface has been modified by human activity).

The Illinoian glacier slowly retreated and, in the intervening 150,000 years, water and other agents have worn down the glacial signatures to a more subdued look. The moraine is now subtle, and requires a second glance: ponds have mostly closed in; streams have enlarged and developed the soil profile; humans have reshaped the veneer. Thousands and thousands of years will do that to a moraine.

(John McPhee points out that some of the great golf courses of the world, such as St. Andrews, are on terminal moraines; moraine

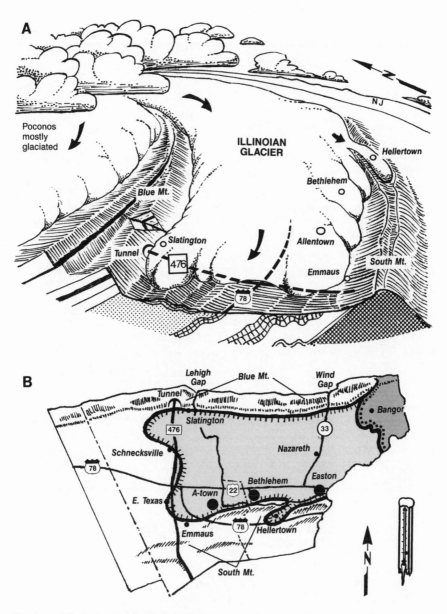

Fig. 2.4 *Glaciation in the Lehigh Valley*

A. Schematic of the Illinoian glacier. Note how the glacier was forced into the valleys (though a small lobe did invade the Hellertown area). This schematic depicts the appearance of the Lehigh Valley about 150,000 years ago. The glacier was approximately 1,000 feet in thickness. All of the present-day tall buildings in the Lehigh Valley would have been deeply buried under the ice. (Redrawn from a sketch by Ken Raniere published in the *Morning Call,* July 23, 1981. With permission.)

B. Map of the area and location of the terminal moraines. The Illinoian glacier margins are marked with a hatch-marked line. The Wisconsinan glacier, which receded about 13,000 years ago, was limited to the northeastern corner of the Lehigh Valley. It is marked here with a line and small squares.

BOX 2.3

Places to See Glacial Signatures

BOULDER FIELDS. Near the terminus of the glacier, diurnal changes of freezing and thawing broke loose large boulders. Hickory Run Boulder Field, a registered national landmark located in neighboring Carbon County, has an extensive field of sandstone boulders. "Devil's Potato Patch" is located on the east side of the crest of the road, just north of Danielsville. "River of Rocks" can be seen from the south lookout at Hawk Mountain (see Box 1.1) and is accessed by hiking trails. Inquire at Hawk Mountain. *Taluses,* the accumulations of rock fragments found at the base of mountains and ridges, are periglacial (around the glacier, or near its terminal extent) signatures along the lower slopes of both the Blue and South Mountains.

ESKER. An *esker* is a long sinuous ridge of glacial drift deposited by a stream beneath a glacier. B. L. Miller mentions an excellent one about one and one-half miles southwest of Portland, in Northampton County. It rises about forty feet above the surroundings and is nearly a mile long.

GLACIAL LAKES. They are especially prominent in the Poconos (Lake Harmony, Saylors Lake, Bruce Lake, and so on) and are of special note in New York State as the Finger Lakes. In Upper Mount Bethel Township, many swamps and some lakes, such as Lake Minsi, were due, in part, to the Wisconsinan glacier. Glacial *till,* or unsorted glacial deposits, covers much of this previous icescape. "Fencerows," composed of a variety of stone types, are characteristically found

topography is naturally suited to elevated tees, bunkers, and the like. In Lehigh County, the Shepherd Hills [public] and Lehigh Country Club [private] golf courses are on the moraine. We will let golfers determine their greatness. We only offer the geology.)

The Wisconsinan glacier was a very recent beat in geological time, and touched only the far northeastern part of Northampton County (see Fig. 2.4). Like the Illinoian, it left a terminal moraine, but—owing to the glacier's relatively recent visit—the moraine is much more conspicuous. It runs from Belvidere through the Bangor area, up and over the Blue Mountain just east of the Little Offset (Route 191). A trip through the area is a convincing ride through Pleistocene glacial geology. The recent glacial scouring and depositional processes left behind a number of poorly drained areas, including the swamps, lakes, and wetlands of northeastern Northampton County, of which Lake Minsi is central.

BOX 2.3 (CONTINUED)

between bordering farm fields; they represent glaciated landscapes cleared of surface rocks for farming.

TERMINAL MORAINE. A *terminal moraine* is a small ridge, typically about a mile wide, of material ("a pile of rubble") deposited at the edge of maximum glacial advance. The Illinoian terminal moraine is relatively subtle, due to its age—150,000 years. It tracks southeastward along the northern base of South Mountain to Emmaus, thence north to East Texas and Wescosville, on to Krocksville, and out to Schnecksville (see also Fig. 2.4). Look for hummocky woodlots and general hill-and-swale topography. The Wisconsinan terminal moraine is very conspicuous from the Foul Rift (at the Delaware River, one and one-half miles south of Belvidere) to Martins Creek, through Factoryville and Ackermanville, to Bangor and north to the Blue Mountain near Fox Gap. The TeKening Hiking Trails, located on the Martins Creek property of the Pennsylvania Power and Light Company facility on the Delaware River, are open to the public and have classic exposures of the Wisconsinan terminal moraine; the site is a few miles east of Route 611, near Martins Creek, and is easily recognized at a distance by the tall cooling towers. The trail runs through a typical mixed tulip tree–ash–oak forest (see Chap. 6).

VALLEY TRAIN DEPOSITS. Outwash from the melting glaciers created the floodplain deposits bordering the Delaware River along Route 611 and continuing south through Route 32.

Trails abound in the area and their scenic delight is enhanced by the northern backdrop of the immutable Blue Mountain.

Though the immense scale of glacial geology may capture the imagination, and though limestone and slate belts helped to steer the economic course of the Lehigh Valley, a more homely resource, perhaps, deserves our most careful consideration: the soil.

LEHIGH VALLEY SOILS

Soil is the loose surface material of the earth in which plants grow. While the definition is simple enough, soil itself is very complex. For most of us, the soil is largely invisible, masked by grass and pavements.

CAMEO 2.2

Richmond E. Myers (1904–1994)

Known affectionately as "Rocky Myers" by his countless students, Richmond Myers was Professor of Geology for many years at Muhlenberg and Moravian Colleges. He was a scholar-teacher of wide interests, including history, literature, agriculture, and music; his passion, though, was for rocks. From 1955 to 1972, he channeled his interests into a weekly parade of colorful popular articles, mostly on Lehigh Valley geology and history, for the local newspapers. The highlights of selected pieces were published in book form in 1972 as *Lehigh Valley the Unsuspected*. He helped the public cross from the unsuspected to the understood.

But to grasp the complexity and variability of the soil system, and to appreciate the nature of the Lehigh Valley soils, we must understand how soil is formed (see Fig. 2.5).

About six major factors contribute to the formation of soils: the parent rock, topographic setting, history/time, climate, biological influences, and composition. Given that there are wide variations within each of the major groupings, the possible combinations of factors are endless. Evolving over time from this collection of influences, the soil develops into layers, or horizons. They typically appear in the following order: the O horizon of surface litter; the A horizon, or organically rich topsoil with maximum biological activity; the B horizon, or subsoil (mostly clay); and the C horizon, or unconsolidated material from the bedrock. The succession of horizons is called the *soil profile*.

Soil scientists now place all soils into one of ten broad soil groupings, or orders, each name ending in the suffix *-sol*, meaning soil. For the Lehigh Valley, the soils are, for the most part, in the order *Alfisols:* they have gray to brown surface horizons, subsurface horizons of clay accumulation, and are usually moist. The Alfisols comprise many different series (somewhat similar to the familiar biological species), and the series names make up the mappable units of the valley.

The Soil Survey Maps of both Lehigh and Northampton Counties are aerial photographs overprinted with reference marks (major roads, schools, and the like) onto which the soil series boundaries and codes are printed. The whole thing looks like a curious monochrome jigsaw puzzle. But it is from these pieces of the puzzle that one can gather much detailed information. For soil mapping units such as Washington, Fleetwood, Trexler, and so on, one can quickly look up information on slope, degree of erosion, depth to bedrock, moisture-holding capacity, mineral composition (gravel, sand, silt, and clay percentages), and bedrock type, as well as the general capabilities of the soil, woodland and building sites, and the soil's suitability for wildlife and for a variety of other uses.

While the above details can readily be extracted from appropriate sources for the dozens of series types in each county (see the bibliography), a broader view of the major soil types is given in Table 2.3. The soil is generally a reflection of the bedrock. For our area, then, both the South and Blue Mountains feature unyielding rocks, steep slopes, and thin, rocky, somewhat infertile soils. By contrast, the valley itself has thick soils derived from shales, dolostones, and limestones—joined by ample flowing water, a comfortable climate, and a workable topography. Such a setting must have been particularly inviting to the early Moravian and German settlers. That story is the focus of the next chapter.

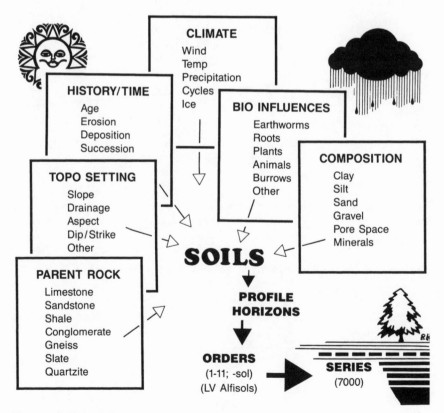

Fig. 2.5 *Soils and their complex development*

Table 2.3 *The major soil types of the Lehigh Valley and some of their characteristics*

Characteristics and Resource Base	Major Soil Types		
	Perma-Berks (Bk)	Appalachian DeKalf-Lehew-Laidig (Dkt)	Alluvial floodplains
Location	Northern half of valley; coincides with shale belt	Blue Mountain (northern border of valley)	Along Delaware, Lehigh, Cedar, Jordan, Bushkill, etc.
Topography	Billowy hills, elevation 650–900 feet; hills flat-topped to rounded	Sinuous ridge, grading into steep colluvial talus slopes; elevation 1,000–1,600 feet	Flat alluvial areas bordering rivers, streams
Mean depth to bedrock, in feet (range)	2.5 (2–5)	4 (0–10)	4+ (3–10+)
pH (range)	5.5–6.0	4.0–4.5	5.0–6.0
Source material	Martinsburg shales; Illinoian glacial	Sandstones, quartzites of ridge	Flood deposits
Major crops/ land use	Potatoes, small grains, corn, soybeans	Non-agricultural: wildlife; trails; wooded; game lands	Corn, pasture, fruit; protected park and recreation land
Texture	Silt loam, shaly	Stony, sandy loam; very stony	Silty to sandy
Moisture storage capacity	Good	Good/moderate	Good to excellent

Table 2.3 (continued) *The major soil types of the Lehigh Valley and some of their characteristics*

Characteristics and Resource Base	Major Soil Types		
	Washington, Hagerstown (Wh, Hg)	Womelsdorf-Annondale (WA)	Northampton-Kistler (Nh)
Location	Southern valley, roughly coincides with limestone	South Mountain	Northeastern corner of Northampton County; Bangor to Belvidere and northeast
Topography	Undulating hills to broad, flat interstream areas; hill elevation 400 feet	Irregular mountains, many steep slopes; elevation 500–1,000 feet	Large swampy areas
Mean depth to bedrock, in feet (range)	2–10+	3–5	3 (2–5)
pH (range)	6.0–6.5	5.5	5.5–6.0
Source material	Limestones; Illinoian glacial	Residual, from gneisses	Martinsburg shales; Wisconsinan glacial
Major crops/ land use	Variety of crops, corn, etc.	Some crops; mostly forested; some development on top	General farming; potatoes
Texture	Silt to silty clay loam	Silt loam to silty clay loam; slopes rocky	Silt loam; shaly silt loam
Moisture storage capacity	Good to very good	Good	Good

SOURCE: Data after Higbee 1967.
NOTE: A narrow band southeast of South Mountain, including Saucon Valley, has some limestone and some Triassic red shale-based soils.

THREE

Human History in the Lehigh Valley

To many western Europeans of the late seventeenth and
eighteenth centuries Pennsylvania was a veritable paradise
and refuge from oppression. Indeed, many commentators
referred to it as "the best poor man's country in the world."

—JAMES T. LEMON, *The Best Poor Man's Country:*
A Geographical Study of Early Southeastern Pennsylvania, 1972

Long before William Penn and his agents were promoting Penn's colony
to western Europeans, people who called themselves Lenape lived in
eastern Pennsylvania, in the region we now call the Lehigh Valley. European colonists referred to these Native Americans as "Delawares," as
many of the Lenape lived along the Delaware River. (The river itself was
named by English officials to honor the first governor of the Virginia
Colony, Sir Thomas West, Lord De La Warr.) How, in what manner, and
especially *when* Native Americans reached the New World are much-
debated topics diligently pursued by archaeologists and historians.

Archaeologists have described a group of humans of modern type,
that is, *Homo sapiens,* who were living as nomadic hunter-gatherers in
northeastern Asia 20,000 years ago. Based on the cultural remains left
by these people, archaeologists assigned them to the Upper Paleolithic
tradition. At that time, the northern hemisphere's climate was extremely

cold, and glaciers covered most of the landmass. When glaciers form, sea levels fall; in this case, the land bridge called "Beringia"—actually more of a subcontinent—formed between Siberia and Alaska, which permitted large mammals to move across into North America. Shortly thereafter, it is argued, the nomadic tribes followed. (Prior visits may have been made by voyagers traveling over the waters of the Bering Strait into the New World. Some evidence of human activity gathered in the Yukon may date from 27,000 years ago.) However, the time of major human invasion into North America is generally believed to have taken place between 15,000 and 12,000 years ago. By about 11,000 years ago, their descendants settled in the region now called Pennsylvania. Our understanding of Early Man in North America and of the origin and early culture of the Lenape—the Native Americans who lived along the banks of the Delaware long before Penn's colony existed—will have to be gained without the aid of a written record; no journals or diaries can be consulted. As the writer Ted Morgan (1993) has noted, "History begins with written records, but prehistory is revealed by buried clues—skeletons, potsherds, flint points, bits of charcoal, burial goods, textile fibers. This is the great subterranean library of Early Man, and the archaeologists are its librarians."

PALEO-INDIAN CULTURE (CIRCA 12,000 B.C.–8000 B.C.)

The Indians of this period lived in a Pennsylvanian landscape that resembled the present-day Arctic tundra. The influence of the retreating glaciers produced a climate that may have been about 18°F colder than the one we enjoy now. Scattered spruce and fir in a vast open grassland would have been the backdrop for herds of caribou and musk ox grazing on the tundra. The occasional woolly mammoth and other now-extinct mammals could have been game stalked by the Indians of this era.

North of the Lehigh Valley, a Paleo-Indian site has been excavated on a river terrace where Brodhead Creek meets the Delaware River in Monroe County. Radiocarbon dates from the earliest levels of the excavation site were determined to be in the range of 9100 B.C. to 7300 B.C. Fluted spear points (termed Eastern Clovis points), scrapers, knives, and other stone tools have been unearthed there. Few remains of Paleo-Indian cultures have been discovered in Pennsylvania, but the impact of those cultures on the landscape would have been minimal, except for their possible role in driving the large mammals to extinction. (Two mastodon fossil sites at Marshalls Creek, in Monroe County, did not contain any artifacts that might have served as clues to human involvement with the death of these animals.) A recently studied site located near Pittsburgh, the Meadowcroft Rockshelter, has been carefully excavated and documented. For some time, experts debated the age of the site, but most authorities now agree that the site predates 12,000 years ago. However, the Meadowcroft assemblage is not greatly different from later Paleo-Indian assemblages.

Melting glaciers would have produced lakes, bogs, and streams comparable to the landscape features of present-day Canada. Indians in Pennsylvania would have hunted the dominant mammals of such habitats—tapir, moose, and giant beaver—but probably relied heavily on fish, mollusks and other shellfish, geese, ducks, auks, bird eggs, and fledglings as dependable sources of food. A wide array of edible plants and seeds were available at that time as well. Archaeological finds of varied tools and weapons—made from stone that originated as far away as central and western New York and as nearby as the jasper quarries of Vera Cruz—suggest that either long-distance travel was conducted to gather specific raw materials or that trade may have been carried out among hunters to secure appropriate raw materials. (See Box 3.1 for details about the Vera Cruz jasper quarries.) Evidence is sparse, but it appears that the transition from the Paleo-Indian period to the next, the Archaic, was marked by changes in spearhead design: spearheads gradually decreased in size and took on the shape of an isosceles triangle.

THE ARCHAIC PERIOD (8000 B.C.–1000 B.C.)

As the glaciers receded, the stage was set for the vegetation and animal life familiar to us today. During the first half of the Archaic period, prairie habitat extended over much of Pennsylvania. About five to four thousand years ago, forests started to replace prairie, and the types of plants and animals well known to us today made their first appearance in Pennsylvania. Interior forests of oaks and hickories developed, which provided better opportunities for hunting game and gathering plant-based foods. Archaic peoples began to stay in somewhat restricted areas; more varied and abundant food sources lessened their need to follow the movements of game such as elk and deer, and allowed them to adopt a village lifestyle. A few sites from the Archaic period reveal that homes may have been circular, dome-shaped, bark-covered structures.

The tools used during this period were grooved axes, pestles and mullers for grinding seeds and nuts, atlatl weights for spear-throwing sticks, scrapers, knives, and stone points with distinctive jagged edges. Such serrated points may have been used as fish spears.

The diet was more varied, as fishing and shellfish gathering may have provided a more steady supply of meat to counterbalance the vagaries of the hunt for deer, bear, turkey, and waterfowl. Notched netsinkers from this period attest to the likelihood that shad, herring, and other fish were becoming more important in the lives of these people. The moderation of climate permitted this more varied lifestyle. Baskets and bark containers, canoes, and other items of manufacture are believed to have been in use, but evidence of the nature and style of these items is absent from excavation sites from the Archaic period. More substantial tools, such as axes and gouges, were devised for woodworking in the construction of dugout canoes, clearing the increasingly forested settings, and building more permanent dwellings. Hunting, gathering, and fishing were still the way of life for these people, but a new method of cooking emerged: the close of the Archaic period is marked by the use of cooking pots made with soapstone (steatite). Vessels carved from blocks of Lancaster County soapstone date from 1800 B.C. to 800 B.C. and distinguish this as a time of transition to the next major cultural period, the Woodland period.

THE WOODLAND PERIOD (1000 B.C.–A.D. 1600)

The early portion of this period is marked by the appearance of pottery. The first ceramic pots had straight sides with lug handles and flat bottoms. Later, cone-shaped pots were produced. Stone and ceramic pipes also made their appearance, evidence of tobacco use for pleasure and for rituals.

Horticultural implements, such as hoes, have also been unearthed from Woodland period sites. American Indian agriculture relied on corn (maize), beans, and a variety of squash as the basis for the revolution in lifestyle. Knowledge of plant cultivation spread slowly from Central America into the American Southwest and Southeast before taking hold in the land of the Lenape and elsewhere in the Northeast. For the Lenape of the Woodland period, the sunny floodplains with more fertile, well-drained soils were the site of this new agricultural venture. The resulting dramatic shift in lifestyle led to the construction of more

Fig. 3.1 *Indian artifacts*
Left to right: conical pot, ceramic vessel, notched points, bone awl, fish hook, axe
head. (Not to scale.)

elaborate houses—some of the dwellings appear to have had excavated
floors, which may have served to give additional protection from cold
winter winds—and to an increase in ceremonial and religious practices.
(A greater reliance on fishing, too, is supported by indirect evidence of
fish smoking and curing activities.)

During the last portion of the Woodland period, before the arrival of
Europeans, the Lenape lived a more or less sedentary life, and villages
were occupied for several years. Agriculture developed more fully
throughout the Middle Atlantic region, but less so in the Delaware Valley, where hunting and gathering were still crucial. During this period,
Indians adopted the bow and arrow, and the small, chipped-stone, triangular arrow tip came into fashion. Villages were surrounded by ditches,
earth embankments, and stockades—more on the order of split-rail
fences—to guard village resources from animal visitors and small-scale
attacks by neighboring tribes. Archaeological investigations of the Middle Delaware floodplain sites have revealed small hearths, small to moderate storage pits, varied tools, and ceramic vessels of all sizes, including
storage size: all of these suggest that groups lived in small extended family bands in dispersed, semipermanent or permanent camps.

COLONIAL PERIOD (A.D. 1600–A.D. 1800)

Pennsylvania land was first purchased from the Lenape in 1638, shortly
after Peter Minuit and Swedish colonists landed near the mouth of Min-
quas Creek in the lower Delaware Valley. This tract was partially

cleared and occupied by Swedish and Dutch settlers, and it was among the first sites sold again to William Penn in 1683. Native American notions about land ownership and property sale were vastly different from those of the colonists, and these differing views were to prove vexing as time passed. Indians retreated from the regions that Europeans were beginning to settle, but it may not have been the presence of settlers that drove them further westward. Some historians argue that the development of the fur trade, coupled with the availability of firearms, resulted in fewer game animals and drew Native Americans away from settlements in the lower Delaware Valley.

William Penn's "Holy Experiment" began with the 1681 charter from Charles II that made Penn the Proprietary of a large tract of land "lying north of Maryland; on the east bounded by Delaware river; on the west limited as Maryland; and northward, to extend as far as plantable"—which was, in fact, about 35 million acres (54,000 square miles). Penn was a good promoter and before he departed from England had sold over 620,000 acres in the new province to over five hundred buyers.

He arrived at New Castle, in northern Delaware, on October 27, 1682 with a colony of Quakers, and shortly thereafter settled in the town laid out a year earlier and named by Penn: Philadelphia. The Indians insisted that the land was theirs, and Penn agreed to buy it from them. Under the famous "Treaty Elm," along the banks of the Delaware, William Penn and Chief Tammany gave pledges of everlasting faith and trust on behalf of their peoples. Penn wanted to attract settlers to the land, and, as a Quaker, believed in religious tolerance. Accordingly, he sent out brochures promoting his colony as a place of "peace, liberty, and fertile soil" to a diverse audience, and during the first thirty years of the colony, significant numbers of Presbyterians, Episcopalians, Lutherans, Calvinists, Mennonites, and other sects came from England, Wales, and Germany. (One of the earliest German settlers in Penn's colony was the Frankfurt lawyer Francis Daniel Pastorius, who was responsible for attracting several dozen German Quakers and Mennonites to Philadelphia. They set about making Germantown a thriving community. Pastorius—unlike Penn—spent thirty-six years in Pennsylvania.)

Penn sailed for England in August 1684, a little less than two years after his arrival in the New World. In 1699, he did revisit a Philadelphia that had grown to a population of five thousand, but Penn himself spent most of his time at Pennsbury. He returned to London in 1701, still struggling with debt, as he had from the first days of the establishment of the province. In January 1709, at the age of sixty-three, Penn was sent to Fleet Prison for almost ten months until he could borrow enough money to settle the suit that had landed him in jail. Shortly thereafter, he suffered a crippling stroke and lingered on in a vegetative state until his death on July 30, 1718. After years of litigation, John, Richard, and Thomas, sons of William's second wife, became the Proprietaries of the colony.

Colonial Settlement in the Valley

Immigration to Pennsylvania increased during the early years of the eighteenth century, with a shift to larger numbers of Scotch-Irish and German settlers. Although some Scotch-Irish made it to the Lehigh Valley, the bulk of the settlers were Germans from the Palatinate and other principalities torn by religious strife. The Germans *(die Deutschen)* became known as the "Pennsylvania Dutch." The spread of settlers into the valley coincided with the Proprietaries deeding over half the lands in the region to themselves or to friends.

As white settlers moved into the region, they initially used the Indian trails as pathways. The Minsi or Minisink Path entered the valley along the course of the Saucon Creek, located north of Philadelphia. The trail then led through Nazareth to Wind Gap. The banks of the Delaware served as a major corridor leading from the south, passing through the sites of Easton, Bangor, and Portland, progressing north through the famed Delaware Water Gap. The Old Warrior's Path came down from the north through the Lehigh Gap, and, at the vicinity of Slatington, split into several forks. One path cut diagonally toward Easton, another followed the Lehigh to a fording site two miles above Bethlehem, and a third passed through the sites of Ballietsville and Dorneyville to the banks of the Little Lehigh and Indian Creeks, thence to Hosensack Creek, and on to the banks of the Perkiomen. Other settlers came to the Lehigh Valley from the west, via the Oley Valley.

Perhaps as early as 1719, Peter Trexler may have settled along Spring Creek where Trexlertown is now. Next to the Penns, William Allen, a London barrister, was the largest landowner. In September 1735, he purchased much of the land now occupied by Allentown, Bethlehem, and the townships that now bear his name, Allen and Williams.

The coming of immigrants to the Lehigh Valley created increased tensions between the Native Americans and the Proprietary government. Councils had been held between the two groups between 1734

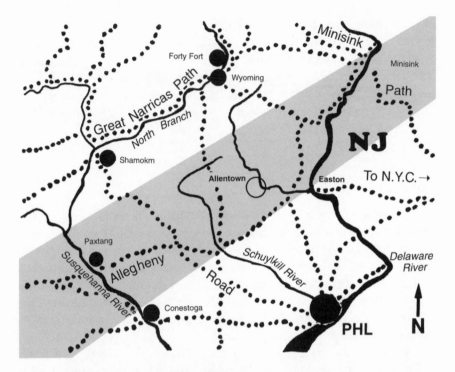

Fig. 3.2 *Indian trails in eastern Pennsylvania*
Dotted lines depict the major Indian trails of the eighteenth century. The shaded
area is roughly the Great Valley. Names are from the period, with a few added as
reference points. The trail mosaic represents a history of people who walked a lot;
paths are attached to natural features, such as valleys, ridges, and rivers.

and 1737, and a decision had been made by the government to set aside
lands just south of the Lehigh Gap as Indian Manor Tract, lands meant
solely for Indian use. The Indians did not agree with this action and continued to roam throughout the region. They did eventually agree, in
1737, to the conditions outlined in the Neshaminy Purchase, now better known as the infamous "Walking Purchase." A "true copy" of an
agreement made by William Penn and three Delaware Indian chiefs
(signed by the chiefs in 1686, two years after Penn had departed from
Philadelphia) was used by James Logan, the agent employed by Penn's
sons, to bully four chiefs—Nutimus, Teeshacomin, Lappawinzoe, and
Manawkyhickon—into reluctantly signing on to the Walking Purchase
on August 25. The initial agreement, now half a century old, outlined
the land that would be given to Penn and his agents; it would be based
on the distance that a man could walk in a day and a half, and from that

point, a line would be drawn eastward to the Delaware River. The chiefs did not know that the map they had been shown had been altered as well. The doctored map placed streams and the Lehigh River—then called the West Branch of the Delaware—in such a manner that the Indians believed that the area was much smaller than it was. The scheme employed by Thomas Penn only came to light more than a century later, when his private papers were discovered.

Penn had used Sheriff Timothy Smith as the subcontractor to carry out a devious plot. Smith secretly engaged three walkers to find the best route and blaze the trail. All three were young, strong, and used to the wilderness. Each man was to be paid five pounds, with an incentive: five hundred acres would be given to the man who walked the farthest. The walk had turned into a race. Edward Marshall, James Yeates (Yates), and Solomon Jennings, who had a place along the Lehigh River, started the walk near the Wrightstown meetinghouse in the early morning of September 19, 1737. After nineteen miles, Jennings gave up, but the other two men continued until they decided to take a fifteen-minute lunch break at Cook's Creek, having covered twenty-eight miles in seven hours! They continued toward Bethlehem, where they crossed the Lehigh River and started inland. At that point, Indian observers objected that the walkers were no longer following the Delaware and that they were going too fast. Marshall and Yeates kept walking, though, and finally stopped near the Indian village of Hockendauqua where they saw Sheriff Smith waiting for them and telling them to "pull up," as time was up. They had traversed forty miles. The next morning, Marshall, with compass in hand to hold his course, moved out briskly as Yeates struggled to keep up. At 1:30 P.M., half an hour before the finish, Yeates collapsed as he was climbing a steep hill, and Marshall knew that he would be the winner. At 2:00 P.M., Marshall stopped four miles from the present-day town of Jim Thorpe, having trekked about sixty-five miles. Then a team of surveyors, in four days, ran a line at a right angle to the line that had been walked, but toward the northeast—not due east, as the agreement had specified—until they reached the Delaware at Shohola Creek. With this chicanery, the Penns collected a large triangular tract of land. The Indians were infuriated, and tensions started to build. Even the work of Moravian missionaries, who arrived in the area in 1740, did little to defuse the situation. By 1742, most of the Indians had vacated the region.

Their departure was accomplished with the assistance of the Iroquois, who had long assumed dominance over the Delawares. Resentment continued to build among the Delawares over the fraud that had

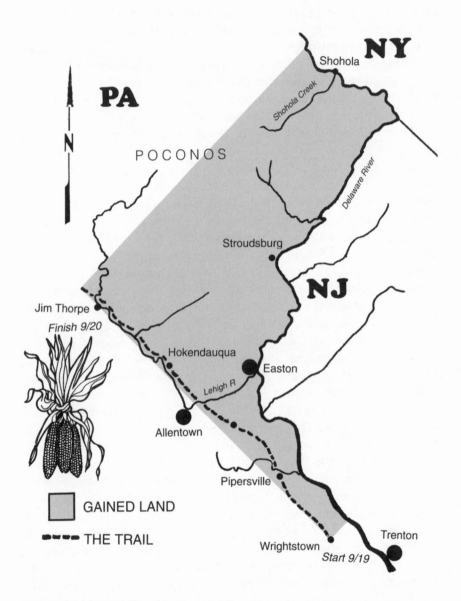

Fig. 3.3 *The Walking Purchase*
In September 1737, the day-and-a-half walk from Wrightstown to the summit of
Broad Mountain, near Jim Thorpe—a distance of about sixty-five miles—established the baseline for the land transfer from the Delawares to the colonists. The
land included much of the Lehigh Valley. (Not all cities and towns on the map
were established by 1737. See text.)

been perpetrated by the Penns. Even Edward Marshall, the winner of the "race," was cheated; he never received the five-hundred-acre prize, but instead purchased land north of Easton. In May 1754, while Marshall was away from his home, a raiding party of Indians attacked his house and killed his daughter. Marshall's wife, eight months pregnant, was taken prisoner. Apparently unable to keep up with the pace of travel, she was killed and scalped as the Indians approached the Poconos. Her body and the remains of unborn twins were later discovered by settlers. In another raid, Marshall's oldest son was killed. Perhaps unwittingly, the Delawares had taken revenge on the walker who had been responsible for carrying out Thomas Penn's scheme. (Marshall himself lived on into his seventies and died peacefully in his home.)

Three Centers: Bethlehem, Easton, and Allentown

In the midst of these disputes over land rights, immigrants continued to move into the Lehigh Valley. Moravians settled first in the Manor (or Barony) of Nazareth. George Whitefield, an English evangelist, purchased the Barony in 1740 and hired a group of Moravians to oversee a variety of building projects for charitable goals. Soon, construction of a stone building known today as the Whitefield House—and nearby Gray Cottage—was begun. Financial difficulties forced Whitefield to sell the entire five thousand acres to the Moravians in 1741.

While activities continued at Nazareth, other members of the community moved a short distance south along the banks of the Monocacy Creek. In April 1741 they completed the first building at the site. By fall, they had started construction of the *Gemeinhaus,* which became the central headquarters for the colony. Count Zinzendorf, spiritual leader of the United Brethren, arrived in December 1741, and, during a Christmas eve vigil, named the new settlement Bethlehem.

Within a few years, the Moravians expanded their colony along the Monocacy, completed the construction of the large stone building in Nazareth, made converts among the German immigrants, and founded a missionary village—Gnadenhutten, near present-day Lehighton—to minister to the Indians. The Moravians' most distinguished missionary was David Zeisberger, who devoted sixty years to missionary activities while creating a legacy of scholarship about the diverse languages and customs of various Indian tribes. Converted Indians served as valuable assistants to the Moravian missionaries, and more than fifty of the converts, including the first, John Wasampa (Tschoop), are buried in God's

Fig. 3.4 *The Sun Inn*
(Collections of the Lehigh
County Historical Society.)

Acre, the first Moravian cemetery in Bethlehem. By 1755, the Moravian settlers had created a waterworks—the first public utility for the valley and the first waterworks in the Commonwealth. By 1756 a thousand Moravians dwelt in the valley; most lived in Bethlehem, but some settled in Nazareth and in Maguntche (later called Emmaus). Increase in travel through the region was the impetus for the construction of a hotel and, by 1760, the Sun Inn in Bethlehem was open for guests.

As early as 1735, the Proprietary government hoped to establish a town at the junction of the west branch of the Delaware (the Lehigh River) and the main stream. Though there were some obstacles to the plan—especially economic competition from Phillipsburg, an established village on the New Jersey side of the Delaware—in 1752 the General Assembly partitioned Northampton County from Bucks and established Berks from portions of Philadelphia, Chester, and Lancaster Counties. A clause in the act designated Easton as the seat of the newly formed Northampton County. These efforts helped to establish Easton—and by 1755, only a few years later, Easton could boast of forty buildings (including five taverns, but no church or school!).

Indian uprisings from 1755 to 1763, in the larger framework of the French and Indian War (during which England and France vied for control of the New World), had minimal impact on the valley. Indians did attack the Moravian missionary colony at Gnadenhutten, killed eleven colonists, and burned buildings. That episode, and the tales told to the valley's settlers by survivors, prompted Governor Morris in Philadelphia to instruct Benjamin Franklin to oversee the construction of a chain of forts and blockades along the northern border of the Blue Mountain, located primarily at the gaps and along the Indian paths. The largest, Fort Allen, was erected at present-day Weissport. By early 1756, when the forts were completed, the Indian raids had diminished. (Accounts of Ben Franklin's travels and tales of where he might have stayed during his visits to inspect the forts are part and parcel of the family legends of many in the region, including the Oplinger clan. It is an "indisputable fact" that "Old Ben" stayed overnight at the frontier post of Nicholas Uplinger [Oplinger] at Lehigh Gap during his trip to inspect Fort Allen.)

Easton was the site of several peace conferences between the Indians and various government officials. Governor Morris and his council met with the Lenape leader Teedyuscung, who had proclaimed himself "King of Ten Nations." The results of the first conference in July 1756 were inconclusive. A second conference was held in November of that year, and Teedyuscung used that occasion to give a passionate recital of the deceptions that occurred in the Walking Purchase nearly twenty years earlier; during the speech, he allegedly exclaimed, "This very Ground that is under me was my Land and Inheritance, and is taken from me by Fraud." Both sides agreed to a truce, provided that the whole matter of the land purchase would be investigated. In July 1757, Teedyuscung led a company of three hundred persons to Easton for a third conference. After extensive deliberations, a peace agreement was conducted with the exchange of decorated belts. Additional conferences at Easton would prove influential in forming closer bonds between the English and the Six Nations. (The Six Nations, also known as the Iroquois Confederacy, was an intricate social and political organization. Composed originally of Mohawks, Oneidas, Onondagas, Cayugas, and Senecas, the sixth group was added when the Tuscaroras moved into Iroquois country in the early eighteenth century.) Without the Indians, the French could not sustain the war, and they surrendered in Canada in 1760, although hostilities did not end on the frontier until 1763.

Despite these gestures toward peaceful relations, Indians remained threatened by the loss of their lands as settlers, especially from Connecticut, moved into frontier parts of Pennsylvania. At Wyoming, on the night of April 19, 1763, Teedyuscung was burned to death when he could not escape from his blazing cabin. Shortly thereafter, news of Indian uprisings in the west led by the Ottawa chief, Pontiac, spurred the Indians in the valley to go on the warpath. Numerous attacks, scalpings, and burnings occurred along the frontier and at farms not too far from valley towns. Captain Bull, Teedyuscung's son, and a war party killed fifty-four persons in the upper section of Northampton County. The stern measures taken by Colonel Henry Bouquet and his troops saw an end to Indian resistance by 1765; whites returned to frontier sites abandoned a few years earlier, and they soon advanced further into the Pennsylvania wilderness. (In the Lehigh Valley, the threat of hostilities actually proved beneficial for the development of the region, since rural folk, villagers, and town dwellers in the three population centers engaged in more cooperative ventures during the periods of siege, lessening the isolation of earlier days.) By 1770, few Indians remained in Pennsylvania. Most had joined their brothers in Ohio, eventually moving on to Oklahoma and to Ontario, Canada.

In 1762, William Allen helped found Allentown (or Northampton Town, as it was then called). The town's plans recalled those employed in the establishment of Easton: blocks were divided into long narrow lots, and two main streets, Hamilton and Allen, crossed at a large plaza. Deeds for lots were not conveyed until 1765, but by year's end several buildings, including a Union church, had been constructed. By 1773 the population had grown to fifty-six.

THE AGE OF AGRICULTURE

Historian W. Ross Yates describes the period from 1763 to 1830 as the age of agriculture in the valley and in the nation. Limestone areas stretching from the Delaware River south into Maryland and Virginia found favor with the German immigrants; the Germans prospered, employed a form of crop rotation, and maintained the fertility of the soil by adding manure and wood ashes and, to a lesser extent, burning limestone. (The northwestern sections of the valley were not considered desirable farm sites by the first settlers—the German term *Allemangel,* still seen on road signs, translates as "lack-all" and forcefully conveys their sentiments!) A prominent Philadelphia physician and political figure, Benjamin Rush, wrote an account in 1789 filled with high praise for the German farmers and tradesmen dwelling in Pennsylvania at that time.

Scholar Henry Hobhouse (1989) has recently explored the relationship of historical development to natural forces: population growth, food supply, and disease. Hobhouse stressed that the Great Valley had the most fertile soil, the most moderate climate, and the best watered area in all of the eastern United States. In addition, by 1776, 150,000 peasants from Switzerland and the Rhineland had been attracted to Pennsylvania. Hobhouse describes them as "immensely hardworking, thorough, thrifty, patient, industrious, and with large families. They had a mystical love of the soil (and of real estate) combined with an intellectual and intelligent application of new methods of husbandry." By the time of the War of Independence, tax lists indicate that almost 75 percent of the inhabitants of the region were farmers. An additional 20 percent were mostly farm laborers. Allentown and Easton were approaching Bethlehem as centers for supplying the surrounding populace with tools, supplies, materials, and the like. Apart from these towns, few settlements qualified as villages.

In 1776, Northampton County was quite large; it comprised parts of what are now seven counties in northeastern Pennsylvania, and included Easton as the county seat. Four distinct cultural groups lived in Northampton County: Germans in the central and southern limestone sections; Scotch-Irish in the hill country to the north (referred to in early documents as Martin's Settlement, the Hunter Settlements, and Craig's Settlement, these regions are now defined as Upper and Lower Mount Bethel Townships); Moravian Germans in Bethlehem and Nazareth; and English settlers primarily in the Easton area. Although most of the citizens were listed in the tax rolls as farmers, only 20 percent or less of the land was under cultivation. Forest cover still prevailed. Gristmills were built on almost every suitable stream and blacksmith shops were set up nearby. A few farmers burned lime on their own farms. The Moravians used local clays to establish a tile works, and as early as 1760, more than fifty manufacturing industries were located in the Moravian industrial area along the Monocacy Creek. The peaceful labors of the Moravians and other settlers were soon to end, however.

Farmers and Fighters

Although no battles were fought on county soil, the valley was an important corridor for the movement of troops and supplies between Washington's army in Philadelphia and colonial forces in New York. Troops from Northampton County commanded by Colonel Daniel Brodhead participated in the battle of Long Island. County men also fought at the battles of Trenton and Princeton. In addition, the Moravian Brethren's House became an army hospital. Over five hundred soldiers who did not recover from their wounds are buried on the west bank of the Monocacy. A monument with the tomb of an unknown soldier of the American Revolution is located along First Avenue in Bethlehem. The most famous of the soldiers who recuperated from their wounds in Bethlehem was the Marquis de Lafayette, considered too

BOX 3 . 1

Places of Archaeological and Historical Interest

Northampton County

WHITEFIELD HOUSE. Built in 1740, the house is now an interesting museum with displays of art, music, the local history of Moravians, and the early history of Nazareth. 214 E. Center Street, Nazareth.

MORAVIAN HALL SQUARE MUSEUM AND CRAFT SHOP. The museum is located in the former headmaster's house of Nazareth Hall Academy, built in 1819, and features guided house tours and a craft area. One Hall Square, Nazareth.

JACOBSBURG NATIONAL HISTORIC DISTRICT. Historic sites are located at Jacobsburg State Park, 835 Jacobsburg Road, Wind Gap. Sites include the Henry Homestead, the remains of the site of Henry's Forge and Gun Works, John Joseph Henry House, and the iron-master's house (Benade House). Occasional open houses and special events are offered. The National Historic District is located off Route 33. Take the Belfast exit north of Easton.

PARSONS-TAYLOR HOUSE. The house was built in 1757 by William Parsons, Surveyor General, and later sold to George Taylor, a signer of the Declaration of Independence. Not open to the public. South Fourth and Ferry Streets, Easton.

FIRST REFORMED (UCC) CHURCH. The scene of the Indian Treaty of 1777, the church was also used as a military hospital during the Revolutionary War. 27 N. Third Street, Easton.

EASTON LIBRARY. Look for the display of the flag flown at the time of the public reading of the Declaration of Independence on July 8, 1776. The library also features other exhibits and an extensive collection of local history manuscripts and texts. 32 N. Second Street, Easton.

NATIONAL CANAL MUSEUM. Interactive exhibits, photomurals, the living quarters of a canal boat, and a knowledgeable staff convey the history of the canal era. The Delaware and Lehigh National Heritage Corridor visitor center, bookshop, and the Crayola Factory tour are all located in the same complex. The Centre Square was the site of one of the three public readings of the Declaration of Independence in the American colonies. The others were at Independence Hall in Philadelphia and Trenton, New Jersey. Two Rivers Landing, 30 Centre Square, Easton.

BOX 3.1 (CONTINUED)

HUGH MOORE PARK. Seasonally, rides may be taken on a mule-drawn replica of a canal boat, the *Josiah White II*. Walk along the towpath to view a locktender's house museum, remains of the Chain Dam, Guard Lock 8, piers of the Change Bridge, and nineteenth-century industrial ruins. 200 S. Delaware Drive, Easton.

HISTORIC EIGHTEENTH-CENTURY INDUSTRIAL AREA. Luckenbach Mill was built in 1869 on the site of the 1743 flourmill. Restored in 1982, the building is administered by Historic Bethlehem, Inc., and serves as an orientation center to the entire Eighteenth-Century Industrial Complex. Other buildings within walking distance include an apothecary (1752), a tannery (1761), and a waterworks (1762) that housed the first pumped municipal water system in the American colonies. There are more than a dozen historic Moravian buildings as well as God's Acre, the old Moravian cemetery that contains the graves of fifty-six Indians—including a Mohican, John Wasampa (Tschoop), who may have been a model for Uncas in James Fenimore Cooper's novel *The Last of the Mohicans*. The Complex is located along the Monocacy Creek, off Main Street, in the historic section of Bethlehem.

MORAVIAN MUSEUM OF BETHLEHEM, INC. The oldest building in the city, the 1741 *Gemeinhaus* (Community House), is now a museum with numerous exhibits that illustrate varied aspects of the early Moravian culture. 66 W. Church Street, Bethlehem.

KEMERER MUSEUM OF DECORATIVE ARTS. The museum houses two centuries' worth of furnishings and art of the Moravians and other regional cultures. 427 N. New Street, Bethlehem.

SUN INN. Built by the Moravians in 1758 as their official *Gasthaus* for travelers, the Inn was visited by many of the nation's founding fathers, European military leaders, and Indian chiefs during the Revolutionary period. It also served as a hospital during the Revolutionary War. The Inn is still operational as a restaurant. 564 Main Street, Bethlehem.

BURNSIDE PLANTATION. (See Box 7.1.) 1461 Schoenersville Road, about one mile north of the Eighteenth-Century Historic District, Bethlehem.

NORTHAMPTON COUNTY HISTORICAL AND GENEALOGICAL SOCIETY. Located in the Mixsell House, a Federal brick building built in

BOX 3.1 (CONTINUED)

1833, this society is the principal contact for additional information on regional history. 101 Fourth Street, Easton.

Lehigh County

LIBERTY BELL SHRINE. The shrine is located in historic Zion's Reformed Church (UCC), where patriots hid the Liberty Bell to protect it from falling into the hands of the British during the Revolutionary War, and includes a replica of the bell, flags of the thirteen original colonies, and related exhibits. 622 Hamilton Street, Allentown.

TROUT HALL. Allentown's oldest home was built as a summer residence by James Allen. The home is furnished in period style. 414 Walnut Street, Allentown.

GEORGE TAYLOR HOUSE. This National Historic Landmark home (1768) was the house of George Taylor, signer of the Declaration of Independence, and is furnished to suggest its original appearance. Lehigh and Poplar Streets, Catasauqua.

TROXELL-STECKEL HOUSE AND FARM MUSEUM. The stone farmhouse, built in 1755, features an adjacent bank barn containing antique carriages, sleighs, and farm tools. 4229 Reliance Street, Egypt.

HAINES MILL MUSEUM. This museum is an operating gristmill, built in 1760 and restored in 1909, with displays of farming and milling techniques from the turn of the century. 3600 Dorney Park Road, Allentown.

CLAUSSVILLE ONE-ROOM SCHOOLHOUSE. Built in 1893, this school was in operation until 1956. The site features a display of items in use from 1893 until the school's closing. 2917 Route 100, Claussville.

LOCK RIDGE FURNACE MUSEUM. Anthracite iron furnaces have been transformed into a museum with exhibits depicting the growth of the region's iron industry in the nineteenth century. Franklin Street, Alburtis.

VERA CRUZ JASPER QUARRIES. In a community park, visitors may view rock outcrops from which jasper was obtained. Vera Cruz, south of Emmaus.

MUSEUM OF INDIAN CULTURE/LENNI LENAPE HISTORICAL SOCIETY. The museum presents dioramas, artifacts, and a slide show and maintains a library of Native American and regional history

BOX 3.1 (CONTINUED)

texts. Lenape ceremonies are held at selected times throughout the year. The museum is located in the Bieber Stonehouse constructed in 1849. 2825 Fish Hatchery Road, Allentown.

SHELTER HOUSE. Constructed in 1734, this house is the oldest continuously inhabited dwelling in the Lehigh Valley. On the slope of South Mountain at the end of South Fourth Street, Emmaus.

1803 HOUSE MUSEUM. This historical landmark is a restored and furnished Georgian-style farmhouse. 55 S. Keystone Avenue, Emmaus.

SAYLOR CEMENT MUSEUM. The museum includes nine Schoefer cement kilns and exhibits that trace the cement industry's history. 245 N. Second Street, Coplay.

LEHIGH CANAL AND LOCKTENDER'S HOUSE MUSEUM. Built by the Lehigh Coal and Navigation Company, this lockhouse—currently being restored—is one of only two remaining stone lockhouses on the Lehigh Canal. Canal towpath south of Route 145, Walnutport.

LEHIGH COUNTY MUSEUM. The museum, located in the old courthouse, features local history exhibits and an extensive library of regional historical and genealogical information. Also located in the courthouse are the offices of the Lehigh County Historical Society, the principal contact for additional information about Lehigh County history. A Geology Garden in the rear of the courthouse helps explain the geological history of the Lehigh Valley. Corner of Fifth and Hamilton Streets, Allentown.

Berks County

DANIEL BOONE HOMESTEAD. A two-story farmhouse stands on the site of the log farmhouse in which Daniel Boone was born. Other buildings on the 579-acre park include a blacksmith shop, homestead barn, sawmill, and smokehouse. The visitor center features exhibits and a museum shop. 400 Daniel Boone Road, Birdsboro (southeast of Reading).

BERKS COUNTY HERITAGE CENTER. The Gruber Wagon Works is now fully restored; the structure had been removed by the Army Corps of Engineers during the construction of Blue Marsh Dam. Exhibits and guided tours convey to visitors how farm wagons

BOX 3.1 (CONTINUED)

were produced during the early 1900s. The C. Howard Hiester Canal Center (with artifacts and exhibits of the Schuylkill Canal), a covered bridge, gristmill, herb garden, and portions of the Union Canal bicycle and walking trail are also located here. A stone farmhouse houses a museum and visitor center. Off Route 183, just north of Reading Airport.

BERKS COUNTY HISTORICAL SOCIETY. The Society is the major source for Berks County history. 940 Centre Avenue, Reading.

special to be housed in the Brethren's House. Instead, Lafayette was cared for in the home of Brother George Frederick Beckel. Other famous visitors to Bethlehem—who often partook of a meal and stayed overnight at the Sun Inn—included Alexander Hamilton, Ethan Allen, John Paul Jones, John Adams, and George and Martha Washington.

This brief review of events relating to the war efforts of Lehigh Valley citizens should not ignore the role played by two Pennsylvania German farmers, Frederick Leasor and Jacob Mickley, in conveying the Liberty Bell and several smaller bells to safety when Philadelphia was threatened by British invaders. The big bell was held for safekeeping in Zion's Reformed Church in Allentown. (See Box 3.1.) And another connection between the valley and the War of Independence cannot be overlooked: the expedition of General John Sullivan. To end the British-inspired Indian attacks in the Wyoming and Upper Susquehanna Valleys, Congress demanded an expedition to punish the Iroquois. George Washington gave the assignment to General John Sullivan, who assembled his troops in Easton. Road-building regiments were sent out to widen the Indian trail that led through Wind Gap to present-day Saylorsburg and across the Pocono Plateau to the Wyoming Valley. Sullivan moved out from Easton on June 18, 1779 with twenty-five hundred men, and they joined forces with Brigadier-General James Clinton's regiments at Tioga Point. After rain delays, the combined force of four thousand men moved into New York by late August. At that time, a decisive and ultimately victorious battle was waged against the Indians and the British troops (who were under the command of Major John "Indian" Butler). Over forty Indian villages were destroyed. In addition, stored foods, farmlands, and orchards were burned as the troops moved

Fig. 3.5 *Long rifle*
Archival photograph from
Henry's Forge and Gun
Works, Jacobsburg State
Park. An early example of
applied technology in the
Lehigh Valley. (Collections
of the Lehigh County His-
torical Society.)

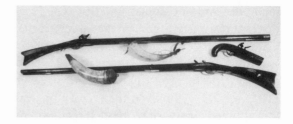

freely through the heart of the Iroquois territory, effectively eradicating British food supplies and eliminating the Iroquois Confederacy as a major force in the Revolutionary War. General Sullivan returned to Easton, and on October 17, he participated in a Thanksgiving service in the German Reformed Church (now the First United Church of Christ).

Throughout the war, Lehigh Valley citizens manufactured items such as clothing, saddles, bayonets, and rifles for use by the military. The most prominent of these industries to continue after the war's end was the gun factory established at Jacobsburg in 1792 by William Henry II, the son of a gunsmith from Lancaster who had supplied guns for the Braddock Campaign of 1755 and the Forbes Expedition of 1758. As early as the 1730s, local Pennsylvania gunsmiths were beginning to produce a rifle with a barrel fifteen or more inches longer than contemporary European rifles. In later years, the rifle design that originated in Pennsylvania came to be known as the Kentucky rifle, and the exploits of many frontiersmen—including Pennsylvania's best-known wilderness wayfarer, Daniel Boone—are intimately intertwined with it.

Like bookends, Henry's Forge and Gun Works on the eastern end of the Lehigh Valley and the Daniel Boone homestead on its far western edge convey something of the dynamics of the valley in the early part of the eighteenth century. It was Daniel Boone's grandfather, George Boone, who had been enticed to venture in August 1717 from Bristol, England, to the place that, in Penn's delightful phrase, lay "six hundred miles nearer the sun." In 1730, Daniel's father bought the tract of land at Oley east of the Schuylkill River on which the Boone homestead now stands. Daniel, the sixth of eleven children in Squire Boone's Quaker family, was born in 1734. Although Daniel Boone left Pennsylvania at the age of fifteen, his early life as a farmhand, herdsman, trapper, and hunter equipped him for his later exploits as an Indian fighter and frontier explorer.

As some colonists, such as the Boones, were moving into uncharted territory, others were building the industries that began to characterize the hinterland of colonial America. The Henrys, in 1808, constructed a forge at the eastern end of the valley to make bar iron for use in gun manufacturing. At the forge, the first bar iron in Northampton County was produced. Matthew Henry, in 1824, erected the Ann Catherine Iron Furnace, the first cold blast iron furnace in Northampton County. In 1812, the Henrys moved the factory to nearby Boulton and produced the famous Henry rifles there for John Jacob Astor's American Fur Company. Indeed, the Henry firearm became one of the most prominent weapons of the western frontier. Prior to and during the Civil War, the Henry Gun Works supplied the Union Army with rifles. In the post–Civil War years, mass production of guns by Remington, Winchester, and other companies brought an end to the Henry Gun Works in 1895.

AT THE TURN OF THE CENTURY

In 1800 the population of the valley was about twenty-five thousand persons, most still living in rural settings; only about two thousand resided in the three largest towns. Rapid growth followed. In thirty years, the population had doubled, and changes in the valley reflected that growth. In 1812, Lehigh County was formed out of Northampton County. The number of villages in the two counties increased to about thirty, although most consisted of only a few dwellings with perhaps one or two industries—a gristmill, tannery, sawmill, or lime kiln. Iron furnaces were built along both mountain ridges, and extensive charcoal production for the furnaces meant that forests were being cleared at a faster rate. As early as 1812, some slate was quarried in Bushkill Township. Roads and bridges became more substantial during the first three decades of the century.

The growth of Easton as the county seat vindicated Thomas Penn's position. Penn had believed that Easton would become a commercial success as well as a political capital of the hinterland. English schools and newspapers were more prominent here than in the other valley towns, Allentown and Bethlehem. The Bushkill Creek provided good waterpower, and Easton became a flour-milling center for the farmers of the surrounding area. By 1830 the population had reached 3,529, and over thirty retail stores, several tanneries, distilleries, sawmills, and nearly six hundred dwellings made Easton the hub of commercial life in the eastern end of the valley. Between 1830 and 1850 the Abbott Street

Fig. 3.6 *The Haines flourmill*
Built around 1760, the flourmill is now the Haines Mill Museum, which focuses on the old method of grinding grain for flour ("grist"). It is located at Haines Mill Road and Walnut Street (just east of Dorney Park), behind Jos. I. Haines Appliances on Broadway, in Cetronia. Seasonal hours. Call (610) 481-9138 for information. (Collections of the Lehigh County Historical Society.)

industrial area in south Easton developed into one of America's early industrial parks and produced an array of goods, including whiskey, rifles, cotton cloth, and—perhaps most significant—a fine quality iron wire. The Rodenbaugh and Stewart Wire Works was located in Easton, within the present-day boundaries of Hugh Moore Park, and wire products from this firm were used by John A. Roebling in the construction of suspension bridges.

Allentown also grew during this period, in part because, like Easton, it had been designated the county seat when Lehigh was formed out of Northampton County. By 1830, Allentown's population was 1,500. A college preparatory school known as Allentown Academy opened its doors in 1816, and a market house was opened the following year on the square at Seventh and Hamilton Streets.

Bethlehem remained exclusively Moravian during this era, and land was reserved solely for sale to Moravians. Building on the success of the waterworks, Bethlehem continued to pioneer the development of utilities: the first fire engine was in use by 1763, and by the turn of the century, an octagonal water tower had been constructed. Early experiments with lead water pipes (in place of wooden ones), curbs, paving, and sidewalks indicate Bethlehem's prominent position among the towns in the advancement of public services. Oil lamps were introduced by 1792. Music and education continued to be central to the life of the Moravians as well, and boarding schools, a "young ladies" seminary, and a theological seminary were all established early in the new century. A church with a seating capacity of 1,500 was built in 1806. By 1823, the town could boast more than seventy buildings in addition to the church, schools, and industrial shops. With the retention of the Moravian theocracy (and the subsequent departure of some of the younger generations), Bethlehem did not experience the growth of the other two population centers, and by 1830 its population was approximately 800. (Accurate numbers are difficult to obtain since the census included the surrounding townships.) The total population of Bethlehem and its surrounding townships was approximately 1,600.

The impact of this population growth on the natural landscape was concentrated on the stream and river edges, where the three main towns of the region were established. Some channeling, small dams, and other manipulation of streambeds resulted as grist- and sawmills were developed; in fact, almost any stream suitable as a source of waterpower was put to use in milling operations. The townspeople's influence was mostly felt, however, on the forested lands cleared for building sites, roads, and—especially—farms. Wheat was the main crop but rye, corn, oats, and some buckwheat were also grown and ground into flour and meal for family use and for animal feed. Forested tracts on both mountain ridges diminished, too, as charcoal was produced for the numerous iron furnaces located in the foothills.

INDUSTRIAL INFLUENCES (1830–1890)

The effect of the Industrial Revolution on the Lehigh Valley is extensive and can only be hinted at here. Building canals and railroads; mining anthracite coal and iron and zinc ores; quarrying slate and limestone; expanding manufactures of varied products from silk to cigars—all brought new challenges and opportunities to the region.

The Brief Canal Era

The Lehigh Canal was the first sign that the Industrial Revolution was about to spread into the valley. As early as 1792, Colonel Jacob Weiss of Fort Allen (now Weissport) and others attempted to develop sites north of Blue Mountain where "stonecoal," as anthracite was sometimes called, had been reported by visitors to the area. Various challenges, especially the lack of transport for the coal and underdeveloped markets, led to little success in these early ventures. However, in 1817, three individuals—Josiah White, Erskine Hazard, and George F. A. Hauto—made a new attempt. Soon the Lehigh Navigation Company and the Lehigh Coal Mine Company were joined, Hauto sold his share to White and Hazard, and in 1822 the company that would be the primary influence on the region for the next half-century, the Lehigh Coal and Navigation Company (LC&NC), was organized.

In the early years of the company's activity, arks laden with coal were floated down the Lehigh River itself: a complex series of ingenious dams and diversion channels created suitable water depths. Such dams, especially the one at Easton, had the effect of altering the reproductive patterns of shad (which head upstream to breed) and may represent the Industrial Revolution's first major transformation of natural drainage patterns in the Lehigh Valley. No longer would shad be caught in the Lehigh River as Indians had done only a century earlier. (Recent efforts to remedy this situation, including the construction of an elaborate shad ladder at the "Forks of the Delaware," are described in Chap. 12.)

The system of dams and diversion channels allowed boats to go downstream but not up. In 1829, a forty-six-mile canal system that extended from Mauch Chunk to Easton was constructed. It had eight dams and fifty-two locks; the mules that supplied the power to haul the barges paced along the narrow towpath that ran along the entire length of the canal. The completion of the Delaware Division Canal in 1831 and the extension of the Lehigh Canal north to White Haven (and eventually to Stoddartsville) created a canal system that totaled eighty-four miles.

In 1830, when the Lehigh Canal was in the first full year of operation, 42,000 tons of coal were conveyed to coastal markets. By 1855 over 1,275,000 tons were transported. This turned out to be the peak year for coal transport, as railroads had started to develop and compete as carriers. The development of canals not only promoted the anthracite coal industry but also played an important role in the initial formation of other industries, such as cement and slate. Canals served as a means of economical transport of beer, charcoal, bricks, tar, and pitch, and general merchandise as well. But the canal era in the United States was brief; railroads ruled within decades of the coming of the "iron horse" to America. (Canal redevelopment will be highlighted in Chap. 12.)

The Rush to Rails

The expansion of anthracite coal mining, begun with the canal era, stimulated the construction of railroads into the valley. The Lehigh Valley

Railroad Company, first incorporated in 1846, floundered until Asa Packer took over in 1851. Packer, ably assisted by a young engineer, Robert H. Sayre, surveyed a route and supervised the construction of a single track, forty-six miles long, between Mauch Chunk and Easton. In the next several decades, the railroad extended its lines to Bethlehem and Allentown and eventually set up a junction at Shimerville with the newly constructed North Pennsylvania line, a line that extended from Philadelphia to Bethlehem. By 1890 the Lehigh Valley Railroad Company had over 1,800 miles of track throughout much of the valley.

The history of railroad competition in the Lehigh Valley, which is largely focused on the courtship of "King Coal," is quite complex. Major rivals for the coal transport market were the New Jersey Central and the Delaware, Lackawanna, and Western Railroad Companies. A mere listing of other companies can perhaps convey the intensity of the competition: consider the Pennsylvania, Poughkeepsie, and Boston Railroad (forerunner of the Lehigh and New England Railroad), the Philadelphia and Reading Railroad, the Berks and Lehigh, the North Pennsylvania, the East Pennsylvania, the Perkiomen, the Catasauqua and Fogelsville, and the Ironton! By the turn of the century, reorganizations, collapses, and mergers resulted in only a few companies dominating the valley's rail system.

Leading the Way with Iron

The development of industry grew apace with that of canals and railroads. And no industry was more intimately linked to the canals, railroad, and anthracite mines than iron making in a blast furnace fueled with anthracite coal. Catasauqua ironmaster David Thomas is considered one of the founding fathers of the Industrial Revolution in the United States because of his pivotal role in the creation of the anthracite iron industry. Thomas was courted by Erskine Hazard, one of the owners of the Lehigh Canal, to come to the United States from his home in Wales to guide the construction of a blast furnace, which would eventually be named the Lehigh Crane Iron Company. After some deliberation and with the encouragement of his wife, Thomas and his family traveled to America. Construction of the furnace began in August 1839 with parts imported from Wales; by July 4, 1840, David Thomas was busy making iron while others celebrated the national holiday. Only ten years later, four furnaces were operating along the Lehigh and area hillsides and farm fields were probed for iron ore; the Thomas Iron Company was established in 1854. (Among the furnace sites scattered throughout the valley, only one, the Lock Ridge Furnace at Alburtis [now a Lehigh County Museum], gives present-day citizens a feel for the legacy of David Thomas. See Box 2.2.) By 1873 iron production was the valley's leading industry, and in Lehigh County alone there were nine companies and twenty-four blast furnaces. The Allentown Rolling Mills and others were producing a variety of iron products, most of them for use by the expanding railroads.

Northampton County had at least five companies operating thirteen furnaces, most along the tracks of the Lehigh Valley railroad from south Easton to south Bethlehem. The Glendon Iron Company, established in 1843, flourished for several decades but lost out to competition from other iron makers. Its massive furnaces were torn down in 1899–1900. Indeed, several furnace foundations are evident in Hugh Moore Park today. The Bethlehem Iron Company situated its plant along the south side of the Lehigh River in south Bethlehem in 1869; when it was formed, it was the largest iron company in the United States.

Other Industries

Aside from the thriving ironworks, railroads, and coal mines of this era, other industries flourished in the valley as well. Flour- and gristmills continued to be important to the valley's economy, ranking second to iron (and later, steel) production. Leather tanning and boot and shoe manufacturing were next in importance in the period from 1880 to 1890. Cigar making, zinc smelting, slate quarrying, and a developing silk industry offered employment to men and women. In the mid-nineteenth century, telegraph lines paralleled railroad lines and provided another connection to the surrounding world. But in 1881, the first long-distance telephone line between Bethlehem and Easton was strung, and the telegraph was displaced even more quickly than the canals had been.

In the midst of this industrial expansion, the significance of agriculture diminished to some extent. Fewer persons were engaged in farming and the value of agricultural products declined. And just as demographic shifts took place in other parts of the United States, the Lehigh Valley also saw towns develop into cities and villages and rural areas lose population.

THE VALLEY AND THE CIVIL WAR

Though it was one of the nation's most momentous episodes, the Civil War only peripherally infringed on the valley. No battles were fought on Lehigh Valley soil. Nevertheless, valley residents responded promptly to the bombardment of Fort Sumter. Three days after the bombardment, on April 15, 1861, Thomas Yeager, captain of the Allen Infantry, went to Harrisburg to tender his services to Governor Curtin. By April 17 Yeager and his forces headed to Harrisburg and thence to Baltimore with four other militia companies. The five militia groups were the first "troop" to arrive in Washington, and they became known as the "First Defenders"—perhaps optimistically, since Yeager's group was armed only with useless flintlocks. A day later they were issued percussion-rifled muskets from the Harpers Ferry Arsenal. (A monument honoring the First Defenders is located in Allentown's West Park.) County regiments were involved throughout the Civil War in battles at Bull Run, Antietam, Chancellorsville, and Cedar Creek. The "War Between the States" gave an added boost to the iron market. Armor plate for Union naval vessels, cannons, muskets, shot, and shells were all provided by the Lehigh Valley ironworks.

A scientific revolution was well underway even in the midst of war. A good indication of this is the number of patents issued: from 1860 to 1890, 440,400 patents were issued by the federal government. The growing use of electricity and the recently invented telegraph, phonograph, reaper (and other farm machinery), and refrigerated freight cars are but a few examples of American ingenuity. By 1890, the valley's urban areas had grown substantially. Easton had a population of 28,000, and Allentown, 25,000. Bethlehem, still under Moravian influence, forced businesses and industries to locate in areas south and west of the town proper; thus, its population in 1890 was about 6,800—but south Bethlehem borough's population by then had exceeded 10,000.

THE TWENTIETH CENTURY

By the end of the nineteenth century, patterns of life in the valley (and in the nation as a whole) were being altered dramatically by a scientific revolution, just as life in the prior two centuries had been changed by the Industrial Revolution. The expanded reliance on electricity, the advent of the automobile, an electric trolley era that spanned only a generation, and technological innovations that put resources such as oil, cement, chemicals, and minerals into service altered both human activity and the natural landscape of the Lehigh Valley profoundly.

Pennsylvania agriculture shifted gradually from a largely self-sustaining way of life into a capitalistic, scientific, commercial enterprise.

However, the family farm remained the dominant pattern in the valley, a pattern probably related to the German traditions of the earliest settlers. Somewhat later in the century, the conservative farmers of the region did not look favorably on governmental programs such as those of the New Deal. Large agricultural complexes such as Trexler Farms in Lehigh County were a rarity in the region.

Industrial Development

This chapter can only survey a few of the Lehigh Valley's industries, but a dominant one in our area is the steel industry. The numerous production plants scattered throughout the valley prospered during the First World War; most succumbed during the postwar depression, but one firm, the Bethlehem Iron Company, most definitely did not. Tycoons had dominated the nation's business life in the last half of the nineteenth century—Carnegie, Rockefeller, Vanderbilt, and Hearst among them—and one member of this eminent group, Charles M. Schwab, was pivotal in the development of the Bethlehem Iron Company. Reorganized by Schwab in 1904 as the Bethlehem Steel Company, the firm survived a turbulent early period, expanding and diversifying by the acquisition of several shipbuilding concerns. A new invention by Henry Grey used to produce rolling steel girders was named the Grey Beam, and in 1908, it helped Bethlehem Steel develop a market for girders suitable for skyscraper construction. Eugene G. Grace assumed the title of President in 1916, and under his direction, the company became the nation's second-largest steel producer.

Two of the nation's landmark suspension bridges, the George Washington Bridge and the Golden Gate Bridge, were fabricated by Bethlehem Steel during the 1930s. And in World War II, Bethlehem yards built more than a thousand naval and merchant vessels, repaired over nearly thirty-eight thousand ships, and armed battleships—such as the USS *Missouri*—with sixteen-inch guns. The last few decades have seen the demise of steel making in the valley, but for much of the twentieth century, Bethlehem Steel's impact on the valley rivaled that of the Lehigh Coal and Navigation Company in the last half of the nineteenth century.

Compared with steel, cement is of lesser importance to the economy of the valley. Nevertheless, the Lehigh Valley has achieved a national reputation for this product, which was first developed successfully here. One of the many effects of the construction of the Lehigh Canal was the start of the cement industry in the valley. A product called "natural

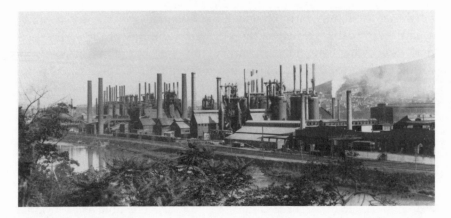

Fig. 3.7 *Bethlehem Steel*
Drawing on area resources, such as iron ore, anthracite coal, the ample flow of
the Lehigh River (foreground), and a receptive community, Steel—as it was locally
known—was a dominant part of the Lehigh Valley until the close of the twentieth
century. Now idle, it is one of many defunct industrial sites that are called
"brownfields" as abandonment and age allow them to rust. Fortunately, some
exciting plans are coming to fruition: redevelopment in the old Steel area is taking
place as part of the creation of the Delaware and Lehigh National Heritage Corridor. See Chapters 2, 3, and 12. (With permission of the Northampton County
Historical and Genealogical Society, Easton.)

cement" was made near Lehigh Gap between 1826 and 1830 and at
Siegfried's Bridge (now Northampton) from 1830 to 1841; it resulted
from a process of calcining cement rock mixed with clay in kilns devised
for the purpose. Most of the natural cement was used in repairing
breaks to the canal from storm damage.

After the Civil War, David O. Saylor and others formed the Coplay
Cement Company and, in 1873, Saylor manufactured the first American
portland cement, which was more durable and uniform in quality than
natural cement. Saylor's cement won the highest award in the nation's
grand Centennial Exposition in Philadelphia in 1876. Another innovation, the rotary kiln, caused an upsurge in production—and in the next
few years, other companies (such as the Atlas Cement Company, the Standard Portland Cement Company of New Jersey, and the Lehigh Portland
Cement Company) formed. Some survived, others failed, and still others
merged into more viable companies. (The Lehigh Portland Cement Company, founded by General Harry Clay Trexler and some of his associates,
was the largest cement company with general offices in the valley.)
Cement production was influential in the growth of numerous towns and
boroughs in the region, including Cementon, Ormrod, Northampton,

Fig. 3.8 *Saylor Park
cement kilns in Coplay*
(Collections of the Lehigh
County Historical Society.)

Coplay, Bath, and Nazareth. (See Box 2.2.) Iron, steel, and cement production required a large labor force, and immigrants from many parts of
the globe—but especially southern and central Europe—increased the
diversity of ethnic and religious groups within the valley.

Textiles

The same forces that drew immigrants to the region for employment in
the iron mills and cement plants contributed to the development of a
textile industry. Pioneers in the silk industry were enticed to the valley
by a group of Allentown businessmen and Allentown's Board of Trade.
The Phoenix Silk Manufacturing Company of Paterson, New Jersey, set
up the first textile mill in Allentown in 1881. Several other companies
followed suit, and by century's end, mills producing raw silk, ribbons,
and broad silks were well established. By 1909, Allentown had sixteen
silk mills; mills were also located in Bethlehem, Easton, Egypt, Vera
Cruz, and other sites in the region.

World War I spurred the growth of the textile industry, and by the
end of the war, 136 companies were located in Northampton and
Lehigh Counties. The Lehigh Valley benefited from the labor troubles
brewing in the garment industry in New York and became a center for
numerous textile products for men, women, and children during the
1920s. However, the Depression that soon followed—along with competition from rayon, nylon, and other synthetic materials—reduced the
market for silk. By 1959 only two companies (Phoenix Clothes, Inc. and
Penn State Mills, Inc.) operated in the valley.

A Diverse Economy

Many other industries can only be touched on here. The revolutionary internal combustion engine gave rise to an array of small and large firms engaged in the manufacture of automobiles, trucks, fire engines, and automotive parts. Only one company persisted in the valley: Mack Trucks. John and Charles Mack founded the Mack Motor Company in Brooklyn, New York in 1903, and the company soon outgrew its original location. The brothers established their first plant in 1905 in south Allentown. For the next half-century, Mack Trucks became a major economic force in the area. Other firms produced foods, chemicals, paper products, industrial machinery, pumps, and even crayons (Binney and Smith was founded in 1885). This diverse economy helped the Lehigh Valley contribute mightily to the war efforts during World Wars I and II, weather the Depression, and sustain population growth.

Shifting industrial patterns during the first half of the twentieth century—including more varied industrial operations and increasing numbers of wholesale and retail trade establishments—manifested themselves throughout the United States as well as in the Lehigh Valley. These new economic imperatives were also reflected in the changing positions of the three population centers in the valley during the same period. Allentown, more than the other cities, was able to expand its territory without infringing on other boroughs. The 1960 census indicates that Allentown's population was over 108,347; by comparison, Bethlehem had a population of 75,408, while Easton was a distant third at 31,955.

RECENT PATTERNS AND TRENDS

As mentioned earlier in this chapter, the natural corridors first used by Native Americans—the trails along streams and rivers—became the entryways for the first colonists into the Lehigh Valley. These same corridors became the sites of stagecoach routes, canal paths, railway beds, trolley lines, and, lastly, the highways that now cut through the valley. The development of Allentown, Bethlehem (along the Lehigh River), and Easton (at the junction of the Lehigh and Delaware Rivers) set the scene for most major transformations of the valley landscape. Running east to west, major roads serve these urban centers; spreading out from the cities, along the transportation corridors, is the suburban sprawl characteristic not only of the valley but also of major portions of the nation. A

CAMEO 3.1

General Harry Clay Trexler
(1854–1933)

During the early part of the twentieth century, General Harry Clay Trexler—more than any other person—was responsible for changing the nature of Allentown and the immediate vicinity. Trexler had extensive real estate holdings throughout the region and maintained a financial interest in almost every branch of the valley's newly developing industries. He founded the major electric utility in the region (Pennsylvania Power and Light) and was a cofounder of the Lehigh Portland Cement Company and the Lehigh Transit Company. Trexler was active in the planning of Allentown, with definite ideas about what constituted a livable city. West Park, the city's first public park, was the start of what would become an extensive park system (initially designed by the Olmsted brothers, famed landscape architects). Now parks run throughout much of the floodplain areas of the city and the adjacent suburbs. Among General Trexler's bequests was his deer park in Lowhill Township, now known as the Trexler Game Preserve.

glance at old valley maps that note roads, railways, and trolley lines readily reveals the locations of towns and villages that soon developed at trolley or train stops. Many outlying stops were built at early industrial sites, such as quarries, mills, or factories. Housing for workers drawn to these sites was soon followed by the construction of taverns, schools, and churches. A "fragmented forest" pattern has been produced during the last fifty years of human interaction with the valley landscape (the focus of Chap. 8). The ways in which this pattern may be altered in the future by decisions reached by today's citizens is assessed in the final chapter of the text. Here, however, we offer a brief summary of the "recent history" of our valley and a look at some important trends.

Population Trends

Population numbers by themselves would not appear to be too exciting. However, examining such numbers and considering the repercussions of

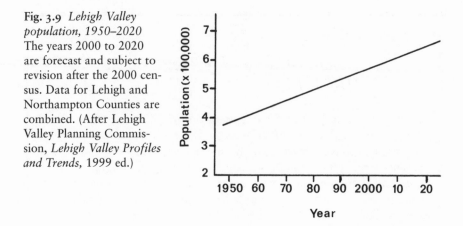

Fig. 3.9 *Lehigh Valley population, 1950–2020* The years 2000 to 2020 are forecast and subject to revision after the 2000 census. Data for Lehigh and Northampton Counties are combined. (After Lehigh Valley Planning Commission, *Lehigh Valley Profiles and Trends,* 1999 ed.)

population pressure can reveal some significant patterns of human inter-action with the landscape. Figure 3.9 presents census data for Northamp-ton and Lehigh Counties from 1950 to 1990. Estimates for the year 2000 and beyond are also provided. Where these people eventually decide to live is pivotal in landscape changes. That said, population projections for the next decade or so have been scaled back from earlier estimates. This bit of "breathing room" should provide planners and government agen-cies with greater opportunities to devise development schemes that could slow the loss of agricultural and open space lands.

Land Use Trends

The Joint Planning Commission, Lehigh-Northampton Counties (JPC) analysis of land use changes in Lehigh and Northampton Counties from the period 1972–92 gives the best assessment of this important pattern. During the twenty years that the study considers, almost fifty-one thou-sand acres of agricultural and "vacant" land (as the category is listed in JPC documents) were converted to other uses, including residential, commercial, industrial, transportation, and parks and recreation lands. In fact, almost 80 percent of the fifty-one thousand acres was recatego-rized as residential land. Residential land use by 1992 made up 21.1 percent of the total acreage of the two-county region; in 1972, that value was 14.9 percent.

As is true elsewhere in the United States, much residential growth occurs in rural and suburban settings. In the valley, a dozen subdivisions with five hundred units or more are all located in townships surrounding the three urban centers. Many of the homes in these subdivisions rely on wells and on-lot sewage disposal. Such developments may alter groundwater and drainage patterns; where a vernal pond or wet meadow once may have harbored an interesting array of plants and animals, a grassy field with a less diverse assemblage of flora and fauna now stands. Several Pennsylvania communities and many grassroots environmental organizations have looked favorably at the proposals to diminish suburban sprawl presented by Thomas Hylton (1995) in his book *Save Our Land, Save Our Towns: A Plan for Pennsylvania*. He suggests that Pennsylvania could adopt comprehensive plans to preserve and strengthen communities and greatly reduce the flight to the suburbs by town and city dwellers.

It is a good sign that during the twenty-year period covered by the JPC study, a little more than fourteen thousand acres was set aside for parks and open space use. However, it should be noted that park settings do not always promote the greatest biodiversity in the frequently "manicured" treatment of the patches of woods and edges that may exist in such parks. The varied uses of these areas also may not be compatible with sustaining a diversity of flora and fauna.

Forests

A detailed survey of woodlands in Lehigh County was conducted by the Soil Conservation Service in 1958. At that time, 37,000 acres of woods were mapped; this is about 17 percent of total land area in Lehigh County. Shortly thereafter, in 1967, a similar survey conducted by Northampton County's Soil Conservation Service revealed that 57,200 acres, almost 24 percent of that county's total land area, was in woodlands. The sizes of the tracts were noted, and it was determined that almost 74 percent of the forests were 50 acres or greater in Lehigh County, whereas in Northampton County, that size was attained by approximately 84 percent of the tracts. In both counties more than two-thirds of these woods were in private hands (industry or other private sources), and slightly less than a third were listed as owned by farmers, with only small amounts owned by the Pennsylvania Game Commission or county and municipal governments. Since that time, some lands adjacent to existing game lands have been acquired, mostly with the assistance of the Wildlands Conservancy, the most active land trust group in the valley. A recent initiative by the Pennsylvania State Forest Service aims at providing private land owners with forest management techniques that strive to address ecosystem considerations. Although no recent governmental agency surveys have been conducted, government officials relayed to us that at least some wooded tracts are increasing in acreage. These observations agree with the prediction made by the Soil Conservation Service in 1958 that growth by an average increase of almost 120 acres per year might be expected. (Some owners of forested tracts have acquired adjacent sites to permit the spread of the forests under their ownership.)

Agricultural Land Use

The JPC's first regional land use survey, performed in 1964, had indicated that 73.5 percent of the two-county area was agricultural and vacant land. By 1972 that figure had dropped to 68.5 percent; by 1992, the figure recorded was 57.7 percent. As noted above, some of that land was preserved as parks and open space; however, the conversion of farmland to subdivisions accounted for almost 80 percent of the loss of agricultural lands. The staff of the JPC suggested that if that trend persists, less than 50 percent of the region will be in agricultural and vacant land by 2006. One movement that may alter this trend is the purchase of agricultural conservation easements. Lehigh County has purchased such easements from ninety-three farms for a total of 9,354 acres. Northampton County has made arrangements with thirteen farms for a total of 2,792 acres.

Commercial and Industrial Development

Another trend noted by the JPC, and again not unique to the Lehigh Valley, is the establishment of commercial and industrial facilities in suburban townships. Between 1972 and 1992, commercial land use in the region increased by almost 2,400 acres, a 53.1 percent increase in this category. Presently, however, commercial land use accounts for only 1.5 percent of the total area of the region. Industrial land use also increased during the same twenty-year period by about 2,000 acres, a rise of 21 percent in this category of land use. Industrial land use comprises 2.4 percent of the total land area in the two counties. Much of the newer commercial and industrial development has taken place in suburban—and what had been previously considered rural—areas.

Transportation, Communications, and Utilities

Land used for roads, rights-of-way for power lines and related communications networks, and airports constitutes the third largest use of land in the region—7.6 percent of the total land area. About 1,480 acres were added to this land use category in the years between 1972 and 1992. With the spread of the suburban housing developments noted above, additional land may well be added to this category in the near future. For example, in the decade from 1960 to 1970, the number of automobiles in the region increased by 47.6 percent; the population, in contrast, had increased by only 9.5 percent during the same period. This pattern persists, and the number of licensed drivers in the two-county area has increased about 1.3 percent annually since 1988. Major corridor development continues along the east-west distribution of the major urban centers. The spread of suburban developments has meant that many of the smaller roads that citizens use, often in a north-south direction, are experiencing more traffic. Expansion of these roads is likely in the near future. Mass transit use has been modest throughout the past decade, showing a slight decline in total passenger trips. A specialized transport service (VAST) has shown a small increase in ridership. The pattern of widespread suburban developments is not conducive to economical mass transit service.

Figure 3.10, adapted from a 1993 Joint Planning Commission report, summarizes the patterns of land use and projects possible land uses by the year 2010.

Governmental Response

Local and county governmental response to the patterns and trends of development within the valley has been varied. Almost all local governments have enacted zoning, subdivision, and land development ordinances. Commonwealth legislation—Acts 515 and 319—has been used by both counties to establish provisions for the preservation of agricultural land. As indicated elsewhere in this chapter, Lehigh County has been much more successful in these efforts than Northampton County has been. However, there have been relatively few examples of larger regional efforts, despite the fact that most environmental dilemmas do not recognize human-made boundaries. One municipality may attempt to protect floodplains while an adjacent municipality tries to promote a particular commercial or industrial development that could adversely

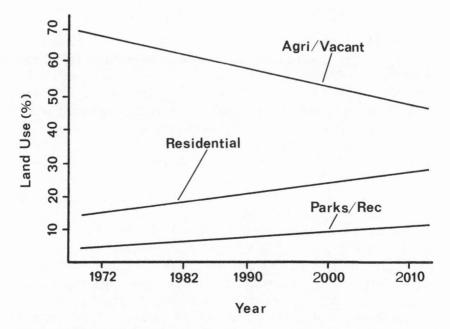

Fig. 3.10 *Lehigh Valley land use trends*
This graph is based on Joint Planning Commission (JPC) figures. See the *Comprehensive Plan for Lehigh and Northampton Counties, PA. The Lehigh Valley . . . 2010*, Table 3. Trend totals do not add up to 100 percent, because *lesser* categories (commercial, industrial, wholesale/warehousing, transportation/utilities, and public/quasi-public) are excluded. Two interesting questions: when will the agriculture/vacant trend line (upper line) intersect with the residential trend line (middle line)? Can—or will—parks and recreation land keep up?

affect the floodplain that occupies both areas. The Lehigh Valley Planning Commission (previously called the Joint Planning Commission, Lehigh-Northampton Counties) has urged greater regional planning for several decades, and more citizens seem to agree with this suggestion, but little has occurred at the governmental level.

Air and Water Quality

Environmental legislation, much of it passed in the late 1960s and early 1970s, had an impact nationally and regionally on air and water quality. (See Chap. 11 for a more extensive discussion of environmental legislation.) The valley saw a considerable reduction in air pollution, especially in particulates. Particulate reduction was achieved largely through the use of electrostatic precipitators and scrubbers at industrial sites and the use of catalytic converters on vehicles. The residents of towns and localities near the numerous cement and steel plants that flourished in mid-century throughout the valley could testify to the poor air quality that often prevailed in those areas. Longtime residents of these towns (and other sites throughout the valley) believe, however, that the air is getting cleaner—and Pennsylvania Department of Environmental Protection data support their views. Monitoring data across the state show total suspended particulate (TSP) measurements in 1960 on the order of 150 micrograms per cubic meter of air. Such levels, exceeding those of the primary air quality standard, were recorded for the next two decades. (The *primary air quality standard* for each pollutant is based on human health studies used by government officials to determine exposure of humans without noticeable ill effects.) However, pollution abatement activities began to have an effect. In the years between 1988 and 1997, there was a 23 percent decrease in annual TSP concentrations throughout the Commonwealth.

Other air pollutants show a similar pattern. In the valley, ozone levels that reached two or three times the standard in the '60s and '70s dipped below that standard by 1989 and remained there through the 1990s. Sulfur oxide levels averaged 60 parts per billion in 1967 but were found to be just above 10 parts per billion by the mid-1970s. (However, in the case of this particular air pollutant, not much improvement has been detected over the past few decades.) Carbon monoxide levels continue a downward trend, with the largest improvements seen in the Allentown-Bethlehem-Easton air basin (63 percent improvement) when statewide studies are examined. Pennsylvania Air Quality Monitoring Survey data presented by county have typically rated air quality in Lehigh and Northampton Counties as "good" for about 70–75 percent of each year listed for the past decade. On the remaining days, a rating of "moderate" was earned. Rarely, a day or so was listed as "unhealthy."

The Environmental Protection Agency has proposed more stringent regulations to reduce air pollution. Cement kilns—twenty-one located statewide, ten of which are located within the Lehigh Valley—have become special targets for the EPA. Cement kilns that burn hazardous waste, such as the kiln of the Keystone Cement Company in Bath, face even tougher air pollution requirements. Of course, air quality in any region is influenced by activities and events hundreds or even thousands of miles from that region. The enforcement (or lack thereof) of federal and state mandates on power plants in midwestern states would have a significant impact on the direction of the trends observed in various pollutants over the past few decades.

At least fifteen main tributaries and numerous smaller streams enter the Lehigh as it makes its way from its source in Wayne County to its confluence with the Delaware River. Only a few of these tributaries have had extensive monitoring by federal, state, or regional agencies. The Lehigh River itself has been the focus of only a few studies, although six United States Geological Survey gauging stations have been maintained on the Lehigh for some decades. Some of these tributaries, and the Lehigh River, were studied most recently in 1987 and 1988 by staff from the Surface Water Quality Assessment unit of the Department of Environmental Protection.

Principal wastes adversely affecting the water quality of the Lehigh and its tributaries are industrial discharge, sewage, runoff from agricultural, urban, and industrial sites, and, in the upper reaches of the Lehigh, acid mine drainage. Drainage from abandoned mine tunnels and runoff from abandoned strip mines have resulted in sections of the river with high concentrations of sulfate, iron, sediment, and acidity. In recent years, the Department of Environmental Protection's operation of lime neutralization facilities on some of the tributaries has begun to reduce acid mine drainage effects. Improved sewage treatment facilities in many towns and cities, prompted by federal legislation and assistance programs, have also had a beneficial effect on water quality in many parts of the valley.

In a similar fashion—again, due largely to federal legislation and assistance—industrial discharges have been reduced. Of greatest concern from industrial sites are heavy metals such as copper, manganese, cadmium, zinc, lead, nickel, and iron. Instream values of some heavy metals exceeded acceptable limits at the mouths of some of the acid mine drainage tributaries. Some elements such as copper, iron, and nickel were reported in the 1987–88 data to exceed the instream criteria at the mouths of certain tributaries, but mainstream concentrations never exceeded the criteria during the course of the survey. The staff of the Department of Environmental Protection survey did express concern about zinc and cadmium concentrations in the Lehigh and identified the main source of zinc and cadmium: the Aquashicola Creek at Lehigh Gap. The well-known smelting operations at Palmerton devastated the vegetation at the gap and, subsequently, caused heavy erosion and runoff into the adjacent waters.

Non–point source pollution has been harder to combat. Contaminants such as sediments, pesticides, spilled solvents, and high levels of nitrate and phosphate come principally from non-point sources, such as runoff from roadways, parking lots and other paved surfaces, agricultural fields, golf courses, and suburban lawns. Studies designed to monitor this type of pollution have captured the periodic attention of school and college students as well as a more continuous monitoring by staff from the Wildlands Conservancy. The Jordan, Cedar, Little Lehigh, Monocacy, and Bushkill Creeks have all been examined with various degrees of rigor. At several study sites in Cedar Creek, silt carried by storm runoff from surrounding suburban and park areas had an adverse effect on benthic macroinvertebrate diversity and abundance. In fact, sediment from erosion is the most significant pollutant by volume in the state. In the southern portions of the valley, which have a higher clay content in the soil, erosion is particularly bad; limited crop rotation makes the land even more susceptible to erosion. Housing developments can add to this type of pollution, when poorly designed or inadequate erosion devices fail to stop or slow runoff. In addition, sediment may carry other pollutants.

A detailed study conducted by staff members of the Wildlands Conservancy on Allentown's Jordan Creek in 1985 revealed a somewhat degraded stream. Five species made up almost 62 percent of all the macroinvertebrates collected at five sites over the nine months of the study, and the species collected are considered typical of a stream experiencing organic enrichment. Unfortunately, no measurements were made to determine the types of organic compounds that might have led to the condition of the stream. As noted above, excess nitrates and phosphates—mainly from fertilizer runoff from agricultural fields, lawns, parks, golf courses, and the like—often lead to this organic enrichment. Control of non–point source pollution will probably continue to be a major threat to water quality in the valley and elsewhere in the Commonwealth. More attention must be paid to local sources and types of pollution, and most experts are confident that water quality in the Lehigh River and in most tributaries will continue to show improvement in the next millennium.

Two Case Studies

In our view, two episodes in recent decades illustrate the changing nature of human/landscape interactions in the valley. One was a proposal to form Trexler Reservoir by having the U.S. Army Corps of Engineers construct a dam on the Jordan Creek in Lowhill Township, Lehigh

County. The other was a proposal to construct a major interstate high-way (I-78) somewhere through the western and southern region of the valley. The reservoir was not built, but the highway was.

The Trexler Reservoir, which was proposed to serve in flood control and to provide a water supply and sites for water-based recreation, would have flooded about 4,600 acres of land. The $46 million project was to begin in 1974 and be fully operational by 1980. The project would have been one of the largest public works projects in the region and was viewed by some as pivotal for industrial, residential, and commercial expansion in the western portions of the valley. Opposition to the proposed dam came principally from nearby landowners and wildlife enthusiasts (since land at State Game Land No. 205 would have been flooded for the reservoir). Other concerns were raised about the possible decline in water quality for the Jordan Creek and the loss of agricultural lands in Lowhill Township. Still other citizens worried about other effects of a dam, predicting its impact on the residential and commercial development of a largely rural landscape.

Grassroots environmentalism was flourishing throughout the nation and in the valley. An association of a dozen eco-action groups, the Lehigh Valley Environmental Federation, was formed to provide techni-cal arguments about environmental damage resulting from the con-struction of a reservoir. The Northwestern Lehigh Citizens Coalition, composed mainly of individuals who lived and owned land in the area near the proposed dam, led the opposition. Even the U.S. Environmen-tal Protection Agency entered the debate, and a report from the EPA released in December 1972 criticized the Corps' "inadequate and inap-propriate" environmental review. Additional efforts by local activists over several years resulted in a referendum on Trexler Reservoir that was placed on the ballot for the November 8, 1977 election in Lehigh County. The electorate soundly rejected the proposed project by a three-to-one margin. Shortly thereafter, the Trexler Reservoir was placed on the inactive list by the Corps of Engineers.

The other case study, the location of Interstate 78, had a different conclusion in spite of a perhaps more rigorous grassroots activism than that seen in the Trexler Reservoir situation. This environmental activism was led by the Saucon Association for a Viable Environment (SAVE), a group of citizen activists that had also been engaged in the Trexler Dam issue. In the early 1960s, federal officials proposed a thirty-five-mile link of interstate highway—I-78—in eastern Pennsylvania, starting west of Fogelsville, Pennsylvania and extending to an area just east of Phillips-burg, New Jersey. At that time, only a few miles of new highway were to be constructed; most of the remaining corridor would use existing roads, which would be upgraded to handle interstate traffic. In 1968, Pennsylvania Department of Transportation (PennDOT) officials proposed an entirely new route south of South Mountain. Activists, mainly SAVE members, quickly became enmeshed in the discussions at public hearings and in the "letters to the editor" section of the local newspapers. Eventually, these discussions reached the level of litigation: the prestigious Environmental Defense Fund, SAVE, and several individual citizens filed a suit before the United States Federal District Court in Philadelphia. Through the suit, the plaintiffs attempted to stop further expenditure of tax monies for the proposed southern corridor of I-78. The greatest concern of environmentalists was the loss of prime farmland, as much as one thousand acres south of South Mountain, for the actual road construction. They argued that other farmlands would be less accessible to farmers and would be sold to developers. Development pressures at intersections would result in additional loss of productive land and diminished habitat for wildlife. But after more than a decade, the lawsuit was decided in favor of PennDOT. There is now an interstate connection between the western border at Fogelsville and the eastern edge near Phillipsburg, most of it new highway. Short sections of existing roads (Routes 22 and 309) are utilized, but—as SAVE members and other environmentalists point out—any valley dweller can see the loss of farmland and wildlife habitat. Other community members, on the other hand, contend that local traffic conditions in the urban area of Allentown, Bethlehem, and Easton would be even more challenging without an interstate to divert truck and traveler traffic away from urban settings. Sadly, most readers of this text will have experienced similar dilemmas; our love of the automobile and the freedom to travel where and when we wish has exacerbated our impact on the environment. No easy solutions to this problem are forthcoming.

The patterns and trends of human/landscape interactions of the last half of the twentieth century, briefly outlined here, have produced a valley landscape which we've designated the "fragmented forest," the focus of Chapter 8. Chapter 11 describes the federal and state environmental legislation that governs how citizens relate to the environment. But for now, we will turn away from our assessment of the political climate for environmental change, addressing instead the climate—and the weather—of the Lehigh Valley.

FOUR

The Climate of the Valley

The belief in former greater weather extremes is almost
universal among old people in any community, regardless
of the fact that over and over again it has been shown by
instrumental readings and carefully recorded observations
of trained meteorologists that there is little or no basis for
such conclusions.

—BENJAMIN L. MILLER, *Lehigh County, Pennsylvania:*
Geology and Geography, 1941

Notable remarks about the weather are readily available to writers
in search of an appropriate chapter-opener. Indeed, in the witty
words ascribed to a famous Pennsylvania meteorologist, Ben Franklin,
"everybody talks about the weather, but nobody does anything about
it." And talk we do, for the weather affects our moods, travel, businesses, schools, heating and cooling, vacation plans, and just about
everything else in our lives. Even such acts as suicide and lovemaking
are weather-related.

Despite the nearly universal interest in weather conditions, the
words "weather" and "climate" are often confused. *Weather* is the condition of the atmosphere (including wind, temperature, humidity,
cloudiness, and the like) at any particular time and place; *climate,* by
contrast, is the average of daily and seasonal weather conditions over

CAMEO 4.1

James H. Coffin (1806–1873)

We take modern weather forecasting for granted; the process, however, evolved from a series of basic laws that were the fruits of extensive research during the last century. James H. Coffin, Professor of Mathematics and Chair of the Department of Mathematics and Natural Philosophy at Lafayette College, was a major contributor to our understanding of weather—particularly through his study of the movement of the winds. He collaborated with the Smithsonian Institution on two major works: *Winds of the Northern Hemisphere* (1853) and *Winds of the Globe* (finished in 1875 by his son). The *Dictionary of American Biography* notes that "the second of these studies . . . involving years of work, was by far the most exhaustive collection and fullest analysis of wind data that had been made, and its main conclusions are good for all time." Though Coffin's work was conceptual (and thus broadly applied), it continues to make a difference in our understanding of and ability to predict Lehigh Valley weather systems.

time. The best and simplest synopsis of our Lehigh Valley climate may be the statement issued by the National Oceanic and Atmospheric Administration (NOAA) in its Annual Summary for Allentown from the Lehigh Valley International Airport station:

A modified climate prevails. Temperatures are usually moderate and precipitation generally ample and dependable with the largest amounts occurring during the summer months when precipitation is generally showery. General climatological features of the area are slightly modified by the mountain ranges so that at times during the winter there is a temperature difference of 10 to 15 degrees between Allentown and Philadelphia, only 50 miles to the south.

The growing season averages 177 days, and generally ranges from 170 to 185 days. It begins late in April and ends late in October. The average occurrence of the last temperature of 32 degrees in the spring is late April, and the average first fall minimum of 32 degrees is mid-October.

Maximum temperatures during most years are not excessively high and temperatures above 100 degrees are seldom recorded. However, the average humidity in the valley is quite high, and combined with the normal summer temperatures, causes periods of discomfort.

Winters in the valley are comparatively mild. Minimum temperatures during December, January, and February are usually below freezing, but below zero temperatures are seldom recorded.

Seasonal snowfall is quite variable. Freezing rain is a common problem throughout the Lehigh Valley. Snowstorms producing 10 inches or more occur an average of once in two years. The accumulation of snowfall over the drainage area of the Lehigh River to the north of Allentown, combined with spring rains, frequently presents a flood threat to the city and surrounding area. The valley is also subject to torrential rains that cause quick rises in the river and feeder creeks.

The area is seldom subject to destructive storms of large extent. Heavy thunderstorms and tornadoes occasionally cause damage over limited areas.

While the NOAA statement provides a tidy summary of our climate, on a day-to-day basis we are concerned with the weather—and particularly with the forecast. The National Weather Service (a division of NOAA) sponsors a twenty-four-hour weather forecast at 162.40 on the Weather Radio. Commercially sponsored weather forecasts can be heard at (610) 797-5900 or (610) 821-8300 (ext. 6799), or on TV (local Accuweather). Forecasts are frequently given on local radio and television stations and in local newspapers; libraries also receive NOAA publications that cover the local weather.

CLIMATE SCALES

When we speak of the climate of the Lehigh Valley, we are referring to the *mesoclimate,* or the climate of a small region. The *macroclimate* is the climate of a very large area, such as Pennsylvania as a whole, while the *microclimate* is the climate on or near the ground. A slate sidewalk (which is black and absorbs heat well) might possibly slowly cook an egg, as the microclimate may be many tens of degrees above the overall climate. In general, weather is recorded in an enclosed and ventilated shelter with the instruments maintained five feet above the ground. (The typical temperature range over the year for the Lehigh Valley is plotted in Fig. 4.1.) Changing temperature is, of course, a reflection of the constant 23° tilt of the earth in its revolution around the sun.

The setting for our climate is that of mostly rolling hills of countryside, scattered forest patches, and concentrated urban islands. It has been known for more than a hundred years that these cities are generally warmer than the rural areas; such warmth zones are called *urban heat islands*. (A typical forecast might call for "85 degrees in center city and around 75 in the outlying areas.") In a similar manner, open fields will heat up more than forested areas will. The bubble of rising hot air, called a *thermal*, over a field can be sensed by glider pilots and some of the large soaring birds, such as the familiar turkey vulture, that are masters of "making lazy circles in the sky" (as a line from *Oklahoma!* puts it). In an urban area, particularly on a still, clear night, a slight "country breeze" may develop, which can be a mixed blessing: while it brings some cooler circulating air to the sweltering citizenry, it also tends to drive the air pollutants more centrally into the city.

Weather-related guidelines for health and safety have been issued by NOAA. The heat index (HI), introduced in the mid-1980s, combines air temperature and relative humidity in order to determine an *apparent* temperature, or how hot it actually feels. When the apparent temperature climbs above 90°F, a variety of serious physiological problems may develop. At the other end of the temperature spectrum, the wind-chill factor (or index) is the cooling effect of any combination of temperature and wind, expressed as a loss of body heat. With an index at or below -25°F, there is a real risk of frostbite. Charts for both of these temperature-sensitive indices and their interpretation are widely available.

WIND, PRECIPITATION, AND STORMS

Being in the belt of the prevailing westerlies, winds in the Lehigh Valley are mostly light and from the west, southwest, or northeast. Over the year, the air is calm about 23 percent of the time; 64 percent of the time, the winds are light (4–15 miles per hour), and they reach 16–31 miles per hour 12 percent of the time, rarely exceeding 32 miles per hour. The windiest month is March, and the calmest is August. The effects of wind on the valley are varied: the prevailing westerlies blow up and over Blue Mountain, the last continuous eastern ridge of the Appalachian chain.

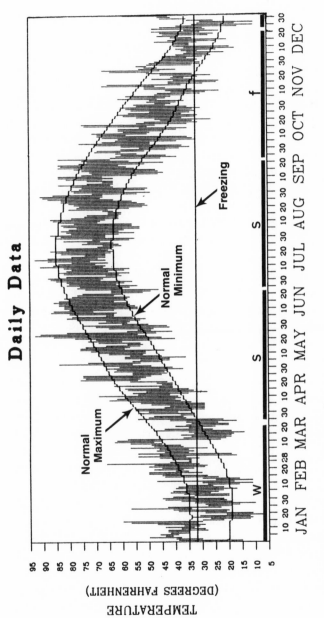

Fig. 4.1 *Temperatures for the Lehigh Valley, 1992*
Normal maximum, normal minimum, and the freezing line are plotted against time and the seasons. (Courtesy of the National Oceanic and Atmospheric Administration [NOAA].)

BOX 4.1

Places to See Temperature-Related Phenomena

PHOTOPERIOD EXTENSION. Look for large street trees with some branches very close to streetlights (particularly to sodium-vapor lamps). These trees will receive enough additional heat, coupled with an extended photoperiod, to encourage the proximal leaves to persist very late into the fall while the tree drops the rest of its leaves.

SLOPE. On a road with a roughly east-west orientation and modest road cut (such as Route 22 or Route 248), snow on the north-facing bank will melt at a decidedly different rate than snow on the south-facing bank. Hemlock Heights, a steep north-facing stand of virgin hemlock near the Kempton approach road to Hawk Mountain, may have residual snow until late May.

THERMALS. The large, slowly rising parcels of warm air are, of course, invisible. But a *kettle* (flock) of broad-winged hawks slowly circling upward is a sure sign that they've caught a thermal.

TREE BASE DEPRESSIONS. After a snowfall, when the temperatures start to rise, watch the areas of snow immediately surrounding tree bases. Being dark, the tree trunks absorb the sunlight better than the snow does, and they reflect the heat back to the adjacent area, causing interesting depressions to form.

(Most of the raptors that spend the warm months in New England and eastern Canada return south along this prominent ridge in the fall. The ridge, which borders the Lehigh Valley on the northwest, plays a prominent role in the Atlantic Flyway for these migrants. See also Chap. 9.)

Tornadoes, those generally destructive whirlwinds, are mostly associated with the flat lands of the southern and midwestern states. Our rolling topography and bordering mountains do not favor the tornado activity that characteristically occurs in April, May, and June—when surface and aloft air masses show maximum differences. A limited number of Lehigh Valley tornadoes are, however, noted in Ben Gelber's 1992 book, *Pocono Weather.* One tornado of particular interest was described in the *Pocono Record* for August 11, 1983: "A small tornado was first sighted near Egypt, five miles northwest of the Allentown/Bethlehem/Easton Airport. The storm continued southeast through Catasauqua before dissipating over Freemansburg. The total path length was

11 miles, though the damage was not continuous. The width of the damage path was 150 yards. As much as $3 million damage was done to the airport, where 20 airplanes and 15 hangars were damaged."

More recently—on May 31, 1998—a tornado of mid-range strength (F-3 on the Fujita measurement scale) created a path of destruction 300 yards wide and 8 miles long in the Berks County towns of Lyons and Bowers. The tornado destroyed or severely damaged about 24 homes and 7 farms, and several dozen other buildings incurred minor damage.

Lehigh Valley wind phenomena also include "dust devils." These are small, rapidly rotating winds made visible by dust and other debris. Being typically only 6–10 feet in diameter and perhaps up to 100 feet in height, they are usually not damaging. They mostly occur on clear, hot days, when a heated surface, such as macadam, has its rising hot air bubble surrounded by invading cooler winds. As the twisting motion develops and the dust devil itself migrates, it becomes particularly visible over dusty or silty surfaces, such as clay tennis courts or dusty baseball diamonds. A dust devil is also called a "whirlwind" or a "willy-willy."

If we add a substantial moisture load to high winds, then there may be trouble. Precipitation in the valley is moderate: the average annual precipitation is about 43 inches and is fairly evenly distributed throughout the year. Included in this figure is snowfall, which is recorded as melted snow and has, roughly, a 10:1 meltdown ratio. (The snow varies in its fluffiness—air spaces—and a 6:1 ratio would indicate dense snow, while 30:1 would indicate loose and light snow.) Moisture-laden storms, such as hurricanes and blizzards, are not unknown in the Lehigh Valley.

A *hurricane* is a severe tropical cyclone with winds in excess of 74 miles per hour, typically laden with moisture. The hurricane season is June through October. If the movement of the hurricane up the coast is "right" and the storm intensity sustains itself, eastern Pennsylvania can take a pounding. A few of our more notable area hurricanes include Hazel (1954), Diane (1955), Agnes (1972), and Gloria (1985). Wind damage and flooding are the most serious consequences.

Add at least 3 hours of snow, high winds (gusts to 35 miles per hour), and a visibility of less than one quarter of a mile, and the event is classified as a *blizzard*. The Lehigh Valley has not been spared from occasional severe blizzards, and ongoing discussions often center on the question, "How severe was it?" Curiously, the National Weather Service does not have a formal mechanism to grade or rank blizzard severity. William Dovico, a meteorologist at the Lehigh Valley International Airport, developed an interesting formula in 1985 from which he could determine a Severity Index for blizzards. (See Table 4.1 for his ranking of Lehigh Valley blizzards.) Although the table may help to settle some arguments, the designation of "the most severe blizzard," like that of "the world's greatest baseball player," will remain elusive and debatable.

Despite the Lehigh Valley's moderate precipitation and occasional blizzards, area residents cannot generally count on a "white Christmas." Based on over 75 years of record, there is one chance in five that measurable precipitation will be on the ground (including "old" snow still in place) at Christmas, and one chance in seven that it will actually snow.

Record-breaking weather events depend on the accuracy of historical accounts, the time frame, the location, the quality of the instruments, and the people involved. And so, at the risk of oversimplification (and in light of the above), Table 4.2 suggests some of the records for the Lehigh Valley. Records, are of course, the exception to the rule; for the most part we enjoy a moderate, continental, mid-latitude climate. Recent hype in the popular media has identified, sometimes erroneously, a strong correlation between *all* anomalous weather behavior and the phenomenon of El Niño.

Table 4.1 *Thirteen worst Lehigh Valley blizzards since 1888*

Date	Severity Index	Snowfall (inches)	Wind Speed During Storm/After Storm (miles per hour)	Temperature (°F)
March 12, 1888	8.5	13.0	37.1/33.5	16
February 11–13, 1899	7.7	20.0	29.8/30.3	5
January 25, 1905	6.1	17.0	30.6/21.7	12
February 14, 1940	6.1	12.0	29.5/31.0	21
February 16, 1958	5.9	16.0	29.3/28.4	19
January 30, 1966	5.6	12.0	27.9/25.9	17
January 7–8, 1996	5.3	25.5	17.9/15.8	14
February 7, 1895	4.9	10.0	25.1/25.3	5
December 24, 1966	4.5	13.3	24.0/24.0	21
February 6–7, 1978	4.4	13.8	23.2/23.0	19
March 13–14, 1993	4.4	17.6	19.2/23.7	25
March 4, 1960	4.4	14.4	24.4/23.4	18
March 2, 1914	4.1	12.0	28.1/20.0	17

SOURCE: Dovico 1985.
NOTE: Drifts of 8–10 feet were common in the blizzard of March 12, 1888.

Table 4.2 *Selected Lehigh Valley weather records*

Weather Condition	Record	Date
Highest temperature	105°F	July 3, 1966
Lowest temperature	–15°F	January 21, 1994
Highest wind speed (sustained one minute)	81 miles/hour	June 15, 1964
Highest gusts	109 miles/hour	June 15, 1964
Coldest month	16.4° average	February 1934
Warmest month	79.0° average	July 1955
Coldest year	48.9° average	1967
Warmest year	55.7° average	1990
Maximum yearly snowfall	75.9 inches	1993–94
Maximum storm snowfall	25.2 inches	February 11–12, 1983
Fastest snowfall rate	5 inches/hour	February 11, 1983
Most severe blizzard	8-10 feet drifts	March 12, 1888
Maximum precipitation/ten minutes	1.05 inches	July 26, 1969
Maximum precipitation/one hour	2.78 inches	August 8, 1982
Worst hurricane	Hazel	October 14, 1954
Highest flood crests—Lehigh River	20.8' (Lehighton)	February 28, 1902
	23.4' (Allentown)	August 19, 1955
	25.9' (Bethlehem)	August 19, 1955

EL NIÑO AND PENNSYLVANIA

In the Lehigh Valley, we tend to look at our climate through the dependable lenses of the National Weather Service, which can issue a report on climate based on dozens of years of solid statistics. Certain occasional seasons—and indeed whole years—can experience perturbations within the system, drifting a bit from the average.

Layered on top of that system has been, most recently, the catchall of El Niño. It is an irregular occurrence of a significant increase in sea surface temperatures (SST) in the eastern Equatorial Zone of the Pacific Ocean (near the coasts of Peru and Ecuador). Although the genesis of these warm water episodes is unclear, there have been about fifteen of them since 1925, each lasting from one to three years. The effects of El Niño, arising in part from moving moister air currents, extend both poleward (north and south) and to other points in the world and change the jet stream patterns. The impact of El Niño seemed most pronounced in 1997–98, with the exceptional precipitation and concurrent flooding and mudslides in California (events that were somewhat predictable from the historical relationship between El Niño and coastal California weather patterns).

For Pennsylvania in general—and the Lehigh Valley in particular—the impact of El Niño is not as readily predictable, and its effect is much more subtle. Penn State University meteorologist Gregory Forbes studied eight of the most recent El Niño events (from 1950 through 1997) for seven Pennsylvania locations, including Allentown. Based on the parameters of temperature, snowfall, and precipitation, and the expected predictability, there is only a weak correlation for Pennsylvania; monthly anomalies over the years were often both positive and negative.

While this is the current status for the Lehigh Valley (at best, an area only marginally affected by El Niño), research continues because of the worldwide importance of accurately predicting El Niño's reach. Michael Glantz, author of a book on El Niño, wrote that forecasting El Niño would be science's gift to the twenty-first century. (Such a development would certainly respond to the recent mandates of the United States Congress and of the scientific community for "usable science.")

But subtracting out the El Niño effect, for the most part, brings us back to the tidy climate summary of the Lehigh Valley with which the chapter opened. And this, in turn, leads us to examine the more predictable seasons and their natural history—the focus of the next chapter.

The Natural History of the Seasons

For everything there is a season, and a time for every matter under heaven: a time to be born, and a time to die; a
time to plant, and a time to pluck up what is planted.

—ECCLESIASTES 3:1–2

At a latitude of 40° north (76° west longitude), and near the middle of the
Temperate Zone, the Lehigh Valley enjoys a vivid seasonal parade. The
Tropical (Torrid) Zone, delineated by the parallel circles of Cancer and
Capricorn at 23° north and south of the Equator, has little change; the sun
is close to overhead for the entire year. The Arctic (Frigid)
Zone, at about 66° north (and extending northward), has but two seasons:
a very short summer and a long winter. The Lehigh Valley is the benefici-
ary of four well-defined seasons. The key lies in the constant 23° tilt of the
earth in its yearly transit around the sun. Simply put: no tilt, no seasons.

According to the position and angle of the earth relative to the sun,
spring officially begins in the northern hemisphere on March 21. At that
time, known as the *vernal equinox,* the tilt of the earth is such that day
and night are both twelve hours long. Only on September 21 (the
autumnal equinox) do we experience similarly equal day and night
lengths, and the date marks the first of three months of fall. The longest
and shortest days of the year are positioned between the equinoxes:
June 21 and December 21, respectively. (See Figs. 4.1 and 5.1.)

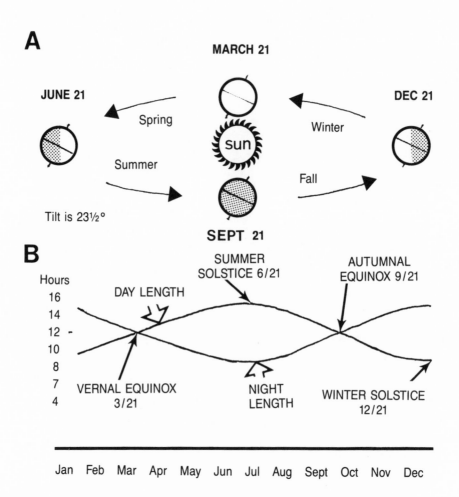

A

MARCH 21

JUNE 21   DEC 21

Spring   sun   Winter

Summer   Fall

Tilt is 23½°

SEPT 21

B

Hours

SUMMER   AUTUMNAL
SOLSTICE 6/21   EQUINOX 9/21

16   DAY LENGTH
14
12 -
10
8
7   VERNAL EQUINOX   NIGHT
4   3/21   LENGTH   WINTER SOLSTICE
                                                    12/21

Jan Feb Mar Apr May Jun Jul Aug Sept Oct Nov Dec

Fig. 5.1 *The earth's revolution and corresponding day length*

PHENOLOGY

Long, short, and transitional days mean seasons. The formal and scientific study of seasonal change is called *phenology*. Primitive peoples probably planted crops in concert with the flowering times of wild plants; biological events linked to the seasons have been recorded since at least 700 B.C. by the Chinese. After years of observation and recording, we can make the following generalizations about spring: events tend to be about four days later for each degree of latitude (equal to 70 miles) north, about the same delay per 400 feet of elevation, and a similar delay for every five degrees of longitude eastward. Put differently, spring moves northward at about 17 miles per day, and its events are delayed by one day for each 100 feet of elevation. The autumn is somewhat reversed (and less studied).

How does all of this translate into the observations of a Lehigh Valley resident? It means that the flowering times of Valley Forge will be about three to four days ahead of those of the Lehigh Valley, and that flowers will bloom roughly a week behind those in the valley at the higher elevations of the Poconos. Within the Lehigh Valley itself, the two extremes might be Hosack, located in the southeastern corner of Lehigh County and at an elevation of 420 feet, and Mt. Minsi, at the northeastern corner of Northampton County and an elevation of 1,460 feet. Discarding *aspect* (slope direction), the distance and elevation differences create a time lag of about twelve days. Slope may add several days to this.

Spring blooms, as every homeowner knows, occur much earlier in warmer, south-facing microhabitats than in those that are north-facing or otherwise shaded. The main agent of flowering (or of leaf drop in the fall) is primarily controlled by genetic factors, temperature, and the photoperiod, but available moisture, wind, cloudiness, human intervention, and additional biotic factors also play their parts. The observational bottom line is this: as one travels north or south, the colorful spring and fall displays will be in cadence with nature's rhythms.

Two Calendars

Humans have always been interested in both the passage and the milestone markers of time. Years, seasons, millennia, and birthdays are illustrative. The earliest people used nature's rhythms, such as flowering periods and bird migrations, to mark time. With advancements in the sciences, we came to adopt a variety of calendars—up to the current twelve-month Gregorian calendar, widely accepted in 1582 and based on precise relationships between the sun and earth.

While the Gregorian calendar by which we schedule our lives is fixed and therefore predictable, natural systems are additionally governed by the vagaries of weather, changing ocean currents, the jet stream, and so on. What follows in the remainder of the chapter, then, is a chronology of nature's plastic seasonal calendar held against the fixed backdrop of our familiar civic calendar. Our dates are for somewhat ideal conditions and may err on the "too early" side; anticipation is a pleasant remedy for a long winter. Without beating the word *usually* to death, the seasonal

CAMEO 5.1

Tom Fegely (1941–)

The best of two worlds—combining an avocation with a vocation—describes the life of Tom Fegely. After spending a number of years teaching environmental subjects in local schools, Tom translated his classroom interests into outdoor pursuits and, in the process, became an expert fisherman, hunter, birdwatcher, photographer, outdoorsman, and environmental advocate. As the widely followed Outdoors Editor of the *Morning Call*, he has been able to communicate his fascination with the outdoors effectively and colorfully for twenty years. For his efforts he has won a number of well-deserved awards.

He writes regular weekly columns, most of them centered on the current Lehigh Valley natural history/seasonal scene. But in addition, he has written a number of books on the outdoors, including some for children. And as a speaker in high demand, he shares not only his seasonal experiences with the audience but also his equally impressive photographic slides.

Tom Fegely has been an attentive and effective observer and translator of the natural history of the Lehigh Valley seasons. Thousands are better informed because of his efforts.

events that follow are just that—usual—and should be treated as observational guidelines. The famed swallows of San Juan Capistrano do punctually arrive at the California mission on March 19 each year (with rare storm delays). They are an exception. Our tree swallows arrive in a window of about two or more weeks and reflect the seasonally less punctual life of the Temperate and Atlantic Coastal Zones.

The familiar "It's been a late spring/short winter/dry summer/wet fall" are typical (usual?) seasonal remarks. As we survey the seasons and calendar months of the year, we leave it to the reader to decide which seasons are the most and least variable in the Lehigh Valley.

JANUARY

Despite being the coldest and one of the cloudiest months, January always provides something stirring and fun for the valley naturalist to see. About twenty or thirty resident birds (see the checklist in Chap. 9) can sometimes be observed on unfrozen ponds, along streams, in shrubbery, and in open fields. If snow is on the ground, it is a particularly good time to check the feeding stations frequently. Regulars may include the mourning dove, junco, white-throated sparrow, black-capped chickadee, tufted titmouse, white-breasted nuthatch, cardinal, house finch, purple finch, blue jay, starling, and, depending on the feeder, a few woodpeckers. (A comprehensive, nationwide study of birdfeeder populations is a current and continuing effort. Interested parties may contact the Cornell Project FeederWatch, c/o Cornell University Lab of Ornithology, Ithaca, NY 14850-1999.)

Although the fall and winter's wet winds, snow, ice, and cold temperatures have long since killed the above-ground parts of the common herbaceous plants, some persist as erect xylem skeletons bearing the remnants of better days. Identifying these plants may seem impossible at first, but the task is actually not too difficult. A number of them can be identified from Figures 5.4, 5.11, 8.6, and 10.4. Figure 5.2 calls particular attention to some of those seeds and fruits that readily attach to animal fur or human clothing, ensuring their wide dispersion. A winter walk through a field, brushy edge, or a forest is a reminder of those persistent attachments. The hooked prickles of the familiar burdock, it has been said, inspired that favorite alternative to zippers and buttons: Velcro.

If, during a casual winter walk, one comes upon a mass of what seem to be moving "pepper dots" on an otherwise still white snow surface, then the encounter is surely with a colony of snow fleas. Also

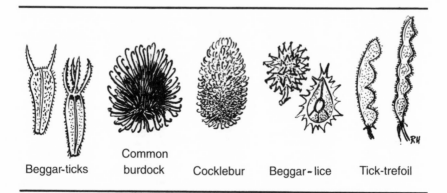

Beggar-ticks   Common burdock   Cocklebur   Beggar-lice   Tick-trefoil

Fig. 5.2 *Selected seeds and fruits with barbed prickles*
These five are among the most common ones picked up on clothing during a fall or winter walk.

called snowlice, these mostly harmless, primitive insects, each about one-sixteenth of an inch in size, jump about with a springy tail (hence, the formal name of springtails) and do attract attention. Late in the month, one may be lucky enough to hear the occasional loud calls of the cardinal or the patterned song of the tufted titmouse; if they are missed, though, one can at least depend on the arrival of the seed catalogues.

FEBRUARY

According to our earth's position in the revolution around the sun, spring officially begins on March 21; according to area climatologists, it begins on the first of March, with the whole of December, January, and February being winter—but according to some of the living organisms in the valley, spring comes around the *end* of February, *if* conditions are favorable, for it's then that early wild garlic may start to push up in south-facing lawns, and the stalks of planted crocus and snowdrops may begin to appear. The vocal announcement of spring comes from the welcome early returns of restless and noisy common grackles, the colorful red-winged blackbirds, and the chevrons of honking Canada geese. (Aldo Leopold rightly described this sound as "goose music," and it surely is the overture to the upcoming spring outdoor concert.)

Some of the hibernating or otherwise quiescent mammals may also begin to move about from their wintering dens or burrows. The most famous (if unreliable) spring prognosticator is the groundhog; every year, on February 2, Pennsylvania's own Punxsutawney Phil is celebrated with lively television and newspaper fanfare. The folk belief is that if he sees his shadow, Phil will return to his den for another six weeks of winter. The prediction is meaningless—but reminds us that pseudophenology can be fun.

MARCH

March is anything but dependable. John Kieran (1959), the famous naturalist and writer, says of March that "it promises much and tries to take it all back." For March is the month of tentative outdoor biking or golf forays on one weekend and a blizzard the next. Four of the thirteen most severe blizzards in the Lehigh Valley (since the famous one of

1888) happened in March. Yet March also provides the segue from February's opening notes to the genuine theme of the springtime concert.

In the valley, we can look about our homes for blooms of crocus, daffodils, and hyacinths. Along the roadsides, clumps of coltsfoot, looking much like the familiar dandelion, come into flower; wild garlic lengthens into so many patches of thin, green, needle-like spires in lawns and waste places; overhead, some of the early flowering elms and maples come into bloom—often in the drapery of a surprise "onion snow." The twigs of the willows start to take on their characteristic hues, giving stream edges a sinuous yellowish look. Early March stirs our spring restlessness, as the forced pussy willows flood the marketplace and the magical Philadelphia, New York, and Lehigh Valley flower shows draw near.

Bird migration, particularly in the period of February through mid-April, is very subject to the vagaries of the weather; expected arrival dates may vary by a week or more. But early March frequently brings the wood duck, woodcock, rusty blackbird, Eastern bluebird, song sparrow, and robin. The robin is probably (and often mistakenly) hailed as *the* first spring arrival because of its familiarity and proximity to people; a few robins also overwinter. (Other birds that overwinter and are visible at winter feeders may stay on for the year, or migrate north in the spring. The latter are simply using the Lehigh Valley as their southern winter residence.) Noisiest of the early arrivals, the killdeer create a great deal of loud squawking and clatter as they try to settle in on open fields, empty lots, and golf course roughs. And in a woodland setting, one may have the good fortune of hearing a grouse drumming on some distant log. (See Fig. 5.7.)

Mid-March is signaled by the arrival of the mourning dove, belted kingfisher, yellow-shafted flicker, Eastern phoebe, Eastern meadowlark and—though sometimes mistaken for a blackbird or starling—the brown-headed cowbird. Into late March the lively music continues with the osprey, tree swallow, golden-crowned kinglet, vesper sparrow, and field sparrow.

While the early migrants are bustling about, vociferously proclaiming their territories, another sound of spring is the reliable mid-March chorus of the spring peepers. Somehow, these vocal wetland tree frogs seem to make the changing season a sure thing. The duck-like call of the wood frog and the trilling of the common toad underscore the month of change. (Details on these and other amphibians are included in Chap. 10.) The first official day of spring, March 21, is marked by "Daffodil Days," the annual local fund-raiser of the American Cancer Society.

Fig. 5.3 *The spring peeper*
Their mid-March choruses
are a sure sign of spring.
(Illustration by Sonja
Schneider.)

But in like a lion, out like a lamb? Hardly. That's about as meaningful as the predictions of Punxsutawney Phil. The one true thing about March in the Lehigh Valley is that it is the windiest month of the year. Kite fliers, tennis buffs, and golfers know this well.

APRIL

April is the month of greening and symbolism. For the most part, the valley has a cold and wintery look as the month begins; by month's end, South Mountain has a soft green glow from the young canopy leaves, and the tired-looking streets take on the freshness of a new overhead paint job. Even lawns start to look green.

In a similar way, a variety of happenings signify the transition out of winter: daylight saving time starts, the bright *Forsythia* blossoms out, trout season starts, the migratory shad reach Easton, the baseball season opens, the first lawns are mowed, Earth Day is celebrated, and winter makes its last stand, hopefully, with a day or so of subfreezing temperatures.

Through the end of March and into April and May, many of the woodland wildflowers blossom while the soil can still absorb the sun's warmth, before the canopy completely closes in. A selection of some of the more common and attractive Lehigh Valley wildflowers is included in Figure 5.4. And along with the wildflowers, the fern fiddleheads start to unravel from their tight winter coils.

While there are dozens of native shrubs in the Lehigh Valley, the most common one in moist woodlands is clearly the spicebush. Standing perhaps eight feet high, typically in groves, the spicebush boasts multiple dull black stems with pale lenticels, alternate simple leaves, and—before

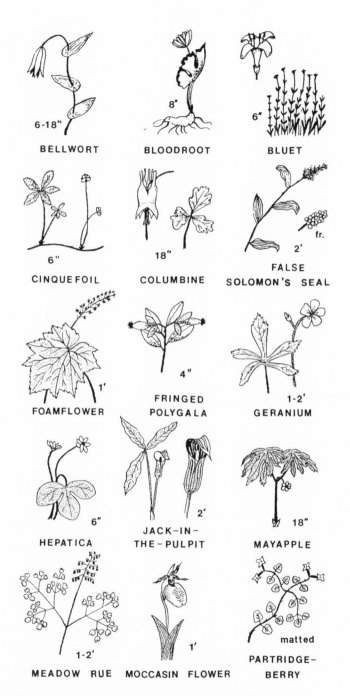

BELLWORT 6-18"

BLOODROOT 8"

BLUET 6"

CINQUEFOIL 6"

COLUMBINE 18"

FALSE SOLOMON'S SEAL 2' fr.

FOAMFLOWER 1'

FRINGED POLYGALA 4"

GERANIUM 1-2'

HEPATICA 6"

JACK-IN-THE-PULPIT 2'

MAYAPPLE 18"

MEADOW RUE 1-2'

MOCCASIN FLOWER 1'

PARTRIDGE-BERRY matted

Fig. 5.4 *Common spring and early summer woodland flowers* (From Oplinger and Halma, *The Poconos* [New Brunswick: Rutgers University Press, 1988]. With permission.)

PHLOX   RUE ANEMONE
6"   6"   SARSAPARILLA
                           2'

SAXIFRAGE   SPRING BEAUTY
8"   6-12"   STARFLOWER
                           6"

prostrate
TRAILING ARBUTUS   TRILLIUM   TROUT LILY
16"   8"

VIOLET   WILD GINGER   WILD LILY-
6"   8"   OF-THE-VALLEY
                         4"

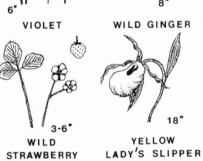
WILD   YELLOW
STRAWBERRY   LADY'S SLIPPER
3-6"   18"

Fig. 5.4 (continued) *Common spring and early summer woodland flowers*

Fig. 5.5 *Spicebush*
This most common moist woodland shrub can grow in excess of eight feet high. Red berries (A), small clustered yellow flowers (B), leaves (C), and small shrub (D) at the base of a tree.

the leaves emerge—small, bright opposite yellow flowers. They bloom through much of April. Sometimes they are so plentiful that they give a light yellowish haze to the woods. Aside from a cheerful color, the flowers, twigs, and crushed leaves also have a refreshing spicy-lemony fragrance. (See Fig. 5.5.)

Just about the time that the spicebush is starting to fade in late April, an even more conspicuous hue dots the subcanopy and edges of the woodlands: that of the shadbush. It is the first of several white-flowering shrubs and trees that blossom just before or at the time that the forest leaves are starting to open. The early settlers along the Atlantic coast gave the plant its name: the shadbush flowers coincide with the migration of the ocean-dwelling shad up the coastal riverways, such as the Delaware, to spawn. Both Easton and Bethlehem traditionally celebrate the shad season in a variety of creative ways. (See also Chap. 12. Typically, the annual Easton-based Shad Tournament is held during the last week of April. For more information, write to the Tournament at Box 907, Easton, PA 18044-0907, or call [610] 250-6711.) By coincidence, the shadbush flowers at the same time as a widely planted, white-flowering tree cultivar—the Bradford pear. A few days to a week after the shadbush starts to bloom, two other similar white trees join in—the flowering dogwood and the pin (fire) cherry—and about a week after that, perhaps in early May, the white-flowering black cherry rounds out the foursome. These four woody plants and some of their distinguishing characteristics are included in Figure 5.6. Appropriately, the last day of the month is traditionally Arbor Day.

The gradually warmer days trigger the emergence of the *poikilothermic* (cold-blooded) wood and box turtles from their quiescent, stuporous winter state. And near a home, one might be startled by an increasingly mobile garter snake. As the calendar days progress through April and

Fig. 5.6 *Four common Lehigh Valley small trees and shrubs with white flowers in the spring*

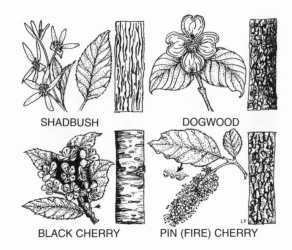

SHADBUSH   DOGWOOD

BLACK CHERRY   PIN (FIRE) CHERRY

into May, bird migration becomes more regular, and hence predictable; the variety and numbers of the spring arrivals peak in early May.

Many of the arriving songbirds are insect eaters. They have been programmed, in part, to the availability of food in the valley: April brings on the hatches, often from sources of water, of gnats, midges, and other insects. From late February through the early spring months one may chance upon two spring butterflies: the occasional and somber mourning cloak butterfly and the contrastingly cheerful spring azure butterfly. Their early appearance is possible because they overwinter in protected places as adults. Both announce the summer ahead.

The spirit of the changing seasons was caught in a phrase from the poet John Lydgate in 1430: "Holsom as the Aprile showr fallyng on the herbes newe." The line now translates as "April showers bring forth May flowers."

Fig. 5.7 *The killdeer*
This noisy, ground-nesting bird favors pasture-lands, golf courses, and fallow land. The two breast bands are distinctive. A master of deception, the killdeer will draw an invader away from the nest area, using loud calls and feigning a broken wing.

Fig. 5.8 *The mourning cloak and spring azure butterflies*
The mourning cloak (right), earliest of all butterflies in the valley, is dressed for its name: dark, purplish brown wings hemmed with yellow-white margins. Its large (three-inch) size makes it conspicuous. The spring azures (left), small and somewhat frail, favor wet areas; their lilac blue color is a welcome note to a chilly spring day.

MAY

May has been called a "runaway" month. Trees array themselves in their full foliage. Fern fiddleheads expand into fronds. Mustard plants give the fields a yellow hue. The moist woodlands are alive with wildflowers just beating the canopy deadline—and the first full week of May is National Wildflower Week. Songbird migration reaches its height. Warbler Weekends, as bird-watching enthusiasts call them, abound both with birdwatchers and with warblers. Edwin Way Teale caught the sense of May in his delightful book from 1963, *North With Spring:* "It is the season of youth, of beginning again; the season of blank pages, of unhurried time, of belief and optimism. The world's favorite season is Spring. All things seem possible in May."

The seasonality of May has a close association, naturally, with the mayfly. Anyone who has spent a few days near water in May is soon impressed by the hundreds of mostly nocturnal adult mayflies that are attracted to nearby street lights. The adults, rather frail and with delicate wings, emerge from the water, mate, and die—all in about a day. Their order name, Ephemeroptera, appropriately reflects their fleeting existence. (The adults, called drakes, are commonly used as models for dry fly-fishing lures—lures that float on the surface—but the nymph stages, which may live for several years on the undersides of rocks in streams, are the template for many flies that are used in the water column itself. Trout are particularly fond of mayflies, either as adults or nymphs. See Fig. 5.9.) April and later months may also bring, unfortunately, the ugly cottony nests of the larvae of the Eastern tent caterpillar. These leaf-chomping caterpillars live gregariously in gradually constructed multilayered nests

Fig. 5.9 *Mayfly adult and nymph*
Adult hatches are commonly seen at lights near water in May, although many species continue to hatch throughout the rest of the summer. The mayfly adult is on the left.

in the forks of certain favored trees, such as poplar, apple, and cherry. (See Fig. 8.9.) Like the seasons, nature has a variety of expressions.

Included in the runaway opening of May is the traditional corn planting ceremony celebrated by the Lenape (Delawares) on the first Sunday in the month. That is followed by Mother's Day somewhere around the tenth of May, concurrent with the expansive woodland displays of the native flowering dogwood. The month closes with the traditional picnics and cookouts of Memorial Day; for most of us, the holiday signals the summer season, although the solstice is still three weeks away.

JUNE

June, a month of brides, blossoms, birds, and butterflies, is one of the best for bird watching; June is the peak month for songbird nesting. The birds are in nearly constant motion—for the mated pair must build a nest, incubate eggs, gather food for the fledglings, fend off invaders, and otherwise attend to being successful in a competitive world. In staking out and defending their territories they are particularly vocal. With a little experience, and some help from an experienced birder or one of the many excellent audiovisual aids available, a novice can quickly learn to associate particular birds with their songs. (The top ten nesting birds in Pennsylvania are detailed in Chap. 9.)

June is also the month in which some of the summer flowering herbs and shrubs bloom. Mountain laurel, that favorite acidophilic native shrub—and the state flower of Pennsylvania—will be in bloom along the acid slopes of both Blue Mountain and South Mountain. (Many of the common spring and early summer woodland flowers are pictured in Fig. 5.4; see Fig. 5.11 for the common summer ones and Fig. 8.6 for roadside flowers.) And look to the treetops for the flowers of several common tree species: the tulip-like, green-orange flowers of the tulip tree; the creamy,

Fig. 5.10 *The multiflora rose*
The multiflora rose has become naturalized and is now common along roadsides, field edges, and disturbed sites. It flowers in early June. Because of its aggressive invasion and extreme difficulty in eradication, it is treated as an undesirable woody weed species. Flowers (A), bristly leaves (B), and bushy growth habit (C) are shown.

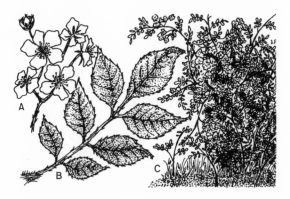

pendulous, fragrant white flowers of the black locust; and the erect white flower clusters of the cultivated horse chestnut. The catalpa, a common cultivar and escape, is better known by its later "Indian cigar" fruits.

The most conspicuous roadside shrub, with an abundance of white flowers, is the "oriental garden flower," the multiflora rose. Initially introduced as an edge and garden plant, this vigorous and prickly bush has naturalized and spread rapidly throughout the Lehigh Valley (see Fig. 5.10).

Crown vetch, the utilitarian but delightful planted ground cover along many of our roadsides, will start to flower in June and continue to thrive through much of the summer. Easily recognized by its "crown" of purple flowers, our variety was developed at the Pennsylvania State University. It does well on slopes with impoverished soils—and thus is used on many rights-of-way. Pennsylvania officially recognizes "Penngift" crown vetch as a Beautification and Conservation plant for the state.

June is also the month during which summer becomes official. On June 21, the tilt of the earth is directly toward the sun: thus, the sun rises close to 5:30 A.M. and sets at 8:30 P.M., DST. This is the longest day of the year, and it is also the day on which the sun, on the meridian at noon, is highest in the sky. Summer is finally here.

JULY

In July, the very vocal birdsong of the previous months starts to diminish, almost as if to recognize summer's sometimes oppressive heat. Young birds appear, and a few breeders will start a second nesting. One character that does sing a variety of other birds' songs throughout the

ASTER

BEDSTRAW

CHECKERBERRY

CLOSED GENTIAN

CORN LILY

COW–WHEAT

FLY–POISON

FROSTWEED

SHINLEAF

SPOTTED
WINTERGREEN

SOLOMON'S SEAL

WHORLED
LOOSESTRIFE

WOOD LILY

Fig. 5.11 *Common summer and early fall woodland flowers*
(From Oplinger and Halma, *The Poconos* [New Brunswick: Rutgers University
Press, 1988]. With permission.)

summer is the familiar mockingbird, which may sing loudly and cease-lessly at 2:00 A.M.—to the dismay of would-be sleepers, known to heave shoes and other missiles at the persistent vocalist.

Dragonflies and the much more delicate damselflies can be seen dart-ing over quiet waters, snagging mosquitoes and other small insects "on the fly." Their speed, acceleration, and ability to change direction and hover predate those of our modern aircraft by about three hundred million years. Similarly hurtling about and sweeping insects out of the sky is the usually crepuscular nighthawk, probably named for its resemblance to a small hawk. It is easily identified late in the afternoon or in the evening by its slender, pointed, and dark wings, swept back like a high-speed aircraft; its erratic wing beats and darting flight pattern; and its loud nasal *beer!* call. (See Fig. 5.12.) Originally a solitary no-nest nester on barren rocks, grav-elly soils, and coarse fields, this bird has taken to nesting on flat gravel and tarred city roofs. The nighthawk is also known as the will-o'-the-wisp.

Other sounds of the hot summer months include the daytime rising crescendo of the snowy tree cricket and the evening sound of "Katy did, Katy she did, Katy did, Katy she did"—the sure greeting of the katydid. And depending on the year, one might be entertained late in the month by the monotonous but sustained daytime chorus of the male periodical cicadas. They continue to buzz throughout July and into August. A number of varieties occur (and two common ones are called "thirteen-year" and "seventeen-year locusts"—their in-ground larval time); the next big seventeen-year hatch in our area is due in 2008.

The early evening firefly, the official insect of Pennsylvania, pursues a very different success strategy. The firefly tends to favor dewy, still nights throughout the summer, and (through a chemical reaction) pro-duces a nearly heatless, pulsating light that is used to attract the oppo-site sex. Biologically, this insect is a beetle, not a fly or a bug, despite its other child-approved name—lightning bug.

Fig. 5.12 *The nighthawk*
The nighthawk is typically seen above city buildings, darting about in pursuit of flying insects in the early evening during the summer.

The roadside wildflower (weed?) show that started earlier in the summer continues to dazzle in July. In the Lehigh Valley, about a dozen particularly prominent edge plants include campion, Queen Anne's lace, black-eyed Susan, evening primrose, goldenrod, mustard, chicory, hawkweed, sweet clover, foxtail, mullein, bull thistle, and ragweed (see Fig. 8.6). Of this quick and dirty list, the "worst" one from a human perspective is, no doubt, the last: ragweed. The "best" one, if colorful action is the gauge, is the bull thistle, a tall (to six feet) and prickly road-side weed; its "thistledown" (silky-hairy tufts on the fruiting head) is the sole nesting material for the beautiful goldfinch. Sometimes called the "wild canary," this bird is readily seen flitting about building its late nest to coincide with its raw material. (The goldfinch-thistle theme appears on the logo of the New Jersey Audubon Society as well as on certain Pennsylvania German distelfinks—and indeed, the word "dis-telfink" literally refers to the "thistle finch.")

AUGUST

July passes into August almost unnoticed, except by the thousands of hay fever sufferers, for whom the transition does signal something important: ragweed season. Ragweed grows through much of the early summer to perhaps eight feet in height; then, in early- to mid-August, it starts producing unbelievable quantities of microscopic pollen grains. Estimates run to about 1,000,000,000,000 grains per plant! Production stops with the first heavy frosts of October. (See Fig. 5.13.)

Although people affected by hay fever may identify ragweed as the leading culprit, other *anemophilous* (wind-loving) plants with princi-pally windborne pollen may also contribute to their misery, including several of the spring-flowering trees and later grasses. (See Table 5.1.) Not surprisingly, windy days are the worst for hay fever sufferers, and the best periods are those that follow an air-cleansing rain. An alterna-tive, of course, is to join the thousands at the seashore who enjoy, among other things, essentially pollen-free ocean breezes.

(Pollen counts, once a regular footnote on newscasts and in the news-papers of the valley, have had a checkered history over the last twenty-five years. But pollen counts for southeastern Pennsylvania are available weekdays from the National Allergy Bureau at 1-800-9-POLLEN. They are not specifically geared to the Lehigh Valley, but they do offer help-ful tips.)

Fig. 5.13 *Ragweed*
This invasive and allergy-triggering plant blooms from mid-August until the first heavy October frost. It is illustrated as (A) general habitat, favoring edges, (B) flowering and leaf detail, and (C) much magnified pollen grains—which even *look* nasty. The mature plant is often in excess of eight feet in height.

Many local fresh fruits and vegetables continue to keep market shoppers happy. Certainly one of the favorites is fresh sweet corn—typically served within hours of picking. The occasion continues to be celebrated on the second Sunday of August with the Roasting Ears of Corn Food Fest at the Museum of Indian Culture.

The somewhat quiet birdsong activity of July nearly stops in August. Nesting is over and many birds are molting. The earlier start of shorebird migration now peaks, and some of the early land bird migrants start their journey.

Although there are splashes of roadside color with butterfly weed, butter 'n' eggs, chicory, thistles, and an assortment of asters, the trees and shrubs of the valley are green—with two exceptions: some of the sumac leaves may start to turn bright red and the leaves of the less common black (sour) gum may start to become a brilliant scarlet. Fall has sent out its early signals.

Indeed, the approach of Labor Day also brings the anticipation of fall, for August is one of the hottest, most humid, and least windy months of the year. Oppressive conditions and "dog days" are equally descriptive terms. Only the psychological marker of Labor Day jump-starts us into fall.

SEPTEMBER

Now, the tempo of the bird migration picks up. The fall migration of broad-winged hawks, which starts in mid-August, peaks through the middle of September. Broad-winged hawks are medium-sized with

Table 5.1 *Pollen-related allergies in the Lehigh Valley*

Group	Examples	Season
Wind-pollinated trees	Elm Hickory Maple Oak Walnut	Late March through May
Grasses	Bluegrass Foxtail Orchard Redtop Timothy	May through July
Weeds	Cocklebur Dock Lamb's-quarter Ragweed (two spp.)	August until frost

NOTE: Oak and walnut trees and ragweed are often the worst culprits, although their effects on individual persons vary.

broad wings and distinctively banded tails, and they are particularly fond of riding the thermals upward and then gliding southeast for many miles. On a good day, especially near the major Lehigh Valley ridges or from valley "hot spots" (fields, macadam, and the like), one may thrill to dozens of these "sky gliders" caught in a rising thermal. Hawk Mountain and Bake Oven Knob are two favorite observation sites. On September 14, 1978, Hawk Mountain recorded one of the most spectacular broadwing flights of all time for one day: 21,448 birds! (The general flight patterns for the fall months are plotted in Fig. 5.14.)

Although thousands of migrating hawks on a crisp September afternoon offer a spectacular view, another less obvious migrant may be discovered wending southward closer to the ground: the monarch butterfly. These well-known black and orange butterflies are best seen in the Lehigh Valley during September, as they migrate to the Gulf States and Mexico. Their flight patterns, of up to sixty miles per day, depend on wind and weather. During north winds they tend to fly high, taking advantage of the tail winds; in south winds, they favor hedgehopping near the ground. The larvae feed on the roadside milkweed, and the adults take in the nectar of a variety of wildflowers. Exactly how the adult acquires its distasteful chemistry is not clear, but most birds shun

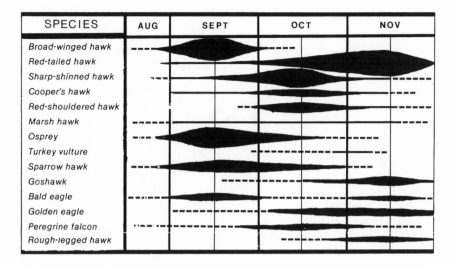

SPECIES	AUG	SEPT	OCT	NOV
Broad-winged hawk				
Red-tailed hawk				
Sharp-shinned hawk				
Cooper's hawk				
Red-shouldered hawk				
Marsh hawk				
Osprey				
Turkey vulture				
Sparrow hawk				
Goshawk				
Bald eagle				
Golden eagle				
Peregrine falcon				
Rough-legged hawk				

Fig. 5.14 *Autumn raptor migration along the Kittatinny Ridge*
(By permission of Hawk Mountain.)

the otherwise conspicuous monarch morsel, thus allowing it to drift southward, uninhibited, with an almost leisurely slow and sailing flight. Although the monarch is the most famous lepidopteran migrant, others also migrate. In the Lehigh Valley, interest in butterfly watching, counting, and gardening is gradually growing—and, no doubt, the press coverage given to Rick Mikula (the expert "Butterfly Man" from nearby Hazleton) has been inspirational.

Some of the butterfly garden plants, such as marigolds, black-eyed Susans, Shasta daisies, and purple coneflowers, all share one common lineage with many of the fall roadside flowers (such as the asters, sunflowers, goldenrods, and thistles): they are all members of the Composite family. This is a large and confusing family of sometimes beautiful plants with small, individual flowers tightly packed into an arrangement called a "head." A dandelion is a good example. Some of these plants, which often flower in September, are illustrated in Chapters 6 and 8; but let the novice beware: the varieties are often distinguished by very technical details. The story goes that a naturalist, once asked to identify a particular fall aster, looked it over, paused, took a deep sigh, and remarked, "Why, it's—it's an A. B. C. . . . . Another *Blasted* Composite."

While broad-winged hawks, monarchs, and daisies add to the quality of September, another doesn't; the fall webworm builds its disfiguring nests on branch tips of cherry, ash, and black walnut. Like the spring tent

Fig. 5.15 *The monarch butterfly*
The larva (rt.) feeds on the roadside milkweed. The adult (l.) migrates from the Lehigh Valley in September to the Gulf States, overwinters there, and returns partway back, lays eggs, and dies. The next adult generation returns to the Lehigh Valley. Such a cycle, different from that of birds, is called generational in nature.

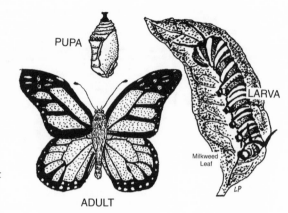

caterpillar, with which it is sometimes confused, it also feeds on tree leaves. Fortunately, both are more repulsive than damaging. (See Fig. 8.9.)

And just as March 21 marks the arrival of spring, September 21 makes it official: it is the first day of fall.

OCTOBER

October, like June, is a fine month, for it sports the best temperatures of both summer and winter, and adds kaleidoscopic color to the mix. After the fall equinox, the days seem to shorten more noticeably, and as the transit of the sun gets increasingly lower in the sky, the temperature continues to drop. By mid-October the Lehigh Valley gets its first frosts. The winter signals are up.

Animals prepare for winter in a variety of ways. Many of the mammals, such as squirrels, mice, and rabbits, will start to store body fat, stockpile food, thicken their coats, and prepare overwintering shelters; a number will eventually go into a sleepy stupor, and a few, like the groundhog and bat, will hibernate. Most insects, small invertebrates, reptiles, and amphibians will hibernate under stones, on pond bottoms, in burrows or bark crevices, and in other protective settings. Some insects, interestingly enough, synthesize glycerol, a chemical not unlike our automobile antifreeze. In all cases, the idea is to avoid the destructive consequences of cellular, needle-like ice crystals that destroy body tissues through membrane disruption. (Mushy tomatoes, the consequence of a hard frost, illustrate cellular ice crystal damage.) Birds, being *homeothermic* (warm-blooded), cope in two ways: they develop a heavier winter plumage and ride out the valley's winter—often with the assistance of generous bird feeder handouts—or they migrate. Although the bird migration that started in August continues to drop off, October is the peak month for the migrating sharp-shinned and red-tailed hawks. (See Fig. 5.14.)

For visitors and valley inhabitants alike, this is a prime time to find a comfortable spot on one of the many rock outcroppings along the top of the windswept Blue Mountain, forget the pace of valley life below, and enjoy the beautiful gliding red-tails and changing foliage. October 19–31, in particular, is the usual height of fall color for the Lehigh Valley. Warm, sunny days and cool nights are ideal for destabilizing the chlorophyll-based green pigments, which results in the exposure of the other colors—always present, but largely masked. The color parade, like the spring flowering sequence in reverse, starts in the cooler, more elevated northern extremes and progresses southward. Typical leaves and their color bands are illustrated in Figure 5.16. Finally, the temperatures get sufficiently low that all pigments break down, soft tissue cells die, and leaves turn brown and drop. The leaf stripping process is often hastened by a driving rain late in October. However, there are two common tree genera that hold many of their dead brown leaves well into the winter, making them easily recognizable: oaks and beeches (see Fig. 6.4). Even as fall grades into winter and the woods start to look cold and somewhat barren, one can be cheered through mid-October and into November by the bright yellow-gold strap-like flower petals of the colorful witch hazel understory tree. It is common in woodlands, in bottomlands, and along fencerows.

October ends with the traditional change back to Standard Time and the last lawn mowing.

NOVEMBER

The late Ned Smith—creative writer, artist, and outdoorsman—caught the spirit of November in one of his many "Gone for the Day" chronicles in *Pennsylvania Game News:*

> November—a month of somber browns and distant purples, of cold rains and soggy leaves . . . the month of transition, the period between the gay foliage of October and the sparkling whiteness of December. Unfortunately, it enjoys little of the glamour of either. After leaf-fall only the brightest sunshine and the bluest skies can

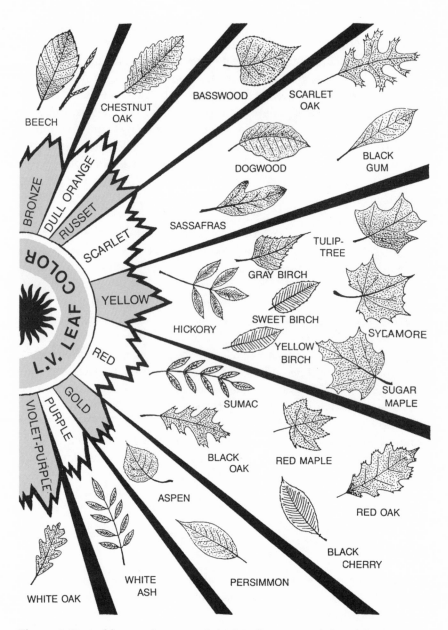

Fig. 5.16 *Typical leaves of common Lehigh Valley trees and their fall colors* October 19–31 is typically the height of fall color change in the Lehigh Valley. (Modified from Oplinger and Halma, *The Poconos* [New Brunswick: Rutgers University Press, 1988]. With permission.)

dispel the somber browns and grays and distant purples of a typical November landscape. But the hunters of Pennsylvania wouldn't swap it for any other month.

November is the right time for hunters to be in the field, for it is the hunting season for small game, waterfowl, turkey, and bear. While the excitement, chase, and satisfaction rightfully go to the hunter, it is also a time of special outdoor caution for the non-hunter. Safety cannot be emphasized enough. It is also a time to remember that hunting is a service to wildlife vitality itself; hunters serve, in many instances, as the predators that are long gone from the original woods.

While the elusive grouse, quail, and pheasant test the hunter's woodsmanship, non-game bird migration continues to decline rapidly. The sharp-shinned hawk, so prevalent in October, all but disappears from the flyways by mid-November. The only relatively abundant migrating raptor through much of November is the red-tailed hawk, and a number of these hawks stay here all winter as residents.

As we try to work our way through the increasingly cold weather, the shortening days and the seemingly endless football episodes, a window of welcome warm weather mistakenly may open for a few days: Indian summer. Saturday afternoon brings out the short-sleeved leaf-raker, who may be startled to find his dormant forsythia in flower. This early spring favorite has been biologically tricked by a short mid-November photoperiod and warm temperatures.

If the surprise summer happens to include November 17, then one might wish to enjoy the evening with one of the best meteor showers of the year, that of the Leonids, which can feature up to one hundred meteor streaks per hour.

The end of November signals the formal beginning of the holiday season: Thanksgiving is followed by Hanukkah, and that means that Christmas and New Year's Day are shortly ahead. Already the valley has had almost a month of department store holiday music and garland—surely a far cry from (and weak substitute for) the song and color of the natural world.

DECEMBER

The somber tones of November continue into December, but we can look for visual relief with the first snowfall. More often than not, it is a strange mix of beauty, traffic headaches, sparkling whiteness, and, for children, wonderment.

Snow is a mixed blessing for the biological world. On the one hand, it signals the arrival of the stressful environment of subfreezing temperatures and sharply reduced food supply; on the other hand, snow brings a benevolent insulating blanket. How does the snow affect animals and plants, and how do they adapt to this harshest of the seasons?

The insulating value of loose fresh snow, measured by its thermal conductivity, is much better than ice, concrete, plain glass, sand, or even sawdust. Its insulating values are higher with a low density (loose packing) and a greater thickness (heavy snowfall). It is also a super reflector, as anyone who has spent time in the snow on a bright and sunny day knows. In fact, it is nature's best reflector, turning back 75–95 percent of the sunlight, although in dirty snow (smudged by gravel, road grime, dust, and the like) that value drops to only about 50 percent. What this means for the small mammals, of course, is that they can overwinter in a *subnivean* (under the snow) environment and benefit from a sizable temperature elevation at the base of the snowpack—often many tens of degrees higher than the surface. They additionally conserve heat by curling, retracting their appendages, and huddling. Many of the voles and mice, for example, that are noncolonial curiously tend to congregate in the winter. (Other winter preparations are described in the October section.) Our smaller Lehigh Valley mammals, then, are hidden by either the snowpack or ground litter or both.

For plants the two major related stressors are low temperatures and dessication. Herbaceous annuals overwinter with resistant seeds, as do perennials with hardy rootstocks (particularly the monocots) such as bulbs, corms, and rhizomes. Most of our Lehigh Valley vegetation, being deciduous, avoids the possibility of severe water loss, and those plants that are evergreen (hemlock, pine, spruce, and so on) have mostly needle-like leaves that minimize water vapor loss. They further avoid the snow burden problem with their spire shapes and their leaves, which have only a small surface area. An evergreen plant completely buried by snow can get along very nicely: adequate light and CO_2 for some photosynthesis, a more favorable temperature than that of the outside air, and protection from desiccation. A half-buried plant, on the other hand, may be subject to "windburn" and bud drying in exposed areas. That was the case for many of our plants during the severe winter of 1993–94. The memorable result was numerous examples of curious "half-flowering" shrubs—forsythia, rhododendron, and the like. For the most part, the damaged upper branches eventually did recover

CAMEO 5.2

Maurice Braun (1906–1979)

Established primarily to stop the senseless mountaintop slaughter of thousands of raptors, Hawk Mountain has evolved in scope and purpose from its touch and go start in 1934 to worldwide recognition today. Much of the credit for the establishment of the sanctuary through its initial growth years was due to the dedication and persistent efforts of Maurice Braun (curator of the sanctuary from 1934 to 1970) and his wife, Erma. The early years are still referred to, informally, as the "Mom and Pop Years" at the sanctuary. Many aspects of Braun's life and times through the years at Hawk Mountain were portrayed in his delightful book, *Hawks Aloft.*

His staunch support of the protection of raptors ultimately led to the 1970 Pennsylvania Model Hawk Law, which protects all birds of prey. He was a naturalist for all seasons; he is best remembered, though, atop the North Lookout in the fall, his jacket and hat brim flapping in a brisk breeze, calling out the names of raptors—only visible as distant moving specks in the sky near the northeastern horizon. Those efforts became part of what is now the longest continuously documented record of raptor migration in the world.

through smaller lateral buds. Someone suggested that "if you were a plant, it would be better to be buried than half-buried." There's some truth in that.

Snow or no snow, the first Monday after Thanksgiving is the much awaited opening day of buck season. Though more remote counties, such as Tioga and Potter, conjure up images of large herds of these beautiful and graceful animals, both Lehigh and Northampton Counties also have large deer populations. (In fact, the deer is the official state animal of Pennsylvania.) In recent years the number of complaints heard from rural landowners in the valley about crop and garden damage by deer has risen measurably. Deer are primarily browsers and thus favor edge, orchard, and second growth hardwoods. As the valley has opened into a variety of rural enterprises, such as truck, tree, orchard, and dairy farms, the changing land use has significantly increased the deer population. Although a country drive is made all the richer when one spots one or more of these agile mammals, the valley also has a high rate of roadkills—a problem intensified by the opening of Route I-78. During the hunting season, in particular, the often frightened deer come down from South Mountain and blindly try to cross the expressway, only to become statistics.

On a much less dramatic level, one can look for the many varieties of galls during the cold months. Just as a tissue responds to some stimulus with a cancerous growth, *galls* are plant deformations caused by insects and are used by them for protection and as a food source. Some of the galls, such as those found on wheat, have economic ramifications; others, such as the spruce aphid galls, are not particularly damaging but are a bit disfiguring. Galls can have many shapes and sizes and are conspicuous in the winter months.

The daylight hours of December continue to shorten until December 21, the winter solstice, when the sun crosses the meridian at its lowest angle in the sky. At noon it is a meager 26° above the horizon. Shadows are long, the days feel cold, and the sky looks like steel. The last nine days of the month start the slow six-month 47° climb of the sun up the meridian—little surprise, then, that diverse celebrations have historically marked the waning days of December and the welcoming of the new six-month cycle.

From the climate and seasons, we move on to the patterns of plant and animal communities, the topic of the next several chapters.

S I X

Native Vegetation

It has been said about Pennsylvania's dense pre-pioneer forest that a squirrel could run from Philadelphia to Pittsburgh without ever touching the ground.

—DAVID J. CUFF, *The Atlas of Pennsylvania*, 1989

Indeed, there was a time when most of Pennsylvania was clothed in a nearly continuous vegetation type—now formally called the Eastern Deciduous Forest. There were, to be sure, occasional exposed rocky ridges, sporadic "barrens," open floodplains, recent burn areas, and the like, but for the most part the forest had a closed canopy of mature trees. Some of the earlier writings about the newly discovered forests of North America suggest that it was pristine, mature, cathedral-like, almost sacred. Even Charles Darwin, according to an entry in his journal, was stirred by this vision. During the voyage of the HMS *Beagle,* he wrote: "Among the scenes which are deeply impressed on my mind, none exceed in sublimity the primeval forests undefaced by the hand of man. No one can stand in these solitudes unmoved, and not feel that there is more in man than the mere breath of his body." Yet our current understandings of the ecology of forests suggest that the forests had their own internal perturbations triggered by the destructive cycles of insect pests, natural fires, plant blights, and hurricanes, among others.

There were human disturbances of the forests in addition to natural ones. Indians (Native Americans, Amerinds) lived in the Lehigh Valley from about 9000 B.C., based on the artifacts found along the Delaware River and elsewhere. The tribe was known as the Lenape (or Delawares) and, like other pioneer groups, its members lived near water sites and on or near floodplains where the land could be cleared for growing maize and other crops. The Lenape cut some of the forests for utensils, canoes, shelters, implements, and fuel, and also set fires to drive game.

It was into this valley setting—featuring large forested tracts of mixed oaks and chestnut trees interrupted by sporadic clearings—that the white settlers arrived. We might well wonder, then, Why a deciduous forest (and not a grassland or a coniferous forest)? And if the Lehigh Valley was abandoned today, what, ecologically, would it become?

THE BIOME CONCEPT

A *biome* is an area "of large geographical extent characterized by a distinctive landscape based on the climax (self-perpetuating) dominant plants." Biomes that immediately come to mind are deserts, tundra, grasslands, and deciduous forests. Further reflection on the definition helps us see that indeed, the Eastern Deciduous Forest *is* large, that it has a cloak of canopy-closed large woody plants, and that the dominant plants are deciduous trees. What causes our area to be a deciduous forest? (And why do other areas become what they are?) According to studies of numerous sites throughout the world by the National Science Foundation, the two *primary* factors are the mean annual temperature and the mean annual precipitation.

In Figure 6.1, the biomes of the world are plotted in the context of these two parameters. Allentown has a mean annual temperature of 62°F and a mean annual precipitation of forty-three inches, for example, and falls neatly into the deciduous forest biome. For each of the biomes, there is a fairly well-defined two-dimensional range that represents the two primary *limiting factors* of a given biome, but also includes within those bounds other, less important limiting factors, such as the photoperiod, wind, soil type, fire tolerance, and light intensity. The successful organisms within the normal distribution range represent a long evolutionary history and have the genetic programs that allow them to thrive. In some cases the two-factor means may be nearly identical but the biomes are different. Those overlap areas in Figure 6.1 represent one or more of the factors other than the two principal ones.

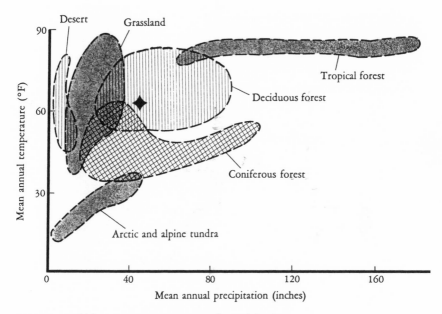

Fig. 6.1 *World biomes, temperature, and precipitation*
The main factors in biome distribution are temperature and precipitation. The Lehigh Valley falls into the deciduous forest realm, as noted by the marker. Movement toward grassland is possible, as in the case of lawns, but would suggest less precipitation and would require more energy for regular maintenance (lawn mowers, fungicides, and so on). (Reproduced from the National Science Foundation.)

The importance of the moisture regime on both the determination of global biomes and the variations *within* individual biomes is underscored by the observation that, early on in the history of ecology, ecologists divided all environments into habitats based on a moisture gradient scale. Thus, we have three major habitat types:

Name	Moisture Content	Lehigh Valley Examples
Mesic	Middle moisture; a midpoint in the gradient; neither excessively drained nor with standing water	Uplands in valley, forests, fields; much of our limestone/shale countryside
Hydric	Wet conditions; sites flooded regularly or occasionally	Floodplains, marshes, swamps; Houdaille Swamp, Monocacy floodplain
Xeric	Dry conditions; poor soil cover and rapid water runoff; limited available water	Ridge tops and exposed rocks, such as South Mountain and Blue Mountain

Table 6.1 *The major vegetation types of the Lehigh Valley and selected characteristics*

| Characteristics | Major Vegetation Types | | |
	Mixed Oak Forest	Blue Mountain Ridge	South Mountain
Dominant vegetation	Red, white, black oaks; American chestnut sprouts, ash, hickory	Pitch pine, chestnut oak, sassafras, red maple	Tulip tree, sweet birch, red oak
Other vegetation, floor aspect	Spicebush, witch hazel, dogwood; many spring wildflowers	Many heaths: blueberry, mountain laurel; few wildflowers	Moderate understory; poison ivy, Virginia creeper, tick-trefoil, and the like
Distribution	Now limited mostly to forest islands	Ridge top and adjacent slopes	On the mountains and slopes
Climate	Moderate	Moderate, but exposed to wind, ice; cooler	Moderate, less severe than Blue Mountain
Moisture regime	Mesic; land generally well-drained	Xeric; water loss with slopes, marginal soil	Mesic-xeric; drains quickly due to slopes
Glaciation	Illinoian, whole Lehigh Valley; Wisconsinan, northeast corner of Northampton County	No, only on the slopes	No, only on the northern slope
Soil	Good: fertile, fairly deep	Shallow, sterile	Shallow, sterile; bedrock unyielding

Table 6.1 (continued) *The major vegetation types of the Lehigh Valley and selected characteristics*

Characteristics	Hemlock Ravines	Floodplains/ Wetlands	Agricultural Fields, Orchards
	Major Vegetation Types		
Dominant vegetation	Hemlock; some white pine and other deciduous trees	Sycamore, cottonwood, silver maple, American elm, willows	Crops, fruit trees; invading weeds
Other vegetation, floor aspect	Few shrubs; floor cover sparse	Vines common; jewelweed, nettles	Invaded by weeds
Distribution	Cool stream ravines or north-facing slopes	Limited to high-water-content soils, flooding	Farmlands, orchards; fallow fields along roads
Climate	Cool, humid, protected	Moderate	Moderate
Moisture regime	Mesic to hydric at stream base	Hydric; many plants obligate to facultative	Mesic
Glaciation	Ravines scoured and depositional	Areas often depositional from erosion	Most
Soil	Acidic, due to needles on floor	Silt, clay, and other fine materials	Good: fertile, fairly deep, productive

These moisture gradient habitats are key in the delineation of vegetation types for the Lehigh Valley. Thus, at least in part, we suggest a division of the Lehigh Valley into six types of habitat: mixed oak forest, Blue Mountain ridge, South Mountain, hemlock ravines, floodplains and wetlands, and fields and agriculture. These groups, with their distinguishing characteristics, are outlined in Table 6.1.

Scientists are fond of putting things into logical orders, patterns, or categories; it removes the apparent disorder and, in turn, defines and organizes the observable. Here, we offer a system that might be helpful to the student, observer, resident, or traveler in the Lehigh Valley. The downside, however, is that the categories grade into each other, and the reader should be alerted to the transition zones among the habitats. They are sometimes quite sharp and clear, as when a xeric cliff suddenly descends into a cool, moist ravine; in other cases, such as that of a gradually rising landscape that grades uphill from a swamp, the location of the hydric-mesic boundary is not always clear. (In many instances such questions are central to litigation cases. Wetlands are explored in Chapter 10.)

THE LEHIGH VALLEY FOREST

A century or more ago, our valley forest might have been appropriately described as an oak chestnut forest. Such a designation, common for most subdivisions of eastern forest, is based on the dominant plants—in this case, the oaks and American chestnut trees. This particular community, with its long-prevailing, self-replicating dominant trees, is referred to as a *climax community*. It should be distinguished from successional, transient communities, such as an abandoned field in the process of invasion and rapid change (see Chap. 8).

In her classic *Deciduous Forests of Eastern North America* (1950), E. Lucy Braun named and described a subdivision of the eastern states as the oak chestnut forest (see Fig. 6.2). While much of her detailed subdivisions are still in wide usage, a substantive change occurred in the former oak chestnut forest. The American chestnut (Fig. 6.3), a magnificent and most useful tree, was nearly decimated by an accidentally introduced fungus from northern China. In a matter of several decades all mature trees became infected, weakened, and, in time, killed back to the ground. Occasionally, shoots up to twenty or so feet tall still sprout from old rootstocks. These, too, eventually get infected. The replacement process is ongoing, but at this time the most stable dominants of the mesic environment are the

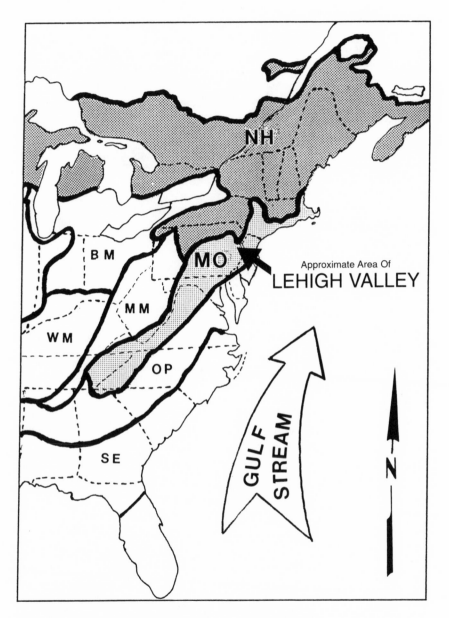

Fig. 6.2 *The subdivisions of the eastern deciduous forest*
The Lehigh Valley is in the mixed oak (MO) forest, formerly the oak chestnut forest, but close to the northern hardwood forest (NH) (also called the hemlock–white
pine–northern hardwood forest) that "starts" in the Poconos. The mixed oak forest
extends from Boston to eastern Tennessee. The roughly NE-SW orientation of the
forest divisions reflects, in part, the proximity to the ocean and gulf stream. (Modified from E. L. Braun 1972. From the collections of Cincinnati Museum Center.)

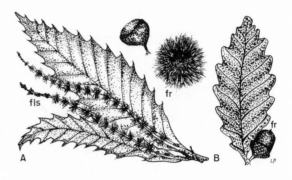

Fig. 6.3 *The American chestnut*
This magnificent tree, once a dominant species of the former oak chestnut sub-division of the Eastern deciduous forest, is now reduced to occasional sucker shoots.
A. Leaves, flowers, and spiny ball-like fruits called "burs" are depicted about one-half size.
B. A leaf of the chestnut oak (not a relative) is included for comparison.

oaks, and hence the botanical subdivision we are part of is called the mixed oak forest; a few refer to it as the Appalachian oak forest.

The Mixed Oak Forest

The mixed oak forest might also be called the upland oak forest, for it characteristically is found in mesic sites throughout the valley on most of the rolling hills between Blue Mountain and South Mountain. On the lower reaches that grade into the bottomlands, floodplains, and wetland areas, the oaks give way to the hydric species, such as sycamore, silver maple, and the willows. The name for the forest is based primarily on three dominant oaks—black, red, and white—although a few other oak species occur occasionally in environments marginal to the mesic condition. Figure 6.4 illustrates many of the trees associated with the general forest type. The composition of the forest trees will vary with history, prior land use, soil type, competition, and other limiting factors. White oak prefers a rich soil but can tolerate a fairly wide moisture regime, while both red and black oaks are confined to the drier uplands. Associate canopy trees may include basswood, elms, silver maple, black cherry, black gum, several hickory species, beech, ash, hemlock, white pine, and, more commonly of late, the Norway maple. The Society of American Foresters (SAF), an organization that has a long history of forest classifications, would categorize most of the Lehigh Valley (as described above) into SAF Type 52: white oak–black oak–red oak. Other groups of their forest taxonomy include SAF Type 59, a tulip tree–white oak–red oak grouping sometimes called "cove hardwoods" and associated with steeper

BLACK OAK   RED OAK   WHITE OAK

BASSWOOD   WHITE ASH   AMERICAN BEECH

BLACK CHERRY   SLIPPERY ELM   BLACK GUM

E. HEMLOCK   SHAGBARK HICKORY   NORWAY MAPLE

WHITE PINE   TULIP-TREE   BLACK WALNUT

Fig. 6.4 *Principal trees of the mixed oak forest*
In addition to the leaves, fruits (acorns, samaras, and so on) are illustrated. All
sketches are about one-half to one-quarter size.

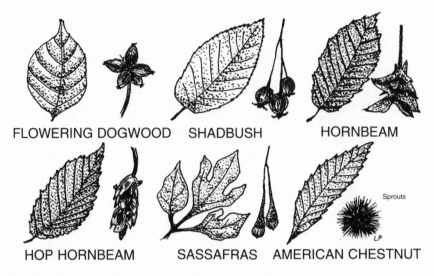

FLOWERING DOGWOOD   SHADBUSH   HORNBEAM

HOP HORNBEAM   SASSAFRAS   AMERICAN CHESTNUT

Fig. 6.5 *Common subcanopy trees of the mixed oak forest*

north- and east-facing slopes, and SAF Type 57, a purer stand of tulip tree that occurs in smaller patches with deep, moist, well-drained soils.

The subcanopy, or understory, includes dogwood, shadbush, hornbeam, hop hornbeam, sassafras, and occasional sprout trees of the American chestnut. These are illustrated in Figure 6.5.

The shrub layer, which includes all of those woody plants growing about three to six feet high, includes deerberry, hobblebush, witch hazel, spicebush, mapleleaf viburnum, arrowwood, American bladdernut, and others. Woody vine growth varies from occasional to rank. In the Lehigh Valley, the three most common forest vines, often competitive with each other, are the Virginia creeper, poison ivy, and fox grape. Poison ivy, in particular, can become a dense ground cover coupled with woody vine growth up into the canopy of host trees; the wand-like laterals from the clambering vine often lead the novice to misidentify a tree. The old poison ivy recognition tale is still a good one: "leaves of three, let it be." Some of these plants are illustrated in Figure 6.6. Other vines include the sporadic but sometimes very pesky Japanese honeysuckle, the occasional (and much less aggressive) Oriental bittersweet, the native climbing bittersweet, and two commonly planted but occasional escapes, the evergreen English ivy and the deciduous Boston ivy.

Herbs are typically abundant in the deciduous forest through the growing season, but are particularly so with the early spring ephemerals

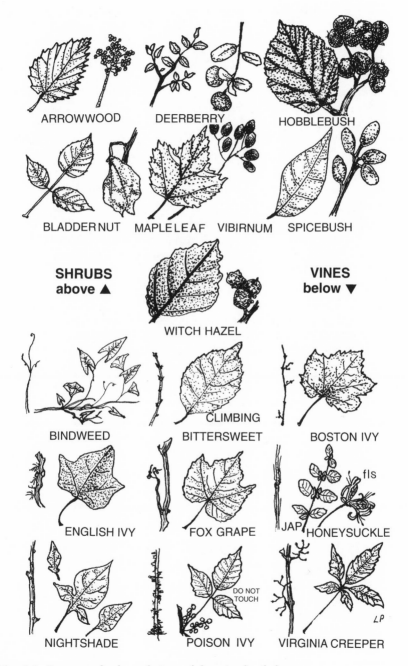

SHRUBS above ▲

VINES below ▼

ARROWWOOD DEERBERRY HOBBLEBUSH

BLADDERNUT MAPLELEAF VIBIRNUM SPICEBUSH

WITCH HAZEL

BINDWEED CLIMBING BITTERSWEET BOSTON IVY

ENGLISH IVY FOX GRAPE JAP HONEYSUCKLE fls

NIGHTSHADE POISON IVY DO NOT TOUCH VIRGINIA CREEPER

Fig. 6.6 *Common shrubs and vines of the mixed oak forest*
Catbrier (*Smilax,* greenbrier) is not included here, as it is mostly limited to the
Blue Mountain and Poconos areas.

BOX 6.1

Places to See the Mixed Oak Forest

BLUE MARSH. About forty-four miles southeast of Allentown on Route 222, take Route 183 northwest (right) and then south (left) on Plum Creek Road. Look for the signs. Trails allow visitors to explore the red oak–white oak forest, especially on the east side. The marsh includes many other passive natural sites and active outdoor recreation areas as well. Brochures and maps are available at the site.

LOUISE W. MOORE PARK. From Route 22, proceed north on Route 33 to the first exit (Hecktown Road). Go west a short distance, and then travel south on Country Club Road to the 113-acre park. It features an arboretum, a natural wildflower meadow, and other environmental areas—but the gem, in terms of native vegetation, is Matson's Woods, located at the very south end of the park. Matson's Woods is a 6.6-acre preserve of a climax white oak forest. Maps and brochures are available. Take Loop Trail 2: black oak, red oak, hickories, and others are typical. Poison ivy is excessive along the walkways, but otherwise the paths are pleasant. This is probably the best example of a remnant of climax oak forest in the Lehigh Valley area.

NOLDE FOREST ENVIRONMENTAL CENTER. Just south of Reading, exit from Route 222 onto Route 625, and travel south for several miles. The Center has about 665 acres and ten miles of hiking trails.

that try to "beat" the overhead leaf canopy. Most are perennials and continue their early conspicuous flowering period as corms, thick roots, or bulbs. Some of the typical herbaceous wildflowers are illustrated in Figures 5.4 and 5.11. (As always, enjoy the early wildflowers, but please do not pick them.)

Most of the plant species of the mixed oak forest in the Lehigh Valley are quite widely distributed throughout the valley. There are, however, a select assembly of plants that are restricted to the limestone formations of the lower valley and favor an elevated pH (see Table 6.2).

The Blue Mountain Ridge Top

Rising sharply along the northern flank of the Lehigh Valley is the Blue Mountain, one of a number of nearly parallel Appalachian ridges that,

Box 6.1 (Continued)

The bedrock, in the rift basin (see Chap. 2), is reddish Triassic/Jurassic sandstone with some igneous diabase. Aside from the planted groves of spruce and pine, the forest has natural areas of tulip trees, several oak varieties, red maple, beech, and so on, along with abundant wildflowers. This is a fine environmental education center.

Parklands. The major cities, such as Allentown and Bethlehem, and many of the townships and counties have parks with natural woodlands open to the public for hiking and nature study. Many of the woodlands are "islands" (see Chap. 8) of forest that boast good representatives of the prevailing mixed oak forest type. Call for maps, brochures, and information from the appropriate park office.

Pool Wildlife Sanctuary/Wildlands Conservancy. This facility, owned by Wildlands Conservancy, is about two and one-half miles south of the Cedar Crest Boulevard (Route 29) exit from I-78. Turn left onto Riverbend Road (which is marked by a light), and later, make a sharp right (there is a street sign with an arrow pointing toward the sanctuary) onto Orchid Place. The sanctuary will be on the right, across the white wooden bridge. The sanctuary maintains several trails, including a Pennsylvania Tree Identification Trail and a Woodland Loop Trail with a fairly typical mixed oak–tulip poplar forest. Maps are available at the kiosk, and many nature programs are held for school children.

in our area, have similar plant communities and are different enough from the mixed oak environment of the valleys below that they merit a separate discussion. Whereas the three oaks (red, black, and white) characterize much of the valley itself, the ridges to the north could properly be called chestnut oak forest (SAF Type 44), as the most common stocking is chestnut oak. (Recall that chestnut oak is not to be confused with the American chestnut). The ridge top setting admirably demonstrates that the two primary factors that determine plant community composition are moisture and temperature. Ridge tops and their attendant steep slopes are xeric communities, owing to the rapid water runoff and the paucity of soil. The chestnut oak, which does not form a tightly closed canopy, creates an environment with wider temperature fluctuations and more exposure to the elements. The resistant bedrock of sandstone and conglomerates favors an acidic (low pH) soil with limited abiotic plant nutrients.

BOX 6.2

Places to See Wildflowers

Many of the places listed in Box 6.1 are also excellent locations for seasonal woodland wildflowers. South-facing protected slopes have the first array of early spring flowers. While one can enjoy the wild-flower parade in almost any patch of woods, four notable spots are described below. Each has detailed checklists available. Using one of the available fine wildflower guides, visitors will find that learning about our native plants can be a rewarding experience.

BOWMAN'S HILL WILDFLOWER PRESERVE. This eighty-acre sanctuary, with twenty-six trails and over a thousand different plants, is one of the wildflower gems in the eastern United States. It is located just west of Route 32, about one-half mile south of New Hope. The sanctuary has trail maps, blooming date guides, and labels for the trail plants. A particularly strong feature is the weekly bloom-ing guide, which not only alerts the visitor to the current flowers in bloom (and even some that are budding!) but is also a useful trans-lation tool for the Lehigh Valley blooming dates. Using the guide-lines from Chapter 5, one can roughly compute the flowering times for the valley. In general, considering an elevation difference of three hundred to fourteen hundred feet and a latitude difference of twenty to forty-five miles, flowering times will differ (excluding slope and aspect) by about one to seventeen days. Exotic (intro-duced) plants and plants of the same species brought in from a dif-ferent geographical area are displayed, and species of special concern—endangered or threatened—have special designations. Picnic area, rest rooms, and a gift shop are located on site. A small fee is charged for admission. For information, call (215) 862-2924.

JACOBSBURG ENVIRONMENTAL EDUCATION CENTER. This state park is located about two miles south of Wind Gap, a few minutes from Route 33 at the Belfast exit. There are good signs. The center

Observations over many years of "typical" deciduous forests sug-gest an average disturbance rate of about 1 percent per year; that is, any given spot will be disturbed about once every fifty to two hundred years. Given the numerous stressors of any ridge top, disturbance there is probably much higher than that of the typical forest. Chestnut oaks, which sprout readily from old exposed rootcrowns, are in much

BOX 6.2 (CONTINUED)

features over one thousand acres of a variety of environments, including mixed oak forests, fields in a variety of stages of secondary succession (see Chap. 8), and a fine example of a one-hundred-acre cool ravine with climax hemlock trees (see Box 6.5). The latter, called Henry's Woods, has a pleasant trail along the Bushkill Creek (Chap. 10) and is itself a good stream study site. The center has excellent year-round environmental programs; plant and animal checklists are available. For information, call (610) 746-2801.

MARITON WILDLIFE SANCTUARY AND WILDERNESS TRUST. This preserve has over two hundred acres of woodlands and other habitats. From Easton, going south on Route 611, turn right (west) onto Spring Hill Road about one mile north of Riegelsville. Travel one-half mile, and make a right onto Sunnyside Road; go one-half mile uphill, and turn left at the sign for the sanctuary. The area boasts woods with dominant vegetation of oaks, tulip poplar, beech, and the like, as well as conifer plantations and open fields. Checklists are available on site, and visitors may wish to use the small museum and library. Reservations are required. For information, call (610) 749-2379.

HERBARIA. A *herbarium* is a collection of dried, mounted, and labeled plants. It is primarily used for reference and research. The most extensive collection on Lehigh Valley plants is in the Biology Department at Muhlenberg College—and largely represents the efforts of Professor Emeritus Robert L. Schaeffer Jr. The herbarium has about seventy thousand specimens. Permission to use the collection is secured through the department. The University of Pennsylvania, in Philadelphia, has an extensive collection from Pennsylvania and elsewhere, as does the Academy of Natural Sciences.

evidence as multiple-stemmed trees—a fact that suggests frequent disruption of growth through blowdowns, ice damage, gypsy moth infestations, and so on.

While the chestnut oak is considered the keystone of the ridge top community, other associates can be found: pitch pine, sassafras, scrub and other oaks, black gum, striped maple, red maple, various hickories,

Table 6.2 *Plants limited to limestone formations*

Meadows	Rocky Outcrops
Bladdernut	Purple cliff-brake fern
False Solomon's seal	Ragwort
Grass-of-Parnassus	Smooth cliff-brake fern
Lousewort	Spleenwort fern
Willow herb	Stiff gentian
	Yellow oak

SOURCE: After Schaeffer 1949.

sprouts of American chestnut, and occasional white pines. The dominant trees and woody shrubs are illustrated in Figure 6.7. The shrub layer is typically quite low and thick with acidophiles such as mountain laurel, various blueberries, deerberry, rhododendron, and sweet fern. The common vines are poison ivy, fox grape, and Virginia creeper (see Fig. 6.6), but with the addition of catbrier, a woody, thorny, round-leaved member of the lily family. The herb layer is somewhat sparse, but includes hay-scented, Christmas, and bracken ferns, wild sarsaparilla, wintergreen, and whorled loosestrife. While the chestnut oak forest dominates most of the ridges, two other communities can be noted.

Pitch Pine–Scrub Oak Forest
On one of the many ridge top trails through the chestnut oak forests, a hiker might be taken aback by an occasional, somewhat bizarre-looking

---

BOX 6.3

Places to See the Chestnut Oak Forest

APPALACHIAN TRAIL. The trail passes along the top of the Blue Mountain and can be accessed at any of the roads crossing it at the various water and wind gaps. State Game Land No. 217 covers much of the ridge in Lehigh County. State Game Land No. 168 is discontinuous in much of Northampton County.

HAWK MOUNTAIN. In Berks County, the trail passes through Hawk Mountain and continues southwestward on State Game Lands Nos. 106, 110, and 80. Many of the Hawk Mountain trails leading up to the two hawk lookouts are classic chestnut oak woods.

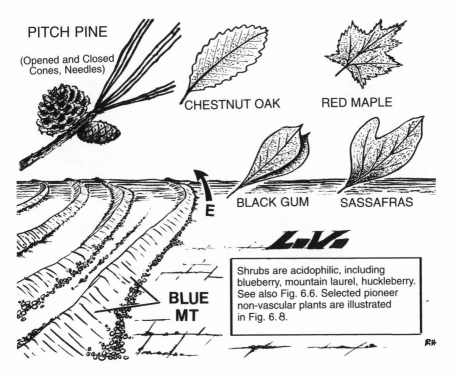

Fig. 6.7 *Typical section of the Blue Mountain and its vegetation*

low-growth opening. These rather unusual spotty parcels, often an acre to tens of acres in size, are called "barrens." Unlike the surrounding woods, the barrens are a rough tangle of low, very slow-growing scrub oaks and heaths punctuated by an occasional emergent scraggly pitch pine, sassafras tree, or taller scrub oak. Being exposed, the taller trees are often shaped by the wind and appear lopsided. The barrens are the result of rigorous environmental conditions, marginal soil, and repeated burnings. Fire was used by Native Americans to drive game and clear underbrush; lightning was another cause of fires. The plants that typically grow in the barrens are fire-tolerant and grow very slowly. Other trees include American chestnut sprouts, the aspens, chokecherry, gray birch, and red maple. Shrubs are mostly heaths—such as blueberry, chokeberry, huckleberry, mountain azalea, mountain laurel, and sheep laurel—and assorted brambles, meadowsweet, and sweet fern. Herbs are rather sparse and include asters, much bracken, checkerberry, fireweed, grasses, sedges, and a few others.

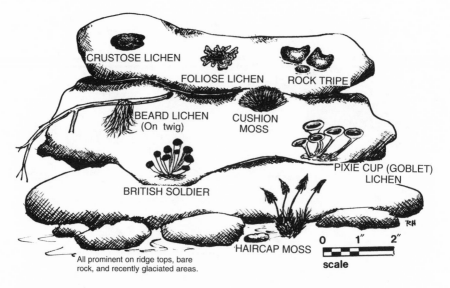

Fig. 6.8 *Selected pioneer nonvascular plants on exposed bedrock*

Rock Outcropping Communities

A hike along the ridge top trails or a near view of the steep slopes from the valley may also reveal occasional exposures of bedrock, simply referred to as outcroppings. These rock outcropping communities are nearly bare rocks that have had their soil mantle and vegetation removed by the scouring action of the glaciers. Extreme xeric conditions result as the two key limiting factors, moisture and temperature, create an inhospitable environment. In the absence of a soil cover, water and any nutrients quickly run off the rocks, and the exposure creates daily temperature extremes. In this setting only the most hardy of the xerophytes can take hold: the lichens. At first the flat crustose lichens, resembling a scruffy, pale green-to-gray paint, invade the surface and are literally cemented to it. In time, the more leafy foliage lichens, such as rock tripe, may start to colonize the surface. Fruticose lichens and mosses may follow, but the process of xeric succession continues to be extremely slow: progress is marked in centuries and millennia.

With the slow breakdown of the very resistant rocks and the development of cracks by the repeated freezing and thawing cycles, seeds may germinate, and a few hardy and tolerant vascular plants (both herbaceous and woody) may grow. Often forced into cracks, woody plants such as scrub oak or pitch pine take on a gnarled and twisted look.

Table 6.3 *Selected northern (Canadian) and southern (Carolinian) plants of the Lehigh Valley*

Canadian Species Near Their Southern Limit—Blue Mountain	Carolinian Species Near Their Northern Limit—South Mountain
Buckthorn	Cancer-weed
Dwarf cornel	Common persimmon
Gold thread	Dangleberry
Golden hardhack	Great-Indian-plantain
Leatherleaf	Jersey (scrub) pine
Mountain ash	Lady fern
Sheep laurel	Powdery catbrier
Shinleaf	Shiny coneflower
Showy lady's slipper	Trumpet honeysuckle
Speckled alder	Velvety beggar's-ticks
Striped maple	Virginia snakeroot
Toothwort	Virginia spiderwort
White basswood	Winter grape

SOURCE: After Schaeffer 1949.

In summary, the northern ridges and slopes of the Lehigh Valley are subjected to moisture and temperature constraints similar to those of Poconos, and the resultant plant species reflect their tolerance of the prevailing conditions. In addition to the common plants described in this section, limited numbers of northern (that is, Canadian/Alleghanian) plants also appear near their southern limit. Typically, they are associated with either the ridges and their slopes or the area just below the slopes but north of the Wisconsinan terminal moraine (see Chap. 2) in the far northeastern corner of Northampton County. (A few of these plants may appear in isolated spots on the acid slopes of South Mountain.) In a similar manner, an assembly of primarily southern plants reaches its northern limit at about South Mountain. About two dozen plants at the southern and northern margins of their distribution are presented in Table 6.3.

South Mountain

Though South Mountain vegetation is not so strikingly different from the baseline mixed oak forest of the valley proper, it deserves separate consideration. The southern geographic counterpart of Blue Mountain,

CAMEO 6.1

Robert L. Schaeffer Jr. (1917–)

For anyone with a question about a Lehigh Valley vascular plant identification, *the* single authority for the last half of the twentieth century has been Robert L. Schaeffer, Professor of Botany (1954–83) at Muhlenberg College. His numerous trips with countless students and his own continued "botanizing" throughout the valley have brought the Muhlenberg herbarium up to nearly seventy thousand specimens. His published dissertation (1949) at the University of Pennsylvania, *The Vascular Flora of Northampton County*, remains a landmark work. It contains keys, descriptions, blooming times, and other details for the serious student or professional.

South Mountain is a metamorphic extension of the New England Province and the southern boundary of the Lehigh Valley. While neither the altitude nor the latitude of South Mountain is that different from those of Blue Mountain, the two ridges do differ in their weather patterns. South Mountain is an isolated, diffuse ridge between the Lehigh and Saucon Valleys, and can be seen as "part of the valley," compared with Blue Mountain (which is at the "weather end" of a series of high-elevation ridges—the Appalachian Mountains and the Poconos). The weather on South Mountain—in terms of moisture and temperature, especially when coupled with a closed canopy—is less demanding.

South Mountain has three dominant trees: the tulip tree, sweet birch, and red oak. Of the three, sweet birch attains a smaller size and may be a less permanent member of the dominant tree community. Although these three species seem to be rather consistently important in the forest composition, a number of associates can be part of the canopy as well: these include red maple, sourwood, white ash, white oak, American beech, shagbark hickory, and black cherry. Their distribution, in turn, is dependent on such limiting factors as past land use, moisture, temperature, aspect, slope, and the like. The subcanopy resembles the mixed oak forest previously described, with such staples as flowering dogwood, sassafras, American hornbeam, hop hornbeam, and common shadbush. Many of the South Mountain shrubs mirror those of the mixed oak forest, as do the three common woody vines on South Mountain—poison ivy, Virginia creeper, and fox grape. Herbs include enchanter's nightshade, jack-in-the-pulpit, false lily-of-the-valley, white baneberry,

Box 6.4

Places to See South Mountain Vegetation

LEHIGH UNIVERSITY, MOUNTAINTOP CAMPUS AREA. From Route 378 near the top of the hill (South Mountain), take Mountain Drive West: after a jughandle to the right, proceed east a few miles to the Mountaintop Campus. Several hundred acres of woodlands surround the campus. The informal paths can be used to explore and study nature.

REIMERT MEMORIAL BIRD HAVEN. This wooded bird sanctuary is on the middle north slope of South Mountain near the western Lehigh County line. From Main Street (Route 100) in Macungie, go west on South Church Street for nine-tenths of a mile and look for the (easily missed) sign on the left. Parking is very limited. The woods include mixed tulip tree, red and black oaks, sweet birch, and American ash. Trails lead through the woods. No facilities. Owned by Wildlands Conservancy in Emmaus. Please call (610) 965-4397 for information.

SOUTH MOUNTAIN PARK. The park provides a hiking and nature study area. Take the route toward Mountaintop Campus (above); South Mountain Park is located near the WFMZ-TV station, only six-tenths of a mile east along Mountain Drive West. Owned and maintained by the City of Bethlehem. Please call (610) 865-7081 for information.

SOUTH MOUNTAIN RESERVOIR. From the junction of Route 309 and Emmaus Avenue, proceed northeast on Emmaus Avenue for about six-tenths of a mile, and turn right (south) onto South Tenth Street. Park and reservoir are located about one-half mile up the hill. There are wooded areas with hiking trails on the north slope of South Mountain. Owned by the City of Allentown. Call (610) 437-7627 for information.

Solomon's seal, false Solomon's seal, perfoliate bellwort, wild sarsaparilla, horsebalm, and others. (In addition, South Mountain hosts those southern plants near their northern border listed in Table 6.3.)

Hemlock Ravines

Downcutting is one of the basic erosion processes of all stream channels: the sediment load, acting much like moving sandpaper, wears away the channel floor. Simultaneously, the erosive processes acting on either side

---

BOX 6.5

Places to See Hemlock Ravines

CAMP HORSESHOE. The camp is operated by the Boys and Girls Club of Allentown. From Route 22, take Route 309 north for several miles; make a left at the Kernsville Road light, and travel just beyond the iron bridge. Make a right on Jordan Road and drive to a stop sign. Turn left onto Horseshoe Road. The camp is at the second right. There is a fine hemlock ravine along the Jordan Creek. Call ahead for visitor information. (The seasonal phone number is [610] 481-9206; the phone number for the Boys and Girls Club is [610] 432-9323.)

HEMLOCK HEIGHTS, HAWK MOUNTAIN. For directions, please see Box 1.1 and Box 4.1. Hemlock Heights is a classic, north-facing virgin hemlock stand lacking a stream, accessible only by a rigorous steep climb from the parking lot below the Schaumbach house.

HENRY'S WOODS, JACOBSBURG STATE PARK. See Box 6.2 for directions. A pleasant trail follows the Bushkill Creek, which is the site of an old stand of hemlock. The look is classic: dimly lit, few shrubs or ground cover plants, and a cool, cathedral-like atmosphere.

TREXLER GAME PRESERVE. From Route 22, go north on Route 309 for several miles to the Schnecksville area. Turn left onto Game Preserve Road (there is a prominent sign for the Trexler Game Preserve).

---

of the channel widen it; the degree of slope retreat and configuration is governed, in part, by the bedrock. Thus, the southern limestone portion of the Lehigh Valley has broad interstream areas with very gentle slopes, while the northern (slate/shale) part has flat-topped stream divides, rounded slopes near the top, and steep slopes near the streams. The latter configuration lends itself to deep (and, if the native trees are not harvested, cool and moist) ravines—a perfect setting for the official tree of Pennsylvania, the Eastern hemlock. Hemlock was abundant on the cool Pocono plateau, where it was mostly lumbered out for the tanning industry; the relatively small patches in the northern Lehigh Valley, being in relatively inaccessible steep ravines or steep north-facing slopes, escaped the lumbermen. The hemlock, an evergreen, perpetuates itself in two ways: it forms tight, closed canopies that create dimly lit, cool and moist conditions (those central limiting factors!) on the ground, which help it to thrive, and it tolerates shade, which encourages "growing up in the shadows of its parents"—so self-replacement is natural. The needles,

Fig. 6.9 *The hemlock tree* The hemlock typically occupies cool, moist ravines in the northern part of the Lehigh Valley. It is often planted in landscapes and can be recognized by the two white parallel lines on the underside of each needle (leaf).

which accumulate on the floor and slowly release their tannic acids, make the floor inhospitable to all but the shade-loving acidophilic plants. (The SAF classifies this as Type 23, an Eastern Hemlock community.)

The scene, then—a somewhat limited one in the northern Lehigh Valley—is that of a steep-sided ravine, the banks clothed in ferns, mosses, and liverworts, the floor devoid of all but occasional shrubs, a sparse ground cover of starflower, Canada mayflower, Christmas fern, trailing arbutus, and others, and large hemlocks presiding over a cool stream environment. Although this vision of a hemlock ravine might be typical, local conditions and history create a number of variations as well. The sometimes nearly pure hemlock stand may have other tree species as well: the oaks, white pine, yellow and black birch, sugar maple, basswood, and red maple.

The future of these ravines is not clear, however. A destructive alien, the hemlock woolly adelgid (a small aphid-like insect native to Asia), has become a serious parasite on the hemlock trees. It sucks the juices from the needles and, if invasion is high enough, may kill the trees. Although the situation is being monitored, the question remains: Will the hemlock go the route of the fabled American chestnut?

As we consider the threat to the hemlock, we should also remember the ecological value of dead trees. It is true, as Malcolm Hunter (1990) notes, that "to many people there is nothing quite so useless as a dead tree, except possibly the fifth wheel on a cart, and when people are called 'deadwood' it is not because they are mature and respected members of an organization. It is hardly surprising that people find dead things unattractive."

But a dead tree, contrary to popular perception, has a plus side. Called a *snag,* it plays host to a variety of insects, fungi, spiders, and other small native creatures of the woodland; a variety of mammals, including flying and gray squirrels, raccoons, and others; and, surprisingly, about eighty-five species of birds in North America. In a forest, at least, maturity and deadwood are relative terms.

Floodplains and Wetlands

While the primary focus of this chapter is on upland environments, we recognize the ecological importance and legislative significance of floodplains and wetlands—where water periodically floods onto the adjacent flat lands or where the soil is saturated with water for a significant part of the year. They are the focus of Chapter 10. Obvious indicator species—such as skunk cabbage, sycamore and willow trees, cattails, and others—signal a wet environment in the Lehigh Valley, but we will defer the discussion of them until the later chapter.

Agriculture and Fields

We will also defer the discussion of this significant habitat within the Lehigh Valley, giving it separate treatment in Chapter 7. There, we will consider crops, fruit trees, arboreta, lawns, and similar kinds of "managed plant" areas in the valley.

NATIVE VEGETATION: THE FUTURE

We have sketched, in the main section of this chapter, an outline of native vegetation in the valley. But a persistent question continues to elude us: What would happen to the forests without man's management? The question of the potential forest landscape applies to regions well outside the borders of the Lehigh Valley. According to numerous studies and observations, our forest would likely continue as a mixed oak forest type. But it took about a century—after the demise of the American chestnut—for oaks to reach their position of dominance. Will the northern hardwoods, i.e., the beech–maple–hemlock–yellow birch community, supplant the current forests? All do well in their own shade, which suggests a possible change, but natural disruptions (the hemlock woolly adelgid, wind episodes, the Dutch elm disease, major hurricanes, the emerging destructive anthracnose disease of flowering dogwood, fires, and so on) all contribute to continued perturbations. And on these, we can superimpose the possibility of the earth's rising temperature—commonly referred to as global warming.

In the past, nature was seen as a repository of balance, harmony, and constancy; more realistically, nature is marked by imbalance, conflict, and perturbation. The current consensus is that *change* itself is the bottom line of the environment. While they may appear a bit abstract and academic in a natural history book, we cannot ignore the many environmental consequences of landscaping with native plants or with cultivars, choosing to plant certain crops, assenting to genetic manipulations, planning woodlot use, or using particular sprays—and these are only a few of the many decisions we must make. (Chapter 12 will take up some of these issues, as it focuses on the valley's future.) For now, we will consider one of the key elements of the Lehigh Valley: its agricultural land.

The Agricultural Lehigh Valley

As a work of art, I know few things more pleasing to
the eye, or more capable of affording scope and gratifica-
tion to a taste for the beautiful, than a well-situated, well-
cultivated farm.

—EDWARD EVERETT, PUBLIC ADDRESS IN
BUFFALO, N.Y., OCTOBER 9, 1857

A tidy farmhouse guarded by old native trees, a colorful red barn, and
a white picket fence, all surrounded by a variety of healthy crops: the
Lehigh Valley has an abundance of these picture-postcard images. In
fact, more than 50 percent of the Lehigh Valley is classified as farmland,
with almost 900 farms set on about 175,000 acres. While many natural
history books either disregard or give token treatment to the agricultural setting, this chapter addresses that important "50 percent plus" of
the Lehigh Valley—including crops, orchards, arboreta, alternative agriculture, and the ubiquitous home lawn.

From the many mom-and-pop seasonal roadside stands to the
almost culturally ingrained institutions such as the Allentown or Ren-
ninger farmers' markets, the message is clear: the Lehigh Valley has an
abundance of quality agricultural products. Indeed, the entire Commonwealth—once earlier noted for its dual resources of lumber and

coal—now ranks strongly among all the states in a variety of crops, and agriculture is still the premier industry in Pennsylvania. For instance, Pennsylvania ranks fourth in producing corn for silage and peaches, and holds fifth place in growing apples, pears, grapes, and tomatoes; the state also ranks in the top ten for many other crops. The Lehigh Valley contribution to this agricultural effort, among others, will be discussed in the rest of this chapter.

CROPS FOR FEED AND FOOD

Cereals, sometimes referred to as the "staff of life," do have the singular distinction of standing between starvation and survival for several billion people. The word *cereal* is derived from the name of the goddess Ceres, the giver-of-grain of ancient lore. True cereals, which include corn (maize), wheat, rice, oats, barley, rye, and sorghum, are all members of the grass family (Gramineae). Small grass flowers and their fruits, called grains, are concentrated in clusters; easily handled, stored, and processed, they have a number of advantages over many other fruit types.

Corn, better known around the world as maize, remains a principal crop in the Lehigh Valley. In fact, the valley is in the top tier of both silage and grain corn production among the Commonwealth's counties. Corn appears to have originated in Mexico about 5000 B.C., but was an established principal crop when Columbus arrived in the Americas. The valley grows field corn—a taller, coarser-grained variety for either grain or silage—as well as sweet corn, a sugary, tender variety intended for direct table consumption. The latter is a welcome addition to the market in late July and for several weeks thereafter. The "picked just hours ago variety" is best, as the (sweet) sugar hasn't started to convert to (not so sweet) starch.

Like corn, wheat is a principal grass of the valley, with Berks, Lehigh, and Northampton all in the top tier of county production. Wheat is a bread cereal and is considered, along with corn and rice, to be part of the top trio of cereal "greats." (Bread, a worldwide staple, is made by adding yeast to wheat dough.) Lehigh Valley wheat is cultivated as winter wheat, which is sown in the early fall, can withstand our moderate winters, and is harvested the following July and August. Even the wheat stalks are useful: like those of oats and other grasses, they make fine animal bedding material, stuffing, and the like, and are marketed as straw.

Fig. 7.1 *Common
economic grass and legume
crops in the valley*
Alfalfa and clover are
legumes (members of the
bean family); the rest are
grasses. Soybeans, also
legumes, are illustrated in
Figure 7.2.

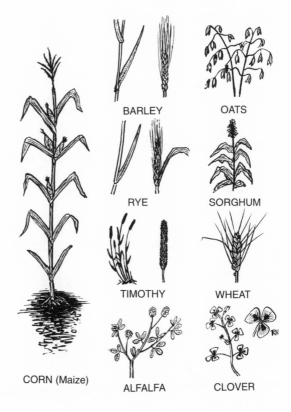

BARLEY   OATS

RYE   SORGHUM

TIMOTHY   WHEAT

CORN (Maize)   ALFALFA   CLOVER

Other Lehigh Valley grasses include barley, timothy, oats, rye, and sorghum. These and some other crop plants that one might observe from a car are presented in Figure 7.1.

Forage crops are those grass and legume plants grown to feed herbivores, which consume the leaves and stems. As such, the food can be consumed in the pasture, as harvested hay, chopped-up feed greens, or silage. Other cereals include timothy and the legumes alfalfa and clover. Alfalfa has been a cultivated forage crop for most of documented history; indeed, the genus name for alfalfa, *Medicago,* was given by Linnaeus in recognition of the introduction of alfalfa to Greece in 500 B.C. by the invading Medes. It is sometimes referred to as the "queen of forage crops" for its long record and worldwide cultivation. It allows for several cuttings per growing season. Berks County is ranked fifth in the state in county alfalfa hay production.

Clover, like alfalfa, is a member of the bean family (Leguminosae), and permits farmers to "grow" their own nitrogen. Legumes biologically fix atmospheric nitrogen (with the symbiotic association of special

---

BOX 7.1

Places to See Lehigh Valley Agriculture

BURNSIDE PLANTATION. Burnside is of particular interest because it is a re-creation of farming in the middle of the eighteenth century. Many of the plants have been grown from "heirloom seeds." The mid-1700s farmhouse is located off Schoenersville Road. Take Route 22 to Route 378, and take 378 south to the Eighth Avenue exit. From the exit, proceed north. At the first traffic light, turn right into Martin Towers Lot D. There is a short walk to the Burnside farmstead.

CROPS. Many of the curbside descriptions are included in Figures 7.1 and 7.2. A casual drive through much of the valley, particularly north of the cities, is a rewarding experience in identification—especially as these very crops may well appear on the kitchen table.

FAIR. The Great Allentown Fair, now approaching the 150th edition, had an original focus on farming, tools, farm animals, and the like. While the fair has become more entertainment-oriented, there are still excellent exhibits of various local products (honey, jams, and so on), prize-winning animals, and other farm-related items. Local granges and 4-H clubs are properly proud exhibitors. The fair is located at Seventeenth and Chew Streets, Allentown, and it is typically held in late summer. Call (610) 433-7549 for information.

FARM TOURS. Both Lehigh and Northampton Extension Services sponsor farm tours. The Lehigh tour has traditionally taken place on the third Sunday in October, while the Northampton tour is the first Sunday of October. Both offer excellent opportunities to visit a variety of farms—including dairy, poultry, horse, Christmas tree, and other farm types—as well as wineries, orchards, nurseries, and greenhouses.

---

bacteria) so that the otherwise useless free atmospheric nitrogen becomes available for plant root absorption. The familiar term "crop rotation" denotes a key factor in agricultural success. Other nitrogen sources include manures and various commercial fertilizers.

Nitrogen, phosphorus, and potassium are essential elements for plant growth. A fertilizer container label often includes a series of numbers, such as 12-30-9; although beginning students have identified these digits as the product's expiration date or zip code, the numbers, in order, actually give the percentages of nitrogen (N), phosphorus (P), and potassium (K) in the fertilizer.

BOX 7.1 (CONTINUED)

Look in the local newspapers late in September for featured farms and directions.

LEHIGH COUNTY CONSERVATION DEMONSTRATION PROJECT. A several-acre parcel of land illustrates sound agricultural practices, such as contour farming, strip cropping, terracing, composting, and the like. (For permission to visit the site, group tour information and guides, a site map, and brochure, call the Lehigh County Conservation District at [610] 391-9583.) From the junction of Routes 100 and 29, go south, and turn left onto Kings Highway. Make a left onto Churchview. Go through the stop sign at Vera Cruz, and cross the train tracks to the driveway on the right (before the Pennsylvania Turnpike overpass).

MARKETS. There are many fine markets that feature fresh local produce. Check the telephone directory, the local newspapers, or the local Extension Service. The Pennsylvania Turnpike service plaza at Allentown was one participant in a few pilot programs for vendors who grow at least 50 percent of their products in Pennsylvania. Started in 1995, this particular program was deemed a success. Travelers on this key toll road may now purchase and enjoy local farm products.

For a free and very informative brochure on the farms in the valley, entitled *Fresh from Lehigh Valley Farms Directory*, call the Lehigh County Agricultural Center at (610) 391-9840 or contact the Northampton County Extension Office at (610) 746-1970. The directory includes an excellent "what's-available-when" chart; farms for various items (fruits, vegetables, herbs, and so on), including addresses, hours, and telephone numbers; listings for milk, eggs, wines, honey, plants, and flowers; and much more.

Alfalfa, with its internally engineered mechanism for assembling useful nitrogen, was the focus of a major local industry in Northampton County in the first half of this century. According to Penn State Cooperative Extension Service Agent Greg Solt, it was processed into pellets (or concentrates) in local drying facilities and used in a variety of ways, including assorted animal feeds. The enterprise faded in the 1960s.

The only forage crop in the legume family to rival alfalfa is clover. It comes in a number of *cultivars* (cultivated varieties) and is variously planted throughout the Lehigh Valley. Like alfalfa, it is a nitrogen-fixing plant, valued in farming; it receives a less than warm welcome in lawns that unfortunately rank cosmetic appearance higher than utility.

THE CHANGING MARKETPLACE

The Irish or white potato sports the appropriate scientific name *Solanum tuberosum* (literally, the tuber of the sun), for it does best with warm sunny days, cool nights, and an acidic soil—conditions prevalent in the north/northwestern tier of the Lehigh Valley. For many years, Lehigh County led the Commonwealth in white potato production, but recent economic changes in the marketplace and increasing competition have greatly reduced the traditional potato farming enterprise. While Lehigh County still ranks sixth among the Commonwealth counties in potato production, the downward shift is substantial, especially in the context of the national potato chip and pretzel industries—in which Pennsylvania holds first place.

White potatoes are considered to be, in terms of worldwide tonnage produced, the number one food; unfortunately, they are about 80 percent water. They store well at low temperatures (to prevent sprouting) and high humidities (to prevent desiccation) and are thus available all year. Nonetheless, a welcome market sign, typically in mid-summer, is the arrival of "new potatoes." Valley cultivars include Chieftain, Norwis, Katahdin, Somerset, and others.

While potato production has decreased, soybean production has increased significantly in the valley. A casual drive through farming country will make this obvious; the bushy plant is typically up to three feet tall, with trifoliate leaves (somewhat resembling the ubiquitous poison ivy!), small flowers, and numerous few-seeded, hairy bean pods (see Fig. 7.2). Soybeans were considered a sacred grain by the ancient Chinese; more recently, they have been called a "Cinderella crop," as they have quickly escalated to the number two cash crop in the Midwest. In Pennsylvania, soybean-planted acres have increased during the last twenty-five years by a phenomenal tenfold. In 1995, our two-county area had twenty-five thousand acres in soybeans at a value of almost five million dollars. (And if we add Berks County to the statistics, the values almost double.)

Shifting economic trends and cultural tastes have, in part, driven the change; a cursory look at the listings of Lehigh Valley restaurants will readily testify to this. Being high in protein (30–50 percent) and oil, the

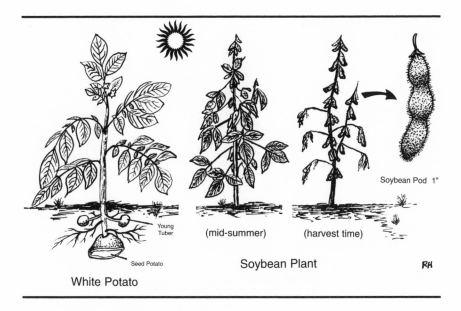

Fig. 7.2 *White potatoes and soybeans*
Potatoes are grown mostly in the northern parts of the valley. Soybeans, which superficially resemble potatoes during the summer months, are grown all over the valley and are referred to as the "Cinderella crop," as their acreage in Pennsylvania has increased tenfold since 1970. Both reach about thirty inches in height. The bristly tan soybean pods put them in the legume (bean) family.

soybean plant has given rise to tofu (a Japanese staple), soybean cakes, the flavoring sauce known simply as "soy," soybean "sprouts," recently introduced soy burgers, and "fortified" breads. Moreover, the leftover meal is a quality stock feed. Small wonder the Chinese, centuries ago, thought of it as sacred—even without soy burgers and fries.

Soybeans and potatoes are market heavyweights; sunflowers are not. Yet they are more apparent now as occasional small fields in the valley, and visitors to the country are typically delighted to come upon one of these colorful brown and gold sun-worshipping plots. Sunflower has an oil similar to those of corn and olive. The several dozens of acres in the valley are planted for direct human consumption or sold mostly through outlets for birdseed. (Twenty years ago, a birdseed store, per se, would have raised eyebrows in the valley; the public's perception and support of nature and biodiversity have changed. This issue will be addressed further in Chap. 12.)

Fig. 7.3 *Sunflower head*
This plant has a tightly
packed inflorescence
("head") of very small flowers, each producing a single
commercial seed. Solar track-
ing (technically called
heliotropism) is conspicuous
in sunflowers, although other
plants—such as cotton, soybeans, and cowpeas—exhibit
the same diurnal ability.

FRUITS

If we define a fruit as a ripened ovary with or without associated parts, then the earlier discussed cereals (grains), corn, soybeans, sunflower seeds, and so on are all fruits. In this section, however, we will look at the more conventional fruits—apples, peaches, grapes, and strawber-ries—that are all Lehigh Valley traditions.

Apples represent a long history of *hybridization*, or crossing among strains. There were about seven thousand apple cultivars at one time, but only several of those—such as McIntosh, Delicious, Winesap, and Granny Smith—have become important. Typically, propagation is by either budding or grafting onto superior rootstock plants; the plant is subsequently trained and pruned to a strong central trunk with several laterals to facilitate harvesting. Pennsylvania ranks fifth in apple pro-duction nationally, and Lehigh and Berks Counties are both in the top ten in Pennsylvania.

Like apples, peaches continue to be significant: Berks, Lehigh, and Northampton Counties all rank in the top ten in Pennsylvania for peach production. Peaches are either freestone (i.e., the edible flesh part separates readily from the pit, or stone) or clingstone (i.e., the flesh maintains a tight adherence to the stone). Peaches are very sensitive to frost, and are mostly planted in locations other than low-lying frost pockets; this is obvious dur-ing a spring drive, when the colorful pink peach flowers, which appear before the leaves do, accentuate the hills. Curiously, nectarines and peaches differ mainly in their surface *pubescence*, or fuzz. Occasional branch mutants on an otherwise normal peach tree produce nectarines.

Strawberries are less important to the valley than some other fruits, but they are still a welcome arrival at local farmers' markets, stores, and roadside stands. Of particular local interest is the advertisement that announces the availability of "pick-your-own" strawberries. This method recognizes the labor-intensive nature of the strawberry economy, and the difficulty of dealing with a perishable and tender-skinned fruit. Look for local "pick-your-own" ads in early May. Additional local fruits include tomatoes, cantaloupes, beans, cherries, pears, and others.

Area farmers' markets and "pick-your-own" events benefit from the general trend away from national commercial food and beverage products to locally produced items. This trend is paralleled in valley wines as well; about a half-dozen wineries offer a nice selection and complimentary tastings. (Detailed information about valley wineries can be found in the *Lehigh Valley Wine Trail* brochure available from Agricultural Extension Service offices.)

The Lehigh Valley features a surprisingly varied array of crops—and this array sustains the valley in more ways than one. Robert Leiby, of the Penn State Cooperative Extension Service, has underscored the value of biodiversity in valley farming and the benefits of not going in the direction of monoculture (as much of the Midwest has done). Not only does the diversity act as a cushion against catastrophic loss due to climate perturbations or pest eruptions, but it also provides the region with an spectrum of fresh products to enjoy.

AGRICULTURE—OTHER

While the term *agriculture* suggests a definition along the lines of "cultivating the ground," it does include, in addition to the production of crops, the production of livestock on farms. (*Agronomy,* by comparison, is more narrowly limited to field-crop production.)

Dairying

Pennsylvania continues to rank among the top five states in butter, ice cream, and milk sherbet production; in fact, dairying is the Commonwealth's primary agricultural activity. The Lehigh Valley, however, has significantly reduced its contribution to the dairy industry over the last few decades. Lehigh County has fewer than twenty farms, with somewhat over one thousand milking cows; Northampton County boasts about one hundred farms; Berks County, around five hundred. The Lehigh Valley Cooperative Farmers building, a large and beautiful Art Deco structure, presides

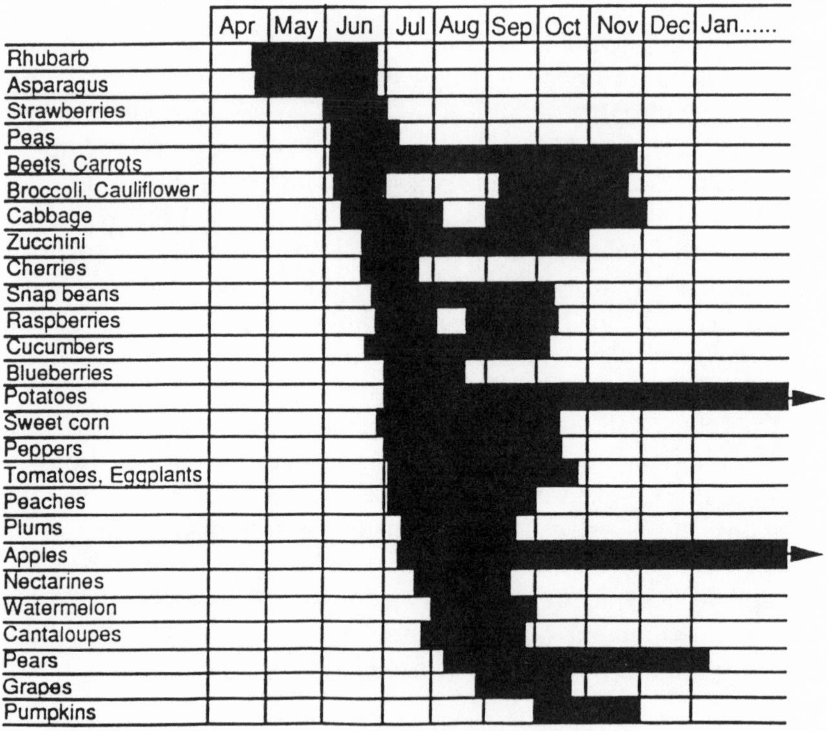

	Apr	May	Jun	Jul	Aug	Sep	Oct	Nov	Dec	Jan......
Rhubarb										
Asparagus										
Strawberries										
Peas										
Beets, Carrots										
Broccoli, Cauliflower										
Cabbage										
Zucchini										
Cherries										
Snap beans										
Raspberries										
Cucumbers										
Blueberries										
Potatoes										
Sweet corn										
Peppers										
Tomatoes, Eggplants										
Peaches										
Plums										
Apples										
Nectarines										
Watermelon										
Cantaloupes										
Pears										
Grapes										
Pumpkins										

Fig. 7.4 *Lehigh Valley calendar of fresh fruits and vegetables*
The "what's-available-when" guide is based on surveys of local farmers by the Lehigh and Northampton Penn State Cooperative Extension Services. (See also Box 7.1.)

over the northern section of North Seventh Street in Allentown, just south of Route 22. Once a bustling processing operation, it now silently reminds the visitor of the changing nature of dairy farming in the Lehigh Valley.

Poultry

Fresh eggs and various poultry products are part of the Lehigh Valley's agricultural focus. The two-county area has a combined production of nearly one-third of a million eggs per year. Perry County leads all the others in turkey production, although over a million turkeys come every year from Jaindl Farms in Lehigh County. (Other farms are minor, compared with the local Jaindl operation.)

Nurseries and Greenhouses

Nurseries and greenhouses are tied to both established and growing affluent urban and suburban developments, institutions, and businesses. In Pennsylvania, both enterprises revolve around the metropolitan areas of Pittsburgh and Philadelphia. While a casual review of Pennsylvania landscapes might support the more conspicuous perception of grains, pastures, and dairies as central, the state does rank third in the nation (behind Florida and California) in nursery- and greenhouse-based sales. This has, no doubt, been bolstered by the establishment of several of the major retail "home builder" stores that include greenhouse plants, nursery sales, and yard accessories. The valley has an ample selection of fine landscaping firms, many of which display their skills and designs at the traditional Lehigh Valley Horticultural Exhibition in Allentown in late February or early March. (Call [610] 437-6020 for more information.) The Philadelphia Flower Show, the largest in the world, is a natural outgrowth in an area historically acknowledged as the birthplace of North American botany and horticulture.

Trees and Such

The original Penn's Woods of the valley has been reduced to isolated island patches, or forest fragments, as described in the next chapter; one would not anticipate a major timber effort in the Lehigh Valley. There are about a dozen sawmills, mostly concentrated in or close to either South Mountain or Blue Mountain. Additionally, the valley grows a substantial number of Christmas trees. Commonly grown species include selected pines, firs, and spruces. Many October "farm tours," open to the public (see Box 7.1), include both sawmills and Christmas tree farms. Grant White offers regular tours of the White Christmas Tree Farm—the perfect name, perhaps, for such an enterprise.

NATIVE VERSUS CULTIVATED PLANTS

Almost all of Chapter 6 dealt with plants that have been here for centuries. Most of our crops, orchards, and landscaping plants, however, have been either introduced or naturalized, or are cultivated strains of some sort. Indeed, it is becoming increasingly difficult to separate the concepts of *natural* and *unnatural*. Generally, the word *natural* means "being or found in its native state." Yet we note that the *native* mulberry leads the woody attack in our *unnatural* mulch beds and that the *unnatural* (alien) Norway maple is an increasingly invasive member of our *native* forests; the latter, in fact, is a *naturalized* plant—one that has become an established resident.

Our crops are mostly derived from "once only wild" plants, now hybridized or genetically engineered to suit our needs. McIntosh, Big Boy, and Snowden are all examples of varieties that feature desirable characteristics, such as large flowers or big yields. Hybrid field corn is much superior to the earliest known cultivated corn (maize) of Mexico from 5000 B.C. But there are disadvantages to non-native plants, including costly pest control, substantial fertilization, and other high-energy inputs (although transgenic crops now are proving very effective in the valley).

Native plants, being of the area, have long since adapted to valley conditions; they require minor (or no) attention and few of the inputs necessary for aliens and cultivars. The renewed interest in our native plants, particularly for residential and public landscaping, has become visible in several ways. A number of organizations, such as the Burnside Plantation (see Box 7.1) and Wildlands Conservancy (see Box 6.1), have scheduled native plant sales. Millersville University has sponsored a very attractive conference on native plant landscaping during the last several summers. And perhaps the *most* visible native plant activities in the valley are the plantings along the major roadways such as Routes 33 and I-78. Federal highway projects mandate that 25 cents of each one hundred dollars are spent on native wildflower landscaping, and in 1990, Pennsylvania initiated Operation Wildflower as an alternative to the monotonous green lawns along rights-of-way. The colorful plantings reduce both visible roadside litter and energy-intensive mowing demands.

Native plants are available by mail from a selected number of mail-order houses. A list is available from Bowman's Hill Wildflower Preserve (Box 6.2). A few nonprofit organizations are devoted to wildflowers, including the New England Wildflower Society (180 Hemenway Road, Framingham, Mass., 01701-2699), which sells seeds, and the Heirloom Seed Project (c/o Landis Valley Museum, 2451 Kissel Hill Road, Lancaster, Pa., 17601-4899), which has a focus on traditional seeds.

REGENERATIVE AGRICULTURE

Up until the 1980s, most of the farming of the valley followed the conventional post–World War II approach: high-yield goals, single-crop

B o x   7 . 2

Where to See Regenerative Agriculture

The Rodale Institute Research Center is located about fifteen miles southwest of Allentown, just north of Route 222. After passing through the town of Maxatawny, take a right (at the Rodale sign) onto Grim Road; at the intersection with Siegfriedale Road, go left to the center. The bookstore and visitor center are on the left. Tours, many workshops, a bookstore, a museum, various plantings, and so on are available. Write to RIRC, 611 Siegfriedale Road, Kutztown, PA, 19530, or call (610) 683-6009 for information.

planting, and substantial use of chemicals such as fertilizers, herbicides, and pesticides. A contrasting approach—long called "organic farming," but more recently termed *regenerative agriculture*—centers on multiple-crop plantings, organic fertilizers, integrated pest management, and the minimal use of chemicals. The physical center is the Rodale Institute Research Center, near Kutztown, Pa. (See Box 7.2.) The sponsor is the Rodale Press, a prolific publishing firm in Emmaus, with many environmentally oriented books and journals to its credit. The research center was founded in 1972 by Bob Rodale (see Cameo 7.1), a strong advocate for personal, public, and general environmental health.

The organic farming concept captured the imagination of the long-haired, back-to-nature types from the 1960s and contributed to the ultimate passage of the National Environmental Policy Act (NEPA) in 1970. The Rodale Institute Research Center estimates that about thirty thousand farms nationwide are now organic operations; a trip to the Rodale facility is a good starting point for a conceptual change. Regenerative agriculture underscores not only the losses from the soil under conventional methods but also the restoration of the land to a viable and continued productivity. The Integrated Pest Management (IPM) approach is one that combines biological controls, such as natural pest enemies, resistant crop varieties, pheromones (attractants, such as Japanese beetle traps), and helpful companion plantings, with limited pesticides. A key part of the approach is that pest populations are monitored as a guide to application, as opposed to the routine use of pesticides for the "general welfare" of plantings. Today's valley farmers are incorporating genetically engineered crops on their farms to limit the use of pesticides further.

CAMEO 7.1

Robert Rodale (1930–1990)

Robert Rodale's obituary notice in the *Lehigh Alumni Bulletin,* Fall 1990, mentions that "Rodale ('52), who built a publishing and research empire around his beliefs in alternative agriculture and wellness . . . has been hailed as the 'guru of alternative agriculture' and a 'friend of the world.' Through his work, Rodale lived in the future and provided a forum for new ideas about farming and fitness. . . . He took old values and applied them to new technologies, and took old technologies and applied them to new values."

His stewardship of the earth and interest in fitness was translated into a number of Lehigh Valley endeavors, including the land donation for the velodrome, the Bob Rodale Cycling and Fitness Park (Trexlertown), and a major land donation for the preservation of South Mountain.

Bob served six years on the board of Wildlands Conservancy and spent three as president of the organization. The Conservancy obituary for him remembered his vision: "The man is gone, but the seeds he planted, the ideas he shared with so many of us, live on and will continue to touch our lives in many ways."

His wife, Ardath Rodale, continues the tradition as an equally strong advocate of fitness, alternative agriculture, and environmental stewardship.

LAWNS AND OTHER MANAGED TYPES

The American lawn is a distinctive landscape: nowhere in the world is there anything comparable. The homeowners' lawns of the United States amount to an area about the size of Pennsylvania—forty-five thousand square miles!—at a maintenance cost of $30 billion per year. Our obsession with the suburban lawn and park image is manifest in our nomenclature. Green Meadows, Fox Meadow, Fair Lawn, Jordan Park, Grassy Knolls, Summit Lawn, Trexler Park—no fewer than 150 town names in the United States include the word "lawn." Forest Lawn may be the last one, in a sense.

The source of our peculiarly American lawn is multifaceted. We evolved in a savanna, a grassland with scattered trees; it, like the later castles of England, provided a vista, a source of protection, and later, status. (Recall the historical insecurity associated with woods: Robin Hood, Little Red Riding Hood, and so on.) The image was translated into major park designs in the 1800s by Frederick Law Olmsted, designer of Central, Prospect, Morningside, Fairmont, and other parks. The popularity of grass sports—including golf, baseball, football, and soccer—along with the affordability of the automobile, the consequential spread of suburbs, the development of Kentucky bluegrass, and, in 1869, the invention of the lawn mower, all promoted the lawn as an American suburban living standard.

Kentucky bluegrass is one of several grasses that are part of a typical lawn seed mix. In grasses, the growing point is at the *base* of the leaves, which allows for repeated mowing (or grazing) with continued renewal. The grasses also produce horizontal *stolons* (runners) which help to "close in" the lawn. If not mowed, the grasses will produce an inconspicuous flower cluster and seed head. Some domesticated grasses are perennials, and the cool season varieties go into a semi-dormant state during the hot and dry part of the summer in the Lehigh Valley. This is when the weekly lawn mowing ritual becomes extended to an on-demand basis.

How does the front lawn fit into a Lehigh Valley natural history book? The lawn is the managed ecosystem closest to home for most residents. And with or without a lawn, many residents find comfort in parks with lawns. Herbert Bormann, Diana Balmori, and Gordon Geballe caught this spirit in *Redesigning the American Lawn:* "Americans' attachment to the lawn is a long and fond one. A lawn is a gathering place for family, friends, and neighbors, a place where we engage in our favorite activities. In cities, it is a place of verdure, a refuge from crowds, traffic, and noise. The green blades feel good to the touch; the cut grass freshens the smell of the air."

Whether in a lawn or park, the exclusion of invading aliens, such as dandelion, clover, crabgrass, or chickweed, is looked upon as a measure of control by the owner. (The reverse is viewed as laziness or lack of interest.) Yet in some cases, new homeowners are dealing with a suburban development on a farm with marginal soil. The most ecologically sound routes toward managing weeds are to avoid heavy herbicides, encourage strong grass root growth with both general fertilization and long cuttings (recycled in place), and add earthworms—a point Charles Darwin made over a century ago.

The principal dilemma of the Lehigh Valley in having a natural grassland lawn, or "peaceful meadow" as some refer to it, is that the natural ecological processes dictate a deciduous forest biome (see Fig. 6.1), not a

BOX 7.3

Places to See Arboreta

CEDAR CREEK PARKWAY. A memorial arboretum sponsored by the Allentown Garden Club is located at the southeastern corner of Hamilton Boulevard (Route 222) and Ott Street in the west end of Allentown. This area is also the site of the annual Mayfair.

FISH HATCHERY, LITTLE LEHIGH PARKWAY. This younger arboretum, also sponsored by the Allentown Garden Club, has labeled its trees and shrubs. From Route 222 (Hamilton Boulevard), proceed south on Route 29 (Cedar Crest Boulevard) for about 1.3 miles. Turn left onto Fish Hatchery Road. The arboretum is at the bottom of the hill, on the left, at the Fish Hatchery; it has ample parking.

WEST PARK. This miniature arboretum (about six acres) in Allentown has many older trees with labels. It is located between Linden and Turner Streets on Sixteenth Street. From Hamilton Boulevard (Route 222), in Allentown, proceed north on Sixteenth Street for one block. The arboretum also features seasonal displays, summer band concerts, and other programs.

CEDAR CREST COLLEGE. The William F. Curtis Arboretum has about 150 tree varieties. The Logan Butterfly Garden is located at the southeast corner of Alumnae Hall. The college is located on the northeast corner of the junction of Route 29 (Cedar Crest Boulevard) and the Hamilton Street (Route 222) bypass. For a brochure, trail guide, and tour information, call (610) 606-4666.

DRIVE-THROUGH ARBORETA. Parts of the I-78 interchanges, such as Summit Lawn, Hamilton Boulevard, and others, are being planted as drive-through arboreta by the Wildlands Conservancy—with the assistance of several corporations, numerous volunteers, and some

grassland, for eastern Pennsylvania. Half of our precipitation and much sunnier days would favor grasslands. Yet one can observe occasional tracts of otherwise monotonous lawn converted into colorful, if somewhat weedy, wildflower meadows. An exceptional area, just east of the Lehigh Valley, is the Pohatcong Grasslands just south of Phillipsburg, New Jersey. This area has been put on a top priority status for the preservation of biological diversity, as the high plateau, with an expanse of open farmland, supports several threatened and endangered field-nesting

BOX 7.3 (CONTINUED)

grant monies. The hundreds of tree additions are a pleasant buffer to the sometimes cold look of the sound barriers.

GERTRUDE R. WHITE MEMORIAL ARBORETUM. This is the newest arboretum in the Lehigh Valley, and it features trees most suitable for urban environments. Upon its completion, it will have a walking trail, a pavilion, and about 250 trees. Located at the Wildlands Conservancy in Emmaus. For directions, see Box 6.1.

GRAVER ARBORETUM. The arboretum holds an exceptional collection of over two hundred conifers, azaleas, rhododendrons, and the like on forty-eight acres of a native beech and oak woodland. It was given to Muhlenberg College by Lee and Virginia Graver. From Route 22, take Route 512 north for about 9.6 miles (Copella sign); turn left onto Bushkill Drive and proceed for 1 mile; then, make a right onto Bushkill Center Road. The arboretum entrance is on the right, 0.2 mile ahead. Information about arboretum visits is available at (610) 759-3132.

RODALE WORKING TREE CENTER. This unique arboretum has trees planted in different sections according to their contributions to the environment, such as producing nuts, controlling erosion, providing excellent wood, and so on. Experimental and organic gardens and greenhouses are also located at this site. From Route 222, proceed south onto Route 29 (Cedar Crest Boulevard) for 1.7 miles to Minesite Road; at Minesite, turn right. The facility with parking is on the immediate left. A corner sign reads "Rodale Experimental Farm/Working Tree Center." The center is open to the public; self-guided tours with brochures can be found at the greenhouse. Call (610) 435-9686 for information.

bird species. The tract is located by Oberly and Carpentersville Roads, just south of Phillipsburg, and is proximal to the Delaware River.

There are a few homes and institutions that have established *Xeriscapes* (dry landscapes), areas that are grass-free and use alternative surface materials: ground covers, such as myrtle and pachysandra; sand; gravel; flat stones; paving blocks; slowly growing trees and shrubs; and decks. All have a resemblance to an ancient, peaceful, and artistic landscape—the oriental garden.

OTHER

Several other kinds of human-modified environments are of interest in the valley. An *arboretum* is a special collection of trees, sometimes with specific focal emphases. Many arboreta are registered with The American Association of Botanical Gardens and Arboreta. The local ones that can be visited are described in Box 7.3.

Butterfly gardens, too, are becoming increasingly popular. They are designed with an assortment of plants that attract butterflies and are typically a colorful mosaic of annuals, biennials, and perennials. (A number of these are identified in other landscape boxes.)

To summarize: the agricultural Lehigh Valley is largely a man-dominated and manipulated ecosystem, divided into about nine hundred farms. These farms often have one or more woodlots, each of which creates biological edges that typically divide fields and farms. The valley is thus fragmented—and that is one of the themes of the next chapter.

EIGHT

Fragmented Forests, Edges, and Patches

> We need to analyze alternatives to continued fragmenta-
> tion, distinguish tradeoffs for management, and recognize
> that there is no real necessity for particular assemblages or
> patterns, only that these are artifacts with which modern
> society must deal. The quandary is still with us.
>
> —ROBERT L. BURGESS, *Forest Island Dynamics*
> *in Man-Dominated Landscapes,* 1981

A bird's-eye view of the valley would reveal a fragmented forest, a view
similar to that seen by airline passengers arriving at Lehigh Valley International Airport. The sequence of events, mostly human-initiated, that
has produced the pattern characteristic of human-dominated landscapes
here in the Lehigh Valley and elsewhere is the first theme of this chapter. The second theme addresses the influence that such a pattern has on
the types and distribution of plants and animals typical of a human-
dominated landscape. Ecologists have quite divergent views about the
relationships of landscape pattern to biodiversity (the focus of several
sections of this chapter). Some ecologists speak of forest "islands" in a
"sea" of mixed landscape terrain, demonstrate boundaries between
communities *(ecotones)* and the resulting "edge effect," and characterize the "remnant forest" as they describe the region—but perhaps the

phrase "fragmented forest" may be the most appropriate label assigned by ecologists to this human-dominated landscape. (See Fig. 8.1.)

FOREST PRIMEVAL

Before European colonization, much of the Lehigh Valley (and all of Penn's Woods) was dominated by forest of a type now designated the "temperate deciduous biome." In our region of Pennsylvania, studies reveal that past climate conditions, especially those dictated by the Illinoian glaciation (150,000 years ago) and the Wisconsinan glaciation (13,000 years ago), had profound influences on vegetation patterns. Botanists believe that the northward advance of deciduous forest into east central North America followed the retreat of the glaciers 10,000 years ago. However, for the early portion of this period (8,000 to 4,000 years ago), prairie extended eastward into what is now forested land. The present distribution of forest zones in eastern North America has developed since about 4,000 years ago—a result of cooling and increased precipitation. At the time of William Penn's arrival to the New World on October 27, 1682, 98 percent of the new province was estimated to have been covered in forests. Although Penn had stipulated that one acre of trees should remain standing for every five acres cleared, the fate of the forests in Pennsylvania was similar to that in other regions heavily colonized by humans.

Several historical accounts convey the impressions of colonists who first ventured into the eastern deciduous forests. Tree species familiar to us today—such as white pine, hemlock, spruce, oaks, and hickories—were present then. Tree stature was larger in the past. An eyewitness account of the primeval deciduous forest in Ohio mentions red and white oaks six feet and more in diameter with trunks shooting up to fifty and sixty feet without a limb; great black walnuts; sycamores, huge in limb and body, along creek bottoms; and tall shell-barked hickories. Travelers remarked on the sweet scent of eastern forests, especially when insect-pollinated trees were in bloom. Accounts also stressed the autumn coloration as well as the edible fruits and nuts. The forests occupied almost all of the land and were interspersed only by rivers and streams, natural prairies, storm-cleared patches, and isolated Indian settlements. An account of settlement in the Lower Jordan Valley in the 1730s described the region which is now Allentown as covered with scrub oak and heath on the flatlands south of the Jordan Creek, where, according to this narrative, Indians had kept the undergrowth down by periodically burning it. Heath was good grouse-hunting country and was the site of a hunting lodge in present-day Wennersville. To the north, the area was described as heavily wooded, mainly with oak, maples, and some nut trees, but few conifers. Natural meadows were also present in the region.

Small populations of Native Americans lived in the forested regions, existing primarily as nomadic hunters until about three thousand years ago. Evidence suggests that forested tracts were cleared and that squash, beans, and corn (maize) were cultivated about this time in Pennsylvania. However, as noted in Chapter 3, the Lenape in Pennsylvania did not engage in horticulture to the extent that it was practiced by Native Americans in some of the other colonies.

Numerous accounts claim that Indians used annual or semiannual fires to clear the forest understory, encouraging the growth of forage plants for wild game and increasing the numbers of edible fruits and other plant parts. In the Lehigh Valley, by the time of European colonization, large trees were rare, and most of these grew along streams and on steep slopes, where timbering was difficult. The state of the forest at that time may have been brought about by the fires set by Indians to drive game through the gaps in the Kittatinny for slaughter by tribal members. Such periodic fires may have also favored increases in the numbers of "sprout hardwoods," such as oaks, hickories and chestnuts. But in recent years, scholars have questioned the impact that these fires had on vegetation patterns. The conclusion reached by one investigator who reevaluated thirty-five historical accounts is that fires set by Indians had little effect on forest vegetation of the eastern United States. But at a minimum, the frequent use of fires for varied purposes by Native Americans probably did increase the frequency of fires above levels caused by lightning—and thus had some effect on vegetation, such as the establishment of more open forest and more extensive grassy areas.

Impact of Colonization

Major changes in the valley's forests occurred with the arrival of the first colonists. As mentioned in Chapter 3, 75 percent of the inhabitants at the time of the Revolutionary War were listed on tax rolls as farmers. Clearing land for planting crops was among the first tasks facing settlers in the valley. Descriptions of large woodpiles, some stacked against the

Fig. 8.1 *A patchy environment* Much of the valley is dissected into fragments of forest patches interrupted by farmland, rights-of-way corridors, and development, all adding to the edge effect.

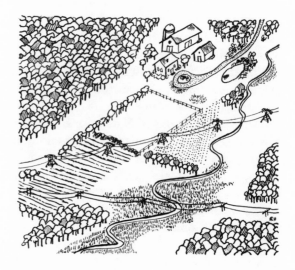

north sides of homes and barns to provide added protection from winter storms, are found in early accounts of colonial life.

The spurt in human population in the early part of the nineteenth century, coupled with industrial development, had a profound impact on the forests. The construction of canals, numerous railroads, and additional streets and roads that crisscrossed the valley produced more fragmentation of the forest and created all sorts of edges and variously sized patches of forest.

Even with the increases in population in the cities and towns of the valley during the first half of the twentieth century—and the development of suburban communities after World War II—Northampton and Lehigh Counties still had a large percentage of land in farms, as data for 1950 indicate. Northampton County farms constituted 81 percent of the total county acreage (192,851 acres), and in Lehigh County, farms accounted for 87 percent of the total acreage (191,650 acres). A strong agricultural tradition, rooted in the lifestyle of many Pennsylvania Germans, favored the passing of farms from one generation to the next; thus, a strong agricultural presence remained until the middle of the twentieth century.

CURRENT LAND USE

A detailed study by the Joint Planning Commission, Lehigh-Northampton Counties (JPC) documents the changes in land use between 1972 and 1992. A major shift in Lehigh and Northampton Counties during this period was the conversion of agricultural and vacant land to other uses. In 1972, agricultural and vacant land composed 68.5 percent of all land in the region, but by 1992 such lands had declined to 57.7 percent. Some of this land, almost 15,000 acres, was converted to parks and other open spaces. But the remaining acres (more than 36,000) were converted to an array of "developed" land categories, i.e., land dedicated to residential, commercial, industrial, transportation, utility, and other public uses. Readers of this book might even live in suburban developments created from previously open land—more than three-quarters of converted agricultural land was used for residential development. Chapter 12 discusses the efforts of varied groups and agencies to minimize the impact of development on the natural landscape of the Lehigh Valley.

THE HUMAN-DOMINATED LANDSCAPE OF THE LEHIGH VALLEY

An aerial view of the Lehigh Valley reveals few extensive wooded tracts. Our valley does have a wonderful northern forested boundary, Blue Mountain, where almost continuous forests form a band running from the Delaware River through the two-county region and into adjacent Berks County. The Applachian Trail along the ridge of Blue Mountain runs more than seventy miles from the Delaware Water Gap to Port Clinton. Several sizable state game lands along the slopes add to the maintenance of the northern border of the valley. (See Fig. 8.2.)

Our southern border, South Mountain, has been influenced much more by human activity than Blue Mountain has been. Native Americans mined flint, quartz, and (perhaps most prized) jasper, to be made into knives, arrowheads, and ornaments. (See the description of the Vera Cruz Jasper Pits in Chap. 3.) European settlers quickly made an impact on the landscape. On the slope of South Mountain, the Shelter House in Emmaus—ca. 1741—served as a wayfarer's refuge (Fig. 8.3).

Starting in 1809, and for almost a century thereafter, numerous iron mines dotted the slopes of South Mountain. Evidence of only a few of the more than three hundred mine sites on South Mountain can be observed; one site is still visible on property managed by the Wildlands Conservancy (the Rodale tract). Most of the mines and pits are overgrown with second-growth woods. Twentieth-century development pressures, in the

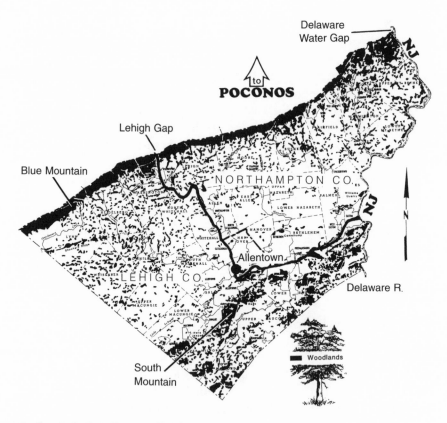

Fig. 8.2 *Lehigh Valley woodlands*
Both Blue Mountain and South Mountain, with their steep slopes, are heavily
wooded. Between the two mountains, the valley itself has hundreds of remnant
woodlots, or "islands" (see text), each of which creates an ecotone. Numerous
smaller woodlots are beyond the scale of this map. (Modified from the Lehigh
Valley Planning Commission, *Lehigh Valley Profile and Trends*, 1993.)

form of housing developments, apartment projects, and roads, have dissected the ridge into smaller forested tracts. (Attempts to lessen human
impact on South Mountain are described in Chap. 12.)

Only a fraction of the wooded tracts in the Lehigh Valley is in public ownership. There are tracts of fifty or more acres in the valley, but
these are privately owned, and trees could be harvested at any time and
the land converted to other uses. Small farm woodlots and narrow strips
of trees along streams and farm field edges do give the valley a bit more
woody vegetation, but even these areas may be degraded.

Several habitat patterns are characteristic of this valley and most
regions in which human activity has flourished for any duration. These

Fig. 8.3 *The Shelter House, Emmaus*

include: (1) bottomland forest, along stream edges, (2) upland forest at higher elevations between stream valleys, (3) suburban with canopy—such as older sections of cities and towns, older developments, and city and county parks, (4) suburban without canopy—newer developments, (5) rural residential—low-density habitation with large treed lots and sometimes woodlots of varied age and size, (6) croplands and pasture lands with hedge and tree line, (7) industrial—light industrial parks, apartment complexes with lawns, planted shrubs, and trees, and (8) the varied vegetational edges formed as the result of the construction of highways and other roads, railways, oil pipelines, transmission lines, and similar human-made corridors. Several of these habitats, forests, and croplands are the focus of other parts of the book (Chaps. 6 and 7), but here, emphasis will be placed on the plants and animals typical of edges and forest patches. Box 8.1 presents some sites at which edge and patch communities may be observed.

Wildlife of Edges, Patches, and Terrestrial Islands

The habitat patterns noted above dictate the types of plants and animals one will encounter in the Lehigh Valley. As we saw earlier, certain kinds of plants and animals tend to thrive in particular locales. Plants found in abundance along the edge of a stream or pond would not flourish in an upland woodlot. In a similar fashion, birds that live and nest at the edge of a woodlot may rarely be found in the interior of a large forest.

There are significant influences on plant and animal distribution that relate to features such as the size and shape of the terrestrial islands, the proximity of the islands to one another, the nature of the intervening landscape, and other subtle components of the larger landscape. Some ecologists base their studies of fragmented forests on a theory of

BOX 8.1

Places to Observe Edge Flora and Fauna

Road Edges

Rural blacktop roads abound in the valley, but even here, increased vehicular traffic makes such sites less desirable for edge walking than they once were. Routes with detailed maps of county roads are described in *Bike Rides: The Lehigh Valley* (copies are available from the Lehigh Valley Planning Commission). These should be suitable for alert walkers as well as bikers. Sections of these several-mile loop bike routes—such as routes around Leaser Lake and Minsi Lake, and through the Lock Ridge Furnace region—should give the nature walker an opportunity to observe edge wildlife.

Canal Towpath

WALNUTPORT. Visitors can walk along a well-maintained four-mile section of the Lehigh Canal from Walnutport north to Lehigh Gap. A shorter section, south of town, goes by a renovated stone locktender's house. Both sections may be reached from Main and Canal Streets at the east end of the Walnutport-Slatington Bridge.

NORTHAMPTON. Riverside Park stretches about 1.5 miles, with only remnants of towpath evident. The north end of the park may be reached from Twenty-first Street (PA Route 329) at the east end of the Northampton-Cementon bridge.

ALLENTOWN TO EASTON. Visitors can walk along the restored towpath at various sites along this seventeen-mile section of the Lehigh Canal. The Allentown section runs from east of the Hamilton Street bridge to Sand Island, Bethlehem—a distance of five miles. The path continues on to Freemansburg, another three miles. Beyond Freemansburg, the walking and bike path joins the Palmer-Bethlehem Township Bikeway. The path continues past Riverview Park and the old Glendon bridge, heading to the "old" Canal Museum at the shad ladder in Easton.

EASTON. The towpath in Hugh Moore Park is a four-mile stretch along a restored portion of the canal (boat rides may be taken in season) and is a good walking trail with views of the canal and the river. The locktender's house may also be visited (contact the park staff about visiting times).

Three miles south of Easton, on PA Route 611, is a Northampton County park (Wy-hit-tuk Park) with a readily accessible walking path along the towpath of the Delaware Canal. The park features edge species and a fine view of the Delaware River. Just south of the county park is Roosevelt State Park, which runs along the southeastern border of the state for more than sixty miles. The state park has numerous towpath areas and recreational sites.

Park Nature Trails

JACOBSBURG STATE PARK. Leading from the education center are several edge-type trails, especially Homestead Trail, a three-mile loop trail in uplands, fields, and second-growth woods.

LOUISE W. MOORE PARK. This is a heavily manicured park, but some edge observations may be conducted along mature woodland areas.

ALLENTOWN CITY PARKS. All three parks—Little Lehigh Parkway, Trexler Memorial Park, and Cedar Creek Parkway—provide opportunities to view edge species. The more open sections of Little Lehigh Parkway offer the best opportunities.

KALMBACH MEMORIAL PARK. Located in Macungie, this small preserve has trails along fields, conifer plantations, and stream edges.

JORDAN CREEK PARKWAY. A Lehigh County park north of Allentown, the Jordan Creek Parkway offers mainly creekside and wooded trails with a few openings for edge viewing.

POOL WILDLIFE SANCTUARY. The sanctuary is located south of Allentown, east of Cedar Crest Boulevard. There are several trails, but the upland trail through an Urban Forest demonstration region allows for some edge viewing.

Rails to Trails

NOR-BATH TRAIL. This trail is a four-mile stretch of old railroad bed along woods and shrubs adjacent to East Allen Township's Bicentennial Park in Northampton County.

PLAINFIELD TOWNSHIP RECREATIONAL TRAIL. A seven-mile trail on a railroad bed between Stockertown and Pen Argyl has a backdrop of woods, fields, creek sections, and suburban settings.

BOX   8.1   (CONTINUED)

PALMER TOWNSHIP–BETHLEHEM TOWNSHIP BIKEWAY. An almost eight-
mile C-shaped bikeway runs through farm fields, woods, and
suburban yards. The bikeway links up to the Lehigh Canal Heritage National Recreation Trail and to Hugh Moore Park.

IRONTON RAIL-TRAIL. Accessible from the North Whitehall Ball
Fields, the trail is also adjacent to the Troxell-Steckel House and
the Saylor Park Cement Industry Museum.

island biogeography. According to this theory, a larger island should
hold more species than smaller islands. Further, the number of species
on an island is a function of immigration rate and extinction rate, rates
that are also related to island size. While other ecologists question the
applicability of island biogeography theory to terrestrial habitats, some
analogies may be worth exploring. (See Fig. 8.4.)

DISTURBANCE

The fragmented forest of the Lehigh Valley (and, for that matter, much
of eastern North America) is largely the result of alterations produced
by humans. However, natural disturbances have always been part of the
history of this planet. Chapter 2 reviewed major geological events—
such as continental movements, mountain building, and glaciation—
that impose profound alterations on the landscape. More localized and
less extensive changes result from other natural disturbances, such as
fires, hurricanes, tornadoes, and floods. Human activities of the type
outlined earlier, including forest clearing, road building, and the like,
have now been added to the more subtle disturbances. As a result of
unwise practices, all sorts of pollution now confront plants and animals.
Some are well-publicized, such as acid rain and cultural eutrophication
(that is, the process by which human activities cause accelerated plant
growth—and subsequent oxygen depletion—in lakes). All of these disruptions, long-term and short, major as well as minor, influence the evolution of plants and animals. Most types of plants and animals

considered to be "invaders" adapt to disturbed land and have varied lifestyle features that enable them to gain a foothold in such settings quickly. These organisms are often termed "opportunistic" species. One prevalent feature of such plants is the ability to produce great numbers of young, often under harsh conditions: for example, certain types of pines have cones that will open after being exposed to the heat from fire. Weeds and other alien invaders that are seen soon after an area is devastated by floods or fire are evidence of the long-term adaptation that life has shown to patterns of disturbance resulting from natural events or from human activity.

OLD FIELD SUCCESSION

Examining the phenomenon of disturbance also provides an opportunity to consider briefly a major type of disturbance pattern witnessed by nearly everyone. When an agricultural field is taken out of cultivation, or a pasture is no longer being used by dairy cattle, the process of ecological succession described in Chapter 1 will take place within a short time. Recall that two types of succession have been identified by ecologists:

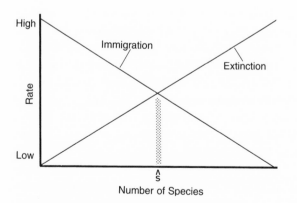

Fig. 8.4 *Island biogeography model*
First applied to oceanic islands, it is also applicable to terrestrial islands (such as forest patches). Notice how Immigration (addition) and Extinction (loss) are related to the number of different species. At some point, $\hat{S}$, I=E, and a balance of sorts may occur. The establishment and design of parks, preserves, and natural areas must take into consideration such factors as island size, age, and proximity to large tracts.

Fig. 8.5 *Old field succession*
Depending on such factors as residual seeds, prior root systems, exotic invaders, slope, soil, proximity to seed trees, and prior land use, succession (or change) may proceed in a variety of formats. In the Lehigh Valley, that change tends to favor a deciduous forest.

primary and *secondary*. Since this is neither bare rock nor a lake setting, we are not witnessing primary succession. Here, in land that has considerable soil present at the time of disturbance, we can observe *secondary* succession. Old field succession is the principal example found in the Lehigh Valley. Plants and animals that have evolved to thrive in the face of disturbances are primed for this opportunity. Pioneering or invading plants quickly dominate the scene; in our region, ragweed and crab grass are common pioneers. The seeds of annuals, in the meantime, can lie dormant in the soil for long periods, while conditions remain unsuitable. But when favorable conditions appear, as in the case of abandoned agricultural lands, annuals flourish and quickly cover the area. By the second year, numerous herbaceous (green, but not woody) plant species make their appearance. A dazzling array of native and alien invaders—the composites, such as asters and goldenrods, wild mustards, knotweeds, peppergrass, Indian hemp, and on and on—makes the scene. (Some of these plants are depicted in Figure 8.6.)

Biennials, which spend the first year getting established and then complete their life cycle during the second year before dying out with the onset of winter, soon make their appearance. Queen Anne's lace, bull thistles, evening primrose, and mullein are common biennials. Perennials, which can live for many years and reproduce annually, follow in the typical succession. Winter cress, also known as yellow rocket, is a conspicuous representative in the valley's old field succession sequence. Other representatives are butter 'n' eggs, several types of

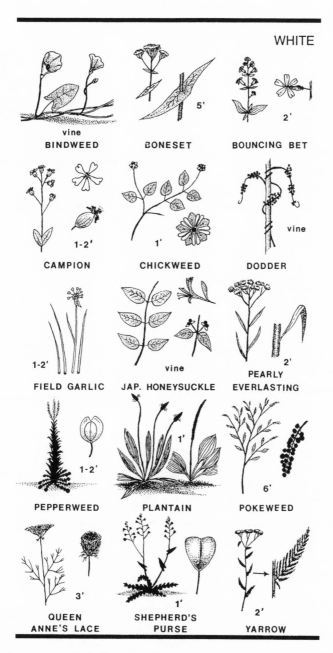

WHITE

vine
BINDWEED

5'
BONESET

2'
BOUNCING BET

1-2'
CAMPION

1'
CHICKWEED

vine
DODDER

1-2'
FIELD GARLIC

vine
JAP. HONEYSUCKLE

2'
**PEARLY
EVERLASTING**

1-2'
PEPPERWEED

1'
PLANTAIN

6'
POKEWEED

3'
**QUEEN
ANNE'S LACE**

1'
**SHEPHERD'S
PURSE**

2'
YARROW

Fig. 8.6 *Common roadside flowers (white)*
Heights are average for all figures. Colors may vary. (Fig. 8.6 from Oplinger and Halma, *The Poconos* [New Brunswick: Rutgers University Press, 1988]. With permission.) In order, this figure shows common white roadside flowers; common yellow roadside flowers; common orange, red, pink, and blue-violet roadside flowers; and common green roadside flowers.

YELLOW

BLACK-EYED SUSAN   2'

BUTTERCUP   1-3'

BUTTER 'N' EGGS   2'

CINQUEFOIL

COLTSFOOT   1'

DANDELION   1'

EVENING PRIMROSE   5'

FIELD DAISY   2'

FLEABANE   3'

GOLDENROD   3-5'

HAWKWEED   1'

MULLEIN   5'

MUSTARD   3'

STICKTIGHT   3'

ST. JOHN'S-WORT   2'

SWEET CLOVER   5'

WILD PARSNIP   5'

WOOD SORREL   1-3'

Fig. 8.6 (continued) *Common roadside flowers (yellow)*

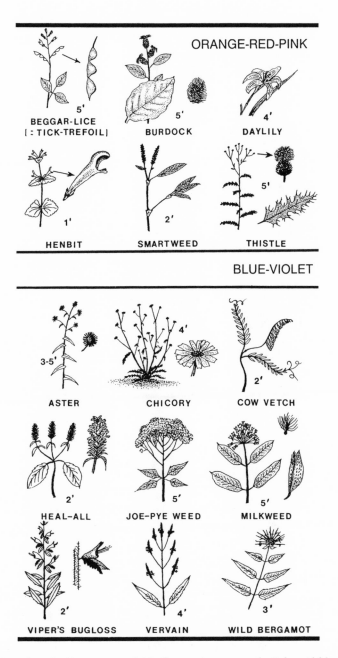

ORANGE-RED-PINK

BEGGAR-LICE
[= TICK-TREFOIL] 5'

BURDOCK 5'

DAYLILY 4'

HENBIT 1'

SMARTWEED 2'

THISTLE 5'

BLUE-VIOLET

ASTER 3-5'

CHICORY 4'

COW VETCH 2'

HEAL-ALL 2'

JOE-PYE WEED 5'

MILKWEED 5'

VIPER'S BUGLOSS 2'

VERVAIN 4'

WILD BERGAMOT 3'

Fig. 8.6 (continued) *Common roadside flowers (orange, red, pink, and blue-violet)*

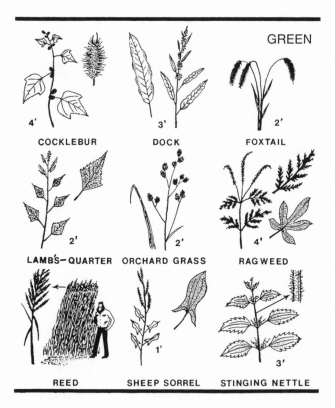

Fig. 8.6 (continued) *Common roadside flowers (green)*

clovers (and their legume relatives, the vetches), sheep sorrel, plantain, and stinging nettle.

Given time, woody shrubs and young tree seedlings can get established. Hawthorns, spireas, shadbush, common juniper, eastern red cedar, sumacs of several species, sassafras, cherries, black locust, and red osier dogwood are typical examples seen during this stage in secondary succession. After some decades, as shade-tolerant tree species assume dominance, a terminal stage forest of the type described in Chapter 6 will complete the succession.

During all of these vegetational sequences, assemblages of animals are also changing, though this is harder to observe. But even the casual observer would note that butterflies, chipping sparrows, and rabbits are inhabitants of open, sunny fields, whereas bark beetles, downy woodpeckers, and gray squirrels dwell in forested woodlots. Some of the other plants and animals seen in ecological succession are described in other sections of this chapter and elsewhere throughout the text.

INVADERS

Dandelions, crab grass, and clover are successful invaders, as any suburban dweller could attest. But what may be surprising is the fact that all three plant species are naturalized aliens, three of more than three thousand plant species from other regions of the world that grow wild in North America. Dock, wild carrot, peppermint, yarrow, tansy, and burdock are some of the plants introduced by colonists to the area. One plant, the European plantain, was called "White Man's Foot" by the Indians—because where he trod, this plant would spring up. (Chap. 10 describes a highly successful plant invader, the purple loosestrife, that uses the river's edge as a corridor for advances into new territory and crowds out native floodplain vegetation.) Some invaders are less troublesome and, in fact, add more color to our roadside edges. Plants such as Queen Anne's lace, oxeye daisy, daylilies, and chicory are European natives now well-established in North America. Multiflora rose was introduced into the eastern United States from Japan in the 1860s as a source of hardy rootstocks for cultivated roses. Wildlife managers eagerly accepted this plant as a "living fence" in wildlife plantings and soil conservation programs. Birds such as American robins and cedar waxwings avidly feed on the fruits, and some experts relate the spread of mockingbirds into the Northeast to the spread of multiflora rose, which provided these birds with winter food. (A viral disease spread by microscopic mites has appeared on multiflora roses in Ohio, West Virginia, and, recently, Pennsylvania, so this troublesome plant's numbers may diminish.)

Bush and climbing vine honeysuckles create a conspicuous tapestry covering the native vegetation along roadsides. These Eurasian natives were introduced in the late 1800s as ornamentals and later were widely planted for wildlife food and cover. Where browsing by white-tailed deer is heavy, bush honeysuckles invade. Indeed, many plants rely on animals to extend their distribution. The fruits, most with easily-detected colors, are readily eaten by birds. Seeds within the fruits are unaffected by their passage through the bird's gut, get distributed with the bird's droppings, and very likely sprout into new plants. Bush honeysuckle (also known as

Table 8.1 *Prominent Lehigh Valley plant invaders*

Trees	Shrubs	Herbaceous Types
European buckthorn	Amur honeysuckle	Bird's-foot trefoil
Norway maple	(and related types)	Dame's rocket
Paper mulberry	Autumn olive	Honeysuckle
Tree-of-heaven	Japanese barberry	Japanese knotweed
	Multiflora rose	Japanese vine
	Privet	Oriental bittersweet
	Wintercreeper	Periwinkle
		Porcelain-berry
		Purple loosestrife
		Reed grass

Amur honeysuckle) has spread to at least twenty-four states in eastern North America and in Ontario, Canada since its deliberate introduction into North America less than a century ago.

Oriental bittersweet, with its distinctive orange fruits and red berries, is another common invader that is crowding out the native bittersweet. And in the last few decades, Japanese knotweed has become a prominent invader along roadside and stream edges. This tall bushy plant, which may reach three to six feet in height, can be recognized by its bright green tubular stems, heart-shaped leaves, and greenish-white flowers arranged in long clusters that extend from the bases of the branched outer stems.

Trees such as Norway maple, hardy mimosa, autumn olive, and tree-of-heaven serve as common examples of exotic trees now well established in the Lehigh Valley. The autumn olive, with gray-green, narrow leaves, is a particularly common invader in the Trexler Game Preserve. The tree-of-heaven (Fig. 8.7), with its large, distinctive, compound leaves, looking almost tropical, is abundant in small clusters along roadsides. This species, sometimes called *Ailanthus,* was first introduced into North America from China by Philadelphian William Hamilton in 1784. (Hamilton also introduced the Norway maple and the hardy mimosa!) The tree-of-heaven is hardy and seems able to break through cement pavements (it found fame in *A Tree Grows in Brooklyn*). It does need sun; thus, it typically invades disturbed areas and grows vigorously by root sprouting and from seeds, which are produced in abundance. *Ailanthus* also engages in a type of chemical warfare termed *allelopathy.* Toxins from stems, roots, and leaves leach into the surrounding soil and inhibit the germination and growth of other types of plants. In time, tree-of-heaven is usually crowded out by more shade-tolerant species. Some of the prominent plant invaders of the Lehigh Valley are listed in Table 8.1.

WEEDS

Almost all of the pioneering plants mentioned in the brief account of old field succession and many of the plant invaders discussed above are generally called "weeds" by most of us. When a homeowner once asked the noted botanist Liberty Hyde Bailey what she could do about the dandelions that kept invading her lawn, he allegedly replied, "learn to love 'em." This may be good advice, but most of us rarely heed it. On the positive side of the ledger, weeds do quickly cover bare soil (and thus preserve it from erosion), conserve water, add to the organic content of the soil, and provide haven and food for numerous animals. Many of us are more sympathetic to the view expressed by the author who compiled a list of America's "Top Ten Least Wanted Weeds." Heading the list is shepherd's purse, tied for first place with large crabgrass. Rounding out the top five are common lamb's-quarter, red root pigweed, and common chickweed. The writer of the article got into the swing of things and listed more than the expected five species that would complete the top ten. Several types of grasses made the list, with quack grass, barnyard grass, green foxtail, and Bermuda grass as specific representatives. Field bindweed, common mallow, annual sow thistle, common ragweed, spotted spurge, common wood sorrel, and, last but not least, wild mustard completed the rogues' gallery. (See Fig. 8.6.)

ANIMAL ALIENS

Aliens—not from outer space, but definitely not native to the valley— are conspicuous animal invaders. Mockingbirds, Carolina wrens, and cardinals are now permanent residents of the valley after extending their range from the south. House finches, native to the western United States, became popular (if illegal) favorites of the pet bird trade in the late 1930s. As agents of the U.S. Fish and Wildlife Service searched out

New York pet dealers who were unlawfully selling the birds, the dealers released the evidence. Within three years of their liberation, house finches were nesting on Long Island. By 1980, house finches had spread from New England to Georgia and west to the Mississippi River. They are readily seen during the winter at bird feeders, where they may be mistaken for a native finch, the purple finch. The male purple finch shows more red than the house finch and has an unstreaked white or rosy belly, whereas the house finch has a streaked belly. Females of both species are more difficult to tell apart; however, the female purple finch does have a bold white eyebrow stripe lacking in the female house finch.

Other aliens, introduced in the hope of controlling some other "pest," soon become pests themselves. Perhaps the best-known example of this phenomenon is the case of the European starling. One hundred starlings were liberated in New York's Central Park in 1890 to control another alien invader, the Japanese beetle. Starlings switched to presumably tastier prey, and now we have both beetles and starlings in abundance.

Opossums have also extended their range northward, and, in all likelihood, only their hairless ears and tails (which give little protection from northern winters) have restricted their movement further into the northeast. Little evidence exists for the spread of other mammals into our area, with the exception of the "wild cat" and "wild dog"—the bobcat and the coyote, discussed in Chapter 9. Only the coyote would be classified as an alien, as bobcats are considered natives of Pennsylvania. Other groups of vertebrates, fishes, amphibians, and reptiles appear to have *diminished* their geographic ranges, not extended them.

The Japanese beetle (the insect that European starlings were meant to exterminate) is but one of the more than two thousand insects that have invaded North America. Foresters estimate that 40 percent of the major insect pests in North American forests are of exotic origin. More than half of these insect invaders are European, a phenomenon explained in part by the high level of trade between North America and Europe. The two areas are biogeographically similar, and it is not surprising that the invasions have occurred in both directions, with many American insects transported with the heavy flow of raw materials and manufactured goods that went to Europe during the colonial and later periods of our history. Gypsy moths have become the dominant spring leaf eater in northeastern mixed oak forests. Sawfly leaf miners, bark beetles, European corn borers, harlequin bugs, and boll weevils are only a few examples of the insect invaders that have gained entry into the United States. Other invertebrates, such as the zebra mussel now invading the waters of

Pennsylvania, reveal that the problem goes beyond insects and terrestrial habitats; the abundance and range of impact of invertebrate aliens on native biota is great and can only be hinted at here.

EDGES

An *edge* may be defined as the junction of two different landscape elements; this junction could be a transition zone, where plant communities grade into one another, or it could be a sharp boundary. Some edges, termed *inherent edges,* are formed by natural features such as local differences in soil type or microclimate. Another type of edge, an *induced edge,* is produced by humans in the construction of roads, power lines and housing developments. Wildlife managers for some decades viewed edges as beneficial, as edges created habitat for game animals (such as ruffed grouse and white-tailed deer) and, in more general terms, promoted species diversity of plants and animals. Such diversity appears linked to the increased complexity of vegetative composition and structure typical of edges. More recently, ecologists have questioned this position: some studies have shown diminished diversity and the loss of certain types of wildlife, particularly nongame species that require extensive stands of forest.

EDGE PLANTS

The openings in the canopy created by edges permit greater amounts of sunlight, and this is the pivotal factor influencing the types of plants generally seen in most edge habitats. It is not surprising that flowering, herbaceous plants thrive in edges. With the pattern of disturbance in induced edges, weeds and alien invaders more easily gain a foothold. (Invasion by exotics and specialized pioneering plants is extremely common along edges and is highlighted earlier in this chapter.)

Lists and descriptions of flowering, herbaceous plants could easily occupy half of this text. Our aim here is to highlight those plants most commonly encountered as one drives, bikes, or walks along our suburban and country roads. Obviously, some of these species might also be glimpsed during travels along the larger roads and interstate highways that traverse the valley, but observation and study there would be ill-advised.

Fig. 8.7 *Tree-of-heaven*
Also called the Chinese
sumac, this introduced eastern Asian tree is an aggressive invader of waste places
and edges. Here it is illustrated (A) as a volunteer in
a poorly maintained factory
edge setting; (B) with flowers and a pinnately com-
pound leaf (up to three feet
long); and (C) with persistent fruit (samara) clusters.
Occasionally advertised as
a "fast-growing and won-
derful tree," it sports weak
wood and disagreeable
odors.

Figure 8.6 should serve as an introduction to this group of roadside
dwellers as well as weeds and plant invaders mentioned earlier. Recall
that Chapter 5 highlighted one exceptionally prominent roadside plant—
the crown vetch. Extensive tangled mats of this plant, with its tiny, compound leaves and heavy cluster of pink-purplish flowers, may be seen
along major roadways here and elsewhere in the Commonwealth.

Numerous sun-loving berry bushes, raspberry, wineberry and
related thorny briar bush types, vines, woody shrubs, and trees are also
evident along edges, with the berry bushes more likely abutting fields
and meadows than roads. Among the most frequently seen shrubs are
mapleleaf viburnum, spicebush, elderberry, and, now most prominent,
the invasive bush and vine honeysuckles. Poison ivy, wild grape,
bindweed, and Virginia creeper—all vines—sometimes smother much of
the other vegetation along some sections of edge communities. Dominant tree species include several types of sumac, sassafras, quaking
aspen, box-elder, several types of cherry, shadbush, dogwood, and that
troublesome invader, the tree-of-heaven.

INVERTEBRATE ANIMALS OF EDGES

Invertebrates are well-represented in edges and ecotones of all sorts. The
varied conditions that promote a diversity of vegetation, especially types
that produce abundant flowers, fruits, and seeds, also assure that inver-

Fig. 8.8 *Bald-faced hornet and the paper nest*
This hornet (A), one of the several species of so-called paper wasps, suspends its large, gray, paper-like globular nest (B) from a branch on a tree or shrub.

tebrates will be on hand to share in the bounty. The close examination of plants, especially flowering ones, should reveal some invertebrate grazers. Most of these animals will be insects, so numerous and varied that they defy useful identification aids for the novice. As is the case with plants, many edge animals are alien invaders. It would be a safe bet to state that beetles—shiny, hard-winged adults or caterpillar-like larvae—will be among the crowd. Japanese beetles, long-horned beetles, weevils, and ladybird beetles are common representatives of the beetle group. The white, bubbly froth placed by the female spittlebug to cover her newly deposited eggs should catch the eye of any summertime edge walker; in addition, the active, brightly marked bees and wasps, attracted to the flowers and fruits of edge plants, are sure to be seen. One relative of the wasp, the bald-faced hornet, often uses trees along the edge to construct its massive, gray, oval paper nest, which can accommodate as many as ten thousand hornets. The nest usually remains undetected except to the most careful observer until the tree leaves fall with the approach of autumn.

The diverse flowers found in edges are equally attractive to butterflies. One common group, the fritillaries, typically displays numerous orange or red spots. Also abundant are the small- to medium-sized nymphs and satyrs, most of which are brownish or grayish with prominent markings called *eyespots* on the wing edges. Small yellow butterflies, appropriately called sulphurs, are frequently seen. Seeing a cloud of sulphurs rising from a drying mud puddle after picking up water and minerals is a memorable sight; it is easy to see how the term "butterfly" might have applied to these creatures. Less common are the larger, brightly colored swallowtails that sport the distinctive long tapered hind wing tips that give this group its common name. The large, plump caterpillars of this group of butterflies are marked with vivid stripes or spots that lead to their ready detection. As is often the case when animals seem to advertise their presence, chemical warfare is generally employed to make the animal less than desirable as prey. One can detect a strong, musky odor emanating from a disturbed swallowtail caterpillar.

CAMEO 8.1

Hugh Moore (1887–1972)

The problem of diseases spread through communal drinking utensils was addressed with the disposable drinking cup. That cup—the Dixie Cup—was Hugh Moore's creative solution to a major public health problem. He returned much of the fruits of his success back to the Easton area of the Lehigh Valley through the Hugh Moore Historical Park and Museums, the Louise W. Moore Park (see Box 6.1), and parts of the Delaware and Lehigh Heritage Corridor.

Beyond the Lehigh Valley, he was an international advocate of peace and population control, having played significant roles with both the Population Reference Bureau and the International Planned Parenthood Federation.

While international in vision, Hugh Moore remained concerned with the local: selecting environmentally sensitive "forests, edges, and patches," he placed them under protection, so that all valley residents could continue to enjoy them.

In our part of the world, most butterflies overwinter in the pupal stage. The larva attaches itself to a firm support (a twig or plant stem in many cases) and undergoes dramatic transformations. The stubby prolegs are lost, and the mouthparts change from the chewing type into the proboscis—looking like a curled-up soda straw—that is used by the adult to withdraw nectar from flowers. Numerous elementary school children have recently had the opportunity of monitoring the emergence of butterflies from pupae collected locally or obtained from biological supply firms. The release of adults as the school year ends is becoming a welcome ritual in the area.

One last remark about these fascinating insects. Not infrequently, a pair of butterflies may be observed engaged in meandering courtship flights that last for many minutes before the couple mates in midair. The male has been attracted to the female, who has released distinctive chemicals into the air. Chemical signals termed *pheromones* are being used to communicate (as they do elsewhere in the insect world). In some instances, the flight proceeds further into the sky and the female continues upward to avoid mating. In such cases, the female is attempting to avoid the male because she has already mated.

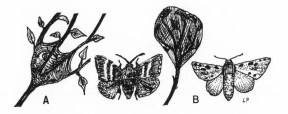

Fig. 8.9 *The tent caterpillar and fall webworm*
The early-nesting tent caterpillar (A) typically builds a nest in the forks of cherry, poplar, and apple trees, while the fall webworm (B), nesting much later, prefers the terminal twigs of black walnut and butternut. Both insects and their nests are ugly, not very damaging, and best handled with the removal and destruction of nests.

Numerous types of moths and their larvae are also abundant in the places that host butterflies. Moths tend to feed at night and are not readily detected by the daytime walker. However, even a short time spent in the vicinity of the light on a back porch might surprise the interested observer: an array of moths and other nocturnal wanderers will be drawn to the light. Moths use light as a navigational device. Normally, this is starlight or moonlight, not the porch lights or candle flames that deflect moths from their normal routes. A few of the largest, most conspicuous moths that are drawn to homesites are discussed in Chapter 9. Many of these moths have striking larvae. One type of moth larva, the woolly bear (the larval form of the Isabella moth), gets the attention of locals who wish to make predictions about the severity of the coming winter. There is an orange band that separates the black front and back ends of the bristly larva, and the width of the band does vary. However, a broad band does not really mean that a severe winter will follow, as the myth suggests.

One final group of edge insects deserves mention. Mid- to late-summer walkers along edges may flush out a flying grasshopper that will noisily whirl off a few yards before settling into the brush again. Grasshoppers and their relatives, the praying mantis and the walking stick (a delightful mimic), should be detected by a careful search of edge vegetation. A host of other invertebrates is also present in ecotones. Snails, slugs, millipedes, centipedes, and spiders of various sizes and shapes are all there waiting to be noticed by the eager observer.

No special effort or observational skill is required to see the activities of two animals found along edges and elsewhere in the valley: the tent caterpillar and the fall webworm. The distinctive—and to our eyes, at least, unattractive—nests seem to be an increasingly common sight. Tent caterpillars are busy in spring with their nest-making activities, often placing the nest in the fork of a cherry tree. Fall webworms construct their nests in late summer and autumn, the nest being a loose gathering of leaves at the ends of a branch. Various trees are used, including ash, maple, and walnut trees. (Fig. 8.9 depicts these animals and their nests.)

VERTEBRATE EDGE DWELLERS

Birds

Probably more studies have been conducted to determine the influence of forest patch size and edge effects on bird species (that is, their distribution, abundance, and breeding status) than on other types of wildlife. Studies conducted in a series of small "islands" in an oak-hickory forest in Maryland demonstrated that the size of the islands, the distances between them, and the nature of the edges related to the adjoining habitat all play roles in determining which birds will dwell and breed in a particular patch of woods. Certain birds—such as the hooded warbler, American redstart, black-and-white warbler, scarlet tanager, and ovenbird, to cite a few examples—require large forest patches (more than 170 acres). Species such as these, so-called area-sensitive species, show diminished populations.

It has also been shown that as habitat fragmentation continues, nest predation and nest parasitism increase, creating an even more negative impact on the populations of area-sensitive species. Potential nest predators such as chipmunks, skunks, raccoons, opossums, crows, jays, and black rat snakes (as well as domestic and feral house cats) are attracted to woody edges. Several studies on nest predation, some with artificial nests and Japanese quail eggs, revealed that nests placed in the interior of large forest tracts, such as Great Smoky Mountains National Park, were robbed by predators at about a 2 percent rate. Similar nests placed in variously sized forest fragments in Maryland had predation rates from 18 percent in the largest tract to 95 percent in tracts surrounded by suburban development. Brown-headed cowbirds are the principal species involved in the curious phenomenon of nest parasitism. Cowbirds do not build their own nests but rely exclusively on laying one of their eggs in the nest of a reluctant host species. Over the course of one breeding season, female cowbirds may lay as many as 20–40 eggs. The open nests of migrant warblers, thrushes, vireos, and flycatchers are most vulnerable to nest parasitism. Although some species of birds recognize and remove cowbird eggs, many forest-interior species have not developed this behavior. Closer to home, a recent study of wood thrush nesting success was conducted by investigators at Hawk Mountain Sanctuary in Berks County. In contiguous forests 82 percent of the nests were successful; in woodlots of more than 250 acres, 72 percent of the thrush nests produced young; in woodlots of less than 250 acres, though, only 43 percent of the nests were successful. Many more nests were lost to predators in the smaller patches of woods than in the larger sections and in contiguous forest. An impressive five-year study conducted by staff of the Patuxent Wildlife Research Center of 75 species of birds in variously sized forest tracts (469 of them in Maryland and adjacent counties in Pennsylvania and West Virginia) supports the view that the degree of isolation and size of the tract are the most significant factors influencing the abundance of species. The ovenbird, veery, red-eyed vireo, scarlet tanager, and numerous warblers are species that are area-sensitive.

This study and similar investigations revealed that some species, such as the cardinal, tufted titmouse, blue jay, and gray catbird, are more adaptable in their requirements and use forest interiors or edges as nesting sites. Other birds, such as mockingbirds, house wrens, American robins, song sparrows, and mourning doves, use forest edges and field edges as feeding and nesting sites. Table 8.2 is based upon the data gathered from numerous studies of the type described here and summarizes the relationships between forest tract size and bird species composition.

In the Lehigh Valley, conspicuous edge species of birds can be encountered not only at the edge of a forest patch but also along roadways and other edges created by humans. At various times of the year, the following species are likely to be seen perched on trees by the roadside: American kestrel, red-tailed hawk, Eastern bluebird, brown thrasher, common grackle, brown-headed cowbird, American goldfinch, chipping sparrow, yellow warbler, Northern oriole, and indigo bunting. Valley inhabitants may also observe Eastern kingbirds, barn swallows, tree swallows, house finches, house sparrows, and European starlings on the wires of transmission lines along roadways. Two of the more prominent birds seen along roadways, the American kestrel and the red-tailed hawk, merit a brief consideration here.

The American kestrel, sometimes called the sparrow hawk, is our smallest falcon; nine to twelve inches long, it sports long, pointed wings

Table 8.2 *Sensitivity of Lehigh Valley forest bird species to habitat fragmentation*

High Sensitivity	Moderate Sensitivity	Low Sensitivity
American redstart	Black-billed cuckoo	American kestrel
Black-and-white warbler	Hairy woodpecker	American robin
Broad-winged hawk	Red-eyed vireo	Black-capped chickadee
Brown creeper	Tufted titmouse	Blue jay
Hermit thrush	White-breasted nuthatch	Brown-headed cowbird
Hooded warbler	Wood thrush	Carolina wren
Least flycatcher	Yellow-billed cuckoo	Downy woodpecker
Ovenbird		Eastern wood pewee
Pileated woodpecker		Gray catbird
Ruby-throated		Great crested flycatcher
hummingbird		House wren
Scarlet tanager		Indigo bunting
Veery		Mockingbird
Yellow-throated vireo		Mourning dove
		Northern cardinal
		Northern oriole
		Red-bellied woodpecker
		Red-tailed hawk
		Rose-breasted grosbeak
		Rufous-sided towhee
		Song sparrow

NOTE: Species with a high sensitivity are least tolerant of habitat fragmentation; those with low sensitivity are most tolerant of fragmentation. (List is based on the studies of Herkert, Hoover, Robbins, Whitcomb, and others mentioned in the text, as well as the observations of local birders.)

and a long tail. A rusty-colored tail and back region are distinctive recognition aids. When not perched on wires, this bird may often be seen hovering twenty feet or so above grassy areas before plunging to the ground in an attempt to catch prey (other falcons try to catch prey in the air). Its prey includes grasshoppers and other insects, small birds, small snakes, and rodents.

The kestrel and the meadow vole—one of our most abundant rodents—have an interesting relationship. Meadow vole populations have been estimated at as many as two hundred animals per acre. Since the world is not overrun with voles, they must fall victim to many predators. Snakes, foxes, weasels, and hawks all consume voles. To defend themselves from these predators, meadow voles use the layer of thatch that covers the meadows and fields in which they reside: they construct

Fig. 8.10 *The red-tailed hawk and American kestrel* The red-tailed hawk (A/a), a common woodlot resident, has adapted to the human suburbs. It mostly soars or perches, looking for squirrels or smaller prey. The much smaller kestrel or sparrow hawk (B/b), a falcon, mostly hovers or perches, looking for small rodents. Both are common visitors to utility lines.

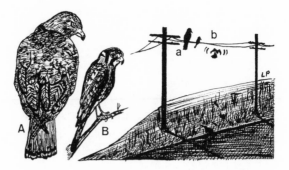

complex inch-wide tunnels that enable them to move about undetected. Nests are also constructed underground, and the animals breed several times over the course of a year. The young develop in twenty-one days, and five to eight young are typically present in each litter. Females reach sexual maturity in four weeks. Voles exhibit population cycles with peaks about every four years; when population levels of voles are low, many predators switch to other prey. However, kestrels have a remarkable ability to locate voles even when population densities are low.

Laboratory experiments and field observations of European kestrels, which are similar to our kestrel, have led investigators to conclude that kestrels can see ultraviolet light! Voles mark their underground trails with urine and feces which, conveniently for the kestrels, absorb ultraviolet light. When kestrels return each spring, they search the area for the active trails marked by feces and urine to determine the prime hunting grounds. Although no studies have been conducted on American kestrels, the assumption is that they possess a similar ability.

The other prominent raptor seen along roadsides is the red-tailed hawk. This large, stocky hawk, eighteen to twenty-five inches long, has a whitish breast and a rust-colored tail. Young birds lack the rust-colored tail and have duller colors and a more streaked breast. This bird is often seen perched on a telephone pole, light standard, tree snag, or other prominent vantage point from which it can survey the ground below for movements of its primary prey, small rodents; an occasional bird or snake may be taken. This hawk, like other *buteos* (or broad-winged hawks), spends considerable time soaring over open country in search of prey and is probably the most common hawk seen by people engaged in outdoor activities.

The relationships between bird species distribution and abundance and the size and type of habitat are complex. A recent study by Scott K. Robinson—based on his analysis of thirty years of data from the North American Breeding survey—argued that the numbers of birds classified as neotropical migrants have remained stable over the past few decades. The study suggests that larger forests in the Midwest may be serving as reservoirs from which younger birds depart to suburban woodlots and parks. Pennsylvania ornithologists, including valley birding enthusiasts consulted by the authors, do believe that at least in eastern Pennsylvania, birds such as the purple martin, wood thrush, Northern oriole, black-billed cuckoo, yellow-breasted chat, grasshopper sparrow, and numerous warblers—golden-winged, Nashville, chestnut-sided, black-and-white, worm-eating, and Canada—have shown population declines. Grassland species, such as meadowlarks, appear to be in even more serious decline.

Mammals

The relationship of mammal distribution to patches and edges has also been studied—but to a lesser extent. Recall the mammals seen on a drive in the countryside or even in the suburbs: these are the typical edge mammals. Woodchucks (also known as groundhogs), cottontail rabbits, skunks, opossums, raccoons, chipmunks, and white-tailed deer are encountered (or, sadly, observed dead) along the roadside. Smaller mammals, such as moles, shrews, deer mice, and meadow mice, are all edge species, but they are only rarely seen scurrying along the road edge. Like birds, mammals are somewhat flexible in the selection of home-sites. The red squirrel is typically found in deep boreal forests in the northern part of its range, but in the southern portions of its range, such as in restricted locales in the Lehigh Valley, it can be found in wooded corridors along fence lines.

In contrast, amphibians and reptiles are not commonly termed edge species—with the single exception of snakes. Again, a dead specimen on a roadway may serve as unpleasant evidence of this. Occasionally, a sunny roadbank will be used for basking by a milk snake, ringneck, red-bellied, black racer, or garter snake. Box and wood turtles may wander across a road from an adjoining woodlot. In early spring, principally during warmer rainy evenings, salamanders, frogs, and toads may be seen on backcountry roads as they make their way to the ponds and water-filled ditches that serve as breeding sites.

Suburban Success Stories

The fragmented forest landscape has been advantageous for numerous plants and animals. In addition to the invaders that are generally assisted by the creation of edges and disturbed habitats, some native and alien animals have flourished. Robins, blue jays, English sparrows, common grackles, American crows, pigeons, mallard ducks, and Canada geese, for example, are thriving in suburban settings. (Indeed, local newspapers recount the capture and removal of Canada geese from city parks and golf courses almost as if these were wartime maneuvers.) Homeowners often request assistance from government officials in removing gray squirrels, raccoons, groundhogs, and skunks from the premises; complaints about these mammals raiding backyard gardens are equally common. Suburban development mainly creates open, savanna-like surroundings. Other human activities, such as eliminating brushy undergrowth and dead trees, mowing, and spraying insecticides, means that some birds like woodpeckers, flycatchers, and swallows will become scarce, but other species will flourish. Humans also provide an array of possible dwelling sites—ledges, crevices, storm sewers, culverts, chimneys, and the like—along with a varied bill of fare. Garbage cans are raided, bulbs are dug up, new shoots of garden plants are sampled, birdfeeders are visited (and not always by the birds): all of these enable suburban opportunists to flourish.

Pigeons and Peregrines

In the suburbs and the city, pigeons are generally viewed as unwelcome guests. The common pigeon developed from the European rock dove and was introduced into the United States as a domesticated bird. Numerous birds escaped, and feral populations now thrive in cities and surrounding areas. In fact, many people consider pigeons the most serious bird pest. Pigeon droppings on buildings, statues, and park benches are objectionable and in large quantities can accelerate the deterioration of these structures. Pigeons have been implicated in the spread of diseases such as salmonella-caused food poisoning, encephalitis, and others. Droppings may harbor the causal agent of histoplasmosis, a fungal disease that affects the human respiratory tract. Various chemical and mechanical repellents, toxic baits, trapping, and shooting have all been employed to reduce the adverse effects of pigeons.

A promising biological control for pigeon populations is also one of the success stories of conservation: the peregrine falcon. This bird was on the road to extinction. Ornithologists conducted a survey of known peregrine *aeries* (nest sites) in eastern North America in 1940 and discovered 275 active sites. In 1964, when biologists issued warnings about the devastating effects of DDT on the eggshells of bald eagles, ospreys, and other fish-eating birds, the same group of birders conducted another survey of peregrine nest sites. To the researchers' dismay, every single site surveyed was found to be deserted.

In 1970, Professor Tom Cade began a research program at Cornell University that devised methods for breeding falcons in captivity. Many young birds were released from high buildings in cities with the hope that as the young matured, they would return to these sites to breed and rear their young; researchers thought that tall buildings might substitute for the steep cliffs that had served as traditional nest sites for peregrines. Urban sites seemed appropriate, since this falcon, commonly called the duck hawk, includes pigeons among its prey. Peregrines have made a recovery, thanks to the efforts of a vast army of professional and amateur ornithologists. Birds have set up nesting sites underneath some of the most heavily traveled bridges that cross the Delaware. And in some local settings, pigeon populations have diminished.

Since 1995, the tallest building in the region—the Pennsylvania Power and Light headquarters in Allentown—has been the site of a peregrine program. Between 1995 and 1997, fourteen falcons were reared and released. To date, no known mortality has occurred and several individuals have been seen feeding in the vicinity. PPL obtains nestling falcons, twenty-five to thirty days old, from licensed breeders in the United States. The birds are raised in a special chamber, a so-called hack box, until they are about forty-five days old. Wildlife biologists from the Pennsylvania Game Commission band the birds just before their release. The project sponsors hope that when the peregrines mature they will return to the area to start nesting.

The status of the peregrine is uncertain. Reproductive success in Pennsylvania has been lower than the national average, and pollution, habitat loss, and disturbance of nesting sites all pose problems for the long-term recovery of a species that was always considered the Commonwealth's rarest raptor. But—even if the pigeon problem is not solved—the possible recovery of the peregrine is still a bright light in the conservation scene.

Contact with edge species brings with it a concern about infectious diseases and parasites that wildlife living in urban and suburban settings might acquire, especially those diseases and parasites that might have public health implications for humans. Canine distemper causes losses among raccoons and skunks in suburban areas. Type C botulism is typically a cause of death of waterfowl in city and suburban parks. Until a few decades ago, most cases of rabies were diagnosed in dogs, but more recently the majority of cases have been diagnosed among wildlife, mainly raccoons, skunks, bats, and foxes. Common sense should lessen the potential dangers of encountering an animal that is carrying an infectious disease. It is not wise to approach wild animals that behave strangely, seem unafraid, and do not attempt to scurry away as would normally be the case. One should avoid handling sick or dead animals without training in the proper procedures. In most situations, control and proper sanitation procedures can help avoid possible human infection.

Alterations in the landscape influence not only the patterns of larger, more prominent animals, but also the patterns of "lesser" forms of life—numerous invertebrates (beyond the few examples presented above) plus an array of the less conspicuous plants, such as mosses and ferns. The effects of human activities on these life-forms are, unfortunately, beyond the scope of this text. But as with so many aspects of the natural world, human impact has profound—and often unpredictable—implications. It is likely that our impact on the nature and abundance of edge dwellers will continue, and we might do better to treat such areas more gently, avoiding the use of herbicides and the grotesque mechanical "pruning" of these special habitats. With the increased interest in walking and biking along less-traveled roads, we should do all we can to be good neighbors to the diverse and fascinating wildlife of edges.

NINE

Animals of the Lehigh Valley

I fervently hope that the "improvers" who are busily clean-
ing up our outdoors will leave a few patches of elders here
and there. Every kid should have the opportunity of finding a catbird nest, of meeting a garter snake face to face. .
. . They'll not do these things on a macadamized play-
ground, and I really believe they'll be poorer for having
missed the fun.

—NED SMITH, *Gone for the Day,* 1971

The present-day vegetation patterns of the Lehigh Valley contrast dramatically with the predominantly forested area that characterized this
region of the world before humans entered the scene. So, too, animal patterns—their nature, distribution, and abundance—are markedly different.

Most ecologists would agree that discerning vegetation patterns is
easier than discerning those of animals. Nevertheless, beginning with C.
Hart Merriam in the 1890s, scientists have attempted to designate life
zones or faunal areas based on vegetation, climate, and terrain. Perhaps
the occurrence of certain indicator animals characteristic of each zone
allows ecologists to retain the concept of faunal areas. The southern
flank of the Blue Mountain marks the northern boundary of the Carolinian faunal area; from the Blue Mountain north, much of Pennsylvania lies within the Alleghenian zone. (Higher elevations within the

Alleghenian show some similarities to the Canadian faunal area farther north.) The area covered in this guidebook, therefore, essentially belongs to the Carolinian zone, but the larger stream valleys between the South and Blue Mountains enable birds and mammals to move from one faunal area to another.

EARLY PENNSYLVANIA

Pennsylvania was a forested wonderland. In the glades dwelt herds of elk; deer lived in more open sites; bison or buffalo herds could be found in open areas and throughout the woodlands. (The trails made by these herds of elk and bison were followed by Native Americans and later by the early colonists.) Mountain lions and timber wolves preyed upon these herd animals. Smaller animals, including fishers, otters, beavers, and mink, lived along streams and sheltered valleys. Overhead flew vast flocks of waterfowl and passenger pigeons. European explorers reported natural fowl similar to those in the homeland—turkeys, swans, geese, ducks, teals, cranes, herons, and heath fowl or pheasants. It was also noted that the rivers had an abundance of fish like those of Europe, i.e., carp, sturgeon, salmon, pike, perch, roach, eel, and the like.

Predators, though plentiful, did not deplete the prey species. The Native Americans who lived in Pennsylvania before European colonization did not exterminate any species of bird or mammal (although there is much conjecture about the impact of human hunting pressure on the mastodons and other large mammals that roamed over much of North America in Pleistocene times). With colonization, conditions changed materially. Trade was established, and trinkets, pots, axes, and whiskey—and, eventually, guns—were given to the natives in exchange for venison and buffalo hides. As towns developed, markets were established and game came to be regarded as a staple, sold along with vegetables and grains. Raccoon pelts were prized, and "coonskin" caps were fashionable among early pioneers. Forests were cut down to provide materials for buildings and for planting sites. Bison and elk were forced westward and wolves and mountain lions moved with them. Men who could have been farming were enticed to become market hunters, lured by the quicker gain from killing ducks by the thousands with cannon-like guns and netting and shooting passenger pigeons.

The last bison in eastern Pennsylvania may have been killed near Wind Gap in 1813. One historian notes that the last native elk was

Fig. 9.1 *The last Pennsylvania bison* The bison was reported to have been seen circa 1813 in Northampton County, near Wind Gap. Habitat loss and excessive hunting contributed to its extirpation.

killed in Pike County in 1845. Bounties were paid on predators: in the 12 years between 1808 and 1820, Luzerne County paid bounty on at least 562 wolf scalps. One mammal species, the fisher (painted from life by John James Audubon), vanished from the state in 1844. By the 1890s, most people finally acknowledged the enormous slaughter of game animals and the destruction of the native habitats of animals large and small. The disappearance of passenger pigeons, which at one time were so abundant that they "darkened the sun" during migration, must have forced this recognition.

Throughout the first two centuries of colonization, laws for the protection of wild creatures were almost nonexistent. But—with considerable difficulty—a group of conservation-minded citizens of the Commonwealth brought about the formation of a Game Commission, the goal of which was to bring back the wealth of wildlife that formerly existed. One of the first moves of the Commission was to stop market hunting. A law was passed in 1897 that prohibited the chasing of deer with dogs. In 1905, the first game refuge was established in Clinton County. Shortly thereafter, numerous hunting and trapping laws were adopted. To protect bears, steel traps, deadfalls, pits, and snares were declared illegal. However, predators were still viewed as competing with hunters, and a bounty system persisted. Wildcats, gray foxes, weasels, goshawks, great horned owls, and even mink were found on the bounty lists in the early part of the twentieth century. Many hawks and owls were shot in the fall hunting season or during "vermin control campaigns" in the spring. Fortunately, the bounty system was abolished a few decades ago, and the proper role of predators in healthy ecosystems is better appreciated now by most Pennsylvanians.

The prevailing patchwork pattern of cities, towns, suburbs, parks, farms, and woodlots has a profound influence on the present-day pat-

Fig. 9.2 *A symbolic dead hawk*
The residents of Drehersville (a town in which the first warden of Hawk Mountain, Maurice Braun, lived in 1934) suspended dead hawks on a nearby bridge to taunt him. Ironically, two seemingly immutable rights— to shoot hawks and to have everlasting steel bridges— fell to time. The bridge was replaced in the early 1950s, and model hawk preservation laws passed in 1970. See Cameo 5.2. (Drawing after a photo by M. Braun, c. 1934, Hawk Mountain Sanctuary Archives. With permission.)

terns of animals in the Lehigh Valley. Statewide, forests have recovered; but while more than half of the state is forested, woodlots and park groves are the rule in the valley. The influence of this patchwork pattern on the natural history of the Lehigh Valley is so extensive that Chapter 8 is devoted to a fuller exploration of the history that produced the pattern. Plants and animals especially characteristic of the "fragmented forest" are also discussed there. By comparison, this chapter focuses on an array of native and introduced animals primarily found in terrestrial habitats that are not highlighted in other sections of the text. (Animals that largely dwell in aquatic settings are featured in Chap. 10.)

DISCOVERING INVERTEBRATES

It is probably safe to say that in any area on land or in water, *invertebrate* animals (those without a spinal column) are dominant. Exploring this vast array of animals is beyond the scope of our natural history guide. Rather, this chapter will highlight some representative animals that readers are likely to encounter. (Some selection was made on the basis of inquiries we've received over the years at our colleges or in response to "mystery" specimens brought or sent to our departments for identification.)

It is clear that land animals, despite their impressive numbers, actually belong to a relatively few major groups (or *phyla*) of the animal kingdom. Living in an air medium is a real challenge, one that poses numerous dilemmas. Animals must prevent dehydration, deal with the lack of support that water provides for movement, obtain oxygen from the air rather than acquire it in its dissolved state in the surrounding water, achieve the union of gametes without the aid of water for sperm transport, enable their young to complete embryonic development in a suitable chamber that mimics water conditions, and handle a host of less obvious activities.

To be sure, many life-forms reside in the thin film coating the surface of soil particles. Here, in the upper inches of soil, dozens of microscopic animal species flourish—in populations of tens of thousands per cubic yard of soil. Protozoans, rotifers, and roundworms are typical representatives. Larger species such as millipedes, centipedes, slugs, snails, mites, and ticks may be evident if moisture conditions are right. These and still larger soil organisms, such as earthworms, spiders, pseudoscorpions, termites, ants, and beetles, are more susceptible to desiccation and avoid it by burrowing more deeply into the soil.

Earthworms are, in fact, some of the most significant burrowers. These humble critters were the focus of Darwin's last major work, *The Formation of Vegetable Mould through the Action of Worms, with Observations on their Habits* (1881). Earthworms ingest soil and organic matter as they construct burrows. Casts of soil and partially or completely digested organic matter thrown up by the worm are deposited on the soil surface or in spaces along the length of a burrow. Surface casting and burrowing slowly overturn the soil. Darwin calculated the weight of worm castings thrown up on the surface of a square yard of pasture soil and determined that for the entire site, in a year's time, eighteen tons of soil were brought to the surface. Darwin's study on these common animals was a pioneering work of quantitative ecology.

A survey of almost any particular habitat will demonstrate that insects and related arthropods unquestionably dominate, both in species and in numbers. As crops, cultivars, and horticultural specimens have been brought to the valley, many insects have been introduced as well. Japanese beetles, army worms, corn borers, apple aphids, cabbage maggots, codling moths, and many others could be cited as crop, lawn, and orchard pests. Insects cause close to a billion dollars' worth of damage to the state's corn crop every year. However, beneficial insects pollinate flowers and play important roles in the dynamics of most ecosystems. As many as fifteen thousand species of insects occur in diverse habitats

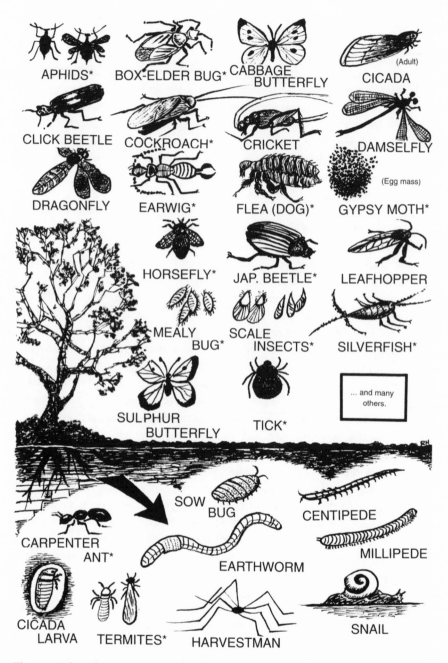

APHIDS* BOX-ELDER BUG* CABBAGE BUTTERFLY CICADA (Adult)

CLICK BEETLE COCKROACH* CRICKET DAMSELFLY

DRAGONFLY EARWIG* FLEA (DOG)* GYPSY MOTH* (Egg mass)

HORSEFLY* JAP. BEETLE* LEAFHOPPER

MEALY BUG* SCALE INSECTS* SILVERFISH*

SULPHUR BUTTERFLY TICK* ... and many others.

CARPENTER ANT* SOW BUG CENTIPEDE MILLIPEDE

EARTHWORM

CICADA LARVA TERMITES* HARVESTMAN SNAIL

Fig. 9.3 *Selected invertebrates*
This medley is representative of commonly seen invertebrates. Some, marked with an asterisk (*), are pests or threats to people, pets, or vegetation. Others, such as earthworms, are more beneficial. Microscopic critters are excluded from this illustration.

across Pennsylvania. (It is not hard to understand why most of the inquiries about invertebrates directed toward us are resolved only by resorting to an insect guide book!)

Moths with wingspreads of three or more inches seem to lead the list of "mystery" invertebrates. These large, showy, slow-moving animals do attract attention. The luna moth, which sports pale, green, long-tailed wings, is one such eye-catcher. Another is the largest North American moth, the cecropia moth, which has a wingspread exceeding five inches. Its wings are gray-brown with distinctive white crescents, and its body is red-orange, with white rings on the abdomen. Almost as large is the polyphemus moth, with its five-inch wings. Distinctive "eye-spots" on the forewings (and, even more prominently displayed, on the hindwings) provided taxonomists with a name derived from Greek mythology—Polyphemus, the one-eyed giant. One last moth that frequently makes the inquiry list is the spicebush moth (also known as the promethea moth). The wingspan of the promethea moth is about four inches, and the color patterns of the wings of the sexes differ. The wings of the male moth are brownish-black, overall, crossed by a pale band, with eyespots at the tips of the forewings. Both sets of wings are edged in tan. The female moth is a bit larger, with reddish-brown wings. The female has markings similar to those found on the male, but they are much more prominent, in contrast to the background color of the female's wings. (Feathery, frond-like antennae give male moths a remarkable sense of smell. Male polyphemus moths are able to detect the scent of potential mates from as far away as seven miles!)

Perhaps it is not surprising that the larvae of these conspicuous moths also prompt inquiries. The caterpillars of all these moths are large—as much as four inches—and plump, generally green to bluish-green, with various bumps and tubercles usually capped with short bristles. Many types of caterpillars are quite specific in their dietary requirements, and some species feed on only one type of plant.

Some telephone queries concern "fuzzy hummingbirds" seen hovering over a flowerbed. These "birds," on closer inspection, turn out to be sphinx (or hawk) moths. They have three-inch wingspans, are rapid fliers, hover over flowers and, with a long straw-like proboscis, sip the nectar of tubular flowers such as honeysuckle and trumpet vine. The moths are more active at dusk and in the evening, feeding on flowers that stay open after dark. While feeding, the moths pollinate the flowers. There are many types of sphinx moths, but three species are common. One, the common clearwing, has transparent sections on the wings where the powdery scales have fallen off. The white-lined sphinx

Fig. 9.4 *Some prominent moths*
These moths are each three or more inches in size and are often brought to university biology departments for identification. The promethea moth (A) has an imposing four-inch caterpillar; the pale lime-green luna moth (B) has been called the "people's choice" for beauty; the cecropia moth (C), also called the "emperor moth," is our largest moth. The bagworm moth (D) is best known for its "bag," an inch-long (or longer) larval "condo" that often attracts the curious homeowner. The inconspicuous adult bagworm moths are not pictured here. None of these moths are serious pests. (Illustrations by Sonja Schneider.)

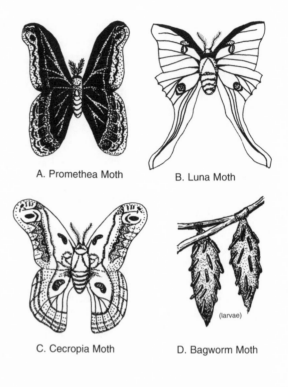

A. Promethea Moth

B. Luna Moth

C. Cecropia Moth

D. Bagworm Moth

(larvae)

has long white lines on the leading wings and rosy-colored, striped hindwings. The five-spotted hawk moth has five or six bright orange spots on each side of the abdomen. It is the larva of this last type of sphinx moth which commonly appears as a "mystery critter." The larval five-spot is more appropriately called the tomato hornworm; like its relatives, it usually has a soft spine which projects like a horn from the posterior. This fat, green, soft-bodied caterpillar is often found eating tomatoes or their leaves. When molested, the larva rears back into a belligerent pose (one that resembles the famous Egyptian monument, thus the common name for the group) to ward off potential predators. Hornworms are sometimes found with numerous white capsules covering most of their bodies. These capsules are the larval cases of tiny wasps, which parasitize the hornworms; the larval wasps burrow into the caterpillar and start to feed on the soft parts. After the caterpillar dies, the larval wasps eat their way out of the dead host, pupate, and emerge as the adult wasps that will continue the cycle. Those hornworms that do survive feed furiously on the fruits and leaves of tomatoes, peppers, petunias, and related plants, molting five times. Then, somewhat atypically for moths and butterflies, the larvae burrow underground to pupate over the winter. (In some sphinx moth pupae, the developing moth's proboscis is so long that the pupa has a sheath curving out from the head to form a loop that resembles a jug handle.)

Other "mystery" invertebrates are even more alarming to homeowners. Some calls about "termites" invading a home are, in fact, false alarms: most often, the specimens brought in for examination turn out to be ants. This may be a mixed blessing, though, if the ants are carpenter ants; they can do considerable damage to the timbers and beams in buildings if their colonies are allowed to spread. (Termites lack the "pinched waist" characteristic of ants, wasps, and bees, and are thus readily differentiated from their ant relatives upon closer examination.) And in autumn, large swarms of bugs—approximately a half-inch long, dull black to gray-brown, with pronounced brick-red markings along each side—may appear around the doors or windows of homes. These are female box-elder bugs searching for a place to overwinter. They are harmless, but their sheer numbers can cause concern.

Late summer or early autumn is also the time when a distinctive song is heard by people enjoying their patios or backyard porches. The call, a shrill "Katy did, Katy she did," mostly heard at night, readily identifies these insects; katydids are two to three inches long, usually bright green, with very long antennae and prominent hind legs (similar to the legs of their relatives, grasshoppers and crickets). Katydid males produce sounds by rubbing together a file (a corrugated surface on the wing cover) and a tooth, or two files, causing special areas in the covers to vibrate. Muscles carry out the movements of the wings in sound production, and in these cold-blooded animals, the muscles work more rapidly at higher temperatures than at lower ones. So if you suspected that you were hearing a more rapid outburst of song on a warm, sultry evening than you did when it was cooler, you were right! Males sing more quickly at higher temperatures. Moreover, female katydids recognize the calls of males of the same species, and their nervous systems correct for temperature differences in the pulses of sound per second. Katydids and other long-horned grasshoppers have their hearing organs on the front legs rather than on the body. This location permits the "ears" to be moved further apart to aid these insects in their use of triangulation techniques to determine the sender of the signals.

Although space limitations dictate that no additional examples can be mentioned here, an abundance of invertebrates (especially insects) awaits your exploration. Any site—inside the home, on a porch, in the garden, or on shrubs and trees—will yield opportunities for discovery and delight. More wooded areas such as parks, game lands, and wood-lots will serve to augment the study of these diverse animals. (The numer-ous invertebrate pests and invaders of woodlots, backyards, and farm fields, such as gypsy moths, tent caterpillars, and Japanese beetles, are discussed in other sections of the text, principally in Chaps. 7 and 8.)

VERTEBRATES OF THE VALLEY

Some special skills and appropriate guidebooks are usually needed to identify the vast array of invertebrates. The situation of vertebrate ani-mals, however, is dramatically different. We encounter many of these animals regularly, and they frequently have features (such as distinctive coloration or characteristic behavior) that permit us to identify them with the assistance of readily available nontechnical guides. The major taxonomic groups of vertebrates are fishes, amphibians, reptiles, birds, and mammals. The first three groups will be discussed in Chapter 10, which highlights aquatic habitats. It is true that some amphibians (and, even more so, reptiles) may be found as one traverses terrestrial habi-tats, but the preponderance of these cold-blooded vertebrates favor aquatic settings. Thus, this chapter will focus on birds and mammals.

Birds

Birds—above all other vertebrates—elicit the interest of nature lovers. Bird clubs, stocked birdfeeders, nesting boxes, and "Christmas counts" are but a few indications of nature enthusiasts' fascination with birds. A Lehigh Valley Bird Club was established in 1946. An early attempt at a detailed list of species seen in Lehigh County was compiled in 1956 by John Trainer and Clint Miller; this was the forerunner of a more recent booklet, *Birds of the Lehigh Valley Area* (1984), featuring data assem-bled by dedicated birders Bernard Morris, Richard Wiltraut, and Fred-eric Brock. This valuable guide lists the times of the year and the habitats in which birds are likely to be seen. Whether a bird is common, uncommon, or rare is also noted. Finally, maps and directions to almost two dozen selected birding areas are provided. (This guide is an out-standing example of the manner in which observations of dedicated amateur naturalists can add to the scientific understanding of a popular

BOX 9.1

Birding Places in the Lehigh Valley

Beginning birders should consult two fine specialized publications, *Birds of the Lehigh Valley Area* and *A Century of Bird Life in Berks County, Pennsylvania*. (These publications are listed in the bibliography for Chap. 9 and give details about the sites that appear below as well as less familiar areas.)

MINSI LAKE. Located in the northeastern corner of Northampton County, this site has been excellent for waterfowl sightings during migration. Several trails, including one around the lake, are good for viewing warblers and other small birds. Edge areas allow visitors to observe edge species of birds and other wildlife. (See Box 10.2 for directions.)

LEASER LAKE. This lake, situated in the northwestern corner of Lehigh County, is also good for migrating waterfowl. Visitors can see woodland birds by taking a pleasant walk along the road that cuts through the mountain slopes north of the lake. Again, edge areas provide opportunities for finding edge fauna and flora. (See Box 10.2.)

FOGELSVILLE QUARRY. Migrating waterfowl visit the pool within this deep limestone quarry, located west of Allentown. Viewing must be conducted outside a fence, and telescopes are needed in order to identify birds accurately.

ONTELAUNEE RESERVOIR. The reservoir is a good spot for migrating waterfowl. In recent years, it has also become a major stopover for snow geese and tundra swans. Some wooded tracts and conifer plantations add to the birding opportunities. (See Box 10.2.)

ALLENTOWN CITY PARKS. As noted in the list of "edge sites," these parks are some of the best spots in which to view wildlife in urban settings. Little Lehigh Parkway, Trexler Park, and Jordan Creek Parkway offer varied habitats, and woodland birds, shorebirds, and waterfowl can be observed.

BETHLEHEM. For decades, the area along the Monocacy Creek has been a favorite of Lehigh Valley birders. A parking area reached from Illick's Mill Road leads to a creekside trail. South Mountain Park, which runs along North Mountain Drive, east from PA Route 378, has some old-growth forests and, on the mountaintop, an open field. The field offers especially good birding during migration.

EASTON. The towpath walks near Glendon and Hugh Moore Park, noted in the "edge sites" list, serve as fine birding sites. South of Easton, along Route 611, Mariton Wildlife Sanctuary and Wilderness

BOX 9.1 (CONTINUED)

Trust has diverse wooded and field areas from which to observe birds. Labeled wildflowers are an added treat for visitors to this site.

JACOBSBURG ENVIRONMENTAL EDUCATION CENTER. As noted in Box 8.1, trails along field edges are frequently good birding spots. A creekside trail through a dense hemlock ravine provides an opportunity to find birds typical of that setting, such as warblers, flycatchers, and chickadees.

NOLDE ENVIRONMENTAL EDUCATION CENTER. This area, at the far western edge of our region, has extensive plantations of conifers; these provide a chance to see birds that frequent this area—such as nuthatches, grosbeaks, and cardinals—in order to feed on cones and other preferred dietary items.

group of vertebrates.) And a fine volume edited by William Uhrich, *A Century of Bird Life in Berks County, Pennsylvania,* will be of great assistance to birders who venture into the western region of the valley. Bird species recorded for the wider Lehigh Valley—based on observations of several local experts—number 260. In addition, 40 species are designated as accidental. However, these species lists include observations made by birders at sites such as Green Lane Reservoir and Penn Forest Reservoir, well beyond the valley itself.

A publication milestone for Pennsylvania was the *Atlas of Breeding Birds in Pennsylvania* (1992), a text that serves as another example of the contributions to be made by dedicated amateur naturalists. Edited by Daniel Brauning, this resource documents those species designated as threatened and endangered and describes the breeding locations of the Keystone State's bird species. From 1983 through 1989, approximately two thousand volunteers contributed over 94,000 records from every region of Pennsylvania. Study sites were based on blocks drawn over topographic maps for the entire state. The blocks varied in area from 9.2 to 9.5 square miles. Statewide, the average number of species per block was 65. For Lehigh and Northampton Counties (Region 5), 139 species of birds were observed and the average number of species per block was 64. Berks County (Region 6) observers recorded 146 species with an average of 66 species per block. The top ten breeding birds in the state were the following, in descending order: American robin, American crow, song sparrow, chipping sparrow, gray catbird, common

Fig. 9.5 *Two thrushes*
The wood thrush (r.), a forest-dwelling bird, was common in the Lehigh Valley when the earliest settlers arrived; the now-familiar robin (l.), an edge species, was uncommon. As the environment changed, so did the relative abundance of these two species.

yellowthroat, blue jay, indigo bunting, American goldfinch, and red-eyed vireo. A detailed account of the 180 species studied statewide is presented in this impressive text. Based upon the works noted above, the observations of avid birders consulted by us, and our own observations, Table 9.1 lists the bird species of the Lehigh Valley along with their preferred habitats. Box 9.1 suggests birding places.

Mammals

The number of books on the natural history of mammals, the group of vertebrates to which we belong, pales in comparison to the burgeoning number of tomes devoted to birds. Although the same "hot spots" visited by birders could probably serve as suitable mammal observation sites, seeing mammals at those sites can be much more difficult. A few mammals are active during the day, and some are more apt to be moving about at dawn and dusk (which are also good birding times), but most mammals are nocturnal. An observer might see or hear several dozen bird species on a morning walk, but that person would be lucky to see a few species of mammals—such as the gray squirrel, chipmunk, cottontail, groundhog, and, perhaps, white-tailed deer. In recent years, some of the Commonwealth's largest mammals—black bears—appear to have developed wanderlust. A few young animals, usually males, are showing up at suburban backyard birdfeeders or garbage sheds some distance from the bears' forest habitats along the Blue Mountain slopes. Such events are destined to make the local newspapers or television newscasts.

Normally, the occasional direct observation must be supplemented by indirect signs of mammalian presence. Muddy or dusty patches can reveal the tracks of an opossum or raccoon. The fecal droppings of many mammals, such as rabbits and deer, have a distinctive shape. The

Table 9.1 *Lehigh Valley birds and their principal habitats*

Species				Habitats				
	Deciduous Forests	Mixed Forests	Hemlock Ravines	Fields, Woods	Floodplains	Lakes	Ponds, Marshes	Bogs
Common loon					•	•	•	
Pied-billed grebe					•	•	•	
Horned grebe*					•	•	•	
Great blue heron					•	•	•	
Green-backed heron					•	•	•	
Great egret*					•	•	•	
Snowy egret*					•	•	•	
Black-crowned night heron					•	•	•	
Mute swan*					•	•		
Tundra swan*					•	•		
Snow goose*					•	•		
Canada goose					•	•	•	
Mallard					•	•	•	
American black duck					•	•	•	
Northern pintail*					•	•	•	
Green-winged teal*					•	•	•	
Blue-winged teal*					•	•	•	
American widgeon*					•	•	•	
Northern shoveler*					•	•	•	
Wood duck					•	•	•	
Redhead*					•	•		
Ring-necked duck*					•	•		
Canvasback*						•		

Table 9.1 (continued) *Lehigh Valley birds and their principal habitats*

| | Habitats | | | | | | | |
Species	Deciduous Forests	Mixed Forests	Hemlock Ravines	Fields, Woods	Floodplains	Lakes	Ponds, Marshes	Bogs
Lesser scaup*					•	•		
Common goldeneye*					•	•		
Bufflehead					•	•	•	
Ruddy duck					•	•	•	
Hooded merganser					•	•	•	
Common merganser					•	•		
Turkey vulture	•	•		•	•			
Black vulture*	•	•		•	•			
Sharp-shinned hawk	•	•	•	•				
Cooper's hawk	•	•	•	•				
Red-tailed hawk	•	•		•				
Red-shouldered hawk	•	•	•	•				
Broad-winged hawk	•	•	•	•	•			
Rough-legged hawk*				•				
Golden eagle*	•							
Bald eagle*					•	•		
Northern harrier				•	•	•	•	
Osprey				•	•	•		
American kestrel				•	•	•	•	
Ruffed grouse	•	•	•					
Ring-necked pheasant				•				•
Wild turkey*	•	•	•			•		
American coot						•	•	

Table 9.1 (continued) *Lehigh Valley birds and their principal habitats*

Species	Deciduous Forests	Mixed Forests	Hemlock Ravines	Fields, Woods	Floodplains	Lakes	Ponds, Marshes	Bogs
Killdeer						•	•	
American woodcock							•	•
Common snipe*				•			•	•
Upland sandpiper*							•	
Spotted sandpiper						•	•	
Solitary sandpiper						•	•	
Greater yellowlegs*						•	•	
Lesser yellowlegs						•	•	
Red knot						•	•	
Pectoral sandpiper						•	•	
Least sandpiper						•	•	
Semipalmated sandpiper*						•	•	
Herring gull					•	•	•	
Ring-billed gull					•	•	•	
Rock dove					•			
Mourning dove					•			
Yellow-billed cuckoo	•	•						
Black-billed cuckoo	•	•						
Barn owl*								
Eastern screech owl	•	•		•	•			
Great horned owl	•	•	•	•	•			
Snowy owl*				•	•			
Barred owl	•	•	•	•				

Habitats

Table 9.1 (continued) *Lehigh Valley birds and their principal habitats*

| | Habitats | | | | | | | |
Species	Deciduous Forests	Mixed Forests	Hemlock Ravines	Fields, Woods	Floodplains	Lakes	Ponds, Marshes	Bogs
Long-eared owl*	•							
Eastern saw-whet owl*			•					
Whippoorwill*	•		•					
Common nighthawk				•				
Chimney swift				•				
Ruby-throated hummingbird				•				
Belted kingfisher					•	•	•	
Northern flicker	•	•	•	•				
Pileated woodpecker*	•	•	•	•				
Red-bellied woodpecker	•	•	•					
Red-headed woodpecker*	•		•					
Yellow-bellied sapsucker	•	•	•					
Hairy woodpecker	•	•	•					
Downy woodpecker	•	•	•					
Eastern kingbird	•			•	•	•	•	
Great crested flycatcher	•			•				
Eastern phoebe		•		•				
Least flycatcher		•						
Eastern wood pewee	•	•		•				
Horned lark				•				
Tree swallow					•	•	•	•
Bank swallow					•	•	•	
Barn swallow						•		

Table 9.1 (continued) *Lehigh Valley birds and their principal habitats*

Species				Habitats				
	Deciduous Forests	Mixed Forests	Hemlock Ravines	Fields, Woods	Floodplains	Lakes	Ponds, Marshes	Bogs
Rough-winged swallow*					•	•	•	
Cliff swallow*					•	•	•	
Purple martin*								
Blue jay	•	•	•	•	•			
American crow	•	•	•	•	•	•	•	
Black-capped chickadee	•	•	•	•	•			
Tufted titmouse	•	•	•	•				
White-breasted nuthatch	•	•	•	•				
Red-breasted nuthatch			•					
Brown creeper			•					
Northern house wren	•		•	•	•			
Winter wren*			•					
Carolina wren			•	•				
Northern mockingbird								
Gray catbird	•			•	•			
Brown thrasher	•			•	•			
American robin	•			•	•			
Wood thrush	•			•	•			
Hermit thrush*		•	•					
Swainson's thrush*		•	•					
Veery*	•	•	•	•				
Eastern bluebird				•				
Blue-gray gnatcatcher*	•	•						

Table 9.1 (continued) *Lehigh Valley birds and their principal habitats*

Species	Deciduous Forests	Mixed Forests	Hemlock Ravines	Fields, Woods	Floodplains	Lakes	Ponds, Marshes	Bogs
				Habitats				
Golden-crowned kinglet	•	•	•					
Ruby-crowned kinglet	•	•	•					
Cedar waxwing				•				
European starling				•	•			
Solitary vireo*	•	•						
Red-eyed vireo	•	•	•					
Warbling vireo*		•				•	•	
Black-and-white warbler	•	•						
Blue-winged warbler*	•			•				
Tennessee warbler*	•							
Nashville warbler*	•							
Northern parula*	•							
Yellow warbler				•	•	•	•	
Magnolia warbler*	•				•			
Cape May warbler*	•		•					
Black-throated blue warbler	•	•						
Yellow-rumped warbler	•	•						
Black-throated green warbler*	•	•						
Blackburnian warbler*	•	•	•					
Chestnut-sided warbler*	•	•						
Bay-breasted warbler*	•	•	•					
Blackpoll warbler*	•	•						
Prairie warbler*		•						

Table 9.1 (continued) *Lehigh Valley birds and their principal habitats*

Species	Deciduous Forests	Mixed Forests	Hemlock Ravines	Fields, Woods	Floodplains	Lakes	Ponds, Marshes	Bogs
Palm warbler*	•							
Ovenbird	•	•						
Northern waterthrush*								
Kentucky warbler*	•				•		•	
Common yellowthroat				•	•	•	•	
Yellow-breasted chat*				•				
Hooded warbler*	•							
Wilson's warbler*	•			•				
Canada warbler*	•	•	•		•			•
American redstart		•	•		•			
House sparrow				•	•			
Bobolink*				•	•			
Eastern meadowlark				•				
Red-winged blackbird	•				•		•	
Northern oriole		•			•			
Common grackle					•	•	•	
Brown-headed cowbird				•				
Scarlet tanager	•				•			
Northern cardinal	•			•				
Rose-breasted grosbeak	•	•		•				
Indigo bunting				•				
Evening grosbeak*		•		•				
Purple finch	•	•		•				•

Table 9.1 (continued) *Lehigh Valley birds and their principal habitats*

				Habitats				
Species	Deciduous Forests	Mixed Forests	Hemlock Ravines	Fields, Woods	Floodplains	Lakes	Ponds, Marshes	Bogs
House finch	•			•			•	
Common redpoll*		•		•				
Pine siskin		•	•	•				
American goldfinch	•	•		•				
Rufous-sided towhee		•		•	•			
Savannah sparrow*				•				
Grasshopper sparrow*				•				
Vesper sparrow*				•				
American tree sparrow				•				
Dark-eyed junco	•	•	•	•				
Chipping sparrow				•				
Field sparrow				•				
White-crowned sparrow*				•				
White-throated sparrow	•			•				
Fox sparrow								
Swamp sparrow*					•		•	•
Song sparrow				•	•		•	

NOTE: Rare and uncommon species are marked with an asterisk (*). Some species on this list may be "common" only at specific seasons or during migration; occasional, exceptionally uncommon species are not included here. Detailed checklists with rarities indicated are available in two sources: see *Birds of the Lehigh Valley Area* (1984), by B. L. Morris, R. E. Wiltraut, and F. H. Brock (Emmaus, Pa.: Lehigh Valley Audubon Society), and *A Century of Bird Life in Berks County, Pennsylvania*, edited by W. D. Uhrich (Reading, Pa.: Reading Public Museum).

Fig. 9.6 *Selected indirect mammal signs*
A sampling of signs suggests mammalian presence. An abundance of woodland dry fruits (such as ash, maple, and elm samaras, acorns, various cones, and so on) typically encourages the populations of small mammals like mice, moles, shrews, and voles. Animal tracks are generalized and vary greatly with surfaces such as mud, dust, and snow. All tracks are moving up (forward) in the panel; *h* signifies the hind foot track, and *f*, the front foot track.

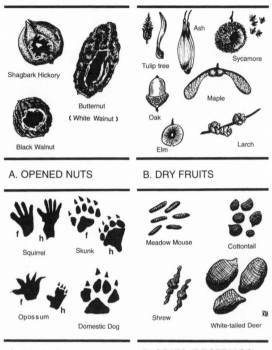

ridges of lawn pushed up by moles may tell homeowners that unwelcome visitors are present. Caches of stored seeds or discarded cherry pits suggest that a white-footed mouse has established residence. With patience and a bit of luck, one can directly observe vertebrates other than birds, and the sighting of a small mammal, amphibian, or reptile can be as rewarding as recording a new species of bird.

The first comprehensive work on the mammals of Pennsylvania was written and privately published by Samuel N. Rhoads in 1903. He lamented the wanton destruction of the virgin white pine and hemlock forest and the accompanying loss of animals. He did express a glimmer of hope when he suggested that an era of reforestation might give a new home to the game and furbearers of early Pennsylvania. The next—and, unfortunately for us, last—statewide mammal survey was conducted from 1946 to 1951 and published in six reports. The Lehigh Valley is included within eleven southeastern counties which were studied during the survey. At that time (1949–51), seventy species and subspecies were collected or observed in these counties. Fifteen years later, J. Kenneth Doutt (senior author of *Mammals of Pennsylvania,* first published in

1966 and largely based on the earlier state survey) commented on reforestation efforts in the forty-five years since Rhoads's statement had been
made. Observing that the hillsides were green with a flourishing forest
in which game could find food and shelter, Doutt expressed the hope
that a full-grown forest might enable the fisher, the marten, and even the
lynx to return to Pennsylvania. Based on Pennsylvania Game Commission studies, comments from other naturalists, and our own studies and
observations in the valley, Table 9.2 lists the Lehigh Valley mammal
species and their typical habitats. A few of the forty-plus species represented in the mammal list will be highlighted in the remaining portion
of this chapter.

Short-Tailed Shrew
Most people would not rank the short-tailed shrew as Pennsylvania's
most common mammal, but many professional mammalogists do just
that. Shrews (and their relatives, moles) are secretive; however, studies
by mammalogists reveal that shrews, especially short-tailed shrews, are
remarkably abundant. Population estimates of one hundred shrews per
acre have been cited in journal accounts. Such studies also indicate that
shrew populations vary. Periods of abundance alternate with those of
scarcity.
   The short-tailed shrew, which is the largest of the eight species
believed to be present in the Lehigh Valley, measures four inches in
length and weighs one half-ounce. Shrews and moles have velvet-like
fur, minute eyes, ears that are hidden in the fur, and a pointed snout. A
short (one inch) and sparsely haired tail is sufficient to distinguish the
short-tailed shrew from other shrew species, which have long tails—
some equal in length to the rest of the body. The short-tailed shrew pos-
sesses normally sized and shaped front paws (unlike moles, which have
paddle-shaped, bulldozing forepaws ideally suited to their burrowing
subterranean lifestyle).
   Shrews may use mole burrows but are more apt to scurry along in
the top few inches of leaf litter. The tiny size of shrews—and their large
surface area, relative to their volume—makes heat conservation difficult. They need steady fuel to maintain the constant body temperature
characteristic of most mammals. As a result, shrews need to consume
food equal to their body weight each day of the year.
   Grasshoppers, caterpillars, spiders, millipedes, slugs, beetles—in
essence, almost any invertebrate animal small enough to be overpow-
ered—is suitable prey for short-tailed shrews. The shrews also consume
insect eggs, cocoons, and carrion and do attack mice, salamanders, and

Table 9.2 *Lehigh Valley mammals*

Species	Preferred Habitat(s)
Opossum	Lowland forests and edges, wooded swamps
Eastern mole	Fields, meadows
Star-nosed mole	Wet bottomland forests, swamps
Masked shrew*	Moist woods, bogs, meadows
Big-tailed shrew*	Rockslides in moist woods
Pygmy shrew*	Hemlock ravines, moist woods
Short-tailed shrew	Widespread; moist to dry woodlands
Least shrew	Meadows, old fields, pasturelands
Little brown bat } Big brown bat }	Retire to hollow trees, caves, tunnels, and the like during the day; feed at night over open land and water
Black bear*	Forests, swamps
Raccoon	Widespread along streams and lake borders
Long-tailed weasel } Short-tailed weasel* }	Open fields, fencerows
Mink	Along streams, marshes, swamps
Striped skunk	Woods, swamps, fields
Coyote*	Woodlands
Red fox	Farmlands, open woods
Gray fox*	Rocky upland forests
Bobcat*	Rocky upland forests
Woodchuck	Fields, meadows, road banks
Eastern chipmunk	Widespread; forests, parks, stone walls
Eastern gray squirrel	Deciduous forests, parks
Red squirrel	Conifer forests, wooded swamps
Southern flying squirrel	Deciduous forests, woodlots
White-footed mouse	Wooded and brushy areas, cabins
Deer mouse	Forests, forest edges
Boreal red-backed vole*	Conifer forests, stream banks
Meadow vole	Grasslands, old fields, orchards
Muskrat	Marshes, swamps, wet meadows
House mouse	Fields, buildings
Norway rat	Fields, farm buildings, dumps
Meadow jumping mouse	Wet meadows, forest edges
Woodland jumping mouse	Forest edges, stream banks
Eastern cottontail	Old fields, forest edges, backyards
White-tailed deer	Open woods, forest edges, farmlands, orchards

NOTE: Species marked with an asterisk (*) are rare or uncommon in the Lehigh Valley.

Fig. 9.7 *Short-tailed shrew*
Here, the shrew consumes
a checkered beetle. The
largely nocturnal short-
tailed shrew is the most
common mammal in Penn-
sylvania. These shrews eat
their weight in small invertebrates (see Fig. 9.3, for
example) each day.

other small vertebrates. With the aid of pincer-action front teeth, poisonous saliva is placed into wounds made in the prey. (It is suspected
that the poison aids in subduing vertebrate prey by adversely affecting
the nervous system.) Shrews are the only mammals, aside from the
duck-billed platypus of Australia, known to be poisonous.

Shrews, in turn, are prey for many predators, including weasels, mink,
foxes, cats, hawks, owls, and snakes. A short-tailed shrew rarely survives
its second winter. However, high mortality rates are counterbalanced by
high natality: females may have three or more litters in a breeding season
lasting from early spring to late fall. After a gestation period of twenty-one
to twenty-two days, a litter of four to eight young are born. The young
grow rapidly and are on their own in about three weeks. In all likelihood,
if you observe a velvet-gray "critter" moving with terrier-like frenzy along
a log, stone wall, or road edge during your outdoor wandering, you've
probably spotted the Lehigh Valley's most abundant mammal.

Bat

Swooping and darting after insect prey in the twilight sky, bats are
unlike any other mammal. Shrews and moles are the bat's closest relatives, but the extensive anatomical modifications that enable bats to fly
make it hard for anyone other than experts to fathom this relationship.

The forelimbs and fingers are tubular and elongate to form the
struts that support the thin, pliable skin that serves as wings for these
mammals. Skin also extends along the side from the modified forelimbs
to the ankle region. An additional membrane that stretches from the
hind limbs to the tail serves as a rudder, a scoop to aid in prey capture,
and even an insulating blanket during hibernation.

The little brown bat is the region's most common species. The body
is about two and one-half inches from nose to rump; however, the

Fig. 9.8 *Little brown bat*
A. Full underside (ventral) display.
B. Suspended.

wingspan is almost ten inches. The color is generally a dark walnut brown, dorsally, with a dull buff-colored ventral region.

Near dusk, the little brown bat begins the evening hunt for insects. Studies indicate that bats are capable of filling their stomachs with prey in an hour's time, suggesting that their hunting times are probably limited to a short period near dusk and another near dawn. The echolocation technique employed by bats for navigational and feeding purposes is truly amazing. While in flight, bats emit twenty to thirty bursts of supersonic sound per second. These sounds last about ⅔₀₀ of a second, and they vary in frequency from 40,000 to 100,000 cycles per second. The sounds echo back from solid objects. The bat's sensitive ears detect these echoes, and the animal processes the information in order to navigate and to locate prey.

It is well established that bats do not maintain the constant and relatively high body temperature typical of most mammals. When resting and sleeping, suspended upside down, a bat allows its body temperature to fall to that of its surroundings—which in the cave, hollow tree, barn, attic, or other suitable site is usually much lower than the body temperature of most mammals (ranging from ninety-eight to one hundred degrees Fahrenheit). This energy conservation technique serves these small-bodied mammals well. Otherwise, bats—with their large surface area relative to their small volume—would require much more fuel to sustain a constant body temperature.

In autumn, bats accumulate extra layers of fat to sustain them during hibernation. In October or early November, bats gather in caves or in abandoned mine shafts. Suspended upside down from walls and ceilings, numbers of bats—sometimes hundreds of them—will go into hibernation. Body temperature drops, heartbeat and respiration rates slow, and a deep, comatose sleep ensues until the following spring.

Chipmunk

Throughout most of the milder months of the year, a familiar and easily recognizable mammal in the valley is the eastern chipmunk, *Tamias striatus*.

Fig. 9.9 *Chipmunk*
It favors stone fences and
both woodland and build-
ing edges.

(Although we have avoided using scientific names in the body of the text, this animal's Latin name is particularly appropriate: *Tamias* means "steward," one who stores and looks after provisions, and the species name *striatus* means "striped"—a fitting designation for the features and behavior characteristic of this small ground squirrel.) Chipmunks possess two large internal cheek pouches into which food is stuffed and carried from place to place. The chipmunk uses its forepaws to maneuver food carefully into the pouches, making sure to load both sides equally. To unload them, the forepaws press externally on the pouches to dislodge the food into the mouth; from there, the food can be dropped into a storage tunnel or in a cache located some distance from the burrow system. The burrow system of chipmunks is remarkable: a typical system includes a nest site, twelve by eighteen inches, with a side chamber that serves as a lavatory, food storage tunnels, and additional side tunnels which may extend for thirty feet from the main chamber. The chipmunk's varied food supply includes nuts, berries, cherries, beetles, snails, fungi, and seed pods, as well as small salamanders, snakes, and young birds and bird eggs. The nuts, berries, seed pods, and fungi are stored away in caches for winter consumption.

Unlike most other ground squirrels, chipmunks are not true hibernators: they do not put on a layer of fat, lower their metabolism extensively, and go into an extreme lethargic state. Chipmunks do awaken during the winter, deep within their burrows, and use the ample stored food to satiate their hunger before returning to sleep. During very hot weather, such as the "dog days" of August, chipmunks retire to the coolness of their underground burrows for a "summer sleep" termed *estivation*. Chipmunks are diurnal, and their keen eyesight is used to detect food and, in turn, to avoid being eaten by diurnal predators such as hawks, foxes, house cats, and weasels. Weasels will pursue chipmunks into their burrows, and it is well documented that a weasel will destroy an entire family of chipmunks in the nest in a few minutes of frenzied attack.

Red Fox

One of the valley's most handsome mammals is certainly the red fox. The fox is the size of a small beagle, and boasts a vivid orange-red coat, black leggings, a touch of white at the throat and cheeks, and a glorious brush or plume tail, fully twelve inches long and tipped with white. Catching sight of this elusive animal is surely a treat for any nature lover. Suburban dwellers, especially those driving about in early morning or at dusk, regularly report a fleeting sight of a red fox. Sadly, some people discover how close to human habitation some red foxes dwell only when a beautiful dead animal is seen along the roadside.

Males may travel over an area of about five square miles in search of food and mates. As is typical of most mammals, females have a smaller home range. If undisturbed, females will use the same den year after year. The den is frequently an enlarged woodchuck (groundhog) burrow, and several openings may be formed, one conspicuous but the others hidden. Mating occurs in late winter and, after a gestation period of fifty-one days, four to seven young are born. The young remain in the den for about a month. When they do emerge, both male and female parents bring food to them. The kits remain with their parents until the fall.

"Dumb like a fox" and "cunning like a fox" are but two of the phrases linked to this attractive mammal. Trappers tell tales of clever foxes that avoided the most well-set traps for years. Numerous accounts of the ways in which foxes outwit pursuing hounds add to their reputation. The fact remains that foxes do get trapped, taken by hounds, or shot by hunters. Disease and parasites take their toll as well, even more than trappers and hunters do: mange and rabies may decimate populations. But a new cycle starts, and populations rebound.

The fable of the fox and the grapes tells something about this mammal's varied diet. Fruits, berries, grains, insects and other invertebrates, small birds and their eggs, mice, shrews, moles, and carrion are among numerous dietary items. The storied "fox in the henhouse" and predation on other farm animals, such as sheep and pigs, are probably overrated by the few farmers who experience such raids. For most of us, glimpsing the cunning, shy red fox is a highlight of a country walk or drive. (The other fox in the valley, the gray fox, is a creature of the forests and much less likely to be found by the casual explorer in the parks and woodlots that cover most of our region.)

White-Tailed Deer

This mammal is perhaps the best-studied mammal in Pennsylvania. Indians and colonists hunted white-tails for food and used the skin to make garments. Native Americans also made utensils, tools, ceremonial rattles, and even weapons of war from the hooves and antlers. In the forested landscape of the colonial period, deer populations would have been sparse, since these mammals are primarily browsers that feed on the tips of woody vegetation. Forest clearing—for farms, housing developments, and light industry sites—created habitats that enabled deer populations to increase. Excessive animal populations generally stem from some kind of habitat destruction (not only the habitat of that particular animal but also those of many other plants and animals). In the case of white-tailed deer, the deer's typical predators, such as wolves and mountain lions, fled from the advance of settlers into the frontier or were killed. In 1895, Pennsylvania formed a Game Commission to regulate recreational hunting. By 1930, Game Commission officials estimated that over a million deer were present throughout the state. Today, the Game Commission permits the harvesting of does as well as bucks in an attempt to control the herd size. (See Kosack [1995] for the history of wildlife conservation activities by the Pennsylvania Game Commission during the past one hundred years.)

Many people are strongly opposed to hunting on ethical grounds, but it would appear that hunters must replace lost predators that might have been able to keep prey populations at levels that would minimize habitat destruction. Even a large mammal such as the white-tailed deer has the potential to reach population levels that can threaten the overall well-being of the entire community of plants and animals: an adult doe, by two and a half years of age, typically has two fawns each spring of her life. Indeed, even with the varied types of licenses, the use of a bonus system to increase the number of licenses that individuals could purchase, and other approaches to controlling the deer population, the number of deer in the state climbed to 900,000 in the early 1980s. White-tailed deer are perhaps our region's best known example of the challenges that arise when population numbers exceed the carrying capacity of the environment for that species. In recent years, the best bucks (heaviest and with the biggest set of antlers) that hunters kill have not been found in the "big woods" counties such as Potter, Tioga, or Warren. Rather, the big deer are coming from "farm country"—Montour, Berks, Washington, Northampton, York, and Lehigh Counties. In such residential areas, deer do extensive damage to gardens and landscape shrubbery, and increasing numbers of vehicular accidents involve encounters with deer. (Although the sheer numbers of deer have intensifed public concern about the spread of Lyme disease, in truth, many warm-blooded birds and mammals can serve as hosts for ticks carrying the spirochete bacterium that causes the disease.)

The influence of expanding deer populations is not only seen in the suburbs. Studies by federal and state scientists in major forested areas, such as Allegheny National Forest, have also documented dramatic shifts in tree species composition (notably the diminished number of oaks) as a result of deer activity. The smaller tracts of forests in the Lehigh Valley have experienced similar consequences, and visitors generally observe diminished understory shrubs and fewer wildflowers in sites that they had previously visited over some span of years. Reduced diversity in vegetation is soon reflected in diminished animal diversity: ecosystem relationships, in all their complexity, make the questions about the morality of hunting even more vexed. Though proponents and opponents of hunting are adamant in their positions, there are no easy answers when it comes to the problems of managing landscapes altered by human activity.

Wild Cats and Wild Dogs

For most naturalists in the not-so-wild Lehigh Valley, wild cats and wild dogs would be rare sights indeed—but some do report catching a glimpse of a bobcat or a coyote. Unsubstantiated sightings of bobcats and coyotes in the Lehigh Valley during the 1970s and 1980s have been superseded, in recent years, by experts' accounts of sightings, duly reported in the local newspapers. Even a brief look at one of these animals would be a highlight of any outing.

Current studies of bobcats carried out by officials of the Game Commission in the southwestern and northcentral sections of the state should provide a better assessment of the present status of this elusive feline, which is about the size of a large male domestic cat. These shy, secretive cats, with the short seven-inch tail signified by their common name, are most active at night, so chances of encountering them are slim. Bobcats—and other predators considered livestock-eating vermin—had bounties placed on their heads almost from the time the Commonwealth was formed. The Pennsylvania Game Commission paid a bounty of $15 on bobcats from 1810 to 1938. The peak year for bounty payments came in fiscal year 1915–16, when 862 bobcats were killed. Protection for these animals came slowly: the efforts of people like Maurice Braun at Hawk Mountain led to a more widespread understanding of the role that predators play in the well-being of the entire wildlife community, and many of the so-called vermin finally received statewide protection. In the mid-1970s, the Game Commission estimated that fewer than 100 bobcats remained in the wild in Pennsylvania. Recently, confirmed sightings and bobcat roadkills indicate that the

CAMEO 9.1

Francis J. Trembley (1904–1978)

It was ironic that the first Earth Day occurred in 1970—the same year that Professor of Ecology Fran Trembley formally retired from Lehigh University. He could hardly fathom the national event of Earth Day: he had been teaching and preaching about the problems of pollution, pesticides, and overpopulation for more than forty years. Countless students were influenced by his informal and delightful lectures; he may be remembered best, though, as a teacher with a mission and an enthusiasm that became pivotal in shaping the ecological conscience of the Lehigh Valley.

In his later years, Trembley wrote a well-received weekly environmental column for the Allentown *Call-Chronicle* newspapers. His articles were peppered with his own field experiences with rattlesnakes, falcons, turkey vultures, trout, and nearly everything else that was alive (or so it seemed). Although his writings often centered on an experience or two—colorful experiences that attracted readers—he always worked in some solid, commonsense ecology. A skillful writer and speaker, he distinctively displayed the strengths of the old-time field naturalist as well as the contemporary ecologist.

Most of his former students, including the authors of this book, would agree that he was *more* than slightly ahead of his time.

population is on the rebound. These animals have a diverse diet and are known to consume small rodents, rabbits, chipmunks, birds, and frogs. Their peak breeding season is between January and March and, generally, two to four young are born after a gestation period of fifty to sixty days. The young stay with the mother for several months before moving out to establish their own territory. It is likely that bobcats will spread from more rugged forested areas into rural and suburban regions. In the valley, reports of bobcat sightings have come from Freemanburg and Hellertown in the last few years, so the chance of seeing Pennsylvania's "wild cat" is now a distinct possibility. Very recently, bobcat hunting was authorized on a restricted basis.

Pennsylvania Game Commission studies suggest that coyotes now reside in every county in the Commonwealth and estimate the statewide population to range from fifteen to twenty thousand individuals. One coyote was shot on South Mountain near Emmaus in 1993, and others have been seen near Lehigh Valley International Airport and along Blue Mountain. The highest concentration of coyotes is in the Poconos and west into northcentral Pennsylvania. There is no closed season on coyotes, and hunters take between six thousand and seven thousand annually. Most of us associate the coyote with the western United States—and it is true that coyotes are abundant and widespread west of the Mississippi River all the way north to Alaska. However, coyotes have moved steadily eastward over the past few decades. Coyotes, about the size of a medium-sized dog, have a prominent black-tipped bushy tail. There is some evidence of coyote-dog crossbreeds and also of coyote–red wolf matings. Coyotes are adaptable animals, seemingly capable of surviving despite the alterations that humans have made to their natural habitat. An extremely varied diet—consisting of plants, animals ranging from birds and small mammals to snakes and insects, and even carrion—is a major factor in the survival skills of this animal. Coyotes have been linked to livestock losses in Pennsylvania, mainly of sheep (primarily lambs) as well as chickens, ducks, geese, and goats. The animals mate in late January to mid-February, and the young are born sixty to sixty-six days later. In Pennsylvania, the average litter size is five to six young. By late August, the family unit, both parents and young, travel and hunt over an area of thirty square miles. Wildlife biologists of the Pennsylvania Game Commission suggest that the recent boom in the state's coyote population is a reflection of the increase in forest habitat as some farms revert to forest. Traveling outdoors in the valley, especially at dawn or dusk, may indeed lead to a "wild dog" sighting that will add to the excitement of the adventure.

The rapidly moving short-tailed shrew, the far-ranging coyote, and other denizens of the valley serve as reminders that the mobility of animals allows them to thrive in a wide range of habitats. But invariably, watercourse and wetland habitats—rich in the water that is key to survival—are home to the greatest abundance and diversity of wildlife. These watercourses and wetlands are the focus of the next chapter.

Watercourse and Wetland Communities

What would the world be, once bereft
of wet and of wildness? Let them be left,
O let them be left, wildness and wet;
Long live the weeds and wilderness yet.

—GERARD MANLEY HOPKINS, "INVERSNAID," 1918

Not surprisingly, many people find watercourse and wetland communities fascinating. After all, most scientists believe that life evolved in an aquatic environment, and water is vital for the sustenance of all types of life: water constitutes about 60 percent of the body weight of humans, for example, and must remain fairly constant over time for human well-being. The earliest clusters of human habitation were believed to be primarily centered on lake and river edges. Wetlands and watercourses provide habitats for varied plants and animals, filter pollutants, conserve precious groundwater, and stabilize the biosphere.

THE PARADOX OF WATER

Water is common: it covers almost three-fourths of our planet. But at the same time, water has unusual physical and chemical characteristics. When water freezes, the molecular arrangement of hydrogen and oxygen atoms forms units that build upon each other to produce a lattice affair that results in a decrease in density; other substances typically exhibit an increase in density when they freeze. Solid water—ice—floats on liquid water. Ponds and lakes have a covering of ice which provides protection for aquatic life in the harshest of winter climates.

Water has other uncommon properties, such as the highest heat of fusion and heat of evaporation of all substances that are liquid at room temperature. Heat is absorbed slowly by and released slowly from water, much more slowly than it is from air, a fact that has profound ramifications for weather and climate. The slow, prolonged temperature changes experienced by water influenced the evolution of aquatic life-forms, such that most aquatic organisms cannot tolerate sudden temperature changes.

Other significant characteristics of water are its viscosity and high surface tension. These properties enable plants to pull in water and move it through narrow conducting networks. Water readily dissolves more substances than almost any other liquid does. Thus, oxygen and carbon dioxide absorbed from the air and mineral salts dissolved from bedrock and soils are available for uptake by aquatic plants and animals.

THE HYDROLOGIC CYCLE

As Ecclesiastes 1:7 proclaims, "All the rivers run into the sea, yet the sea is not full: unto the place from whence the rivers come, thither they return again." The hydrologic cycle plays an important role in sustaining life in the biosphere. Driven by solar energy, water is moved in a global cycle. Oceans cover 71 percent of the earth's surface. Fresh water composes but 3 percent of the earth's supply, and three-quarters of *that* small amount is in the form of ice in glaciers and polar ice sheets. The atmosphere contains only 0.035 percent fresh water as water vapor.

Water vapor in the atmosphere cools as the air rises, condenses, and coalesces into raindrops. Some rain is intercepted by vegetation as rainfall occurs over land, some runs into surface waters, and some percolates through spaces within the soil and ends up in groundwater. Surface runoff does indeed get to the oceans to replace water lost from the oceans through evaporation into the atmosphere.

Water evaporates from the earth's surface at rates governed by the moisture content of the atmosphere in contact with various regions of the earth's surface. Plants also emit water vapor through the surfaces of the leaves, a process termed *transpiration*. At any one time, the atmosphere holds about a ten- to eleven-day supply of rainfall.

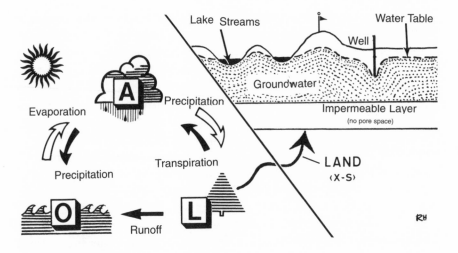

Fig. 10.1 *The hydrologic cycle*
Water moves through the (A) atmosphere, (L) land, and (O) oceans. About 97 percent of the earth's available water is in the oceans. The cycle is powered by solar
energy. The diagram (right) of a cross section through the land underscores the
importance of the water table.

Lehigh Valley Aquatic Communities

Designating aquatic communities is challenging, since they change over
time and space. Many lowland areas, now existing as swamps and
marshes, represent later stages in succession from their earlier incarna-
tions as lakes and ponds; streams and rivers, too, have a "life history"
from youth to maturity. For biologists, aquatic communities fall into
two major categories: *lotic* (running water) and *lentic* (standing water)
habitats. These useful terms will help us explore some of the varied
aquatic communities in the Lehigh Valley.

Lotic Communities

The continuous, one-way flow of water is *the* characteristic that governs
much of the anatomy, physiology, and behavior of aquatic life found in
streams and rivers. Plants and animals are adapted to stay in position
and avoid being carried downstream to unfavorable settings. The
bedrock of the site and the varied terrestrial communities bordering the
watercourse also influence the abundance and diversity of life in lotic
habitats.

What is not widely appreciated is how important the banks, stream edges, and adjacent land areas are to the well-being and productivity of any stream. In the last few decades, many biologists have engaged in detailed studies of stream dynamics, and it is now clear that the material carried into the stream from the adjacent land area is a major energy source for stream life. (Some studies, such as the one conducted at Bear Brook in northern New Hampshire's Hubbard Forest, have determined that over 90 percent of the energy input for the brook came from the surrounding forested watershed.) The energy sources are (1) coarse particulate organic matter (CPOM)—leaves and woody debris; (2) fine particulate organic matter (FPOM)—leaf fragments, invertebrate feces, and dissolved organic matter; and (3) dissolved organic matter (DOM)— even tinier materials that seep through the subsurface from adjacent forests, fields, and lawns. Much of the larger organic matter is colonized by fungi and bacteria. The partially degraded matter is termed *detritus*. Many stream insects—larvae and adults—serve as shredders, using the matter, bacteria, and fungi as food. Stoneflies, caddisflies, and dipterans are among this group of aquatic feeders. Finer matter drifts into the pools, where other stream invertebrates use filtering devices to trap nutrients. Larval types such as net-spinning caddisflies, blackflies, and midges gather food in this manner. Predators such as hellgrammites (the larval stage of dobsonflies), dragonfly nymphs, and small fish enter the food chain here as well.

Brooks and Springs

Where groundwater seeps out from rock fissures, brooks form on some of the steeper slopes of the ridges that border the Lehigh Valley. These rivulets find their way into creeks and streams. Springs emerge where groundwater moves through a porous layer of soil or rock onto the surface, forming habitats called *seeps*.

Even as water flows over the rocks on the bed, a motionless boundary on the rocks' surface, only a fraction of an inch thick, provides a site for primitive plants that are able to attach themselves to rocks with adhesives of their own manufacture. Microscopic green desmids and yellow-brown diatoms anchor here and serve as the base of the food chain. More conspicuous are the numerous filamentous green algae, aquatic mosses, and liverworts, but even the somewhat larger plants would be hard to identify more precisely without resorting to a hand lens or a microscope.

Animals must also master the challenge of maintaining their position in this one-way flow of water. Some, such as net-spinning caddisfly larvae, employ the adhesive method to anchor themselves for short or

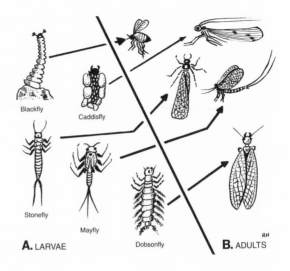

Fig. 10.2 *Common stream insects*
Aquatic larvae (A) typically lodge on the undersides of rocks for several years and emerge as terrestrial adults (B) for a short life. Blackfly larvae are associated with marginal or poor water quality; the others are indicators of good water quality.

long periods. Others, including mayfly and stonefly nymphs, use the sharp claws at the ends of appendages or the hooks projecting from underside or posterior to cling to cracks in the rocks. Here in brooks and in larger streams, other types of caddisfly larvae use adhesives to form tiny stone cases that provide anchorage.

As in most other habitats, insects—largely in larval form—are dominant in brooks and springs. Insect larvae are perhaps the most conspicuous organisms found by removing rocks from the stream bed for more detailed study. Some insects will remain attached to the rock, while others will quickly wriggle away to avoid detection. (Be sure to carefully return any rock to its original position, since you've taken the "home" and its occupants away from the neighborhood.)

Representatives from other animal phyla, such as sponges, hydroids, flatworms, and snails, can sometimes be noted by the careful observer. One particular flatworm, a planarian, may seem familiar to readers of this book: in a beginning biology class, it is often the first live animal studied with the aid of a microscope. The tiny flatworm with a triangular head, distinctive crescent-shaped eyes, and earlike projections, slowly crawling along the slide or dish on the microscope stage, is not easily forgotten.

Even relatively larger animals, such as brook fish, are still tiny, fast-moving, and difficult to study without specialized equipment. Species diversity in brooks is low; dace (relatives of minnows), darters, with highly modified pectoral fins, and young brook trout might be present, but the distinctive features needed for their identification are not easy to discern.

With a bit of effort, visitors to valley brooks and springs may locate stream salamanders. Rocks at the edge and the immediately adjacent moist areas are ideal sites in which to search for these elusive amphibians. Abundant and widespread throughout the state, the northern dusky salamander is the most likely one to be discovered: it is one of a large and fascinating group, the lungless salamanders. These accurately named animals do not possess lungs; instead, they take in most of the oxygen they require through their moist, thin, heavily vascularized skin. Finding a female coiled against a cluster of eggs in some moist, sheltered site beneath a rock or rotting log would certainly be a highlight of any trip to a seep habitat.

A few other types of salamanders occupy sites similar to those favored by the dusky salamander. The two-lined, long-tailed, northern spring, and northern red salamanders may also be found in these seepage areas. (The spring and red salamanders might be observed a bit further away from the wettest edges or may even be seen resting on the shallow bottom of a brook.)

Spring water is cold throughout the year, ranging from 48–54°F, and generally holds less oxygen and more carbon dioxide than surface water. A distinctive, but sparse, biota is characteristic of this habitat. Stones in the spring bed serve as attachment sites for filamentous algae, diatoms, and mosses. Watercress is one of the few vascular plants that do thrive in springs.

Streams

While most of us might agree that a stream is likely to be broader and deeper than what is typically considered a brook, the distinction between a stream and a river may prove more challenging. What differentiates a stream from a river is a bit vague, but usually, a stream has a narrower channel, often with a steep gradient or pitch. Rivers are larger, with a broader channel, and tend to have a low gradient. *Limnologists*, scientists who specialize in the study of streams and lakes, classify streams by order, with the smallest, headwater stream being a first-order stream. When two streams of the same order join, the stream falls into the category of the next order. In this fashion, headwater streams are orders 1–3; medium-sized streams, orders 4–6; and rivers, orders greater than 6.

Numerous streams, including some outstanding trout steams, meander through the Lehigh Valley. Of these, the Jordan, Little Lehigh, Cedar, Saucon, and Monocacy Creeks are most accessible to the public. Box 10.1 highlights these streams, which provide ideal settings for birding, botanizing, and other nature studies, as well as for fishing.

BOX 10.1

Places to Observe Lotic Communities

LEHIGH RIVER. The best vantage points from which to note floodplain vegetation along the river are the towpath trails noted in Box 8.1. The section north of Walnutport and the various towpath stretches between Allentown and Easton deserve special attention.

STREAM SITES. Again, the sites listed in Box 8.1 (as well as the birding sites along the Little Lehigh, Cedar, Jordan, and Monocacy, which are listed in Box 9.1) are prime examples of the fascinating lotic community. A pleasant nature trail runs along a stretch of the Little Lehigh located on the Pool Wildlife Sanctuary; it provides an additional opportunity to visit a preserve near urban centers.

Along the Little Lehigh in Allentown there is a trout fish hatchery. Once a city operation, the hatchery is currently maintained by volunteers from several fish and game associations. Visitors may purchase fish food pellets and toss them to the trout fingerlings in the numerous pools. As many as thirty-five thousand young (two- to three-year-old) brook, brown, and rainbow trout are given by the associations to the Pennsylvania Fish and Boat Commission for release into county waters.

At the far western edge of the region, a well-maintained trail along the Tulpehocken Creek (with parking at the Berks County Heritage Center in Wyomissing) provides walkers with a delightful experience in any season. The Gruber Wagon Works and C. Howard Hiester Canal Center, also at the site, give history buffs an added reason to visit. (Check with the staff for hours and fees for historical sites.)

Less disturbed or "manicured" sections of a stream afford the greatest opportunity to observe some of the wildlife characteristic of flowing water communities. If stones from the shallow stream edge are removed for detailed observation of stream invertebrates, remember to return the stones, so that the "critters" can return to their homes after you depart from the site.

Riffles and Pools

The topography of the region strongly influences the character and structure of a stream; the width, depth, and gradient of the channel play important roles in the velocity of the current. Fast-flowing streams have stony bottoms. As the velocity diminishes, silt and decaying organic matter are deposited on the bottom. Most streams have two different but interrelated habitats: riffles and pools.

Riffles are shallow, fast-flowing, well-aerated sections of streams with rocky substrata, and they feature more abundant and diverse life than that usually present in the quieter pools. Varied, mostly tiny plants and small animals collectively called *periphyton* live attached to plants, rock surfaces, and debris. Attached algae, diatoms, and mosses serve as the producer base of the food chain within the stream community. Microscopic protozoans, rotifers, flatworms, and segmented worms live in, on, and among the producers. (Recall that the detritus food chain starts with plant matter coming into the stream from adjacent lands and serves as the major energy source for the stream community.) In most aquatic communities, insects, crustaceans, and fish are the larger, more conspicuous members of the riffle zone.

Even the most casual observer should find some typical representatives of the riffle community. Indeed, sometimes a rock will be covered with one type of insect. Blackfly larvae have a distinctive swollen posterior, laden with hooks, which enables the larvae to stay in position in fast currents. These larvae, after two to six weeks of development, transform into resting pupae, and emerge shortly thereafter as small terrestrial adults. Most of us have experienced the irritating bites of female blackflies searching out a blood meal from warm-blooded vertebrates.

Case-building caddisfly larvae may also be readily observed. This diverse group of insects comprises more than a thousand species. The distinctive shapes and the composition of the cases can help the novice identify these animals. Small stones, sand grains, bits of bark or leaves, and twigs are all used to build the case, which may take the shape of a long, hollow tube, a bean or flask, or even a turtle or snail shell. The larval life may last almost a year and is followed by a brief pupal stage. Adults emerge from the water to live near streams for a few weeks. During this time, the adults mate, and the female deposits the fertilized eggs in the stream—or nearby, so that newly hatched larvae fall into or get washed into the water.

The active nymphs, which belong to various orders of insects, tend to cooperate less with the naturalist wishing to observe them. Mayfly and stonefly nymphs mimic each other in anatomy, behavior, and life cycle. Active nymphs of both groups are streamlined and equipped with claws, bristles and other structures that allow them to maintain their position in the riffles. More abundant, though tinier and more secretive, are dipteran (two-winged fly) larvae, especially midges and their relatives. Other riffle community animals include dobsonfly larvae, well-known to fishermen as hellgrammites; some beetles, both adults and larvae (such as the appropriately named riffle beetle larvae); dragonfly

Fig. 10.3 *Crayfish and chimney*
Crayfish often build tunnels proximal to water. The crayfish deposits the excavated mud pellets in a cluster (called a chimney) around the entrance to the tunnel system. A typical chimney height is five to six inches.

and damselfly nymphs; flatworms; segmented worms; snails; the occasional limpet; and crustaceans, such as crayfish and isopods.

Crayfish, which look remarkably like miniature lobsters, are likely to be the largest invertebrates seen by the casual visitor. However, trying to catch one is not easy for the inexperienced person—or even the novice natural predator, such as a raccoon. Surprisingly, the escape route of this crustacean is backward! The prominent muscle mass in the tail region permits the crayfish to flex the abdomen underneath the body, producing a rapid backward motion.

Adult crayfish are nocturnal, but they are sometimes seen on cloudy days in shady sections of a stream. Young animals are active during the day. Distinctive crayfish chimneys, composed of clusters of pea-sized mud pellets, reveal the presence of crayfish burrows; such chimneys are generally about six inches high. The pattern and extent of the burrows varies with the species, the nature of the stream bank soil, and the depth of the water column. Adults spend most of the daylight hours in their burrows, which (except during the breeding season) house a single animal.

A phenomenon familiar to anglers is the hatch of aquatic insects. Many such "hatches" in the Lehigh Valley occur in late winter or early spring. Early brown stoneflies and dark brown caddisflies are examples of early season hatchers. However, other stoneflies, caddisflies, and mayflies emerge at other times throughout the summer and fall. Anglers remark that the classic hatches, which featured great numbers of adults emerging in a short period of time, have not been witnessed in recent years. (The mayfly life cycle is highlighted in Chap. 5 as one of the signal events of the month of May.)

Fish typically found in riffles are blacknose and longnose dace, darters, shiners of various species, chubs, fallfish, small catfish called "madtoms," and white suckers. If the stream is stocked by the Pennsylvania Fish and Boat Commission, younger brook, brown, and rainbow trout also dwell in the cool, well-aerated water.

Bart Snyder (1907–1998)

Bart Snyder was best known in the Allentown region as the curator of the largest private bird egg collection in North America. In his basement museum were huge cabinets filled with more than sixteen thousand eggs; the eggs represented over five hundred North American species. More than a third of the collection was gathered between 1844 and 1898, the heyday for amateur natural history collectors in this country and elsewhere. Mounted bird specimens (largely window kills) added to the educational value of the museum, which he regularly opened to Scouts, church groups, and clubs. Bart prepared transportable displays that he exhibited at schools, libraries, museums, and colleges. (The vast majority of his collection was given to Messiah College.)

Bart was also one of the original members of a committee incorporated to run the Queen City Fish Hatchery, and he served as treasurer of the organization for almost fifty years. He helped establish an informative exhibit of trout and other fishes: visitors to the Lil-Le-Hi Trout Hatchery in Allentown (off Cedar Crest Boulevard on Fish Hatchery Road in Lehigh Parkway) can enjoy the exhibit as they view the hatchery operations. Active in numerous fish and game associations and conservation groups, Bart was recognized for thirty-five years of service by the Pennsylvania Fish and Boat Commission. This native and lifelong resident of Allentown, devoted to the wise use of our natural resources, was eager to share his love of wildlife and the outdoors with young and old throughout his lifetime.

Pools are interspersed with riffles, and these quiet sections of streams have a less diverse assemblage of aquatic life: the slower velocity of the water means that silt and mud settle to the bottom, covering the rocks that provide a superior substratum for most types of plants and animals. (However, these fine sediments do permit anchorage for vascular plants. By midsummer, prominent patches of river weeds, milfoils, and pondweeds may be seen.) In the poorly aerated sediments at the bottoms of pools, fewer types of invertebrate animals will be found: perhaps the most abundant will be wormlike fly larvae, especially the larvae of midges, craneflies, and horseflies. Some types of damselfly and dragonfly nymphs, burrowing types of mayfly nymphs, and fingernail clams round out the sparse assemblage in this challenging setting. Larger representatives of riffle-type fish—such as chubs, shiners, fall-fish, and trout—as well as common white suckers, channel catfish, smallmouth bass, and various types of sunfish will spend a portion of their time in shady sections of deeper, quieter pools.

At the edges of the pools, insects that can utilize the surface tension of water, such as water striders, water boatmen, and whirligig beetles, will catch the eye of anyone strolling along the stream. From this vantage point, a group of whirligig beetles swerving over the surface of the water, bumping into one another before careening off in another direction, resembles a pile-up of bumper cars at an amusement park.

Limestone Streams
We in the Lehigh Valley can claim a kind of kinship with Izaak Walton. Walton (1593–1683) wrote what is considered a masterpiece on fish and thought—*The Compleat Angler*. The English streams about which Walton wrote hundreds of years ago, with their whitish, chalk-colored water, are world-renowned as outstanding trout streams—and we have counterparts to those chalk waters here: fifteen limestone streams have been recorded by the Pennsylvania Fish and Boat Commission for Lehigh and Northampton Counties. A limestone stream, in simple terms, is one that flows through a bedrock of limestone. Limestone streams may gather water through a far-ranging network of underground channels. The water is clear, but great quantities of dissolved limestone are present. (If water from such a stream is boiled, the residue left behind on the walls of the container will testify to that!)

The high levels of salts, primarily calcium carbonate, produce a slightly alkaline pH of 7.5 to 8.0 year-round and make the limestone streams extremely fertile. Plants flourish—not only periphyton but also, in pools, waterweeds and milfoils. Abundant and diverse insect and crustacean populations are the rule. Mayflies, midges, crayfish, isopods, and, in particular, scuds are typically abundant in limestone streams. (Scuds, which are freshwater shrimp, are commonly called "sideswimmers," due to their tendency to roll onto their backs or sides and skitter along with sweeping motions of their appendages.) Sadly, many of our limestone streams do not harbor the wily, brightly colored trout of the English chalk waters. Although some of the Lehigh Valley's limestone streams are good trout streams, many now are home to suckers, carp, and other less desirable fish species. Human activities from farming, timbering, industry, and housing projects have altered the watershed such that harmful runoff and wider temperature fluctuations have taken their toll. Wiser management of the watersheds for these intriguing streams could mean the return of more "chalk water" trout streams for the enjoyment of valley inhabitants and visitors.

Monocacy Creek, the Lehigh Valley's premier limestone stream, flows through nine municipalities in Northampton County, from its headwaters in Moore Township to its juncture with the Lehigh River at Bethlehem. (The Monocacy was the site of the first successful waterworks, begun by the Moravians in 1754. The second waterworks, a stone, two-story building, still stands and is a National Historic Landmark.) Several studies conducted by professors and students at nearby institutions reveal that severe soil erosion, excess nutrient load, poorly treated effluent discharges, and increased warming have had adverse effects on the quality of this aquatic jewel in our midst. Increased warming is a particular threat to the well-being of the native brook and brown trout, which are rare in the valley's waters. Several organizations—including the Monocacy Creek Watershed Association, the Wildlands Conservancy, the Pennsylvania Rivers Conservation Program, and numerous cities, boroughs, and townships—have endorsed a project designed to restore the Monocacy. Ideally, the project will revitalize the creek and restore its original beauty. An early Moravian settler, Anna Nitchmann, reminisced about the creek as it appeared in 1740: "When I think back to the Monocacy, I remember the gently flowing water at my feet, with the mighty run of shad rippling the surface as they returned upstream to spawn and the beauty of the Red-shouldered Oriole inhabiting the extensive thickets of reed and reed mace."

Rivers

Much of the aquatic life of rivers will go undetected by visitors who walk along the river's edge. Anglers and boaters have the best opportunity to observe some of the more conspicuous biota. The major habitats in rivers are, once again, riffles and pools; bottom-dwelling life in rivers parallels the aquatic life found in the riffles and pools that are located in streams.

Our river, the Lehigh, flows south from its headwaters for 103 miles before joining the Delaware River at Easton and forming the "Forks of the Delaware," which served several times as a conference site for governors, their agents, and Indian chiefs during the early days of Penn's colony. Numerous access points along the river permit us to engage in recreational pursuits and in the study of river life.

By mid- to late summer, river weeds, pondweeds, milfoils, aquatic mosses, and patches of filamentous diatoms and algae may be noted.

Filter-feeding mollusks, mussels with black shells, dig into the silty bottom. These shellfish are fed upon by fish, muskrats, and raccoons. A pile of empty mussel shells—and, perhaps, crayfish shells—may be found on the river's edge, suggesting that some animal, probably a raccoon, had a nocturnal feast.

In centuries past, the Lehigh River served as a spawning ground for American shad, alewives, and other sea-run species. But as the canal age began in the valley, wooden dams constructed to aid in the transport of coal prevented the migration of fish to and from spawning areas. Deposits of coal silt, pollutants from mining operations, and—more recently—acid mine drainage resulted in low-pH waters in the upper reaches of the river, a condition that destroyed spawning and nursery areas. Domestic and industrial pollution from population centers in the lower Lehigh River basin produced additional habitat degradation for migrant and resident fish species, principally as the result of diminished dissolved oxygen and excessive amounts of ammonia, nitrate, and phosphate in these sections of the river.

The most extensive study of the Lehigh River was a multi-agency study conducted in 1968. It revealed a river with both fish and benthic (bottom-dwelling) populations that were depressed in terms of biomass, numbers of individuals, and numbers of species. Since that time, spot surveys and brief studies show evidence that conditions are improving slightly. Muskellunge stocked in the river below Bethlehem are doing well. Smallmouth and largemouth bass are well-established in the lower stretches. Other species recorded in Pennsylvania Fish and Boat Commission surveys include brown and brook trout, chain pickerel, rock bass, bluegills, crappie, fallfish, darters, suckers, eels, bullheads, and several types of shiners and dace. Attempts to bring shad back into the Lehigh River with a "shad ladder," an elaborate passageway constructed at Easton, are described in Chapter 12.

In June 1997, the state's Bureau of Recreation and Conservation selected the Lehigh River to promote its "Pennsylvania Rivers Month" program—a good indication that the recovery of the Lehigh is proceeding apace. Rafting in the upper sections and canoeing in the lower sections of the river gave participants in the program an opportunity to appreciate the recovery that the Lehigh has undergone in recent years. For some years now, in fact, the upper reaches have been a favorite of kayakers, experienced canoeists, and those who wish to float on rafts over the rapids of this section of the Lehigh. Scheduled and publicized releases of water from the Francis E. Walter Dam in the upper Lehigh augment the white water flows.

Gentler trips can be taken by canoe in the valley section of the river; one of the best is a six-mile paddle between Bethlehem and the Glendon (Chain) Dam. Along this stretch of the river, visitors can observe flood-plain vegetation and aquatic birds and can glimpse past glories of the valley's industry and commerce, including Bethlehem Steel buildings and furnaces and remnants of the Lehigh Canal. Near the end of the trip, canoeists will encounter Island Park—a one-hundred-acre island, once an amusement park (complete with picnic grove and merry-go-round), which is now part of Hugh Moore Parkway. Between the bank of the river and the island edge, there is a quiet water section in which submergent and emergent plants such as water lilies and spatterdock become abundant in midsummer. (Downstream from this site, the Lehigh Canal shifted from the north side of the Lehigh to the south, and a bridge was constructed from the island to the south bank of the river. The mules walked across the bridge while continuing to pull the barges behind them until they reached the other section of the canal.)

As the river quality continues to improve, more and more residents and visitors to the Lehigh Valley will likely include a canoe trip among their outdoor adventures. A healthy river is key to any long-range regional plan designed to sustain natural ecosystems, maintain or increase biodiversity, and assure outstanding recreational opportunities in the area. Fortunately, several local, regional, and state groups have dedicated themselves to the vital mission of restoring the Lehigh to its former grandeur—the splendor that greeted the first settlers to the valley.

Floodplains

The land that borders rivers and larger streams is frequently covered in spring by spillover water as spring runoff raises the water level in the main river channel. However, for most of the year, these floodplains are dry. The major public parks in Allentown, Bethlehem, and Easton, and those in the surrounding boroughs and townships, are largely located in floodplains. The sand and silt left behind when floodwaters recede are influential in determining the characteristic vegetation of the floodplains in the Lehigh Valley. The most conspicuous trees are sycamores, silver maple, river birch, American elm, cottonwood, and willow. All of these species have adapted to floodplain conditions: they grow rapidly, are supple enough to tolerate bending by floodwaters, and can send up new sprouts from a main trunk so pressed down by floodwaters as to remain in a prone position. Willows are the outstanding example of this latter trait. A shrub layer is generally wanting, although an occasional spice-bush, elderberry, or silky dogwood may be present. More common are

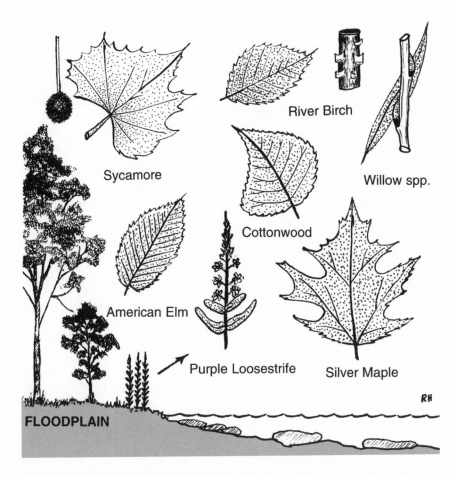

Fig. 10.4 *Common floodplain vegetation*
These plants are common along the flat, flood-prone areas of rivers and streams such as the Monocacy, Jordan, Bushkill, and others. Purple loosestrife has become a colorful, but pesky, invader of the water's edge in recent years. Vines and some shrubs are also common along floodplains. (See Fig. 6.6.)

numerous vines such as poison ivy, Virginia creeper, catbrier, and wild grape, which cover the ground before extending into the tree canopy. Figure 10.4 illustrates a typical floodplain vegetational array.

Along the edge of the Lehigh River (as elsewhere in the Northeast), purple loosestrife, an alien plant, is the plant most commonly seen in the summertime. This Eurasian perennial began to invade early in the nineteenth century, when the plant was introduced; it had been a contaminant of European ship ballast. Some escapes from plants brought to this country as medicinal herbs contributed to the spread of purple loosestrife from New England into the mid-Atlantic states. Now the plant occurs in scattered stands in many midwestern and western states and Canadian provinces. Native vegetation, bulrushes, spike rushes, and other species are crowded out by this aggressive invader. Botanists have estimated that a single loosestrife plant will release almost three billion seeds each year, seeds that are dispersed by water, wind, and the muddy feet of marsh birds. Even the foraging activities of muskrats have aided the spread of this prolific marsh weed. Currently, investigators are attempting to rely primarily on biological controls for purple loosestrife, employing root-mining weevils and leaf-feeding beetles of species known to be natural enemies of the plant. Not all annuals and perennials are obliterated by purple loosestrife, however: dense stands of jewelweed, mints, wild phlox, and nettles can be observed by midsummer along the river's edge. (An accidental brush against the tiny, stinging nettle hairs will give a positive, if unpleasant, identification of the nettle plant.)

Animals tend to be transient visitors to the floodplains. Water snakes, pond sliders, snapping turtles, and the common toad are found here, just as they are in other semi-aquatic settings. Purple grackles, red-winged blackbirds, yellow warblers, mourning doves, and purple and house finches are birds frequently noted by valley residents. Of course, waterfowl, herons, egrets, sandpipers, and other species characteristic of marshes, ponds, and lakes will also be found, though more sporadically, along floodplains. Less likely to be directly observed are numerous mammal species. Often, only tracks left behind in the mud and silt will reveal that deer, muskrats, skunks, raccoons, mink, and foxes come to the plains in search of food and drinking water.

Officials of the Allentown park system have tried to re-create wetlands from the more manicured landscape of a city park. Formally known as the Little Cedar Creek Lower Section Restoration project, this is a pioneering attempt at "bioengineering" or "restoration ecology" in the Lehigh Valley. Visitors to the site in Trexler Park (located at the northwestern corner of Cedar Crest and Broadway Boulevards) can see the results of the restoration, which was begun in the spring of 1991. In midsummer, numerous herbaceous plants—such as coneflowers, brown-eyed Susans, asters, turtlehead, blue flag iris, and, perhaps most conspicuous, rose mallow—are readily seen. At other times of the year, visitors can observe trees specifically planted here as representatives of species that do well in floodplains. Most distinctive is the bald cypress; its usual haunts are southern swamplands, such as Big Cypress National Preserve or Okefenokee Swamp. Older trees have characteristic cone-shaped knees projecting above the water. The light green needles, one-half to three-quarters of an inch in length, are borne singly in two rows on thin green twigs. The needles are lost in autumn—hence the common name for this conifer. At the restoration site (as elsewhere in the valley), planting schemes are at the mercy of the invaders, many of which are alien weeds that can establish themselves given the slightest opportunity. Thistles, Queen Anne's lace, bindweed, and other aggressive invaders are abundant now, only a few short years after the restoration activities were initiated. (Plant invaders and weeds are discussed more fully in Chap. 8.)

Lentic Communities

Standing water (lentic) communities are rare in the Lehigh Valley. Unlike regions to the north, in which glaciation effects left behind the numerous potholes and depressions now filled to form ponds and lakes, the valley has no natural bodies of standing water. The valley's lakes, actually man-made, are more properly called *impoundments*.

Lake Stratification and Zonation

Deep lakes exhibit thermal stratification throughout the year. As surface water is warmed to about 39.2°F, where maximum density occurs, a lighter layer, the *epilimnion*, develops. At about ten to fifteen feet, a narrow layer, the *thermocline*, exhibits a sharp temperature drop. Below is the cold, dark *hypolimnion*. As the epilimnion cools in autumn, the now-heavier surface layer sinks, and the fall turnover occurs. Winter temperatures, in colder climates, bring an insulating layer of ice to deep lakes. Sometimes, sustained bacterial decomposition depletes oxygen levels in the hypolimnion so that a winter "fish kill" may occur. When the ice melts in spring, surface waters again reach maximum density, sink, and the spring turnover follows. Both fall and spring turnovers bring nutrients to the lighted zone from below and appropriate light and temperature conditions permit algal blooms. Further details and typical temperature and dissolved oxygen (D.O.) profiles for deep lakes are noted in Fig. 10.5.

Distinctive biotic assemblages have adapted to these zones. In the littoral region, plants exhibit a well-defined zonation determined by their stature after initial germination. Starting at the moist edge of the lake, plants that start their growth while covered with water soon extend into the air. These plants, the *emergents*, are familiar to many of

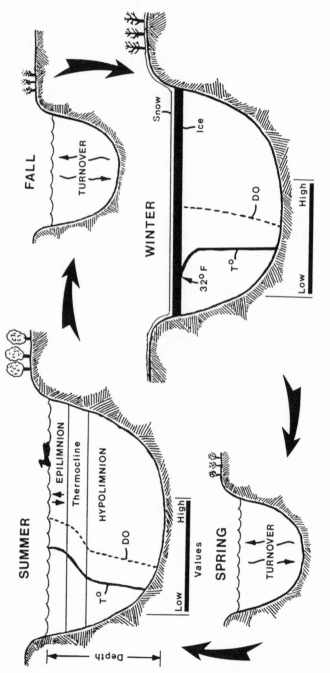

Fig. 10.5 *Lake stratification and zonation*

These temperature (T°) and dissolved oxygen (D.O.) profiles are typical of deeper temperate zone lakes, such as Beltzville, Blue Marsh, Leaser, and Nockamixon. Farm ponds and the like have rapid turnover times, which bring the bottom nutrients up into the water column—often triggering a surge of algal growth (called a "bloom") of pea-soup proportions. (From Oplinger and Halma, *The Poconos* [New Brunswick: Rutgers University Press, 1988]. With permission.)

us. Cattails, bulrushes, bur reeds, sedges, arrowheads, and pickerel-weed, with its showy spikes of purple flowers, are prime examples of emergent plants. Emergents are also found in marshes and wet meadows, interspersed with woody shrubs such as buttonbush and water willow. (Perhaps not surprisingly, these shrubs find lake edges equally suitable habitat, and can generally be viewed here.)

Away from the lake edge, located in water that is generally one to three feet deep, stand plants that are anchored on the mud bottom by extensive roots and thick rhizomes; their leaves, however, float at or on the surface. Spatterdock, water shield, and water lilies are common examples of floating leaf plants. Beyond this zone (but frequently interspersed with the floating leaf plants), *submergents* become dominant. Submergent plants include several species of pondweeds as well as milfoil, water celery, and bladderwort, many of which have finely dissected leaves and are buoyed by air-filled stems. (Bladderwort is a most unusual plant of the type designated as *insectivorous*. Readers may have seen other insectivorous plants at specialty landscape dealerships that sell Venus flytraps and sundews. Bladderworts have thin, dissected leaves on thin stems. Interspersed with the leaves are tiny swellings, the bladders, which have trapdoors to snare tiny aquatic animals. Bladderwort reveals its presence in midsummer, when tiny flowers extend on thin stalks above the water surface.) Many of these submergent plants are also *dimorphic*—that is, the shape of their leaves depends on whether the leaf is below or above the water.

Found still further away from shore are types of submergent plants that extend only a few inches above the bottom, including waterweed, water nymph, and hornwort. Floating on the surface and scattered among all of these aquatic and semi-aquatic plants is one of the smallest flowering plants in the world, duckweed. Late in the summer, some ponds and lakes are almost covered by a green carpet of plants, each a half-inch oval frond with one or more roots.

The stems and leaves of aquatic plants in the littoral zone are home to even more aquatic life. Attached to the plants are other plants and animals, ranging from tiny to microscopic, termed *periphyton*. The open water is home to *phytoplankton*, microscopic algae, especially types classified as green algae, blue-green algae, and diatoms. These microscopic plants are found throughout the pond or lake, wherever adequate sunlight permits them to engage in photosynthesis. Figure 10.6 depicts some of the aquatic vegetation typical of lentic communities.

Microscopic *zooplankton* also live where phytoplankton dwell. However, zooplankton can and do live in the dark, and some types

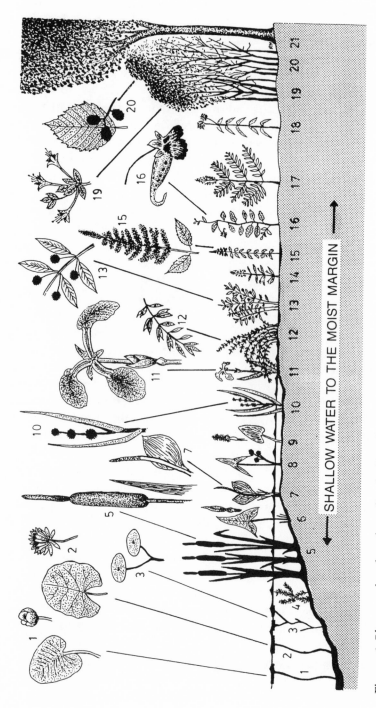

Fig. 10.6 *Plants at the edge of standing bodies of water*

Lake margins, marshes, ponds, sluggish streams, swamps, and floodplains may have a variety of these plants. 1. Spatterdock. 2. White water lily. 3. Water shield. 4. Milfoil. 5. Broad-leaved cattail. 6. Arrow arum. 7. Golden club. 8. Arrowhead. 9. Pickerelweed. 10. Bur reed. 11. Blue flag. 12. Water willow. 13. Buttonbush. 14. Swamp candle. 15. Hardhack. 16. Jewelweed. 17. Royal fern. 18. Swamp milkweed. 19. Swamp azalea. 20. Alder. 21. Red maple. (From Oplinger and Halma, *The Poconos* [New Brunswick: Rutgers University Press, 1988]. With permission.)

engage in daily migrations through the water column, typically moving toward the surface as night falls and returning to lower regions at dawn. Larger animals such as snails may be seen grazing on plant stems, and young fish and amphibians use the tangle of vegetation for refuge and feeding sites. Additional animals live in or on the mud bottom throughout a pond or lake. Some examples of this group of aquatic life, termed *benthos*, are worms of all sorts—round, flat, and segmented—and wormlike insect larvae, tiny clams, and snails.

Two animals often warrant a call to a local college "expert" for identification. Jellyfish, familiar to seashore visitors, are not exclusively marine. Almost every summer, someone finds small jellyfish in a pond or quarry swimming hole. They are only about a half-inch wide across the typical half-dome bell, but they do have the distinctive array of tentacles around the rim and move in the pulsating fashion of all jellyfish. The other attention-getting animal is a grapefruit-sized (or even larger) "ball of jelly" attached to a submerged branch or other support. This is an encrusting colony of tiny hydra-like critters, only a quarter-inch long, called *zoids;* they belong to a primitive type of animal called a *bryozoan* (moss animal). Like jellyfish, bryozoans are abundant in marine habitats, but this freshwater representative does catch the eye of a pond or lake visitor.

To complete this overview of lentic community zonation, the active swimmers should be noted. These, the *nekton*, are most evident to visitors. Active insects such as whirligig beetles, water striders, and other less active invertebrates (such as snails and crayfish) may be seen. An array of fish, amphibians, reptiles, birds, and mammals are lake and pond dwellers. Some representatives of this large group of vertebrate animals are highlighted in other sections of this chapter and in other chapters.

Minsi Lake

Minsi Lake was created in 1975 by the Pennsylvania Fish and Boat Commission and leased to Northampton County. This 117-acre impoundment has seven miles of blazed hiking trails through varied habitats. One trail encircles the lake and provides visitors with an opportunity to observe lake edge plants and animals. By midsummer, several stands of cattails are probably the most conspicuous plants. Both broad-leaved and narrow-leaved arrowhead plants (with prominent white flowers and seed balls on the stalk, as well as the appropriately named leaves) are readily identified. Bur reed, with linear, one-inch-wide leaves and distinctive green or brown seed balls, is also easy to see. Pickerelweed's showy violet-blue flowers are in evidence here as well. Various types of smartweeds, with tiny white-to-pink flowers on a spike, are visible to the careful observer. Much harder to identify are the abundant grasslike plants; some of these are true grasses, but others are various species of sedges and rushes.

The largest turtle that would be encountered at Minsi Lake, or in most aquatic settings in our valley, is the snapping turtle. These reptiles may grow to reach a foot and a half in length and weigh up to forty-five pounds. Captive animals in zoos exceed seventy-five pounds. This animal is easy to recognize: it boasts a massive head, powerful jaws ending in a hook, an upper shell (carapace) that is tan to dark brown with three rows of ridges over the top and a prominent saw-toothed posterior border, and a tail as long as the shell. If a "snapper" is approached on land, it will usually rise up on its hindquarters and open its mouth, emitting a loud hissing sound to ward off the intruder. Unlike many of our aquatic turtles, the snapping turtle does not move out onto rocks or logs to bask in the sun. Most are observed resting in shallow water with just the nostrils and the front of the head above water. Egg laying takes place in early summer, and the female may move some distance from water to a sunny bank where she will dig a cavity six or seven inches into the soil with the use of her hind limbs. Several test cavities may be made before she finally deposits twenty-five to fifty eggs, each about the size and shape of a Ping-Pong ball, into the deep, flask-shaped chamber. She then covers the eggs by scooping soil over them.

As with other turtles and many other types of reptiles, incubation of the developing embryos will require heat from the sun. Depending upon the location and the local weather conditions, nine to sixteen weeks may be required for the young to complete their development. Not all of the young will survive this challenging phase of the life cycle. Numerous mammals, including skunks, mink, and (primarily) raccoons, are known to uncover even the most well-hidden nests. Birds—and, perhaps surprisingly, other turtles—have also been reported to feed on snapper eggs. One study suggests that as many as 60–70 percent of all nests are found by animals looking for an easy meal. If leathery, split "Ping-Pong balls" are spotted along an embankment near a stream, pond, or lake, the visitor can rest assured that one clever predator had a grand breakfast or late-night snack. Snapping turtles themselves have hearty appetites and consume a varied diet, one that includes aquatic plants, carrion, invertebrates, fish, frogs, young mice, and ducklings. Although many anglers are not enamored of snappers, the turtles do not take many game fish, birds, or mammals. (Bass, bluegills, crappies, and other game fish are maintaining their populations, and restocking for these species is not required in the lake. Walleye, tiger muskellunge, and several types of trout—brown, brook, and rainbow—are the only species currently stocked by the Fish and Boat Commission.) And in fact, snapping turtles are a highly desirable menu item for many persons who consider the meat a delicacy and who will travel some distance to a restaurant that features "snapper soup."

Leaser Lake

Leaser Lake, in the northwestern corner of Lehigh County, is the other frequently visited lentic environment. This impoundment was built in 1970 and covers 117 acres. Leakage in the dam prompted a drawdown of the water in the early 1990s, and after repairs, the reservoir slowly filled. These recent events mean that there has not been much time to establish a shoreline of semi-aquatic vegetation characteristic of older lentic habitats.

Bluegill, sunfish, yellow perch, largemouth and smallmouth bass, walleye, and channel catfish are among the species stocked. Visitors who stroll along the shallow margins of the lake should easily observe cleared bottom areas, the size of dinner plates, that mark the location of bluegill nests. The male bluegill will usually be seen nearby, ready to chase any intruders away from the developing young that he has been guarding ever since the female deposited the eggs during mating activities.

Much of the lake edge is in grass and open fields. Due to the fairly recent drawdown, only the borders, along a few shallow coves, have a modest number of emergent and submergent aquatic plants. In such coves, visitors will have the best opportunity to view not only plants but also animals. Painted turtles are commonly seen as they sun themselves on a partially submerged log or exposed rock. A green frog (or related animal) might quickly jump into the water upon being approached. A brown water snake might also move away, but in a much more leisurely manner.

One of the more intriguing episodes that may be witnessed during a springtime visit to the shallows of Leaser Lake, or comparable lake settings, is the courtship ritual of the red-spotted newt. This salamander has an unusual three-stage life cycle: the larvae and adults are completely aquatic but, in a variation not seen in most amphibians, the subadult newt (called a red eft at this stage) lives a completely terrestrial life. The adult newt—which remains active throughout the year, even under the cover of ice—can easily be recognized by the row of conspicuous red dots, bordered in black, along the flank. The adults reach three to four inches in size, and their overall color ranges from olive to dark brown. The tail, which is compressed laterally, serves as an effective rudder. In

BOX 10.2

Places to Observe Lentic Communities

MINSI LAKE. This 120-acre lake was formed by damming several small creeks and flooding an adjacent swamp. Lake Minsi may be reached by taking Route 191 north through Bangor and Roseto. About a mile north of Roseto, turn right onto Lake Minsi Road. Cross Fox Gap Road, bear right at the Ts, and pass the archery range. The lake will be seen shortly beyond the range, and the Bear Swamp nature trail is near the range as well. The lake edge trail circles the lake. It is a fine spot for viewing spring and fall migrants on the lake and in the woods.

LEASER LAKE. From Allentown, the lake may be reached by traveling north on Route 309 and turning west onto Route 143. Just before reaching the village of Jacksonville, turn right onto a small blacktop road that heads directly to the lake, which is largely surrounded by open grassy areas. The small cove west of the parking and boat launch area is probably the only suitable site from which to observe a modest assemblage of shallow-water plants and animals.

ONTELAUNEE RESERVOIR. The reservoir for Reading is located west of the city. Take Route 222 to Maiden Creek, where Route 73 crosses Route 222. Turn north on Route 73. The first section of the reservoir is about 1.2 miles from the intersection. Other roads essentially circle the reservoir, and several walking trails head toward the water from parking sites along the roads.

LENTIC COMMUNITIES FARTHER AFIELD. There are three large impoundments north, south, and west of the Lehigh Valley that provide additional

early spring, the male's hind limbs become swollen, and black, horny protuberances appear on the inner thighs and the tips of the toes. The male maneuvers himself in front of the female, waving his tail from side to side and moving his body from side to side in a serpentine fashion. The hind limbs may also swing from side to side. All of these movements are meant to entice the female toward him. If she approaches, he then moves slowly away, releasing a stream of air bubbles from his mouth. As the male continues to move along the lake bottom, the female follows, and she soon nudges the male's *cloaca,* or ventral opening. This stimulates the male to deposit a *spermatophore,* a small conical mass of jelly with a packet of sperm on the tip, onto the bottom. The female proceeds along the path, and as she does so, she uses her cloaca to pick up the sperm

BOX 10.2 (CONTINUED)

opportunities to observe plants and animals typical of quiet water settings: Beltzville Lake, Nockamixon State Park, and Blue Marsh Lake, respectively, are all within easy driving distance of the Lehigh Valley.

BELTZVILLE STATE PARK. At the park, the 950-acre Beltzville Lake—almost six miles in length—was created by damming Pohopoco Creek. To visit the lake, take the Pennsylvania Turnpike to Exit 34. At the exit ramp, go across Route 209, and follow the signs to the park. Some trails run along the lake, and there is an interesting loop trail along both sides of Sawmill Run. Other trails can be found in the woods and along fields.

NOCKAMIXON STATE PARK. Located about four miles east of Quakertown, the 1450-acre Lake Nockamixon was created by damming Tohickon Creek; it offers an opportunity to view waterfowl and other birds. Travel south on Route 309, turn east onto Route 313 and north onto Route 563, which skirts the north edge of the park. Nature trails run along the edge of the lake and stream region, and there are several loop trails through the woods.

BLUE MARSH LAKE. This lake is located on Tulpehocken Creek, about six miles northwest of Reading. Visitors will find nature trails along the lake edge and in the nearby woods. There are several access routes from Route 183. To reach the lake, drive north on Route 183 from Route 222 at Reading, or drive south on Route 183 from the I-78 exit near Strausstown.

packet. (In this manner, internal fertilization is assured; most amphibians rely on external fertilization.) Females lay fertilized eggs singly on the leaves and stems of aquatic plants. The young develop in one to two months, and they spend the next two months feeding on small aquatic invertebrates found on and among the plants along the shallow margins of the pond or lake. The juveniles then leave the water and live in the leaf litter and shallow soil of woodlots; some animals have been found a quarter of a mile away from any significant source of water. During this intermediate stage, the animal is bright red or orange-red and may be seen on the forest floor on rainy days. If handled, the red eft feels dry to the touch, more like a lizard than a typically slippery and moist salamander. This skin modification may enable the salamander to survive the one to three years of terrestrial life that make up the middle stage of its life. During this time on land, the red efts eat a vast array of soil invertebrates, especially mites, springtails, and snails. The transformation to the adult coloration begins at the close of the red eft stage, and the red-spotted newt returns to water to spend the remainder of its life—an active, aquatic animal always on the prowl for food, particularly for immature aquatic insects and tiny zooplankton.

Ontelaunee Reservoir

At the western edge of the Lehigh Valley, in Berks County, the Ontelaunee Reservoir—the impoundment that serves as a reservoir for Reading—provides additional opportunities to see the plants and animals mentioned in connection with Minsi and Leaser Lakes. However, more than any other quiet body of water in the region, Ontelaunee has become a stopover site during the spring migration of snow geese, birds that spend the winter farther south along the Atlantic coast at various wildlife refuges and protected estuary sites. On their way north to their Arctic nesting grounds, these large (twenty-two to thirty inches in length) white birds with distinctive black wing tips are literally "traffic stoppers" wherever they decide to rest and feed during their journey. Snow geese had been rare sights in the Lehigh Valley, but in the past year or two, these showy birds have made the front-page news in the local papers. Flocks numbering several hundred birds have been seen feeding among the cornstalk stubble in fields adjacent to major highways and country roads. At the reservoir, a favorite resting place for snow geese is the area on Route 73 crossed by a bridge, about one mile north of Route 222, near Maiden Creek. Other waterfowl, such as mergansers and several types of ducks, may occasionally be seen in the same area. Fortunate visitors may also glimpse the tundra swan, an even larger (about forty-eight to fifty-five inches in length) and showier bird, all white with a long neck held straight up. Not surprisingly, watercourses of all sorts are favorites with birders and naturalists who wish to have the best opportunity to view a diversity of plants and animals. (See Box 10.2.)

AMPHIBIANS AND REPTILES IN WETLANDS AND WATERCOURSES

Animals belonging to these two classes of vertebrates can be seen in other habitats, but the amateur naturalist will have the best chance of encountering amphibians and reptiles along wetlands and watercourses.

Adding to the specific examples presented in other sections of this chapter, an overview of the Lehigh Valley's "herps" (a term derived from *herpetology*, the scientific study of these animals) follows.

Amphibians

Amphibians, as the name suggests, are adapted for life on land and in water. These vertebrates, to a greater or lesser degree, rely on gas exchange across moist skin to pick up oxygen and release carbon dioxide. Some species have lungs; others, such as lungless salamanders, rely solely on cutaneous gas exchange. Probably the most readily observed amphibians are toads and frogs.

In the valley, even the most casual observer is likely to see the American toad. In fact, this amphibian is more likely to be found in the backyards of homes located some distance from permanent bodies of water. Toads have a drier skin and depend much more on gas exchange via the lungs than do their relatives, the frogs. Toads have rough, warty skin, with enlarged glands located on each side of the neck just above the disk-like tympanum. These glands serve as effective deterrents against any potential predator: a viscous white toxic secretion oozes from the glands at the slightest provocation. The toxins are known to cause nausea, irregular heartbeat, and, in extreme cases, death to the would-be predator. Survivors of such an episode rarely attack a toad a second time.

In early spring, at almost any body of water, the long trill of the male American toad can be heard. Each trill can last for thirty seconds, and the call attracts females to the breeding site. After mating, long strings of jelly-covered eggs can be seen at the site. One-inch black tadpoles hatch in three to twelve days; after about two months as tadpoles, the toads metamorphose and begin their life on land. (Two close relatives, Fowler's toad and the Eastern spadefoot toad, are less abundant in the valley.)

Often considered a harbinger of spring, the spring peeper is one of the first amphibians to come out of its hibernating places beneath the forest litter. The males then travel, sometimes as much as one-half of a mile, to breeding ponds. By mid-March, when air temperatures hover around 55°F, the shrill "peep" of the calling males can be heard at a distance of a half-mile. As the evenings get warmer, choruses may be heard from late afternoon through much of the evening hours. Although easily heard, these tiny tree frogs are challenging to detect visually. Calling

Fig. 10.7 *American toad and leopard frog*
More than any other amphibian, the American toad (l.) is likely to be seen in one's backyard garden. The leopard frog is the most common amphibian, but it is usually found close to water.

males seem to have a ventriloquist's skill and appear to be somewhere other than at their calling site. Adults are about an inch in length and have a distinctive dark-brown *x*-shaped mark in the middle of the back (documented in the scientific name for the species—*Pseudacris crucifer*). More secretive relatives of the spring peeper are the Eastern gray tree frog and the northern cricket frog, both of which are less abundant in the valley.

A major group of amphibians are the members of the genus *Rana*, the true frogs. The largest, the bull frog, has the distinctive low-pitched, loud, "jug-o'-rum" call, which can be heard from a quarter of a mile away. Green, leopard, and pickerel frogs are smaller-sized relatives of the bull frog. All of these frogs have greenish-brown skin with bands, blotches, and spots (ranging from reddish-brown to dark brown or black) scattered over much of the dorsal surface.

One relative deviates from this typical coloration and pattern: the wood frog. This member of the genus has a fairly uniform tan to brown skin color, with only a bit of the darker bands on the hind limbs and even less banding on the fore limbs. The most distinctive marking is a dark brown mask that covers the eye and extends backward to the tympanum. This "Lone Ranger" of the frog world is, along with the spring peeper, one of the earliest amphibians to call, mate, and breed. The call is a wonderful imitation of a duck call, with a series of short, raspy quacks, each lasting about one second. The common name accurately describes the habitat of this frog, which ranges farther from water than any of the other true frogs. It is so well-camouflaged against the dead leaves of the forest floor that it will remain undetected except to the most observant visitor. Tables 10.1 and 10.2 list these amphibians as well as other amphibians and reptiles of our region.

Table 10.1 *Lehigh Valley amphibians*

Amphibians	Preferred Habitat(s)
Eastern spadefoot toad*	Floodplain woods
Fowler's toad*	Floodplain sandy shores, lake shores
American toad	Widespread; woods, meadows, lawns, gardens
Eastern gray tree frog	Woodland ponds, shrub swamps, marshes, wooded swamps
Northern spring peeper	Woodland ponds, shrub swamps, marshes, wet meadows
Northern cricket frog*	Shrub swamps, ponds
Northern leopard frog	Ponds, marshes, wet meadows
Pickerel frog	Widespread; ponds, lakes, stream banks, marshes
Wood frog	Wooded swamps, moist woods
Green frog	Ponds, lakes, stream banks, swamps
Bullfrog	Ponds, lakes, stream banks, marshes
Marbled salamander*	Woodland ponds, swamps, drier slopes
Jefferson salamander*	Woodland ponds, adjacent slopes
Spotted salamander	Woodland ponds, adjacent slopes
Red-spotted newt	Widespread; ponds, lakes, marshes (terrestrial stage: moist woods)
Northern dusky salamander	Brooks, springs, seepage areas, small streams
Eastern red-backed salamander	Upland forests, wooded swamps, gardens, wooded parks
Slimy salamander	Upland forests, wooded swamps, hemlock ravines
Four-toed salamander	Sphagnum bogs, seepage areas, small streams
Northern spring salamander	Springs, brooks, small streams
Northern red salamander	Springs, brooks, small streams
Long-tailed salamander*	Seepage areas, rocky crevices near caves, springs
Northern two-lined salamander	Brooks, seepage areas, moist woods

NOTE: Species marked with an asterisk (*) are rare or uncommon in the Lehigh Valley.

The other major group of amphibians that may be observed in wetlands and along watercourses is salamanders. Several of the representatives most characteristic of seepage areas along springs, brooks, and streams were noted earlier. Some are more likely to be discovered if one turns over rocks and fallen logs in the damper portions of the woods bordering lakes and other quiet bodies of water.

The red-backed salamander is the most common type in such habitats. Some individuals of this species of lungless salamander do have a
broad red dorsal stripe, but sometimes this band is replaced with a light
gray to black color (the so-called leadback phase). In the same habitat,
one might detect a slimy, spotted, or marbled salamander, but these are
generally less common. Spotted and marbled salamanders are members
of a family termed mole salamanders, a well-named group: these animals spend the greater portion of the year underground, and use animal
burrows and other fissures in the soil as dwelling sites. Only in spring—
before, during, and shortly after the breeding period—will they be visible to the average person.

Reptiles

Reptiles ruled the world in the Mesozoic era—the Age of the Dinosaurs.
In the present era, reptiles are minor role players in most regions of the
world; in the entire state of Pennsylvania, only thirty-eight species have
been recorded. In the Lehigh Valley, turtles and snakes are the major
groups represented. In more southern climes, lizards, alligators, and
their relatives would typically be among the representative species, but
in the Commonwealth, only four species of lizards are found. And in
our region, only the rough and scaly northern fence lizard and the five-
lined skink have been occasionally detected by herpetologists.

In addition to the turtles mentioned elsewhere in this chapter, one
common species and one uncommon species are worthy of brief consideration. Though less common now than it was a few years ago, the
Eastern box turtle is still the species most likely to be encountered by
most of us in our outdoor pursuits. The high domed carapace, usually
patterned with a brown or black background featuring orange, yellow,
or olive blotches, assures easy identification. The lower (ventral) surface
has a broad, movable hinge that permits this turtle to close the upper
and lower shells tightly together. Males have bright red eyes, while the
eyes of females are yellowish-brown. They are most likely to be seen
early in the day, when dew is on the vegetation, or after a rain. In the
heat of summer they may retire to swampy regions. Box turtles have
been known to eat earthworms, slugs, strawberries, and mushrooms
that are poisonous to humans.

Numerous box turtles have had numbers or initials carved into their
shells by persons who hope to encounter the same turtles months or
years in the future. But this species has been the focus of some fascinat-

ing (and more scientific) studies as well. John Nichols, a naturalist who worked at the American Museum of Natural History in New York City, studied box turtles at the family home in Long Island in the early decades of this century. This area is now part of Fire Island National Seashore, and a few years ago, one of the park rangers encountered one of the turtles that Nichols had apparently inscribed in 1934. Nichols had marked more than four hundred turtles and kept records of where and when he had found them. These records are now being used by Park Service officials and a volunteer crew who regularly search for box turtles in the areas examined by Nichols. This study and others suggest that box turtles live a long time, perhaps eighty to one hundred years. An equally intriguing nineteen-year study is that of a husband and wife team, Charles and Libbie Schwartz, who studied a subspecies of the Eastern box turtle on their property in Missouri with the help of Labrador retrievers. Over the span of the study, nine different dogs were used to scent, trail, and find turtles. The dogs did this very well and could even locate hibernating turtles. These and related studies have shown that box turtles have home ranges that average twelve to thirteen acres, but in some instances, turtles may spend their entire lives in an area no more than 250 yards in diameter.

Box turtles do not seem to be quite as common in more recent years; increased auto traffic and unscrupulous collectors dealing in the pet trade may factor into their apparent decline. But of all of the turtles that occur in the Lehigh Valley region, the bog turtle is the most threatened with extinction—and was the first turtle to be placed on Pennsylvania's list of endangered species. Indeed, the U.S. Fish and Wildlife Service has recently listed the northern population of the bog turtle as a "threatened species" nationally. Sometimes referred to as the Muhlenberg turtle, this animal is easily identified by the prominent orange or red blotches located on each side of the head. The threat to the well-being of this reptile centers on the particular habitat that it prefers, that is, bogs, marshes, and swamps. Wetland areas are often unappreciated and undervalued here and throughout the nation; frequently, people view them as waste areas that need to be "drained and converted to useful purposes." Various national, state, and local agencies are attempting to prompt the conservation of wetlands, with limited success. The fate of this little turtle (and those of many other animals and plants) hinges on an increased appreciation of wetlands. The areas in which bog turtles live are often small patches of land with little standing water, such as spring-fed fens, sphagnum bogs, marshy meadows, and pastures with slowly-moving shallow ditches of water. Unlike larger wetlands, such

Fig. 10.8 *The Muhlenberg (bog) turtle*
This secretive turtle, three to four inches long, was the first turtle to be placed on the Pennsylvania list of endangered species. Loss of its wetland habitat and earlier pet trade both contributed to its endangered status.

microhabitats are frequently not the focus of protection programs. Yet shifts in the water table caused by nearby housing projects, road construction, or other major land alterations have a drastic impact on such tiny areas. In addition, these smaller wetland patches are slowly invaded by the type of woody plant succession typical of this region, which can make woodlots unsuitable as bog turtle habitat. And as is too often the case, unethical collectors serving the pet trade industry compound the challenges facing the survival of a species—a species that was first described in 1801, based on specimens collected in Lancaster County by the distinguished colonial botanist Gotthilf Heinrich Ernst Muhlenberg and sent to the Swedish taxonomist Linnaeus.

Snakes are perhaps the one group of reptiles that the hiker, backyard explorer, or visitor is happiest *not* encountering. For the most part, snakes have an ill-deserved reputation as dangerous or menacing. To be sure, a few snakes may be potentially dangerous, since they do possess venom that their fangs can inject into prey. Of the three venomous snakes in Pennsylvania, only the northern copperhead is likely to be found in the Lehigh Valley—and as is true of all of Pennsylvania's venomous snakes, copperheads have a well-defined head with a distinct triangular shape. (Nonpoisonous snakes have a head only slightly wider than the neck.) In addition, poisonous snakes have catlike elliptical pupils, while other snakes have round pupils. Finally, a facial pit located between the eye and nostril is present in copperheads and in all other pit vipers, the family to which Pennsylvania's snakes belong.

Copperheads are strikingly colored, with a copper or hazel-brown background interspersed with bold crossbands of reddish-brown. The crossbands are frequently described as resembling flattened hourglasses. The belly is mottled, with white and gray blotches. This feature helps distinguish the rarer copperheads found in the valley from the more commonly collected milk snakes. The milk snake is one of fourteen

Table 10.2 *Lehigh Valley reptiles*

Reptiles	Preferred Habitat(s)
Common snapping turtle	Widespread; all aquatic and semi-aquatic sites
Musk turtle*	Rivers, sluggish streams, ponds, lakes
Spotted turtle*	Shallow lakes, ponds, wet meadows
Wood turtle	Swamps, moist woods, meadows
Bog turtle*	Sphagnum bogs, swamps, wet meadows
Eastern box turtle	Upland woods, meadows
Eastern painted turtle	Ponds, lakes, slow streams
Map turtle*	Rivers, larger streams
Five-lined skink*	Moist woods, woodlots
Northern fence lizard*	Woodland edges, rocky outcrops
Northern red-bellied snake*	Moist woods, cut-over woodlots
Northern brown snake*	Fields, meadows, swamps, vacant lots
Eastern worm snake*	Primarily subterranean in moist woods
Northern water snake	Most aquatic and semi-aquatic sites
Eastern garter snake	Widespread; semi-aquatic to terrestrial sites, near homes
Eastern ribbon snake	Swamps, stream banks, bogs
Eastern hognose snake*	Upland woods, forest edges
Northern ringneck snake	Wooded slopes, banks of roadways
Northern black racer	Swamps, lowland forests, woodlots
Black rat snake	Rocky hillsides in mature woods, barnyards, old fields
Smooth green snake*	Meadows, grassy fields, forest edges
Eastern milk snake	Widespread; semi-aquatic to terrestrial sites, barnyards, near homes
Northern copperhead*	Rocky upland forests, rocky ledges, farm areas
Timber rattlesnake*	Mature upland forests along Blue Mountain

NOTE: Species marked with an asterisk (*) are rare or uncommon in the Lehigh Valley.

species of nonpoisonous snakes in the Lehigh Valley. These harmless (and in fact, quite beneficial) snakes are often killed by persons who believe that they are ridding the world of venomous copperheads. The milk snake does have dorsal coloration that slightly resembles the copperhead pattern, but the belly of the milk snake has a distinctive black and white "checkerboard" pattern.

Of all of the types of snakes found in our region, the Eastern garter snake is far and away *the* snake likely to be seen by anyone who spends even a limited time outdoors. Three yellow-brown or green stripes extend down the back and sides for the full length of the animal, and typically, a double row of spots is seen between the stripes. A close relative, the ribbon snake, has the same three-stripe arrangement as the garter snake; however, the stripes of the ribbon snake are bright yellow, not mixed with brown or green. The ribbon snake prefers more moist habitats than does the garter snake and tends to move away quickly so as to avoid detection.

Sighting a black-colored snake is not an uncommon event for those who spend time around barns, old sheds, garages, and other buildings in suburban and rural regions of the valley. If the snake is large (three feet or longer) and heavy-bodied, one has probably chanced upon the black rat snake, the state's largest snake. Unlike the rounded body common to most snakes, the black rat snake has a shape described as resembling a loaf of bread seen from one end. The other black snake in our area is a somewhat thinner, round-bodied animal, the northern black racer. It too is a shiny black color, but there is usually a small bit of white on the chin and throat which can help distinguish it from the black rat snake.

One other snake deserves brief consideration here, partly due to its unusual behavior. The Eastern hognose snake, attempting to ward off potential predators, will widen its neck to produce a hood-like appearance and follow this with a hissing sound. (Its behavior has given rise to a variety of nicknames for the hognose: puff adder, spreading adder, and hissing adder.) If this maneuver fails to do the trick, the snake may employ another technique; it "plays possum" by rolling over on its back, perhaps even opening its mouth and extending the tongue, in an effort to deceive a would-be attacker. The stout-bodied hognose has a variable color, ranging from yellow, tan, and brown to reddish-brown and gray, and usually has prominent dark black and reddish-brown blotches and spots along the back and sides. A slightly upturned snout explains the common name and also insures easy identification. (Table 10.2 lists the remaining species of snakes and their preferred habitats, and includes comparable information about the other reptiles in our region as well.)

BIRDS

Some of the easiest birding can be done along watercourses and wetlands. Boxes 10.1 and 10.2 list some of the best of these sites in the Lehigh Valley, where birds (and usually at least a few other animals) may be seen with a limited amount of time and effort. In addition, Table

9.1 provides a listing of all of the birds recorded in the valley, with the preferred habitat of each species, and Box 9.1 lists various birding sites in diverse habitats.

ENDANGERED SETTINGS: MARSHES AND SWAMPS

Sadly, marshes and swamps—which bring joy to the heart of the naturalist—are frequently the regions most adversely affected by human activities. Generally, marshes and swamps have an earlier history as lakes, ponds, or other wet areas produced by a meandering stream or river. Over time, soil and moisture conditions determine the pattern of succession that usually follows in these wet areas. In some sites, grasses and related plants dominate, and a marsh is produced. In others, woody plants, trees, and shrubs are evidence of a swamp.

Naturalists adore these sites, which allow a wide array of plants and animals to flourish. Botanists, birders, and those interested in "herps" and mammals all head to marshes and swamps. However, most Lehigh Valley sites available to earlier generations of naturalists have been drained for agricultural, industrial, municipal, or residential use. (In adjoining regions, such as the Poconos, several marshes and swamps were acquired by the state and are open to the public.) At Lake Minsi, in the far northeastern corner of our valley, Bear Swamp now provides the best opportunity to study marsh and swamp biota. But the many landings and nature walk opportunities that are being planned for the 150 miles of the Delaware and Lehigh Canal National and State Heritage Corridor (see Chap. 12) are certain to become popular and accessible watercourse settings for natural history study as well.

As noted in the opening section of this chapter, humanity's links to aquatic settings have had a long evolutionary history. A visit to any of the valley's wetlands or watercourses should be a rewarding and refreshing experience. Wetlands deserve our appreciation—and more crucially, our protection. By protecting them, we will insure that not only we but generations to come will continue to enjoy the diverse plants and animals found in wetlands and watercourses.

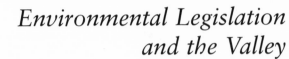

Environmental Legislation
and the Valley

The people have a right to clean air, pure water, and to the
preservation of the natural, scenic, historic and esthetic
values of the environment.

—PENNSYLVANIA CONSTITUTION, ARTICLE 1, SECTION 27

Since its inception as William Penn's colony, the Commonwealth of Pennsylvania has enjoyed an abundance of natural resources. Although the
state constitution itself now addresses the "right" to a clean environment,
anyone alert to the condition of our natural surroundings can attest to
deterioration in many areas of the Commonwealth. This chapter will provide some historical perspective on environmental concerns and issues in
the United States, paying particular attention to the Lehigh Valley.

HISTORICAL ROOTS

Historian Lynn White Jr., who published an essay in *Science* entitled
"The Historical Roots of Our Ecological Crisis" (1967), is often given
credit for introducing the view that the Judeo-Christian religion brought

with it a particular way of interacting with nature. He argued that Western society's relationship to nature is one of exploitation, and that this exploitation arose from a philosophy based on a special understanding of man's dominant position in the existing order. It is certainly the case that as Christianity spread throughout the civilized world, Christians applied innovation and technology to make use of environmental resources. By the seventeenth century, western Europe was in the midst of the dramatic cultural shifts brought by the emerging scientific-industrial revolution. Again, historians have argued that some scientists of that time, such as Johannes Kepler and Sir Isaac Newton, were motivated in their endeavors by Judeo-Christian traditions.

The notion of controlling and dominating nature was not only confined to western Europe: it also invaded the shores of North America as Europeans arrived to establish and settle colonies. In little more than a century, the initial settlers and their descendants transformed the lands and waters of the coastal regions of the New World with the techniques, machinery, and devices brought along or newly developed to meet the ongoing challenges of colonial life. (The notion of clever tinkerers still lingers in the phrase "Yankee ingenuity.") Application of the technology coming out of the industrial revolution was put to ready use in the Lehigh Valley, for example, as valley residents began processing the iron ore of the region. Valley initiatives also include the structural I beam, portland cement, the manufacture of the transistor, and many others.

The vision of a world that operated according to basic laws of chemistry and physics was revolutionary thinking, difficult for many people to accept. However, another monumental change in thinking about humanity's place in the scheme of things was to come with Charles Darwin's theory of natural selection. His major work, *The Origin of Species* (1859), replaced a static view of nature with a dynamic, ever-changing view, one that posited a mechanistic process of interaction of organisms with the environment—and his theory of evolution continues to be unsettling for many in today's world.

MANIFEST DESTINY—AND MODERATION

The colonies rapidly grew, and in the early to mid-1800s, a movement termed "Manifest Destiny" took hold: Americans believed that it was their God-given right to continue territorial expansion. Numerous historians have made the claim that railroads were largely responsible for opening the frontier to occupation. Indeed, government-sponsored westward expansion was epitomized by the linking of two railways, the Union Pacific and the Central Pacific, with a "golden spike" placed at Promontory Point, Utah on May 10, 1869. (By that time, the Lehigh Valley had had twenty years of railroads; they extended in spiderweb fashion across the entire valley.) Unfortunately, in the general enthusiasm for "progress," there was considerable myopia about its impact on the environment.

There were a few voices being raised, however, that questioned the frenzied growth and expansion that prevailed in the young nation. Toward the middle of the nineteenth century, Ralph Waldo Emerson and Henry David Thoreau wrote extensively to promote harmony between man and nature through a holistic philosophy diametrically opposed to the notion of Manifest Destiny. And by the close of the nineteenth century, John Muir was perhaps the most ardent proponent for wilderness preservation. His writings were influential in the establishment of Yosemite National Park in 1890 and in the formation of the Sierra Club two years later. (Today, the Lehigh Valley chapter of the Sierra Club actively reminds us of the legacy of John Muir. Other environmental groups inspired by the likes of Emerson, Thoreau, and Muir continue their work as well: the Wildlands Conservancy, for example, has already placed over twenty thousand acres of land into public trust—forever.)

At the beginning of the twentieth century, a new view of nature led to the conservation movement that represented just one phase of the Progressive Era (1900–1920). But environmental concerns were not the prevailing theme of the Roaring Twenties. The automobile era blossomed at this time, and the auto's profound impact on the environment probably could not have been envisioned by early promoters of the new technology. Trucks and automobiles required many natural resources, including iron ore (steel), rubber, gasoline, and lead. Allentown, through the famous Mack Truck (with its bulldog mascot), became the "Truck Capital of the World." Regional firms such as Exide Batteries, Bethlehem Steel, numerous iron ore industries, and others grew with the expanding transportation industry. As the twentieth century continued, little (if any) thought was given to the declining quality of the soil, land, water, and air—a decline that, by century's end, could no longer be ignored.

Franklin Delano Roosevelt's New Deal focused on the many social problems growing out of the economic depression of the 1930s but also paid some attention to environmental dilemmas. Young unemployed men enrolled in the Civilian Conservation Corps carried out projects on public lands and on state and national parks, many of which resulted in

Fig. 11.1 *The Twenties—a contrast*
A. Gifford Pinchot (1865–1946), governor of Pennsylvania, was a strong environmental advocate. In 1898, he was the first appointed director of the newly formed U.S. Forest Service. The Pinchot Institute, in nearby Milford, is a testament to his advocacy.
B. The Roaring Twenties—a period of carefree spirit, optimism, consumption, and environmental negligence.

roads, bridges, and other features that can still be noted today. Lehigh Valley examples include Cedar Beach Park and Jordan Park, in Allentown, and Monocacy Park in Bethlehem.

MOBILIZATION OF THE ENVIRONMENTAL MOVEMENT

During the years of World War II and shortly thereafter, science and technology flourished, but with little concern about potential harm to the environment; in 1947, for instance, the United States produced about 125,000,000 pounds of DDT. Du Pont's advertising slogan, "Better Things for Better Living Through Chemistry," neatly expressed the prevailing

Fig. 11.2 *The Civilian Conservation Corps* The CCC planting seedlings in 1934—and the trees of today.

attitude. After Rachel Carson (herself a Pennsylvania native) published *Silent Spring* (1962), some of the American public began to consider the possible disadvantages of much of the postwar technology—and even then, harsh critics of Carson's views received equal time in the media.

Well-respected scientist Paul Ehrlich, though, joined Carson in voicing the urgent need to renew the environment. His powerful, best-selling book, *The Population Bomb* (1968), was (like *Silent Spring*) widely read against a backdrop of high-profile disasters, such as the infamous case in which the Cuyahoga River, in neighboring Ohio, actually caught fire! In our region, itself a natural air trap, smog and haze presided over the valley, as did the smelly fumes from steel; fishermen bemoaned the sad state of local streams; the shad migration up the Delaware River was blocked at Philadelphia by the low oxygen levels. The public mood was one of broad dissatisfaction with the quality of life. Environmental advocacy groups began to spring up like weeds. The political and legislative types got the message and discovered great legislative opportunities: who could be *against* a healthy environment? The stage was set for the single most important piece of environmental legislation in human history: the National Environmental Policy Act (NEPA) of 1969–70.

The National Environmental Policy Act of 1969–1970

NEPA was a paradigm: a Magna Carta-like federal program, it was designed to manage our whole fragile environment. While other acts preceded it, working in a piecemeal fashion, NEPA addressed the environment as a *national* concern, and thus extended beyond the prior limited management of public lands. It ensured that proposed federal activities would take into account their potential environmental effects, and that the public would be informed of and given participatory opportunities to react to federal proposals. A classic example of NEPA's effectiveness took place in the Lehigh Valley in the 1970s. The U.S. Army Corps of Engineers had proposed to dam the Jordan Creek with the to-be-designated Trexler Dam. The public response, at all levels of environmental resistance, was so great that the project was stopped cold.

Broadly speaking, some of the aims of the NEPA policy were to encourage productive harmony between people and the environment; to act as a trustee of the environment for future generations; and to preserve high-quality environmental places (historic, cultural, and so on). In the Lehigh Valley, some registered places include Hawk Mountain, the Delaware and Lehigh National Heritage Corridor, the King George Inn, the Sun Inn, and many others. The Act also created the Council on Environmental Quality (CEQ), which reports directly to the President on policies, surveys, changes, and other matters of national environmental interest and concern.

THE NEPA AFTERMATH

With every paradigmatic change, there is a follow-up stage, one that reinforces, supports, and challenges the new paradigm. To understand the scope of the new legislative attitude toward the environment, we must examine not only (a) the series of legislative acts meant to "detail" the paradigm—for example, the attempt to legally define the concept of clean air for all citizens (a concept supported by NEPA as well as the Pennsylvania Constitution) and the enactment of subsequent enforcement laws (e.g., the Clean Air Act, which sets quantitative standards for clean air)— but also (b) the public response, history, and backdrop to the legislative process. The review of legislative acts lends itself readily to a tabular format, which lacks the excitement of storytelling but can be convenient for those interested in the significance of a particular law in time and the law's bearing on our natural history. Analyzing the public response, on the other hand, is less well-defined; it requires a more qualitative sense of people's perceptions and reactions to the changing laws. Thus, at this point in the book, we present the legislative acts in Table 11.1 and continue the narrative account of the changes in legal and public arenas in the text.

Table 11.1 *Major environmental legislation, 1950–2000*

Date(s)	Environmental Laws, Statutes, Acts	Purposes, General Remarks	General Impact and Effect on Lehigh Valley Environment
1955	Clean Air Act; numerous amendments in 1963, 1970, 1977, 1990	Revised, tightened up in amendments to 1990; act was to protect against airborne pollutants, including auto exhaust	Particulate matter greatly reduced in Lehigh Valley, partly due to the smaller number of operating cement plants (from 23 to 5); smog standard violations very high in PA and Lehigh Valley; pre-1977 exempt power plants and air from Ohio River Valley blamed
1959	PA Act 787, Air Pollution Control Act		
1956	Water Pollution Control Act; renamed Clean Water Act in 1977	Grants for water treatment plants, initially; defined discharges, point sources, and water quality	Improvements, additions for water treatment plants; water quality improved
1961	PA Act 268, Delaware River Basin Compact	Management of water basin, flood control, use allocation, and the like; creation of Delaware River Basin Commission (DRBC)	Improved this key watershed, of which the Lehigh River sub-basin is an important part
1964	PA Act 8, Project 70: Land Acquisition and Borrowing Act	Preservation of open space, land conservation, reclamation of mined lands	Land preservation
1967	PA Act 442, Preserving Land for Open Air Space		
1968	PA Act 443, Project 500		
1966	Endangered Species Act; several reauthorizations over the years, but some recent resistance in Congress	Habitat preservation and rare species protection (habitat loss is the primary cause of extinction)	Bald eagle, osprey restored to the Delaware River; peregrine falcon reintroduction program successful in Allentown and Reading

Table 11.1 (continued) *Major environmental legislation, 1950–2000*

Date(s)	Environmental Laws, Statutes, Acts	Purposes, General Remarks	General Impact and Effect on Lehigh Valley Environment
1968	PA Act 275, creation of the Department of Environmental Resources (DER)	Consolidation of seventeen different pollution/resources groups in PA government	Efficiency increased; pollution management more central
1969–1970	National Environmental Policy Act (NEPA)	Major legislation to manage environmental protection; created Council on Environmental Quality (CEQ) and Environmental Protection Agency (EPA)	Wide, national impact; EPA the responsible agent, involved in all aspects of pollution control in Lehigh Valley
1968 1972 1982	National Wild and Scenic Rivers Act PA 283, Pennsylvania Scenic Rivers Act PA 71, Lehigh River Scenic Rivers Act	Designation of rivers with unique scenic, wild, or recreational values	Parts of the Lehigh and Delaware Rivers designated as scenic
1970	Occupational Safety and Health Act (OSHA)	Designed to promote safe working conditions; new employment-related perspective on "the environment"	Mandatory safety glasses, dust masks, helmets, and other sensible regulations for worker safety; inspections
1972	Noise Control Act	Protection against noise levels that may affect health and welfare	First "Quiet Community Program" in North America located in Allentown; develops model legislation to be used elsewhere
1974 1981 1987	PA Act 319, Clean and Green Program PA Act 43, Agricultural Area Security Law (amended 1992) PA Act 70, Pennsylvania Farmland Preservation Program	Farmland preservation; agricultural security areas; easements	Noteworthy participation by Lehigh and Northampton Counties; Wildlands Conservancy a leader

Table 11.1 (continued) *Major environmental legislation, 1950–2000*

Date(s)	Environmental Laws, Statutes, Acts	Purposes, General Remarks	General Impact and Effect on Lehigh Valley Environment
1976	Resource Conservation and Recovery Act (RCRA)	Derived from 1965 Solid Waste Disposal Act; goals to reduce waste, conserve energy; in 1984, amended by Hazardous and Solid Waste Amendment	"Cradle to grave" tracking system changes handling of hazardous wastes
1976	Toxic Substance Control Act	To protect human health and environment, requires EPA to maintain an inventory of chemicals with unknown/dangerous characteristics	Prevents introduction of such past chemical problems as DDT and the PCBs into the environment
1980	Comprehensive Environmental Response, Compensation, and Liability Act (CERCLA), known as Superfund	To clean up hazardous waste sites and spills; to focus on groundwater contamination problems	Several Lehigh Valley Superfund sites in remediation; many risky dumps and landfills closed
1982	PA Act 170, Wild Resource Conservation Act	Board created to protect endangered plants and animals	Construction and development areas mandate plant and animal checklists from Harrisburg for the protection of species of concern; special auto license plates
1980	PA Act 97, Solid Waste Management Act	To manage, regulate, and dispose of solid waste; plans required by certain population densities	Most municipalities in Lehigh and Northampton included in plan

Table 11.1 (continued) *Major environmental legislation, 1950–2000*

Date(s)	Environmental Laws, Statutes, Acts	Purposes, General Remarks	General Impact and Effect on Lehigh Valley Environment
1980–89	Amendments to Superfund, Clean Air Act, and others	New standards, additional regulations, other initiatives	General fine-tuning and changes in the law to cope with an ever-changing environment
1988	PA Act 101, Municipal Waste Planning, Recycling and Waste Reduction Act	Eventually to recycle 25 percent of waste stream; composting encouraged; elimination of lawn clippings in dumps	Lehigh and Northampton establish recycling centers; yard waste returned to consumer as mulch and compost; curbside recycling pickup
1989	PA Act 31, Phosphate Ban Act	To eliminate phosphate in laundry detergents in order to prevent algal blooms, excessive foaming in surface waters	"Foam-head" glasses of affected well water stopped; surface water foaming and blooms halted; water quality improved
1990	PA Act 188, Rails-to-Trails Program	To establish program in which abandoned rail lines and rights-of-way become hiking trails	Wildlands Conservancy and others active in acquiring and promoting rights-of-way in Lehigh Valley; hiking/walking gets a boost
1990	National Environmental Education Act	To establish a nonprofit national environmental education and training foundation; funding of K–12 environmental education programs	Broad-based environmental education expanded; field trip centers in Lehigh Valley note increased participation; school environmental projects get increased press coverage

Table 11.1 (continued) *Major environmental legislation, 1950–2000*

Date(s)	Environmental Laws, Statutes, Acts	Purposes, General Remarks	General Impact and Effect on Lehigh Valley Environment
1993	PA Act 1, designation of each April 22 as Earth Day	Recognition of our environment and our earth as a precious spaceship that mandates our care and stewardship	In Lehigh Valley and elsewhere, often spread over a loosely defined Earth Week in late April
1993	PA Act 40, extension of Industrial Development Program	To provide funding for "brownfields" cleanup; to restore old industrial locations	Development of key areas of deterioration along the Lehigh River in Allentown and Bethlehem
1995	PA Act 4, Abandoned Industrial Sites Environmental Assessment Act		
1999	PA Growing Greener ($646 million plan)	To expand environmental protection, recreation trails, general maintenance, local parks, conservation easements	Important open land to be preserved; Lehigh Valley, under a farmland–urban sprawl strain, to benefit from this "millennium" initiative

Note: Unless otherwise noted, the acts are federal. Many acts were followed by subsequent renewals, amendments, revisions, and so on; Pennsylvania (PA) enacted parallel laws or others for the environment. This is *not* a complete listing. Our emphasis is on the quality of the environment.

Fig. 11.3 *A hiking trail*
Abandoned railroad rights-of-way, now sometimes privately secured and part of
the Rails-to-Trails system, offer a variety of outdoor opportunities—allowing people of all ages and interests to walk, bike, and run. The region boasts a range of
trails, from level canal towpaths to the famously challenging Appalachian Trail.

THE FIRST EARTH DAY AND THE 1970S

The first Earth Day, on April 22, 1970—the brainchild of Senator Gay-
lord Nelson—spotlighted the numerous environmental woes that faced
the nation. Local Lehigh Valley colleges, including Cedar Crest and
Muhlenberg, canceled classes and conducted rallies, demonstrations,
and panel discussions. Nationally known environmentalists, including
Paul Ehrlich and Barry Commoner, presented lectures to large audi-
ences. Most of the colleges in the region had student groups that took
on specific projects, such as stream cleanups or air pollution monitoring. Soon, a League of Concerned Voters was created to track the vot-
ing records and position statements of members of Congress.

Environmental groups expanded their efforts in the 1970s. The
Environmental Defense Fund, for instance, led most environmental battles in the courts. Alternative groups—much less conservative than the
old-style conservation organizations—also took up the environmental
cause. Greenpeace was confrontational in its approach, while Earth
First! resorted to "eco-sabotage" techniques—the most widely publicized being "monkey wrenching." In their efforts to halt timber
clearcutting, for example, they would spike trees with large nails that
could damage the cutting saws or the operators or both.

Even so, the first oil crisis experienced by U.S. citizens in 1973 damp-
ened much of the enthusiasm for environmental concerns, and rollbacks
on environmental standards for air and water quality were quickly
sought by some of the public and their elected officials. The Carter

CAMEO 11.1

Gertrude Fox (1917–1995)

Known as "Mrs. Monocacy" to many local environmentalists, Gertrude Fox was a native of Boston whose first association with the Lehigh Valley was as an industrial biologist and metallurgical investigator at the Bethlehem Steel Corporation. She later taught math at Moravian Preparatory School, Notre Dame High School, and Lehigh County Community College and helped establish innovative methods of environmental education for the Lehigh County School District. She was interested in historical preservation (especially at Burnside Plantation) and in regional planning, and she served as a member of the Planning Commission of Hanover Township. But Gertie Fox was best known for her long-term involvement with the Monocacy Creek Watershed Association.

She highlighted—earlier than many others in the environmental movement—the importance of streamside vegetation to the well-being of aquatic ecosystems. She also assisted volunteers in monitoring water quality, and she readily testified before the U.S. House and Senate Appropriations Committees and the state Department of Environmental Resources on varied environmental issues. Gertie kept close watch on the activities of local industries and developers to insure that waterways would not experience further degradation. Her efforts, along with those of others in the Bethelehem area, started the Monocacy on the road to recovery—to the extent that a section of the waterway won a distinction shared by only a few other Pennsylvania streams: "Trophy Trout Area." In 1987, Northampton County Council named a section along the Monocacy the "Gertrude Fox Conservation Area." In 1990, she was one of seventy-five persons honored by President George Bush with the first Theodore Roosevelt Conservation Award. Gertrude Fox's example demonstrates that an individual, with determination and dedication, can be an effective advocate for the environment.

administration was generally sympathetic to the goals of the environmentalists, but economic woes undermined most of President Carter's attempts to address important environmental issues. Even the creation of a new cabinet department, the Department of Energy, accomplished little in the way of energy conservation and the development of renewable energy sources. At the end of Carter's term, Congress did pass the Comprehensive Environmental Response, Compensation, and Liability Act, better known as Superfund. But *The Global 2000 Report,* a Carter-inspired major interagency publication that outlined major environmental problems, was ignored by President Reagan.

Some earth-watchers have referred to the 1970s as the Legislative Period: the National Environmental Policy Act triggered a number of important legislative acts throughout the decade. Key advocacy groups, such as the Lehigh Valley Sierra Club and SAVE (Saucon Association for a Viable Environment), continued to press for environmental improvement. Interestingly enough, public interest waned somewhat—perhaps due to a sense that the government, having gotten the message, would now fix things up and punish the "bad guys" of heavy industry.

SAGEBRUSH REBELLION AND THE 1980S

Most environmental historians view the 1980s as a time of reversal for environmentalism, a reversal initiated by the "Sagebrush Rebellion." This movement was started in the western United States by those who opposed federal government regulation of public lands. Ronald Reagan cut government regulatory agency budgets, attempted to repeal environmental legislation, and appointed individuals such as James Watt (seen by environmentalists as entirely unsuited to the post) to key environmental agencies. However, two major environmental concerns—global warming and ozone layer depletion—served to refocus the public's attention on the environment, as did the grounding of the *Exxon Valdez* off the coast of Alaska's Prince William Sound on March 24, 1989. This accident resulted in some eleven million gallons of crude oil washing up on the sound's pristine shores; television news coverage featured clips of oil-covered birds and mammals, which heightened the concern of many citizens about technological abuses of modern societies. The growing recognition of acid deposition (popularly called "acid rain") as a major cause of lake failures in the Poconos and elsewhere resulted in the National Acid Precipitation Assessment Program (NAPAP, 1980).

Polling data suggest that although public concern about the environment remained high throughout the 1980s, the issue of job losses versus environmental interests persisted—as it had since the beginning of the conservation movement at the turn of the century.

THE 1990S

Earth Day 1990—the twentieth anniversary of the very first Earth Day—could boast more participation and media coverage than any other celebration since that first one in 1970. Local Lehigh Valley community groups, colleges, and school clubs renewed their past commitment to environmental issues. *Time* magazine, in an unusual departure from its Person of the Year tradition, named the earth the Planet of the Year and designated the 1990s the Decade of the Environment.

Such apparent environmental interest was confirmed by the passage of the National Environmental Education Act (1990), which provided support for school students—from kindergarten all the way through twelfth grade—to become better informed about their environment. Many of our schools have been leaders in environmental education, and field trips to our local natural areas, such as Hawk Mountain, Pool Wildlife Sanctuary, Trexler Game Preserve, and local arboreta, have become a regular feature of school programs. Two other events fueled the initial optimism about the Decade of the Environment as well: in 1992, then-President Bush attended the Earth Summit in Rio de Janeiro, Brazil, and recent Vice-President Al Gore published a pro-environment text called *Earth in the Balance: Ecology and the Human Spirit*. Even with these positive developments, however, pragmatism and legislative opposition prevailed.

Locally, the Superfund seemed to be working, if slowly, in the Novak, Dorneyville, and Palmerton sites that are high on the EPA's priority list for cleanup and restoration. In Northampton County, concern about the use of cement kilns for burning hazardous waste initiated, in the 1990s, the formation of a grassroots organization concerned about the safety of this enterprise. In December of 1997, firefighters spent hours at the hazardous waste fuel site in East Allen Township, near Bath, after a near-explosion forced the evacuation of sixteen hundred people in and around the Keystone Cement Company site. (Seven months after the incident, the Department of Environmental Protection reinstated Keystone's permit after fining the company $488,000 for negligence.) Changes in laboratory procedures and new requirements for independent safety checks have done little to relieve many local citizens of their concern about the merits of burning hazardous waste. However, Pennsylvania is in the vanguard in the identification and environmental cleanup of hazardous waste sites located on military bases. Priority sites include the former Marine Corps Training Center in Freemansburg, Northampton County, and the Birdsboro Army Tank Foundry in Berks County.

Fig. 11.4 *Typical noise barrier along I-78*
While the noise barriers have reduced the sound level by about 50 percent (or ten decibels), they offer about as much visual excitement as a penitentiary wall. Occasional graffiti on the walls—along with litter and unnecessary horn blowing—lowers the environmental quality of life in the Lehigh Valley a notch.

Recycling efforts, in the meantime, have been expanded from urban centers to the surrounding townships. In July 1998, Bethlehem officials estimated that 92 percent of the city's residents had used the voluntary drop-off center on Illick's Mill Road. Allentown may have one of the highest curbside participation rates—90 percent—in the state. Hazardous waste collection sites have been established as well; four counties (Northampton, Lehigh, Schuylkill, and Monroe) have formed a regional collection program for the pickup of household hazardous waste.

Another local environmental event—the opening of I-78—marked the Lehigh Valley during the 1990s, despite the pro-environment opposition (spearheaded by SAVE) to the four-lane bypass south of the valley. More than anything else, the issue reminded the citizenry of the precious commodity of open space. In fact, recent letters to the editor in local newspapers continue to focus on the dual problems of city decay and urban sprawl.

As the 1990s came to a close, Governor Tom Ridge authorized the "Growing Greener" plan, sounding a positive note for the environment. The five-year plan, signed in nearby Chester County, assigns the largest share of its $646 million budget to protecting the environment, dedicating other monies to state park maintenance work, recreational trails, and local parks. It will inject about $100 million into the farmland preservation program to support local conservation easements.

Having provided this overview of the history of environmental legislation and changing attitudes toward our natural resources, the final chapter of our natural history guide now turns to the future of those natural resources in the Lehigh Valley.

TWELVE

Envisioning the Environmental
Future of the Lehigh Valley

In my mind, there is nothing that ties the Lehigh Valley together more effectively than the Lehigh River. Not the highways, not the airport, not the mall. The river's a spiritual thing.

—Tom Kerr, "Lehigh River: The Tie That Binds," 1996

Early on in this book, we sketched the Lehigh Valley's geological and human histories. This, in turn, was followed by descriptions of the valley's climate, flora, fauna, wetlands, and other familiar themes from natural history; we then moved on to the environmental movement and legislation that helped our nation—and the valley—address some environmental dilemmas. How successful has the legislative process been? Have attitudes toward the environment changed in any substantial fashion? Is the Lehigh Valley cleaner and healthier for humans and for other life? And as we pass the thirtieth anniversary of the first Earth Day, what can we predict about the valley's environmental future?

Assessing that future is a daunting task. In our view, the development of the Delaware and Lehigh Navigation Canal National and State Heritage Corridor will be a key factor in any environmental equation—a factor that deserves particular attention here. We believe that many decisions concerning development, zoning, and governmental regulations will relate to the establishment of this corridor that, like the Lehigh River itself, meanders through the center of the Lehigh Valley. We therefore open the chapter with a consideration of the Heritage Corridor and a brief overview of land, water, and air quality in the valley.

Since predicting the valley's environmental future is a risky business, we asked specially qualified individuals to give their forecasts on this topic. We were delighted by their willingness to participate and are gratified by their thoughtful and insightful responses, which we have summarized later in the chapter. We end, finally, with our own predictions, based on our "reading of the landscape."

THE HERITAGE CORRIDOR

Although local groups have worked for several decades to restore sections of the Delaware and Lehigh Canals, the action of the U.S. Congress in 1978 provided the headline news that heightened citizen awareness of the corridor: in that year, the Delaware Canal was declared a National Historic Landmark, and sections of the Lehigh Canal were placed on the National Register of Historic Places. Legislation introduced by Rep. Peter H. Kostmayer of Bucks County and Rep. Don Ritter of Northampton County was signed into law by President Ronald Reagan on November 18, 1988. (The law permitted the canal section to be designated a National Heritage Corridor and an affiliated unit of the National Park Service. However, there is little federal government land acquisition. Private, local, and state groups are expected to work together to preserve and revitalize the corridor.) In 1993, Governor Robert P. Casey designated the corridor a State Heritage Park.

The Delaware and Lehigh Navigation Canal National Heritage Corridor (NHC) extends 150 miles between Wilkes-Barre and Bristol, running along the route of the Delaware and Lehigh Canals (and, in the upper reaches of the corridor, sections of the Lehigh & Susquehanna/Central Railroad of New Jersey). The canal is a narrow, shallow waterway, largely parallel to the Lehigh and Delaware Rivers, through which coal, lumber, and other goods were towed in elongated, shallow-draft barges by mules guided by mule tenders who walked with them along the towpath. In several places, the barges were diverted to slack water sections of the rivers. As the canal followed the rivers, occasional elevation changes were accomplished through a system of locks. (See Fig. 12.1.) This historic corridor

Williams
office - 610-261-3850
cell - 610-217-8987

610-248-7953
Nestor

Trail Tender volunteers aid in the
f the trails and trail environment, special
of the trail experience.

xists to organize trail tasks and functions in
hip to plan, direct, control and evaluate trail

vhich need to be addressed in the long-term
e include the following issues.

teer program

ers involved so that the same people are not

for trail promotion: including newsletter
d membership development.

lementation

served as the primary coal transportation system that extended from the anthracite mines of Carbon and Luzerne Counties to the major users of the coal, the Lehigh Valley iron and steel industries. (Consult Chap. 3 for brief descriptions of the formation of the canal and the iron and steel industries.) Additional coal was conveyed via the Delaware Canal to numerous industries and towns established along the ancient Indian trails and colonial stagecoach routes that paralleled the Delaware River.

The development and management of such a historic and diverse complex will be a monumental undertaking. As the late Gerald Bastoni, Executive Director of the Delaware and Lehigh Canal National and State Heritage Corridor, put it, "this project is going to leave a big footprint on all of eastern Pennsylvania for years to come." Major support in 1999, through a PennDOT grant of $2.1 million over six years, continues to aid corridor design and the acquisition of land—including the rails-to-trails programs. Eventually, ten "landings"—where visitors may obtain area information and directions to nearby sites—will be established. To date, landings have been developed in Easton and Jim Thorpe (Mauch Chunk). Multimillion-dollar projects are planned for landings in Allentown and Bethlehem. (Interestingly, the Allentown and Bethlehem sites are *brownfields*. These contaminated areas have been identified by the Environmental Protection Agency as sites that can be cleaned up to levels that will permit specified uses, thus "recycling" sites that otherwise would be left abandoned.) The landings will not only aid visitors in planning their recreational pursuits along the corridor but should also serve to educate citizens about how their activities and lifestyle choices influence the environmental future of all of the valley's human and non-human inhabitants.

Over 80 percent of the navigation system's route is in public ownership, and throughout the corridor, numerous groups are working to restore sections of the towpath as a continuous trail. Municipalities and townships adjacent to the corridor have expressed interest in developing linkages to corridor trails. One good example of such an effort is the Ironton Rails-to-Trails project, in which a section of the Ironton trail links up to the canal towpath. Another proposed project would connect the trail between Northampton and Bath (the Nor-Bath Trail) to trails on the corridor. An extensive trail project is planned to extend from Catasauqua to Lehigh Gorge State Park. Areas such as these will serve as refuges for various plants and animals that might be crowded out of suitable habitat elsewhere in the valley. Habitat fragmentation, a major challenge for many plants and animals, could be partially reduced by the development of corridor trails.

Fig. 12.1 *The Lehigh Canal*
A locktender's house, canal lock, and towpath are pictured. The mules walked the
towpath, pulling the coal-laden barges from the anthracite region to viable markets. (Collections of the Lehigh County Historical Society.)

Other organizations have a different concern: the protection and
restoration of historic structures related to corridor activities. For
instance, the Walnutport Canal Association coordinated the reconstruc-
tion of Lehigh Canal Lock 23, located in front of the previously restored
locktender's house. Money for the project came from state and federal
grants as well as donations from corporations and citizens. Such
endeavors, starting at the grassroots level, are envisioned as the model
for the development of the NHC; indeed, the federal government's
involvement in the development of National Heritage Corridors is similar to its role in the enforcement of environmental regulations. This
kind of involvement emphasizes a bottom-up approach (rather than
issuing dictates from on high) and promotes voluntary compliance with
regulations. Key to the success of the corridor project is the involvement
of many citizens in projects that will benefit the entire community as
well as the wildlife of the region.

An informative account that serves as a guide to the corridor was
published in 1994 under the auspices of the Lehigh River Foundation.
The text, with major contributions and editorial direction provided by

Willis M. Rivinus, contains detailed descriptions of major historic and natural history sites along the entire length of the corridor and should be consulted by readers who want to obtain information and directions to particular sites. (Fig. 12.2 provides an overview of the corridor, highlighting the major sites.) Here, however, we wish to highlight selected portions of the corridor within the Lehigh Valley that will, we believe, serve as nodes for the restoration and preservation of the natural environment. As noted above, we also believe that the presence of this corridor will influence the activities and decision-making processes of local governments, community associations, and environmental activists.

One of these nodes lies just beyond Blue Mountain, the northern border of the valley, but is of such special natural history interest that it is included in this overview. The most natural section of the NHC, designated as Audubon's Lehigh Reach, certainly merits brief consideration. More than ten thousand acres of land of this area are in public ownership. The Wildlands Conservancy and other organizations placed a high priority in having this splendid section of the corridor be accessible to the public. The scenic waterfalls at Lehigh Gorge, a National Natural Landmark, make it a jewel in this tract of land, and it is protected as the Lehigh Gorge State Park. A twenty-six-mile trail on an abandoned right-of-way of the Lehigh & Susquehanna Railroad provides an opportunity for hikers and mountain bikers to experience the region visited by John James Audubon in 1829. (The Audubon Society in that region is also compiling an audiotape with commentary about Audubon's travels, so that visitors to the area can link their journeys to those of Audubon as they admire the same terrain.)

The section designated the Canal Towns Reach includes towns north and south of the Blue Mountain that derived some of their economic viability from canal operations. As noted above, the section of the Lehigh Navigation Canal that runs through Walnutport is one of the better-restored portions, and a towpath along the canal was highlighted as a place to see edge flora and fauna (see Box 8.1). Along the section of the NHC that runs north of Blue Mountain, communities such as Weissport and Parryville have initiated restoration efforts. These examples support our view that corridor presence will promote environmental protection and restoration in the valley.

The next section of the NHC, the Lower Lehigh Valley Reach, runs through the industrial heart of the Lehigh Valley. All three urban centers—Allentown, Bethlehem, and Easton—were intimately linked to the Lehigh Navigation transportation route, first with the canal and shortly thereafter with railroads that paralleled the canal route. Landings are

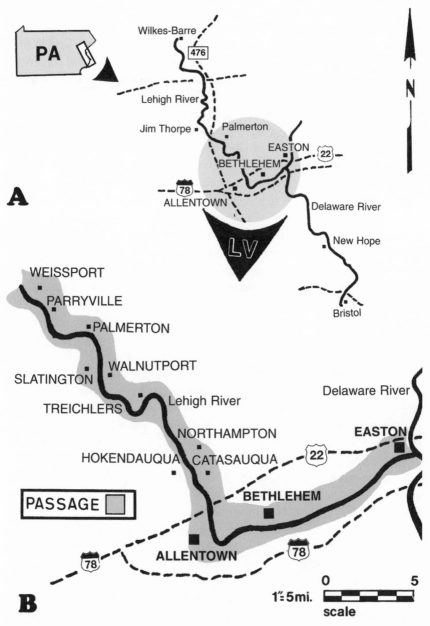

Fig. 12.2 *Delaware and Lehigh National Heritage Corridor*
A. General map of the 150-mile corridor extending between Bristol and Wilkes-
   Barre. The major connectors of the subdivisions, called *passageways,* include
   the rivers, canals, and proximal communities.
B. Detail of the Lehigh Valley. Wider surrounding areas are called *reaches,* and
   include important cultural and natural resources. The short area on the map
   north of Palmerton is in the Appalachians. (After Rivinus 1994, with permission from the Lehigh River Foundation.)

Fig. 12.3 *The good life*
This is the adopted symbol of the Friends of the Delaware Canal, one of many
groups that support the Delaware and Lehigh Navigation Canal National Heritage
Corridor. (With permission from the Friends of the Delaware Canal.)

planned for each of the cities; at the Easton landing, visitor response has
been greater than anyone had imagined. The development of hiking,
auto, and boat routes along this urban section of the corridor is an
excellent example of cooperative efforts by citizen groups and governmental agencies.

Another positive note in the future of the Lehigh Valley is the very
recent (2000) federal move—twenty-two years after the bill was first
proposed—to designate the lower sixty-five miles of the Delaware River
as "wild and scenic." Of those sixty-five miles, a good number fall
between the Delaware Water Gap and Easton. Thus, the whole eastern
boundary of the Lehigh Valley will enjoy this favored status. Lehigh Valley environmentalists and conservationists have joined in to praise the
federal action. The status will prohibit highways, dams, and other fed-
erally funded encroachments on the river. Participating communities
will be asked to subscribe to the goals of high water quality, resource
protection, and open space preservation—thus advancing environmental awareness and concern.

WATER QUALITY IN THE VALLEY

Although we view the Heritage Corridor as pivotal to the environmental well-being of the valley, the quality of life in any region ultimately
depends on clean water, air, and soil. The health of streams is intimately
related to adjoining land use, and various agencies and citizen groups
are devoting time and effort to promote the appropriate use of such
boundaries in the valley. Important park areas need to be expanded

along stream corridors, and several communities are working toward that goal; the proposed Riverside Park on the south bank of the Lehigh River, a joint project of Allentown, Salisbury Township, and Lehigh County, is but one example. The Lehigh River Watershed Initiative of the Wildlands Conservancy hopes to create and maintain a platform for regionally focused, comprehensive watershed education and management in order to protect and improve the watershed's natural systems. Many other exciting projects all along the 150-mile corridor could be cited—but we hope that we have adequately demonstrated that the National Heritage Corridor will serve as the focal point for many of the Lehigh Valley's environmental efforts over the next fifty years.

Support from the state and federal government has enabled the three cities in the valley to upgrade their sewage treatment facilities (although documents from the Lehigh Valley Planning Commission [LVPC] suggest that there is a need for additional treatment capacity). Most of the smaller communities in the region have, to varying degrees, addressed point source pollution within their boundaries. Industries throughout the region have increasingly complied with federal and state regulations, which helps to improve water quality as well. But the cleaner water is largely due to the fact that Pennsylvania has set more stringent regulations than those put in place by the federal government. (That said, there is some worry among environmentalists that these regulations may be modified by the state legislature.) In most areas within the valley's boundaries, non–point source pollution—such as the inappropriate application of lawn fertilizer, poorly sited and functioning septic systems, and the improper disposal of household waste—are now major threats to the continued improvement of water quality. Again, some townships and municipalities have taken measures to address these sources of pollution (or plan to do so in the near future), especially the problem of on-site sewage disposal.

LAND USE ISSUES

Land use issues are clearly crucial to the future environmental well-being of the Lehigh Valley. Numerous groups have directed their efforts toward this issue. The Wildlands Conservancy, for example, took the lead in acquiring vital habitats, especially along the mountain ridges. Many of the Wildlands Conservancy's land purchases in the 1980s and early 1990s went toward the establishment of state game lands or the expansion of existing game lands. More recently, the Conservancy has expanded its efforts, attempting to preserve open space in areas not connected to state game lands. In the two-county region, Conservancy efforts have resulted in the protection of over four thousand acres. Another early example of land preservation efforts in the valley was that made by a consortium of local environmental groups, extensively aided by the Rodale family and others in the Emmaus region, to set aside sizable tracts—such as the Walter tract—along South Mountain as nature preserves. These tracts, combined with Allentown's adjacent parkland, now form almost a square mile of greenbelt along the southern boundary of the valley. Setting aside such tracts will be part of the environmental solution for the valley; Lehigh Valley Planning Commission documents reveal that over a thousand acres of agricultural and vacant land are converted yearly to other uses, and typically, well over three-quarters of those acres go for residential development. In their publications and public statements, LVPC officials contend that combating suburban sprawl will be key to slowing the fragmentation of open space and natural settings (including those discussed in depth in Chap. 8).

In 1997, Governor Tom Ridge launched a project designed to establish Pennsylvania's environmental priorities for the coming century. Forty representatives from diverse organizations engaged in year-long deliberations and debate. Their efforts culminated in a thought-provoking document: the *Report of the Pennsylvania 21st Century Environment Commission*. The *Report* presents a statewide blueprint for the future of the Commonwealth; its basic premise is that a healthy environment is linked to a dynamic economy and community well-being. More than any recent document that we've encountered, this report outlines the manner in which sprawl threatens the natural environment and endangers farming and other activities related to rural life. Depleted groundwater supplies, an increased risk of water pollution, and increased air pollution are also linked to suburban sprawl. A key recommendation of the 21st Century Environment Commission, one supported by the LVPC staff, is that a series of amendments to the Municipalities Planning Code be adopted by the state legislature in order to insure regional planning. If state laws remain unchanged, local officials concerned about these issues point to Lancaster County as a possible model for regional planning, since countywide urban growth boundaries have been established there. Some citizen groups hope that voters in the valley will support bond issues directed toward the purchase of land for park and preserve use, as was done recently in Chester County. And a newly formed environmental group, the Green Valley Coalition, has adopted appropriate land use as

CAMEO   12.1

Charles H. Nehf Sr. (1910–1996)

He may be best known to the Lehigh Valley community as the long-time (56 years!) writer of an outdoor column for the *Morning Call*—a column that frequently focused on one of Charlie's passions, trout fishing—but this dedicated conservationist's most lasting legacy will result from his role in land preservation. He served as the volunteer chairman and driving force of the Land Trust Committee of the Wildlands Conservancy. In that capacity, Charlie garnered support from anglers, hunters, wildlife enthusiasts, and others—so that by the time of his death, he had helped to preserve almost twenty-two thousand acres of wildlife habitat in sixteen counties in eastern Pennsylvania.

Charlie was a native of the region, a graduate of Muhlenberg College, and—for forty years—a teacher of math and science and an administrator in the Allentown school district. He also served as a school board member and as a valued member of the public library board. All who knew and worked with him admired his ability to convince all sorts of people to support a particular project, doing so with good humor and steady determination until the goal was attained. The environmental future of the Lehigh Valley will be in good hands if more of us can follow the path set by this good-natured conservationist.

its primary mission. This group might advance land preservation efforts within the Lehigh Valley by promoting many of the approaches successfully used in nearby counties.

AIR QUALITY IN THE VALLEY

Aside from water and land, the other obvious environmental component is air—and public health issues are easily linked to air quality. We are reminded of such linkages when we hear announcements about ozone levels during weather forecasts. (Such announcements are, of course, much more typical of regions south of the valley in and around the Philadelphia metropolitan area.) High levels of fine particulate matter were common in the air over the Lehigh Valley during the era of the valley's steel, cement, and other heavy industries. With the decline in manufacturing and the abatement procedures instituted by existing firms, particulate pollutants from these sources have diminished dramatically. Now, the increased traffic activity linked to suburban sprawl is a major contributor to fine particulate pollution throughout the valley. Although citizen groups and some public officials have called for improved mass transit and the expansion of rail freight, those calls have not yet been heeded.

Electricity generation is the primary source of air particulate pollution and is a major contributor to smog, acid deposition, global warming, and toxic waste. (Acid deposition, which has sped the decline in environmental health of Pocono lakes and forests, is countered in the lower regions of the valley by the more alkaline limestone conditions.) Currently, one possible approach to the problem of electricity generation is seen in Northampton's cogeneration plant, which is designed to produce marketable steam and electricity from previously unusable coal. Nearby anthracite regions provide the coal, which is presently found as unsightly waste heaps (culm banks). Located on the south side of Route 329 at the eastern edge of the Borough of Northampton, the Northampton Generating Company returns its ash for mine reclamation. In addition, the recently established energy choice program in Pennsylvania has received high marks from environmentalists. It is too early, however, to ascertain whether citizens will be influenced by fuel type and environmental impact when they choose an energy supplier or whether other factors will prevail in the decision-making process.

The related issues of waste handling, abuses in landfill operations, and varied levels of recycling have become important topics in particular towns and cities within the valley. Almost every municipality and township now has a mandatory recycling effort. Programs have been established so that residents in the valley can phone a "hotline" number to arrange for the collection of household hazardous wastes. The long-term maintenance of such programs is always in doubt, however, as continued financial assistance from state and federal agencies remains uncertain. And throughout the Commonwealth, citizens are voicing concern that Pennsylvania is too willing to accept waste from neighboring states. Various community groups have insisted that their elected officials re-examine the issue of waste disposal. All residents surely wish to avoid the dilemmas and the decade-long lawsuits that resulted when a Lehigh County landfill located in South Whitehall Township became one of the Superfund sites on the EPA's National Priorities List of the most hazardous and toxic waste sites.

PERSPECTIVES ON THE FUTURE

Two individuals who have been involved with Lehigh Valley environmental matters over the long term have agreed to provide their perspec-
tives on the environmental future of the valley. The statements of
Frederic H. Brock, Assistant Director of the Lehigh Valley Planning
Commission, and Thomas J. Kerr, Executive Director of the Wildlands
Conservancy, warrant the careful attention of those who wish to insure
a healthy sustainable future for both Lehigh Valley citizens and the
plants and animals of our region. (While these guest commentators are
experienced naturalists and are associated with respected organizations,
their essays reflect their own observations, not necessarily those of the
organizations with which they are professionally affiliated.)

The Future of the Lehigh Valley

BY FREDERIC H. BROCK

In 1969 my family moved to the Lehigh Valley so I could take a
position with the Joint Planning Commission (now the Lehigh Valley Planning Commission). One of my responsibilities has been to
monitor land use, population, and housing changes in Lehigh and
Northampton Counties.

I definitely have seen changes in the Lehigh Valley. The population has grown from 469,849 in 1970 to 554,992 in 1997, an
increase of 18.1 percent. During the same period the number of
housing units increased from 156,303 to 225,517, 44.3 percent.
Most of this housing growth took place in the region's townships.

What we are experiencing in the Lehigh Valley is a major redis-
tribution of the population. Between 1970 and 1997, the region's
cities and boroughs lost 12,478 persons. During the same period,
the townships grew by 98,150 persons—nearly 59 percent. I do not
see this pattern changing any time soon.

The result of this housing growth is a loss of farmland and open
space. In 1970 about 70 percent of the Lehigh Valley was in agriculture or vacant land. In 1997, only 55 percent was agricultural or
vacant. Over 37,000 acres, about 58 square miles, have been used
for residential development. Much of this housing growth occurred
on large lots in rural townships. *Classic urban sprawl.*

One positive land use change is the increase in park acreage.
The region's supply of parks and other outdoor recreation space
grew from 20,373 acres in 1970 to 34,096 acres in 1998, an

increase of 67 percent. I believe valley residents will continue to support the purchase of park and open space land.

It is going to be a big challenge to retain farmland. At one time, farming had a major role in the Lehigh Valley. Although the economic importance of agriculture has declined, much of the region remains in farmland. The conversion of some farmland to urban uses is inevitable and necessary. However, many areas are not needed for development and should remain in agriculture. Lehigh County has been successful in acquiring farms under the agricultural conservation easement program. As of September 1998, Lehigh County had purchased agricultural easements for 71 farms with a total of 7,235 acres. That is an impressive start, but the effort must continue well into the twenty-first century if a really significant amount of farmland is to be permanently preserved. I think more should be done in Northampton County, where only 2,792 acres of farmland have been protected. Almost nothing has been done at the township level to protect farmland. Only three townships have strong agricultural zoning.

The Lehigh Valley is a small region—only about 730 square miles. If the current pattern of development continues for a few more decades, we will become much like the counties surrounding Philadelphia. A key to our future will be how we accommodate population growth and economic development and still maintain much of the farmland and open space that are so much a part of our quality of life. Nothing I have seen makes me think that the current patterns of development will change anytime soon.

The Future of Environmental Quality in the Lehigh Valley

BY THOMAS J. KERR

Since important federal legislation regarding our water and air resources was passed in the 1960s and 1970s, the Lehigh Valley area has enjoyed a substantial improvement in its water and air quality. Our streams and rivers no longer suffer the "big-pipe" pollution problems of yesteryear; the now-beautiful Lehigh River is cleaner—and more usable recreationally—than it has been in 170 years. For various reasons, smokestacks billowing sulfurous fumes are becoming only a memory. Flagrant violators of our environmental laws are being snared and brought to justice more vigorously and with more regularity than ever before.

While there certainly are negative things one could—and should—contemplate (abandoned mine drainage, the loss of farmland, wetlands depletion, forest fragmentation, species loss of flora and fauna and their habitat, etc.), one overarching circumstance is nevertheless encouraging: our citizens, corporate and government leaders, and institutional entities are showing an increasingly sophisticated awareness of the state of the environment, man's relationship to it, and his effect upon it. Concerning the environment, there is much less tolerance on all levels for the reckless, the criminal, the sloppy.

Through a holistic, integrated approach to environmental management, some local industry leaders are taking the initiative to go beyond compliance regarding emissions of all types—looking for "cleaner, cheaper, smarter" solutions. Whether it's economics or conscience that drives them—or both—we in the Lehigh Valley are benefiting.

On the other side, progressive government leaders are not finding it easy to change the entrenched "sledgehammer" system of enforcing compliance with environmental regulation. But some are discovering new ways to assure it through a system of monitored self-regulation based on total outcome rather than micro-monitoring. It may sound risky, but the results, so far, are impressive. If the trend continues—and it looks very promising—we in the Lehigh Valley stand to gain substantially, both economically and environmentally, as the coupling of economic and environmental well-being becomes increasingly ingrained. We absolutely can have economic growth in an atmosphere of care and concern for the environment.

On another important front, the Lehigh Valley (along with the rest of Pennsylvania) is struggling with inadequate land-use laws. As one example, government is paradoxically trying to preserve our valuable farmland (through the state/county agricultural easement purchase program) and destroy it (by funding of infrastructure that makes it easier and cheaper to build in a cornfield than in a vacant, inner-city lot). Some municipal leaders, who can't (or won't) look beyond their boundaries to see the broader effects of their decisions, would spiral us down into a quagmire of sprawl. There are others, however, who see more clearly that a broad encouragement of inter-municipal cooperation, coupled with a stronger planning voice granted to our regional planning organizations, would help stanch the flow of inappropriate development. It is certainly too early to tell if this is really a groundswell, but one could be encouraged by the intensity of discussion being advanced by many, including those in the highest levels of government.

Environmentally, we have come a truly great distance in the last thirty years; real conquests have been made. While it's difficult to paint an altogether rosy picture of the future of environmental quality in the Lehigh Valley without some concomitant pessimism, it seems unlikely that we would retreat in any substantial way from these gains. I am encouraged that we seem more thoughtful and concerned than ever before about these issues and that public discourse on these matters is commonplace. Bob Rodale once said that one sure way to engender the growth of plants is to disturb the soil. Just the fact that we are earnestly discussing these issues is reassuring and useful. I believe good is coming out of the turbulence, and will grow.

Our Reading of the Landscape and Our Predictions

Ecologists often speak of "reading the landscape" as a way of getting an overview of the data gathered for a specific research project. Our training—added to several decades of teaching students and guiding research projects in the Lehigh Valley—gives us some perspective on environmental conditions in the valley and a way of "reading the landscape" as we predict the valley's environmental future. (See Table 12.1.)

Both of us, sadly, can point to specific habitats that are no longer available to us for field trips and study sites. Wetland areas and vernal springs are particularly diminished. Road construction and highway improvements have often degraded adjacent streams. Hedgerows in farmlands, shrubby sections of public parks, and low-maintenance roadsides that harbored an array of interesting plants and animals are also greatly diminished in extent and numbers. With more "manicured" farms, parks, and roadsides, there has been a noticeable reduction in biodiversity. As we noted earlier in the book, such conditions also tend to promote the proliferation of a few common species of plants and animals. Matson's Woods, in Louise Moore Park (see Box 6.1 and Chap. 6), is the last remnant of climax old-age forest in the region. To be sure, such losses are perhaps most intensely felt by those of us who engage in the observation and study of plants and animals. However, avid birders have mentioned the reduction in sightings of particular species. We've heard similar comments from others who regularly go afield to observe butterflies, wildflowers, and amphibians and reptiles. We would assess this feature of the landscape as boding ill for the environmental well-being of the valley. The one bright light in this somewhat pessimistic forecast would be the return of shad into the Lehigh River—a potential success story that might serve as a model for efforts in this area. The Easton Fish Passageway, known as the shad ladder, provides this important game fish access from the Delaware River into the Lehigh. The passageway was constructed in 1994, and 87 shad made it through that year. Since then, video cameras have documented increasing numbers of shad moving through the passageway. A record 3,621 shad moved into the Lehigh in 1998. To repeat this kind of success with other creatures will require a dedicated group of individuals devoted to the well-being of a particular species, as anglers and "river watchers" and certain governmental agencies demonstrated in the shad recovery effort.

To be sure, some farmers and rural landowners are re-establishing hedgerows and restoring wetlands on their properties. More knowledgeable citizens continue to urge municipal authorities to reduce maintenance in parks and roadsides, not only to save money but also to promote wildlife habitats. As we noted earlier in this chapter, the greater awareness of changes in land use practices along with the increased activity of citizen groups devoted to this issue should be beneficial in rectifying past abuses. It is our opinion that citizen activists will continue to urge the Commonwealth's legislators to pass laws that will permit more regional planning of zoning regulations. As noted previously in this chapter, numerous local government officials voiced support for the recommendations concerning land use given by the 21st Century Environment Commission. Nevertheless, we believe that the prevailing patterns of suburban sprawl, increased traffic congestion, new malls, and increased human population in the two-county region will continue to diminish wildlife habitats.

As Tom Kerr noted, the coupling of economic and environmental well-being can be achieved. It may be worth noting that the Greek word *oikos,* meaning "house," is the prefix of both *ecology* and *economics.* Our many years of teaching in the Lehigh Valley (and the childhood recollections of one of us [CO] who was born and raised in the area) have allowed us to note the significant improvements in air and water quality over the past two decades. To be sure, some of this improvement has been due to the dramatic reductions in steel and cement production during that same time period. But in other instances, more stringent laws

Table 12.1 *Selected trends in the Lehigh Valley environment*

Characteristics	Before 1970	At 2000	Next Century
General			
"Ecology"	Term weakly recognized or abused	Term recognized and accepted	A working term
Environmental attitude	Ignorance; avoidance; vagueness	Awareness; concern; focus	Continued awareness; through advocacy, awareness level raised to that of economics; complacency seen as risk
Approach to problems	Fragmented; short-term; avoided	Holistic; longer-term; addressed	Informed public recognizes the environmental value system; long-term approach is basic
Growth			
Land use	Classic urban sprawl	Same, mostly housing; suburban tensions rise with "intrusions" into farmlands	Conservation easements and parks grow in importance
City centers	In the classic city cycle—Birth, Growth, Maturation, Decline, Renewal—pains in the latter two	Malls and "edge cities" grow; peripheral cores become more central	Brownfields emerge as vital to cities; demise of A & B Packing and Bethlehem Steel illustrative
Population growth	About 8 percent	Rate of increase declines slightly	Touchy population issue is central; advocacy for zero population growth gains ground; recognition at family level imperative

Table 12.1 (continued) *Selected trends in the Lehigh Valley environment*

Characteristics	Before 1970	At 2000	Next Century
Pollution-related matters			
Environmental regulations	Seen as nuisance, annoyance, costly	Obligatory compliance; voluntary self-regulation rising	Long-term corporate strategies imperative
Air and water quality	Systems strained, inadequate, unhealthy; key legislation after 1970	Substantial improvements through continuing legislation; air quality much better	Legislation continues to improve the quality of the environment
Biodiversity	Of marginal concern; interests mostly qualitative, not necessarily yielding environmental insights	Concern; habitat loss blamed; concept debated in legislatures	Reintroductions of the extirpated osprey, bald eagle, and peregrine falcon signal optimism in the Lehigh Valley
Soil loss	Addressed in a general way	Focus of serious attention; holding basins and new construction barriers become important	Continuing efforts help minimize development effects
Excessive noise	Not addressed	Noise legislation a helpful guide; minor vehicle enforcement	Problematic; quality of life issues in unwanted noise levels parallel those raised by graffiti and litter, for example
Recycling	Nominal	Act 101 makes it mandatory; public readily accepts concept and practice	A continuing and expansive concept; yard waste recycling increases; positive changes

Table 12.1 (continued) *Selected trends in the Lehigh Valley environment*

Characteristics	Before 1970	At 2000	Next Century
Landfills	Weak regulations; water table invasions by nasty chemicals	Several shutdowns; Superfund sites designated	Regulations tightened; groundwater gets equal recognition
Non-point source pollution	Common, from all accounts, via agricultural runoff and the like	Continuing, but mitigated somewhat by mandatory holding basins, barriers	Integrated pest management (IPM) more widespread, reducing chemical dependency
Habitat preservation	Mostly pragmatic, local, limited	Preservation increases, riding on the environmental movement; resistant cores	Optimistic forecasts, through efforts of WC, SAVE, and other groups
Education			
Support organizations	Diffuse, often disorganized; goals unclear; lacking adequate financial support	Wildlands Conservancy emerges as key group in 1973; SAVE and others continue as important focus groups	Elevate the quality of the environment; they deserve support
Planning groups	Joint Planning Commission established in 1961; prior groups short-term or local	JPC (now Lehigh Valley Planning Commission) continuing as excellent catalyst, with guidelines for future	Central to environmental quality; hopefully gaining more power (not relegated to advisory status)
Environmental education	Nothing formal in schools	Environmental education becomes mandatory in schools; in 1999, required for K–12	Should increase to the level of competence required for history, English, and other basics

(and more rigorous monitoring and enforcement of these regulations by governmental agencies) forced individuals and corporations to alter their past practices.

Several local controversies—such as the continuing debate over the merits of hazardous waste burning in Northampton County, the landfill issues in Bethlehem, and others—suggest that not all agree on the proper approach to solving environmental dilemmas. Fortunately, voluntary compliance (based in part on economic considerations) has become a more widespread practice. Recycling efforts, combined with the assistance given to homeowners with the removal of hazardous wastes, have greatly aided in the restoration of cleaner air and water. Special county recycling centers have returned what would otherwise be yard waste (and thus "dumpfill") to consumers as useful mulch products. Educating the public about agricultural runoff, malfunctioning septic systems, urban storm water management, and similar water quality issues has also been useful in revitalizing streams and rivers.

While noise, air, water and other pollutants tend to trigger our immediate attention, we find a common theme in the words of both of our guest writers—a theme also taken up by other environmentalists—that is more sustained, broadly based, and thorny: growth and expanding population. Just as a finite world can only support a finite population, so, too, a finite valley can only support a finite population. To separate the issues of pollution and quality of life from the question of population is to avoid the obvious.

The two elements that comprise growth are *immigration,* over which there is little control unless the issue is debated at the national level, and *family size,* which is a sensitive issue. It should be noted that no fewer than seventeen developed countries have now achieved ZPG (zero population growth), primarily through education. In a seminal paper, "The Tragedy of the Commons" (1969), Garrett Hardin portrays a shared pasture of finite size—the commons—with a growing number of cattle permitted to graze. If unchecked, the result is ruinous. If we consider the "commons" as our air, scenery, water, quietude, space, resource base, and the like, then his analogy suggests a mandatory trend toward zero population growth if we jointly wish to preserve the commons and strive for a high-quality life.

In the context of the Lehigh Valley, we think that a central part of that quality is the natural history of the region—its plants, animals, open space, ecosystems, geology, and all else we identify with our natural environment—and we further advocate conservation for now and for future generations. Aldo Leopold wrote in his classic *A Sand County*

Almanac (1949): "The art of land doctoring is being practiced with vigor, but the science of land health is yet to be born." As we all grow in our understanding of land health, we look forward, with quiet optimism, to a better quality of life—one that unites a compatible economy and a renewed environment.

Nomenclature

Flowering plants and vertebrates mentioned in the text, figures, or tables are included below. Section 1 converts common names to scientific names; Section 2, the reverse. The common names are those generally used in eastern Pennsylvania or in the larger community of naturalists. Synonyms are generally not given. Scientific names (genus and species) are technical and presumably fixed—although they do change with new information and technologies. *Spp.* (the plural of species) is added when common names refer to any one of a number of similar species. Subspecies are not used in our lists, although specialists do recognize some subspecies in the same group (such as in the reptiles and amphibians). The scientific names are based on standard professional reference books.

1 COMMON NAMES TO SCIENTIFIC NAMES

Alder	*Alnus* spp.
Alfalfa	*Medicago sativa*
American beech	*Fagus grandifolia*
American black duck	*Anas rubripes*
American chestnut	*Castanea dentata*
American coot	*Fulica americana*

American crow	*Corvus brachyrhynchos*
American eel	*Anguilla rostrata*
American elm	*Ulmus americana*
American goldfinch	*Carduelis tristis*
American kestrel	*Falco sparverius*
(Sparrow hawk)	
American redstart	*Setophaga ruticilla*
American robin	*Turdus migratorius*
American shad	*Alosa sapidissima*
American toad	*Bufo americanus*
American tree sparrow	*Spizella arborea*
American widgeon	*Mareca americana*
American woodcock	*Philohela minor*
Apple	*Malus pumila*
Arrow arum	*Peltandra virginica*
Arrowhead	*Sagittaria* spp.
Arrowwood	*Viburnum dentatum*
Aspen	*Populus* spp.
Aster	*Aster* spp.
Autumn olive	*Elaeagnus umbellata*
Bald cypress	*Taxodium distichum*
Bald eagle	*Haliaeetus leucocephalus*
Bank swallow	*Riparia riparia*
Barley	*Hordeum vulgare*
Barn owl	*Tyto alba*
Barn swallow	*Hirundo rustica*
Barnyard grass	*Echinochloa crusgalli*
Barred owl	*Strix varia*
Basswood	*Tilia americana*
Bedstraw	*Galium* spp.
Beggar-lice (Tick-trefoil)	*Desmodium* spp.
Beggar-ticks	*Bidens* spp.
Bellwort	*Uvularia* spp.
Belted kingfisher	*Ceryle alcyon*
Bermuda grass	*Cynodon dactylon*
Big brown bat	*Eptesicus fuscus*
Big-toothed aspen	*Populus grandidentata*
Bindweed	*Convolvulus arvensis*
Bird's-foot trefoil	*Lotus corniculatus*
Black-and-white warbler	*Mniotilta varia*
Black bear	*Ursus americanus*

Black-billed cuckoo	*Coccyzus erythropthalmus*
Blackburnian warbler	*Dendroica fusca*
Black-capped chickadee	*Parus atricapillus*
Black cherry	*Prunus serotina*
Black crappie	*Pomoxis nigromaculatus*
Black-eyed Susan	*Rudbeckia serotina*
Black gum	*Nyssa sylvatica*
Black locust	*Robinia pseudoacacia*
Blacknose dace	*Rhinichthys atratulus*
Black oak	*Quercus velutina*
Blackpoll warbler	*Dendroica striata*
Black rat snake	*Elaphe obsoleta*
Black-throated blue warbler	*Dendroica caerulescens*
Black-throated green warbler	*Dendroica virens*
Black walnut	*Juglans nigra*
Bladdernut	*Staphylea trifolia*
Bladderwort	*Utricularia vulgaris*
Bloodroot	*Sanguinaria canadensis*
Blueberry	*Vaccinium* spp.
Blue flag	*Iris versicolor*
Bluegill	*Lepomis macrochirus*
Bluegrass	*Poa pratensis*
Blue-gray gnatcatcher	*Polioptila caerulea*
Blue jay	*Cyanocitta cristata*
Bluet	*Houstonia* spp.
Blue-winged teal	*Anas discors*
Blue-winged warbler	*Vermivora pinus*
Bobcat	*Lynx rufus*
Bobolink	*Dolichonyx oryzivorus*
Bog turtle	*Clemmys muhlenbergii*
Boneset	*Eupatorium perfoliatum*
Boreal redback vole	*Clethrionomys gapperi*
Boston ivy	*Parthenocissus tricuspidata*
Bouncing bet	*Saponaria officinalis*
Box-elder	*Acer negundo*
Bracken (Brake)	*Pteridium aquilinum*
Bradford pear	*Pyrus calleryana* "Bradford"
Broad-leaved cattail	*Typha latifolia*
Broad-winged hawk	*Buteo platypterus*
Brook trout	*Salvelinus fontinalis*
Brown creeper	*Certhia americana*

Brown-headed cowbird	*Molothrus ater*
Brown thrasher	*Toxostoma rufum*
Brown trout	*Salmo trutta*
Buckthorn	*Rhamnus* spp.
Bufflehead	*Bucephala albeola*
Bullfrog	*Rana catesbeiana*
Bullhead	*Ictalurus* spp.
Burdock (common)	*Arctium minus*
Bur reed	*Sparganium* spp.
Bush (Amur) honeysuckle	*Lonicera* spp.
Buttercup	*Ranunculus* spp.
Butterfly weed	*Asclepias tuberosa*
Butter 'n' eggs	*Linaria vulgaris*
Buttonbush	*Cephalanthus occidentalis*
Campion	*Lychnis* spp.
Canada goose	*Branta canadensis*
Canada warbler	*Wilsonia canadensis*
Canada yew	*Taxus canadensis*
Cancerroot	*Conopholis americana*
Cancer-weed	*Salvia lyrata*
Canvasback	*Aythya valisineria*
Cape May warbler	*Dendroica tigrina*
Carolina wren	*Thryothorus ludovicianus*
Catalpa	*Catalpa bignonioides*
Catbrier	*Smilax* spp.
Cattail	*Typha* spp.
Cedar waxwing	*Bombycilla cedrorum*
Cerulean warbler	*Dendroica caerulea*
Channel catfish	*Ictalurus punctatus*
Checkerberry	*Gaultheria procumbens*
Chestnut oak	*Quercus prinus*
Chestnut-sided warbler	*Dendroica pensylvanica*
Chickweed	*Stellaria* spp.
Chicory	*Cichorium intybus*
Chimney swift	*Chaetura pelagica*
Chipping sparrow	*Spizella passerina*
Chokeberry	*Aronia* spp.
Chokecherry	*Prunus virginiana*
Christmas fern	*Polystichum acrostichoides*
Cinquefoil	*Potentilla* spp.
Cliff swallow	*Petrochelidon pyrrhonota*

Climbing bittersweet	*Celastrus scandens*
Closed gentian	*Gentiana clausa*
Clover	*Trifolium* spp.
Club moss	*Lycopodium* spp.
Cocklebur	*Xanthium* spp.
Coltsfoot	*Tussilago farfara*
Columbine	*Aquilegia canadensis*
Common alder	*Alnus serrulata*
Common goldeneye	*Bucephala clangula*
Common grackle	*Quiscalus quiscula*
Common juniper	*Juniperus communis*
Common loon	*Gavia immer*
Common mallow	*Malva neglecta*
Common merganser	*Mergus merganser*
Common nighthawk	*Chordeiles minor*
Common redpoll	*Carduelis flammea*
Common shiner	*Notropis cornutus*
Common snapping turtle	*Chelydra serpentina*
Common snipe	*Gallinago gallinago*
Common yellowthroat	*Geothlypis trichas*
Coneflower	*Rudbeckia* spp.
Cooper's hawk	*Accipiter cooperii*
Corn	*Zea mays*
Corn lily	*Clintonia borealis*
Cottonwood	*Populus deltoides*
Cow vetch	*Vicia cracca*
Cow-wheat	*Melampyrum lineare*
Coyote	*Canis latrans*
Crabgrass	*Digitaria sanguinalis*
Crappie	*Pomoxis* spp.
Creek chub	*Semotilus atromaculatus*
Crocus	*Crocus* spp.
Crown vetch	*Coronilla varia*
Daffodil	*Narcissus* spp.
Dame's rocket (Phlox)	*Hesperis matronalis*
Dandelion	*Taraxacum* spp.
Dangleberry	*Gaylussacia frondosa*
Dark-eyed junco	*Junco hyemalis*
Darter	*Etheostoma* spp.
Daylily	*Hemerocallis fulva*
Deerberry	*Vaccinium stamineum*

Deer mouse	*Peromyscus maniculatus*
Dock	*Rumex* spp.
Dodder	*Cuscata* spp.
Dogwood	*Cornus* spp.
Downy woodpecker	*Picoides pubescens*
Duckweed	*Lemna minor*
Dwarf cornel	*Cornus canadensis*
Dwarf mistletoe	*Arceuthobium pusillum*
Eastern bluebird	*Sialia sialis*
Eastern box turtle	*Terrapene carolina*
Eastern chipmunk	*Tamias striatus*
Eastern cottontail	*Sylvilagus floridanus*
Eastern garter snake	*Thamnophis sirtalis*
Eastern gray squirrel	*Sciurus carolinensis*
Eastern gray treefrog	*Hyla versicolor*
Eastern hognose snake	*Heterodon platyrhinos*
Eastern kingbird	*Tyrannus tyrannus*
Eastern meadowlark	*Sturnella magna*
Eastern milk snake	*Lampropeltis triangulum*
Eastern mole	*Scalopus aquaticus*
Eastern painted turtle	*Chrysemys picta*
Eastern phoebe	*Sayornis phoebe*
Eastern red-backed salamander	*Plethodon cinereus*
Eastern ribbon snake	*Thamnophis sauritus*
Eastern screech owl	*Otus asio*
Eastern spadefoot toad	*Scaphiopus holbrookii*
Eastern wood pewee	*Contopus virens*
Eastern worm snake	*Carphophis amoenus*
Elderberry	*Sambucus canadensis*
Elm	*Ulmus* spp.
Enchanter's nightshade	*Circaea quadrisulcata* var. *canadensis*
English ivy	*Hedera helix*
European buckthorn	*Rhamnus cathartica*
European starling	*Sturnus vulgaris*
Evening grosbeak	*Hesperiphona vespertina*
Evening primrose	*Oenothera biennis*
Fallfish	*Semotilus corporalis*
False (Wild) lily-of-the-valley	*Maianthemum canadense*
False Solomon's seal	*Smilacina racemosa*
Field daisy	*Chrysanthemum leucanthemum*

Field garlic	*Allium* spp.
Field horsetail	*Equisetum arvense*
Field sparrow	*Spizella pusilla*
Fire cherry	*Prunus pensylvanica*
Fireweed	*Erechtites hieracifolia*
Five-lined skink	*Eumeces fasciatus*
Fleabane	*Erigeron* spp.
Flowering dogwood	*Cornus florida*
Fly-poison	*Amianthium muscaetoxicum*
Foamflower	*Tiarella cordifolia*
Forsythia	*Forsythia* spp.
Four-toed salamander	*Hemidactylium scutatum*
Fowler's toad	*Bufo woodhouseii*
Fox grape	*Vitis labrusca*
Fox sparrow	*Passerella iliaca*
Foxtail	*Setaria* spp.
Fringed polygala	*Polygala paucifolia*
Frostweed	*Helianthemum canadense*
Geranium	*Geranium* spp.
Gold thread	*Coptis groenlandica*
Golden club	*Orontium aquaticum*
Golden-crowned kinglet	*Regulus satrapa*
Golden eagle	*Aquila chrysaetos*
Goldenrod	*Solidago* spp.
Grass-of-Parnassus	*Parnassia glauca*
Gray birch	*Betula populifolia*
Gray catbird	*Dumetella carolinensis*
Gray fox	*Urocyon cinereoargenteus*
Great blue heron	*Ardea herodias*
Great crested flycatcher	*Myiarchus crinitus*
Great egret	*Casmerodius albus*
Greater yellowlegs	*Tringa melanoleuca*
Great horned owl	*Bubo virginianus*
Great-Indian-plantain	*Cacalia muhlenbergii*
Great (Rosebay) rhododendron	*Rhododendron maximum*
Green-backed heron	*Butorides striatus*
Green frog	*Rana clamitans*
Green-winged teal	*Anas crecca*
Ground cedar (pine)	*Lycopodium* spp.
Hairy woodpecker	*Picoides villosus*
Hardhack	*Spiraea tomentosa*

Hawkweed	*Hieracium* spp.
Hawthorn	*Crataegus* spp.
Hay-scented fern	*Dennstaedtia punctilobula*
Heal-all	*Prunella vulgaris*
Hemlock	*Tsuga canadensis*
Henbit	*Lamium* spp.
Hepatica	*Hepatica* spp.
Hermit thrush	*Hylocichla guttata*
Herring gull	*Larus argentatus*
Highbush blueberry	*Vaccinium corymbosum*
Hobblebush	*Viburnum alnifolium*
Honeysuckle	*Lonicera* spp.
Hooded merganser	*Lophodytes cucullatus*
Hooded warbler	*Wilsonia citrina*
Hop hornbeam	*Ostrya virginiana*
Hornbeam	*Carpinus caroliniana*
Horned grebe	*Podiceps auritus*
Horned lark	*Eremophila alpestris*
Hornwort	*Ceratophyllum demersum*
Horsebalm	*Collinsonia canadensis*
Horsetail	*Equisetum* spp.
House finch	*Carpodacus mexicanus*
House mouse	*Mus musculus*
House sparrow	*Passer domesticus*
Huckleberry	*Gaylussacia* spp.
Hyacinth	*Hyacinthus* spp.
Indian hemp	*Apocynum* spp.
Indigo bunting	*Passerina cyanea*
Interrupted fern	*Osmunda claytoniana*
Jack-in-the-pulpit	*Arisaema triphyllum*
Japanese barberry	*Berberis thunbergii*
Japanese honeysuckle	*Lonicera japonica*
Japanese knotweed	*Polygonum cuspidatum*
Jefferson salamander	*Ambystoma jeffersonianum*
Jewelweed	*Impatiens capensis*
Joe-pye weed	*Eupatorium* spp.
Killdeer	*Charadrius vociferus*
Knotweed	*Fallopia japonica*
Lady fern	*Athyrium filix-femina*
Lamb's-quarter	*Chenopodium album*
Largemouth bass	*Micropterus salmoides*

Least flycatcher	*Empidonax minimus*
Least sandpiper	*Erolia minutilla*
Least shrew	*Cryptotis parva*
Leatherleaf	*Chamaedaphne calyculata*
Lesser scaup	*Aythya affinis*
Lesser yellowlegs	*Tringa flavipes*
Little brown bat	*Myotis lucifugus*
Long-eared owl	*Asio otus*
Longnose dace	*Rhinichthys cataractae*
Long-tailed salamander	*Eurycea longicauda*
Longtailed weasel	*Mustela frenata*
Longtail shrew	*Sorex dispar*
Lousewort	*Pedicularis lanceolata*
Magnolia warbler	*Dendroica magnolia*
Mallard	*Anas platyrhynchos*
Map turtle	*Graptemys geographica*
Mapleleaf viburnum	*Viburnum acerifolium*
Marbled salamander	*Ambystoma opacum*
Margined madtom	*Noturus insignis*
Marigold	*Tagetes* spp.
Masked shrew	*Sorex cinereus*
Mayapple	*Podophyllum peltatum*
Meadow jumping mouse	*Zapus hudsonius*
Meadow rue	*Thalictrum* spp.
Meadow vole	*Microtus pennsylvanicus*
Meadowsweet	*Spiraea* spp.
Milfoil	*Myriophyllum* spp.
Milkweed	*Asclepias syriaca*
Mink	*Mustela vison*
Mint	*Mentha* spp.
Moccasin flower	*Cypripedium* spp.
Mountain ash	*Sorbus americana*
Mountain azalea	*Rhododendron* spp.
Mountain laurel	*Kalmia latifolia*
Mourning dove	*Zenaida macroura*
Mullein	*Verbascum thapsus*
Multiflora rose	*Rosa multiflora*
Muskellunge	*Esox masquinongy*
Muskrat	*Ondatra zibethica*
Musk turtle	*Sternotherus odoratus*
Mustard	*Brassica* spp.

Mute swan	*Cygnus olor*
Narrow-leaved cattail	*Typha angustifolia*
Narrow-leaved milkweed	*Asclepias* spp.
Nashville warbler	*Vermivora ruficapilla*
Nettle	*Urtica* spp.
Nightshade	*Solanum* spp.
Northern black racer	*Coluber constrictor*
Northern brown snake	*Storeria dekayi*
Northern cardinal	*Cardinalis cardinalis*
Northern copperhead	*Agkistrodon contortrix*
Northern cricket frog	*Acris crepitans*
Northern dusky salamander	*Desmognathus fuscus*
Northern fence lizard	*Sceloporus undulatus*
Northern flicker	*Colaptes auratus*
Northern harrier (Marsh hawk)	*Circus cyaneus*
Northern house wren	*Troglodytes aedon*
Northern leopard frog	*Rana pipiens*
Northern mockingbird	*Mimus polyglottos*
Northern oriole	*Icterus galbula*
Northern parula	*Parula americana*
Northern pintail	*Anas acuta*
Northern red-bellied snake	*Storeria occipitomaculata*
Northern red salamander	*Pseudotriton ruber*
Northern ringneck snake	*Diadophis punctatus*
Northern saw-whet owl	*Aegolius acadicus*
Northern spring peeper	*Pseudacris crucifer*
Northern spring salamander	*Gyrinophilus porphyriticus*
Northern two-lined salamander	*Eurycea bislineata*
Northern water snake	*Nerodia sipedon*
Northern waterthrush	*Seiurus noveboracensis*
Norway maple	*Acer platanoides*
Norway rat	*Rattus norvegicus*
Norway spruce	*Picea abies*
Oats	*Avena sativa*
Opossum	*Didelphis virginiana*
Orchard grass	*Dactylis glomerata*
Orchard oriole	*Icterus spurius*
Oriental bittersweet	*Celastrus orbiculatus*
Osprey	*Pandion haliaetus*
Ovenbird	*Seiurus aurocapillus*
Oxeye daisy	*Chrysanthemum leucanthemum*

Palm warbler	*Dendroica palmarum*
Paper mulberry	*Broussonetia papyrifera*
Partridgeberry	*Mitchella repens*
Peach	*Prunus persica*
Pear	*Pyrus communis*
Pearly everlasting	*Anaphalis margaritacea*
Pectoral sandpiper	*Calidris melanotos*
Peppermint	*Mentha piperita*
Peppergrass	*Lepidium campestre*
Peregrine falcon	*Falco peregrinus*
Perfoliate bellwort	*Uvularia perfoliata*
Periwinkle	*Vinca minor, V. major*
Persimmon	*Diospyros virginiana*
Phlox	*Phlox* spp.
Phragmites reed (Common reed)	*Phragmites communis*
Pickerel	*Esox* spp.
Pickerel frog	*Rana palustris*
Pickerelweed	*Pontederia cordata*
Pied-billed grebe	*Podilymbus podiceps*
Pigweed (Lamb's-quarter)	*Chenopodium album*
Pileated woodpecker	*Dryocopus pileatus*
Pine siskin	*Carduelis pinus*
Pitch pine	*Pinus rigida*
Plantain	*Plantago* spp.
Poison ivy	*Rhus radicans*
Pokeweed	*Phytolacca americana*
Polypody fern	*Polypodium virginianum*
Pondweed	*Potamogeton* spp.
Porcelain-berry	*Ampelopsis brevipedunculata*
Prairie warbler	*Dendroica discolor*
Privet	*Ligustrum* spp.
Pumpkinseed	*Lepomis gibbosus*
Purple cliff-brake fern	*Pellaea atropurpurea*
Purple coneflower	*Echinacea purpurea*
Purple finch	*Carpodacus purpureus*
Purple loosestrife	*Lythrum salicaria*
Purple martin	*Progne subis*
Pussy willow	*Salix discolor*
Quack grass	*Agropyron repens*
Quaking aspen	*Populus tremuloides*
Queen Anne's lace	*Daucus carota*

Raccoon	*Procyon lotor*
Ragweed	*Ambrosia* spp.
Ragwort	*Senecio* spp.
Rainbow trout	*Salmo gairdneri*
Raspberry	*Rubus* spp.
Red-bellied woodpecker	*Centurus carolinus*
Red-breasted nuthatch	*Sitta canadensis*
Red cedar	*Juniperus virginiana*
Red-eyed vireo	*Vireo olivaceus*
Red fox	*Vulpes vulpes*
Red maple	*Acer rubrum*
Red oak	*Quercus rubra*
Red-ozier dogwood	*Cornus stolonifera*
Red-shouldered hawk	*Buteo lineatus*
Red-spotted newt	*Notophthalmus viridescens*
Red squirrel	*Tamiasciurus hudsonicus*
Red-tailed hawk	*Buteo jamaicensis*
Redtop	*Agrostis* spp.
Red-winged blackbird	*Agelaius phoeniceus*
Rice	*Oryza sativa*
Ring-billed gull	*Larus delawarensis*
Ring-necked duck	*Aythya collaris*
Ring-necked pheasant	*Phasianus colchicus*
River birch	*Betula nigra*
Rock bass	*Ambloplites rupestris*
Rock dove	*Columba livia*
Rose-breasted grosbeak	*Pheucticus ludovicianus*
Rose mallow	*Hibiscus* spp.
Rough-legged hawk	*Buteo lagopus*
Rough-winged swallow	*Stelgidopteryx ruficollis*
Royal fern	*Osmunda regalis*
Ruby-crowned kinglet	*Regulus calendula*
Ruby-throated hummingbird	*Archilochus colubris*
Rue anemone	*Anemonella thalictroides*
Ruffed grouse	*Bonasa umbellus*
Rufous-sided towhee	*Pipilo erythrophthalmus*
Rye	*Secale cereale*
Sarsaparilla	*Aralia* spp.
Sassafras	*Sassafras albidum*
Savannah sparrow	*Passerculus sandwichensis*
Saxifrage	*Saxifraga* spp.

Scarlet oak	*Quercus coccinea*
Scarlet tanager	*Piranga olivacea*
Scotch pine	*Pinus sylvestris*
Scrub oak	*Quercus ilicifolia*
Sensitive fern	*Onoclea sensibilis*
Shadbush (Juneberry)	*Amelanchier* spp.
Shagbark hickory	*Carya ovata*
Sharp-shinned hawk	*Accipiter striatus*
Shasta daisy	*Chrysanthemum* spp.
Sheep laurel	*Kalmia angustifolia*
Sheep sorrel	*Rumex acetosella*
Shepherd's purse	*Capsella bursa-pastoris*
Shining clubmoss	*Lycopodium lucidulum*
Shinleaf	*Pyrola* spp.
Short-eared owl	*Asio flammeus*
Short-tailed shrew	*Blarina brevicauda*
Short-tailed weasel	*Mustela erminea*
Showy lady's slipper	*Cypripedium reginae*
Silver maple	*Acer saccharinum*
Skunk cabbage	*Symplocarpus foetidus*
Slimy salamander	*Plethodon glutinosus*
Slippery elm	*Ulmus rubra*
Smallmouth bass	*Micropterus dolomieu*
Smartweed	*Polygonum* spp.
Smooth cliff-brake fern	*Pellaea glabella*
Smooth green snake	*Opheodrys vernalis*
Snowdrop	*Galanthus nivalis*
Snow goose	*Chen caerulescens*
Snowy egret	*Egretta thula*
Solitary sandpiper	*Tringa solitaria*
Solitary vireo	*Vireo solitarius*
Solomon's seal	*Polygonatum* spp.
Song sparrow	*Melospiza melodia*
Sorghum	*Sorghum bicolor*
Sourwood	*Oxydendrum arboreum*
Southern flying squirrel	*Glaucomys volans*
Sow thistle	*Sonchus* spp.
Soybean	*Glycine max*
Spatterdock	*Nuphar* spp.
Speckled alder	*Alnus rugosa*
Spicebush	*Lindera benzoin*

Spirea	*Spiraea* spp.
Spleenwort fern	*Asplenium ruta-muraria*
Spottail shiner	*Notropis hudsonius*
Spotted salamander	*Ambystoma maculatum*
Spotted sandpiper	*Actitis macularia*
Spotted spurge	*Euphorbia* spp.
Spotted turtle	*Clemmys guttata*
Spotted wintergreen	*Chimaphila maculata*
Spreading dogbane	*Apocynum androsaemifolium*
Spring beauty	*Claytonia virginica*
Starflower	*Trientalis borealis*
Star-nosed mole	*Condylura cristata*
Sticktight	*Bidens* spp.
Stiff gentian	*Gentiana quinquefolia*
Stinging nettle	*Urtica* spp.
St. John's-wort	*Hypericum* spp.
Strawberry	*Fragaria* spp.
Striped maple	*Acer pensylvanicum*
Striped skunk	*Mephitis mephitis*
Sugar maple	*Acer saccharum*
Sumac	*Rhus* spp.
Sunfish	*Lepomis* spp.
Sunflower	*Helianthus annuus*
Swainson's thrush	*Catharus ustulatus*
Swamp azalea	*Rhododendron viscosum*
Swamp candle	*Lysimachia terrestris*
Swamp milkweed	*Asclepias incarnata*
Swamp sparrow	*Melospiza georgiana*
Sweet birch	*Betula lenta*
Sweet clover	*Melilotus officinalis*
Sweet fern	*Comptonia peregrina*
Sycamore	*Platanus occidentalis*
Tansy	*Tanacetum vulgare*
Tennessee warbler	*Vermivora peregrina*
Thistle	*Cirsium* spp.
Tick-trefoil (Beggar-lice)	*Desmodium* spp.
Timber rattlesnake	*Crotalus horridus*
Timothy	*Phleum pratense*
Tomato	*Lycopersicon esculentum*
Toothwort	*Dentaria* spp.
Trailing arbutus	*Epigaea repens*

Tree-of-heaven	*Ailanthus altissima*
Tree swallow	*Iridoprocne bicolor*
Trillium	*Trillium* spp.
Trout lily	*Erythronium americanum*
Trumpet honeysuckle	*Lonicera sempervirens*
Tufted titmouse	*Parus bicolor*
Tulip tree	*Liriodendron tulipifera*
Turkey vulture	*Cathartes aura*
Turtlehead	*Chelone glabra*
Veery	*Catharus fuscescens*
Vervain	*Verbena hastata*
Vesper sparrow	*Pooecetes gramineus*
Violet	*Viola* spp.
Viper's bugloss	*Echium vulgare*
Virginia creeper	*Parthenocissus quinquefolia*
Virginia snakeroot	*Aristolochia serpentaria*
Walleye	*Stizostedion vitreum*
Warbling vireo	*Vireo gilvus*
Water celery	*Vallisneria americana*
Water nymph (lily)	*Nymphaea odorata*
Water shield	*Brasenia schreberi*
Waterweed	*Elodea* spp.
Water-willow	*Decodon verticillatus*
Wheat	*Triticum aestivum*
White ash	*Fraxinus americana*
White baneberry	*Actaea pachypoda*
White basswood	*Tilia heterophylla*
White-breasted nuthatch	*Sitta carolinensis*
White crappie	*Pomoxis annularis*
White-crowned sparrow	*Zonotrichia leucophrys*
White-footed mouse	*Peromyscus leucopus*
White oak	*Quercus alba*
White pine	*Pinus strobus*
White potato	*Solanum tuberosum*
White sucker	*Catostomus commersonii*
White-tailed deer	*Odocoileus virginianus*
White-throated sparrow	*Zonotrichia albicollis*
White water lily	*Nymphaea odorata*
Whorled loosestrife	*Lysimachia quadrifolia*
Wild bergamot	*Monarda fistulosa*
Wild celery	*Vallisneria americana*

Wild garlic	*Allium* spp.
Wild ginger	*Asarum canadense*
Wild grape (Summer grape)	*Vitis aestivalis*
Wild lily-of-the-valley	*Maianthemum canadense*
Wild parsnip	*Pastinaca sativa*
Wild strawberry	*Fragaria virginiana*
Wild turkey	*Meleagris gallopavo*
Willow	*Salix* spp.
Willow herb	*Epilobium strictum*
Wilson's warbler	*Wilsonia pusilla*
Wineberry	*Rubus* spp.
Winter grape	*Vitis vulpina*
Wintergreen	*Pyrola* spp.
Winter wren	*Troglodytes troglodytes*
Witch hazel	*Hamamelis virginiana*
Woodchuck	*Marmota monax*
Wood duck	*Aix sponsa*
Wood frog	*Rana sylvatica*
Woodland jumping mouse	*Napaeozapus insignis*
Wood lily	*Lilium philadelphicum*
Wood sorrel	*Oxalis* spp.
Wood thrush	*Hylocichla mustelina*
Wood turtle	*Clemmys insculpta*
Yarrow	*Achillea millefolium*
Yellow-bellied sapsucker	*Sphyrapicus varius*
Yellow-billed cuckoo	*Coccyzus americanus*
Yellow birch	*Betula lutea*
Yellow lady's slipper	*Cypripedium calceolus*
Yellow (Chinquapin) oak	*Quercus muhlenbergii*
Yellow perch	*Perca flavescens*
Yellow rocket	*Barbarea vulgaris*
Yellow-rumped warbler	*Dendroica coronata*
Yellow warbler	*Dendroica petechia*

2 SCIENTIFIC NAMES TO COMMON NAMES

Accipiter cooperii	Cooper's hawk
Accipiter striatus	Sharp-shinned hawk
Acer negundo	Box-elder

Acer pensylvanicum	Striped maple
Acer platanoides	Norway maple
Acer rubrum	Red maple
Acer saccharinum	Silver maple
Acer saccharum	Sugar maple
Achillea millefolium	Yarrow
Acris crepitans	Northern cricket frog
Actaea pachypoda	White baneberry
Actitis macularia	Spotted sandpiper
Aegolius acadicus	Northern saw-whet owl
Agelaius phoeniceus	Red-winged blackbird
Agkistrodon contortrix	Northern copperhead
Agropyron repens	Quack grass
Agrostis spp.	Redtop
Ailanthus altissima	Tree-of-heaven
Aix sponsa	Wood duck
Allium spp.	Field garlic
Allium spp.	Wild garlic
Alnus spp.	Alder
Alnus rugosa	Speckled alder
Alnus serrulata	Common alder
Alosa sapidissima	American shad
Ambloplites rupestris	Rock bass
Ambrosia spp.	Ragweed
Ambystoma jeffersonianum	Jefferson salamander
Ambystoma maculatum	Spotted salamander
Ambystoma opacum	Marbled salamander
Amelanchier spp.	Shadbush (Juneberry)
Amianthium muscaetoxicum	Fly-poison
Ampelopsis brevipedunculata	Porcelain-berry
Anaphalis margaritacea	Pearly everlasting
Anas acuta	Northern pintail
Anas crecca	Green-winged teal
Anas discors	Blue-winged teal
Anas platyrhynchos	Mallard
Anas rubripes	American black duck
Anemonella thalictroides	Rue anemone
Anguilla rostrata	American eel
Apocynum spp.	Indian hemp
Apocynum androsaemifolium	Spreading dogbane
Aquila chrysaetos	Golden eagle

Aquilegia canadensis	Columbine
Aralia spp.	Sarsaparilla
Arceuthobium pusillum	Dwarf mistletoe
Archilochus colubris	Ruby-throated hummingbird
Arctium minus	Burdock (common)
Ardea herodias	Great blue heron
Arisaema triphyllum	Jack-in-the-pulpit
Aristolochia serpentaria	Virginia snakeroot
Aronia spp.	Chokeberry
Asarum canadense	Wild ginger
Asclepias spp.	Narrow-leaved milkweed
Asclepias incarnata	Swamp milkweed
Asclepias syriaca	Milkweed
Asclepias tuberosa	Butterfly weed
Asio flammeus	Short-eared owl
Asio otus	Long-eared owl
Asplenium ruta-muraria	Spleenwort fern
Aster spp.	Aster
Athyrium filix-femina	Lady fern
Avena sativa	Oats
Aythya affinis	Lesser scaup
Aythya collaris	Ring-necked duck
Aythya valisineria	Canvasback
Barbarea vulgaris	Yellow rocket
Berberis thunbergii	Japanese barberry
Betula lenta	Sweet birch
Betula lutea	Yellow birch
Betula nigra	River birch
Betula populifolia	Gray birch
Bidens spp.	Beggar-ticks
Bidens spp.	Sticktight
Blarina brevicauda	Short-tailed shrew
Bombycilla cedrorum	Cedar waxwing
Bonasa umbellus	Ruffed grouse
Branta canadensis	Canada goose
Brasenia schreberi	Water shield
Brassica spp.	Mustard
Broussonetia papyrifera	Paper mulberry
Bubo virginianus	Great horned owl
Bucephala albeola	Bufflehead
Bucephala clangula	Common goldeneye

Bufo americanus	American toad
Bufo woodhousei	Fowler's toad
Buteo jamaicensis	Red-tailed hawk
Buteo lagopus	Rough-legged hawk
Buteo lineatus	Red-shouldered hawk
Buteo platypterus	Broad-winged hawk
Butorides striatus	Green-backed heron
Cacalia muhlenbergii	Great-Indian-plantain
Calidris melanotos	Pectoral sandpiper
Canis latrans	Coyote
Capsella bursa-pastoris	Shepherd's purse
Cardinalis cardinalis	Northern cardinal
Carduelis flammea	Common redpoll
Carduelis pinus	Pine siskin
Carduelis tristis	American goldfinch
Carphophis amoenus	Eastern worm snake
Carpinus caroliniana	Hornbeam
Carpodacus mexicanus	House finch
Carpodacus purpureus	Purple finch
Carya ovata	Shagbark hickory
Casmerodius albus	Great egret
Castanea dentata	American chestnut
Catalpa bignonioides	Catalpa
Cathartes aura	Turkey vulture
Catharus fuscescens	Veery
Catharus ustulatus	Swainson's thrush
Catostomus commersonii	White sucker
Celastrus orbiculatus	Oriental bittersweet
Celastrus scandens	Climbing bittersweet
Centurus carolinus	Red-bellied woodpecker
Cephalanthus occidentalis	Buttonbush
Ceratophyllum demersum	Hornwort
Certhia americana	Brown creeper
Ceryle alcyon	Belted kingfisher
Chaetura pelagica	Chimney swift
Chamaedaphne calyculata	Leatherleaf
Charadrius vociferus	Killdeer
Chelone glabra	Turtlehead
Chelydra serpentina	Common snapping turtle
Chen caerulescens	Snow goose
Chenopodium album	Lamb's-quarter (Pigweed)

Chimaphila maculata	Spotted wintergreen
Chordeiles minor	Common nighthawk
Chrysanthemum spp.	Shasta daisy
Chrysanthemum leucanthemum	Field daisy
Chrysanthemum leucanthemum	Oxeye daisy
Chrysemys picta	Eastern painted turtle
Cichorium intybus	Chicory
Circaea quadrisulcata var. canadensis	Enchanter's nightshade
Circus cyaneus	Northern harrier (Marsh hawk)
Cirsium spp.	Thistle
Claytonia virginica	Spring beauty
Clemmys guttata	Spotted turtle
Clemmys insculpta	Wood turtle
Clemmys muhlenbergii	Bog turtle
Clethrionomys gapperi	Boreal redback vole
Clintonia borealis	Corn lily
Coccyzus americanus	Yellow-billed cuckoo
Coccyzus erythropthalmus	Black-billed cuckoo
Colaptes auratus	Northern flicker
Collinsonia canadensis	Horsebalm
Coluber constrictor	Northern black racer
Columba livia	Rock dove
Comptonia peregrina	Sweet fern
Condylura cristata	Star-nosed mole
Conopholis americana	Cancerroot
Contopus virens	Eastern wood pewee
Convolvulus arvensis	Bindweed
Coptis groenlandica	Gold thread
Cornus spp.	Dogwood
Cornus canadensis	Dwarf cornel
Cornus florida	Flowering dogwood
Cornus stolonifera	Red-ozier dogwood
Coronilla varia	Crown vetch
Corvus brachyrhynchos	American crow
Crataegus spp.	Hawthorn
Crocus spp.	Crocus
Crotalus horridus	Timber rattlesnake
Cryptotis parva	Least shrew
Cuscata spp.	Dodder
Cyanocitta cristata	Blue jay

Cygnus olor	Mute swan
Cynodon dactylon	Bermuda grass
Cypripedium spp.	Moccasin flower
Cypripedium reginae	Showy lady's slipper
Cypripedium calceolus	Yellow lady's slipper
Dactylis glomerata	Orchard grass
Daucus carota	Queen Anne's lace
Decodon verticillatus	Water-willow
Dendroica caerulea	Cerulean warbler
Dendroica caerulescens	Black-throated blue warbler
Dendroica coronata	Yellow-rumped warbler
Dendroica discolor	Prairie warbler
Dendroica fusca	Blackburnian warbler
Dendroica magnolia	Magnolia warbler
Dendroica palmarum	Palm warbler
Dendroica pensylvanica	Chestnut-sided warbler
Dendroica petechia	Yellow warbler
Dendroica striata	Blackpoll warbler
Dendroica tigrina	Cape May warbler
Dendroica virens	Black-throated green warbler
Dennstaedtia punctilobula	Hay-scented fern
Dentaria spp.	Toothwort
Desmodium spp.	Beggar-lice (Tick-trefoil)
Desmognathus fuscus	Northern dusky salamander
Diadophis punctatus	Northern ringneck snake
Didelphis virginiana	Opossum
Digitaria sanguinalis	Crabgrass
Diospyros virginiana	Persimmon
Dolichonyx oryzivorus	Bobolink
Dryocopus pileatus	Pileated woodpecker
Dumetella carolinensis	Gray catbird
Echinacea purpurea	Purple coneflower
Echinochloa crusgalli	Barnyard grass
Echium vulgare	Viper's bugloss
Egretta thula	Snowy egret
Elaeagnus umbellata	Autumn olive
Elaphe obsoleta	Black rat snake
Elodea spp.	Waterweed
Empidonax minimus	Least flycatcher
Epigaea repens	Trailing arbutus
Epilobium strictum	Willow herb

Eptesicus fuscus	Big brown bat
Equisetum spp.	Horsetail
Equisetum arvense	Field horsetail
Erechtites hieracifolia	Fireweed
Eremophila alpestris	Horned lark
Erigeron spp.	Fleabane
Erolia minutilla	Least sandpiper
Erythronium americanum	Trout lily
Esox spp.	Pickerel
Esox masquinongy	Muskellunge
Etheostoma spp.	Darter
Eumeces fasciatus	Five-lined skink
Eupatorium spp.	Joe-pye weed
Eupatorium perfoliatum	Boneset
Euphorbia spp.	Spotted spurge
Eurycea bislineata	Northern two-lined salamander
Eurycea longicauda	Long-tailed salamander
Fagus grandifolia	American beech
Falco peregrinus	Peregrine falcon
Falco sparverius	American kestrel (Sparrow hawk)
Fallopia japonica	Knotweed
Forsythia spp.	Forsythia
Fragaria spp.	Strawberry
Fragaria virginiana	Wild strawberry
Fraxinus americana	White ash
Fulica americana	American coot
Galanthus nivalis	Snowdrop
Galium spp.	Bedstraw
Gallinago gallinago	Common snipe
Gaultheria procumbens	Checkerberry
Gavia immer	Common loon
Gaylussacia spp.	Huckleberry
Gaylussacia frondosa	Dangleberry
Gentiana clausa	Closed gentian
Gentiana quinquefolia	Stiff gentian
Geothlypis trichas	Common yellowthroat
Geranium spp.	Geranium
Glaucomys volans	Southern flying squirrel
Glycine max	Soybean
Graptemys geographica	Map turtle

Gyrinophilus porphyriticus	Northern spring salamander
Haliaeetus leucocephalus	Bald eagle
Hamamelis virginiana	Witch hazel
Hedera helix	English ivy
Helianthemum canadense	Frostweed
Helianthus annuus	Sunflower
Hemerocallis fulva	Daylily
Hemidactylium scutatum	Four-toed salamander
Hepatica spp.	Hepatica
Hesperiphona vespertina	Evening grosbeak
Hesperis matronalis	Dame's rocket (Phlox)
Heterodon platyrhinos	Eastern hognose snake
Hibiscus spp.	Rose mallow
Hieracium spp.	Hawkweed
Hirundo rustica	Barn swallow
Hordeum vulgare	Barley
Houstonia spp.	Bluet
Hyacinthus spp.	Hyacinth
Hyla versicolor	Eastern gray treefrog
Hylocichla guttata	Hermit thrush
Hylocichla mustelina	Wood thrush
Hypericum spp.	St. John's-wort
Ictalurus spp.	Bullhead
Ictalurus punctatus	Channel catfish
Icterus galbula	Northern oriole
Icterus spurius	Orchard oriole
Impatiens capensis	Jewelweed
Iridoprocne bicolor	Tree swallow
Iris versicolor	Blue flag
Juglans nigra	Black walnut
Junco hyemalis	Dark-eyed junco
Juniperus communis	Common juniper
Juniperus virginiana	Red cedar
Kalmia angustifolia	Sheep laurel
Kalmia latifolia	Mountain laurel
Lamium spp.	Henbit
Lampropeltis triangulum	Eastern milk snake
Larus argentatus	Herring gull
Larus delawarensis	Ring-billed gull
Lemna minor	Duckweed
Lepidium campestre	Peppergrass

Lepomis spp.	Sunfish
Lepomis gibbosus	Pumpkinseed
Lepomis macrochirus	Bluegill
Ligustrum spp.	Privet
Lilium philadelphicum	Wood lily
Linaria vulgaris	Butter 'n' eggs
Lindera benzoin	Spicebush
Liriodendron tulipifera	Tulip tree
Lonicera spp.	Bush (Amur) honeysuckle
Lonicera spp.	Honeysuckle
Lonicera japonica	Japanese honeysuckle
Lonicera sempervirens	Trumpet honeysuckle
Lophodytes cucullatus	Hooded merganser
Lotus corniculatus	Bird's-foot trefoil
Lychnis spp.	Campion
Lycopersicum esculentum	Tomato
Lycopodium spp.	Club moss
Lycopodium spp.	Ground cedar (pine)
Lycopodium lucidulum	Shining clubmoss
Lynx rufus	Bobcat
Lysimachia quadrifolia	Whorled loosestrife
Lysimachia terrestris	Swamp candle
Lythrum salicaria	Purple loosestrife
Maianthemum canadense	False (Wild) lily-of-the-valley
Malus pumila	Apple
Malva neglecta	Common mallow
Mareca americana	American widgeon
Marmota monax	Woodchuck
Medicago sativa	Alfalfa
Melampyrum lineare	Cow-wheat
Meleagris gallopavo	Wild turkey
Melilotus officinalis	Sweet clover
Melospiza georgiana	Swamp sparrow
Melospiza melodia	Song sparrow
Mentha spp.	Mint
Mentha piperita	Peppermint
Mephitis mephitis	Striped skunk
Mergus merganser	Common merganser
Micropterus dolomieu	Smallmouth bass
Micropterus salmoides	Largemouth bass
Microtus pennsylvanicus	Meadow vole

Mimus polyglottos	Northern mockingbird
Mitchella repens	Partridgeberry
Mniotilta varia	Black-and-white warbler
Molothrus ater	Brown-headed cowbird
Monarda fistulosa	Wild bergamot
Mus musculus	House mouse
Mustela erminea	Short-tailed weasel
Mustela frenata	Longtailed weasel
Mustela vison	Mink
Myiarchus crinitus	Great crested flycatcher
Myotis lucifugus	Little brown bat
Myriophyllum spp.	Milfoil
Napaeozapus insignis	Woodland jumping mouse
Narcissus spp.	Daffodil
Nerodia sipedon	Northern water snake
Notophthalmus viridescens	Red-spotted newt
Notropis cornutus	Common shiner
Notropis hudsonius	Spottail shiner
Noturus insignis	Margined madtom
Nuphar spp.	Spatterdock
Nymphaea odorata	Water nymph (lily)
Nymphaea odorata	White water lily
Nyssa sylvatica	Black gum
Odocoileus virginianus	White-tailed deer
Oenothera biennis	Evening primrose
Ondatra zibethica	Muskrat
Onoclea sensibilis	Sensitive fern
Opheodrys vernalis	Smooth green snake
Orontium aquaticum	Golden club
Oryza sativa	Rice
Osmunda claytoniana	Interrupted fern
Osmunda regalis	Royal fern
Ostrya virginiana	Hop hornbeam
Otus asio	Eastern screech owl
Oxalis spp.	Wood sorrel
Oxydendrum arboreum	Sourwood
Pandion haliaetus	Osprey
Parnassia glauca	Grass-of-Parnassus
Parthenocissus quinquefolia	Virginia creeper
Parthenocissus tricuspidata	Boston ivy
Parula americana	Northern parula

Parus atricapillus	Black-capped chickadee
Parus bicolor	Tufted titmouse
Passerculus sandwichensis	Savannah sparrow
Passer domesticus	House sparrow
Passerella iliaca	Fox sparrow
Passerina cyanea	Indigo bunting
Pastinaca sativa	Wild parsnip
Pedicularis lanceolata	Lousewort
Pellaea atropurpurea	Purple cliff-brake fern
Pellaea glabella	Smooth cliff-brake fern
Peltandra virginica	Arrow arum
Perca flavescens	Yellow perch
Peromyscus leucopus	White-footed mouse
Peromyscus maniculatus	Deer mouse
Petrochelidon pyrrhonota	Cliff swallow
Phasianus colchicus	Ring-necked pheasant
Pheucticus ludovicianus	Rose-breasted grosbeak
Philohela minor	American woodcock
Phleum pratense	Timothy
Phlox spp.	Phlox
Phragmites communis	Phragmites reed (Common reed)
Phytolacca americana	Pokeweed
Picea abies	Norway spruce
Picoides pubescens	Downy woodpecker
Picoides villosus	Hairy woodpecker
Pinus rigida	Pitch pine
Pinus strobus	White pine
Pinus sylvestris	Scotch pine
Pipilo erythrophthalmus	Rufous-sided towhee
Piranga olivacea	Scarlet tanager
Plantago spp.	Plantain
Platanus occidentalis	Sycamore
Plethodon cinereus	Eastern red-backed salamander
Plethodon glutinosus	Slimy salamander
Poa pratensis	Bluegrass
Podiceps auritus	Horned grebe
Podilymbus podiceps	Pied-billed grebe
Podophyllum peltatum	Mayapple
Polioptila caerulea	Blue-gray gnatcatcher
Polygala paucifolia	Fringed polygala
Polygonatum spp.	Solomon's seal

Polygonum spp.	Smartweed
Polygonum cuspidatum	Japanese knotweed
Polypodium virginianum	Polypody fern
Polystichum acrostichoides	Christmas fern
Pomoxis spp.	Crappie
Pomoxis annularis	White crappie
Pomoxis nigromaculatus	Black crappie
Pontederia cordata	Pickerelweed
Pooecetes gramineus	Vesper sparrow
Populus spp.	Aspen
Populus deltoides	Cottonwood
Populus grandidentata	Big-toothed aspen
Populus tremuloides	Quaking aspen
Potamogeton spp.	Pondweed
Potentilla spp.	Cinquefoil
Procyon lotor	Raccoon
Progne subis	Purple martin
Prunella vulgaris	Heal-all
Prunus pensylvanica	Fire cherry
Prunus persica	Peach
Prunus serotina	Black cherry
Prunus virginiana	Chokecherry
Pseudacris crucifer	Northern spring peeper
Pseudotriton ruber	Northern red salamander
Pteridium aquilinum	Bracken (Brake)
Pyrola spp.	Shinleaf
Pyrola spp.	Wintergreen
Pyrus calleryana "Bradford"	Bradford pear
Pyrus communis	Pear
Quercus alba	White oak
Quercus coccinea	Scarlet oak
Quercus ilicifolia	Scrub oak
Quercus muhlenbergii	Yellow oak
Quercus prinus	Chestnut oak
Quercus rubra	Red oak
Quercus velutina	Black oak
Quiscalus quiscula	Common grackle
Rana catesbeiana	Bullfrog
Rana clamitans	Green frog
Rana palustris	Pickerel frog
Rana pipiens	Northern leopard frog

Rana sylvatica	Wood frog
Ranunculus spp.	Buttercup
Rattus norvegicus	Norway rat
Regulus calendula	Ruby-crowned kinglet
Regulus satrapa	Golden-crowned kinglet
Rhamnus spp.	Buckthorn
Rhamnus cathartica	European buckthorn
Rhinichthys atratulus	Blacknose dace
Rhinichthys cataractae	Longnose dace
Rhododendron spp.	Mountain azalea
Rhododendron maximum	Great (Rosebay) rhododendron
Rhododendron viscosum	Swamp azalea
Rhus spp.	Sumac
Rhus radicans	Poison ivy
Riparia riparia	Bank swallow
Robinia pseudoacacia	Black locust
Rosa multiflora	Multiflora rose
Rubus spp.	Raspberry
Rubus spp.	Wineberry
Rudbeckia spp.	Coneflower
Rudbeckia serotina	Black-eyed Susan
Rumex spp.	Dock
Rumex acetosella	Sheep sorrel
Sagittaria spp.	Arrowhead
Salix spp.	Willow
Salix discolor	Pussy willow
Salmo gairdneri	Rainbow trout
Salmo trutta	Brown trout
Salvelinus fontinalis	Brook trout
Salvia lyrata	Cancer-weed
Sambucus canadensis	Elderberry
Sanguinaria canadensis	Bloodroot
Saponaria officinalis	Bouncing bet
Sassafras albidum	Sassafras
Saxifraga spp.	Saxifrage
Sayornis phoebe	Eastern phoebe
Scalopus aquaticus	Eastern mole
Scaphiopus holbrooki	Eastern spadefoot toad
Sceloporus undulatus	Northern fence lizard
Sciurus carolinensis	Eastern gray squirrel
Secale cereale	Rye

Seiurus aurocapillus	Ovenbird
Seiurus noveboracensis	Northern waterthrush
Semotilus atromaculatus	Creek chub
Semotilus corporalis	Fallfish
Senecio spp.	Ragwort
Setaria spp.	Foxtail
Setophaga ruticilla	American redstart
Sialia sialis	Eastern bluebird
Sitta canadensis	Red-breasted nuthatch
Sitta carolinensis	White-breasted nuthatch
Smilacina racemosa	False Solomon's seal
Smilax spp.	Catbrier
Solanum spp.	Nightshade
Solanum tuberosum	White potato
Solidago spp.	Goldenrod
Sonchus spp.	Sow thistle
Sorbus americana	Mountain ash
Sorex cinereus	Masked shrew
Sorex dispar	Longtail shrew
Sorghum bicolor	Sorghum
Sparganium spp.	Bur reed
Sphyrapicus varius	Yellow-bellied sapsucker
Spiraea spp.	Meadowsweet
Spiraea spp.	Spirea
Spiraea tomentosa	Hardhack
Spizella arborea	American tree sparrow
Spizella passerina	Chipping sparrow
Spizella pusilla	Field sparrow
Staphylea trifolia	Bladdernut
Stelgidopteryx ruficollis	Rough-winged swallow
Stellaria spp.	Chickweed
Sternotherus odoratus	Musk turtle
Stizostedion vitreum	Walleye
Storeria dekayi	Northern brown snake
Storeria occipitomaculata	Northern red-bellied snake
Strix varia	Barred owl
Sturnella magna	Eastern meadowlark
Sturnus vulgaris	European starling
Sylvilagus floridanus	Eastern cottontail
Symplocarpus foetidus	Skunk cabbage
Tagetes spp.	Marigold

Tamiasciurus hudsonicus	Red squirrel
Tamias striatus	Eastern chipmunk
Tanacetum vulgare	Tansy
Taraxacum spp.	Dandelion
Taxodium distichum	Bald cypress
Taxus canadensis	Canada yew
Terrapene carolina	Eastern box turtle
Thalictrum spp.	Meadow rue
Thamnophis sauritus	Eastern ribbon snake
Thamnophis sirtalis	Eastern garter snake
Thryothorus ludovicianus	Carolina wren
Tiarella cordifolia	Foamflower
Tilia americana	Basswood
Tilia heterophylla	White basswood
Toxostoma rufum	Brown thrasher
Trientalis borealis	Starflower
Trifolium spp.	Clover
Trillium spp.	Trillium
Tringa flavipes	Lesser yellowlegs
Tringa melanoleuca	Greater yellowlegs
Tringa solitaria	Solitary sandpiper
Triticum aestivum	Wheat
Troglodytes aedon	Northern house wren
Troglodytes troglodytes	Winter wren
Tsuga canadensis	Hemlock
Turdus migratorius	American robin
Tussilago farfara	Coltsfoot
Typha spp.	Cattail
Typha angustifolia	Narrow-leaved cattail
Typha latifolia	Broad-leaved cattail
Tyrannus tyrannus	Eastern kingbird
Tyto alba	Barn owl
Ulmus spp.	Elm
Ulmus americana	American elm
Ulmus rubra	Slippery elm
Urocyon cinereoargenteus	Gray fox
Ursus americanus	Black bear
Urtica spp.	Nettle
Urtica spp.	Stinging nettle
Utricularia vulgaris	Bladderwort
Uvularia spp.	Bellwort

Uvularia perfoliata	Perfoliate bellwort
Vaccinium spp.	Blueberry
Vaccinium corymbosum	Highbush blueberry
Vaccinium stamineum	Deerberry
Vallisneria americana	Water celery
Vallisneria americana	Wild celery
Verbascum thapsus	Mullein
Verbena hastata	Vervain
Vermivora peregrina	Tennessee warbler
Vermivora pinus	Blue-winged warbler
Vermivora ruficapilla	Nashville warbler
Viburnum acerifolium	Mapleleaf viburnum
Viburnum alnifolium	Hobblebush
Viburnum dentatum	Arrowwood
Vicia cracca	Cow vetch
Vinca minor, V. major	Periwinkle
Viola spp.	Violet
Vireo gilvus	Warbling vireo
Vireo olivaceus	Red-eyed vireo
Vireo solitarius	Solitary vireo
Vitis aestivalis	Wild grape (Summer grape)
Vitis labrusca	Fox grape
Vitis vulpina	Winter grape
Vulpes vulpes	Red fox
Wilsonia canadensis	Canada warbler
Wilsonia citrina	Hooded warbler
Wilsonia pusilla	Wilson's warbler
Xanthium spp.	Cocklebur
Zapus hudsonius	Meadow jumping mouse
Zea mays	Corn
Zenaida macroura	Mourning dove
Zonotrichia albicollis	White-throated sparrow
Zonotrichia leucophrys	White-crowned sparrow

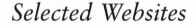

                                        A P P E N D I X   B

Selected Websites

This appendix is divided into two sections. In the first section, websites devoted to the Lehigh Valley are arranged by chapter. The second section offers more general environmental sites. A few words of caution are in order, however: website addresses are case-sensitive (that is, the addresses should be reproduced exactly, with special attention to capitals and lowercase letters), and they may change—or even disappear—without warning.

LEHIGH VALLEY WEBSITES BY CHAPTER

1. *Lehigh Valley Patterns and Places*
Allentown—Bethlehem—Easton: Sister Cities of the Lehigh Valley
http://www.dced.state.pa.us/PA_Exec/DCED/film/e.beth.htm
> A short review of the ABE metropolitan area from the Pennsylvania Film Office. It includes tourist information, some brief historical notes, and a description of weather patterns.

Pennsylvania Heritage Park System
http://www.dcnr.state.pa.us/recreation/heritage/delawareandlehigh.htm
> The Heritage Park System website includes photographs and a brief description of the Delaware and Lehigh Canal Heritage Corridor: "Scenic rivers, historic canals and towns, green mountains and valleys, natural

areas, remnants of early industries, distinctive religious heritage and active cultural arts are waiting as you follow the 150-mile historic route of the Delaware Canal and Lehigh Navigation System stretching from Wilkes-Barre in the northeast to the tidewaters of Bristol in the southeast."

2. The Geological History
Lost River Caverns
http://www.lostcave.com/

A commercial enterprise, the cave—located in Hellertown—is one of Pennsylvania's natural limestone caves. The site has its own Gilman Museum of fossils, minerals, and gems and provides links to the National Speleological Society, the National Caves Association, and the U.S. Geological Survey.

Pennsylvania Topographic and Geologic Survey: Appalachian Mountain Section—Ridge and Valley Province
http://www.dcnr.state.pa.us/topogeo/map13/13ams.htm

The site provides descriptive text along with geological maps of the Appalachian Mountain region.

Pennsylvania Topographic and Geologic Survey: Topographic Maps and Aerial Photographs
http://www.dcnr.state.pa.us/topogeo/topomap.htm

Find geological maps and aerial photographs for the state, download information, or order maps from the U.S. Geological Survey.

Pennsylvania Topographic and Geologic Survey: Directory of Non-Fuel Mineral Producers in Pennsylvania
http://www.dcnr.state.pa.us/topogeo/mineral/intro.htm

Pennsylvania rocks, their products, and more: "The majority of the 695 operations listed in the Directory are sources of construction aggregate, such as crushed stone, sand, and gravel, and borrow-and-fill material. The Directory also includes information on agricultural minerals, dimension stone, high-quality carbonate rocks, topsoil, and many specialized rock products." (Directory information is available in PDF format; printed copies can also be purchased.)

3. Human History in the Lehigh Valley
Pennsylvania Technology Atlas: Lehigh County Profile
http://ltl0.sis.pitt.edu/atlas-98/ctyprofiles/lehighprof.htm

The Pennsylvania Technology Atlas site links to a brief profile of Lehigh County. Statistics relating to county land area, historical and cultural sites, and schools—along with other figures largely geared toward businesses—are presented in tabular form. (The Technology Atlas covers all of the counties of the state, including Northampton and Berks.)

National Canal Museum: Hugh Moore Historical Park and Museums
http://www.canals.org/hmpark.htm
> Information about Hugh Moore Park, the Lehigh Canal, and the history of Easton. Directions to the Park and links to related sites are provided.

4. The Climate of the Valley
The Pennsylvania State Climatologist
http://www.ems.psu.edu/PA_Climatologist/
> The Pennsylvania State Climatologist website originates in the Department of Meteorology at Penn State. Numerous links offer climatic data, hourly observations, daily weather archives, means and extremes, and current weather for the state as a whole as well as for regions and cities—including Allentown.

5. The Natural History of the Seasons
Fall in Pennsylvania: Rails to Trails
http://www.fallin.state.pa.us//hike/hb_rails.html
> The Rails to Trails site describes three rail-trails, including the Lehigh Gorge State Park trail. Information on biking and hiking in the area, fall foliage, driving tours, and bird watching is included. The website features video and photos and requires a QuickTime viewer.

6. Native Vegetation
Wild Resource Conservation Fund
http://www.dcnr.state.pa.us/wrcf/wrcfmain.htm
> Through public financing of its efforts, the WRCF supports research on and protection of Pennsylvania's "natural heritage—[its] unique collection of native nongame animals and wild plants."

The Pennsylvania Department of Conservation and Natural Resources: Plants
http://www.dcnr.state.pa.us/wrcf/plants.htm
> The DCNR website offers information on endangered native plants of Pennsylvania. Data for each plant include identifying characteristics, biology, natural history, habitat, and Pennsylvania locations.

The Rodale Institute
http://www.rodaleinstitute.org/home.html

The Rodale Institute "works with people worldwide to achieve a regenerative food system that renews environmental and human health working with the philosophy that 'Healthy Soil = Healthy Food = Healthy People.®'"

Keystone WILD! Notes
http://www.dcnr.state.pa.us/wrcf/keynotes/wnotessp.htm
The online version of the Wild Resources Conservation Fund's official newsletter offers information about the organization and its ongoing projects.

7. *The Agricultural Lehigh Valley*
Penn State Cooperative Extension and Outreach
http://www.cas.psu.edu/docs/COEXT/
Penn State's Cooperative Extension office provides the citizens of the Commonwealth with access to knowledge that will enhance their lives—knowledge ranging from agriculture, natural and community resources, and nutrition to youth and family development. Follow the links to reach cooperative extension websites for specific counties, such as Lehigh and Northampton.

Penn State Department of Horticulture: Vegetable Newsletters
http://hortweb.cas.psu.edu/vegcrops/newsletterlist.html
The Vegetable Gazette, a monthly publication from the Department of Horticulture, provides extensive coverage of Pennsylvania crops, timely notices about meetings, and contact information for extension agents.

Penn State University College of Agricultural Sciences
http://www.cas.psu.edu
The homepage of the College of Agricultural Sciences allows users to search the CAS website; it also features numerous links to sites related to the varied aspects of agriculture (everything from agronomy and consumer issues to veterinary science).

8. *Fragmented Forests, Edges, and Patches*
Pennsylvania Forestry Association
http://www.cas.psu.edu/docs/casdept/forest/pfa.html
The Pennsylvania Forestry Association homepage presents information about the Association—including a guide to its publications and activities—and links to other sites. The PFA describes itself as "a broad-based

citizens group devoted to good forest management and wise stewardship of the forest resources in the Commonwealth of Pennsylvania among all owners and users of forest land. The Association encourages widespread public support for all forest values including timber, water, wildlife, recreation, aesthetics, and minerals."

Pennsylvania Bureau of Forestry
http://www.dcnr.state.pa.us/forestry/forestry.htm

The homepage of the PBF offers information about state forests, biodiversity, trees, and forest management and usage. It also describes the Pennsylvania Natural Diversity Inventory, a joint effort of the Western Pennsylvania Conservancy, the Pennsylvania Bureau of Forestry, and the Nature Conservancy.

9. Animals of the Lehigh Valley
Game Preserve
http://www.gamepreserve.org

The Game Preserve, located in Schnecksville, was founded by Harry C. Trexler and is now owned by Lehigh County. Its primary mission is to help preserve wildlife and wildlife habitats in as natural a setting as possible.

Hawk Mountain Sanctuary
http://www.hawkmountain.org

The nonprofit organization was established in 1934 to provide a refuge for raptors. Hawk Mountain Sanctuary is a leader in conservation, research, and education efforts involving birds of prey.

Wild Resource Conservation Fund
http://www.dcnr.state.pa.us/wrcf/contents.htm

This link to the WRCF homepage details the agency's efforts to protect the endangered and threatened species of the Commonwealth. Photographs accompany the descriptions of specific species of birds, mammals, invertebrates, fish, reptiles, amphibians, and plants. This page also provides a link to "Keystone WILD! Notes."

Lehigh Valley Audubon Society
http://www.lehigh.edu/~bcm0/lvas.html

The local Audubon Society page presents birding sites, activities, Christmas counts, and an online newsletter.

10. *Watercourse and Wetland Communities*
U.S. Geological Survey: Water Resources of Pennsylvania
http://pa.water.usgs.gov/

This U.S. Geological Survey site contains preliminary data on current streamflow conditions in the Delaware and other rivers. A search mechanism can be used to link to data for individual counties from survey stations located along the Lehigh River, Little Lehigh Creek (for example, at East Texas), Saucon Creek, Jordan Creek, and so on.

Lehigh Valley Trout Streams
http://www.lvstreams.com

Trout fishing is vital to the economic and personal lives of Lehigh Valley residents. Along with photographs of valley streams, this site provides data for each stream—such as the type of streambed, the water temperature and quality, and the best dates and times for fishing.

Pennsylvania Rivers
http://www.dcnr.state.pa.us/rivers/riverhome.htm

This Pennsylvania Department of Conservation and Natural Resources site includes maps and information on river projects under the Rivers Conservation Program and the Pennsylvania Scenic Rivers Act. The Lehigh River, which originates in Carbon County, is a designated scenic river.

The Hydrogeologist's Home Page
http://www.thehydrogeologist.com/

This site is an extensive collection of hundreds of links to organizations, software and data repositories, publications, and other resources of use to scientists and others interested in the effects of water functions, especially erosion and deposition, on the geology of a region.

11. *Environmental Legislation and the Valley*
Pennsylvania Department of Environmental Protection (DEP)
http://www.dep.state.pa.us

This site amply covers environmental issues of concern that a Pennsylvanian may have. In addition to an alphabetical list of articles covering topics from Abandoned Mine Reclamation to Waste Reduction, this site includes an interactive topographic map and links to timelines of Pennsylvania environmental history. Visitors can also link to county, state, and federal governmental directories, learn how to participate in the legislative process—and more.

12. Envisioning the Environmental Future of the Lehigh Valley
Pennsylvania 21st Century Environment Commission
http://www.21stcentury.state.pa.us
>The Commission's homepage is dedicated to its 1998 final report and its recommendations for the Commonwealth.

Wildlands Conservancy
http://www.wildlandspa.org
>Wildlands Conservancy, founded in 1973, is a nonprofit organization dedicated to preserving precious land, keeping waterways healthy, teaching the community about nature, and caring for injured and orphaned wildlife.

General Environmental Sites

Amazing Environmental Organization WebDirectory!
http://www.webdirectory.com
>Subject categories include agriculture, arts, business, design, health, land conservation, parks and recreation, and sustainable development, among others. Search by keyword or by organization name on "Earth's Biggest Environment Search Engine."

Best Environmental Directories
http://www.ulb.ac.be/ceese/meta/cds.html
>This site provides links to environmental sites that are evaluated by the Center for Economic and Social Studies on the Environment (CESSE) at the Université Libre de Bruxelles. The site is updated bimonthly. Visitors may use the English version of the database or may choose one of several European languages; links to annotated international environmental databases are available.

Center for Environmental Philosophy
http://www.cep.unt.edu
>The University of North Texas hosts the Center for Environmental Philosophy (which publishes the journal *Environmental Ethics*) as well as the International Society for Environmental Philosophy, which maintains the most extensive bibliography on the subject.

Delaware and Lehigh National Heritage Corridor
http://www.nps.gov/dele/

This National Park Service site describes the Heritage Corridor in detail. Its introduction notes that "Settlement patterns, from Native Americans to today's immigrants, continue to change the patterns in the tapestry known as the Delaware and Lehigh National Heritage Corridor." Today, the Corridor is a joint project of federal, state, and local agencies.

Earth Times
http://www.earthtimes.org/index.html
Earth Times is an online newspaper reporting on artistic, cultural, environmental, and political issues worldwide, with a special emphasis on global environmental concerns.

ECOMALL
http://www.ecomall.com
This site is a clearinghouse for environmental and educational businesses, advocacy groups, and other organizations. Take an online tour of natural history museums and botanic gardens; locate environmentally friendly businesses along the way; find a listing of vegetarian restaurants. This source also provides information about investment opportunities in "socially responsible" companies.

EcoNet
http://www.igc.org/igc/econet
This site is part of the Institute for Global Communication, a nonprofit organization designed to assist activists in using global communications and the Internet to further their goals. It includes abstracts and the full texts of selected ecological articles as well as links to other information sources and related sites.

EnviroLink Network
http://www.envirolink.org
This award-winning site boasts that it is one of the largest environmental websites. Animal Concerns and the Sustainable Business Network are two of the many regular features on this page.

Environmental Protection Agency (EPA)
http://www.epa.gov
This extensive site offers a wide range of services for users; for example, it provides maps of air quality, details air pollution by specific particulates, discusses a variety of EPA programs, and offers an overview

of land use. The full text of federal environmental regulations and of environmental legislation (existing and under consideration) is available as well. Visitors can link to other sources of information and find out details about the environmental state of their own communities.

Greenpeace International
http://www.greenpeace.org
Greenpeace was founded in 1971. Its mission is to use "non-violent, creative confrontation to expose global environmental problems, and to force solutions that are essential to a green and peaceful future."

Lehigh Earth Observatory (LEO)
http://www.leo.lehigh.edu/
Developed by Lehigh University (Bethlehem), this site is dedicated to active observation of earth and environmental systems. It includes Lehigh programs, active and ongoing research projects, faculty contacts, and the like.

Sierra Club
http://www.sierraclub.org
The Sierra Club boasts a membership of over 600,000. It focuses on conservation and environmental protection; its homepage links to other organizations and related sites. Listservs help environmentally conscious citizens track and influence key legislation. And the Sierra Club's online newsletter, "The Planet," offers valuable tips on planning and organizing effective grassroots campaigns.

U.S. Department of the Interior
http://www.doi.gov/
The site contains a fully searchable index of Interior news releases, the DOI newsletter ("People, Land, and Water"), and information on the Interior Museum. Not just one site, it provides direct links to the informative web pages of bureaus within the Department of the Interior, such as the Bureau of Reclamation and the U.S. Fish and Wildlife Service (which offers, for example, an endangered species list), and to individual offices within the DOI.

U.S. Geological Survey: Water Resources of the United States
http://water.usgs.gov/
The site includes data and contact information on surface water and groundwater, water quality, water use, and acid rain, as well as descriptions

of programs such as the Toxic Substances Hydrology (Toxics) Program and the National Water Quality Assessment Program. The Water Resources site connects to state water websites (with local offices) and provides general information and preliminary data on current stream-flow conditions in the state's rivers and creeks.

Bibliography

PREFACE AND ACKNOWLEDGMENTS

Cuff, D. J., W. J. Young, E. K. Muller, W. Zelinsky, and R. F. Abler, eds. 1989. *The atlas of Pennsylvania*. Philadelphia: Temple University Press.

Hill, R. J., and D. Folland. 1986. *Poisonous plants of Pennsylvania*. Harrisburg: Pennsylvania Department of Agriculture and Plant Industry.

Lehigh Valley Convention and Visitors Bureau (LVCVB). 1998. *Visitor guide and map: Lehigh Valley*. Lehigh Valley, Pa.: Lehigh Valley Convention and Visitors Bureau.

Martin, J. P. 1992. Lehigh Valley: Where is it? *Allentown (Pa.) Morning Call*, 19 July.

Oplinger, C. S., and R. Halma. 1988. *The Poconos: An illustrated natural history guide*. New Brunswick: Rutgers University Press.

Zegers, D. A., ed. 1994. *At the crossroads: A natural history of southcentral Pennsylvania*. Proceedings of the conference at Millersville University, November 6, 1993. Millersville, Pa.: Millersville University.

CHAPTER 1

Kendeigh, S. C. 1954. History and evaluation of various concepts of plant and animal communities in North America. *Ecology* 35:152–71.

Merriam, C. H., V. Bailey, E. W. Nelson, and E. A. Preble. 1910. *Zone map of North America*. Washington, D.C.: Biology Survey, U.S. Department of Agriculture.

Miller, B. L. 1939. *Northampton County, Pennsylvania: Geology and geography*. Harrisburg: Commonwealth of Pennsylvania, Bureau of Topographic and Geologic Survey.

———. 1941. *Lehigh County, Pennsylvania: Geology and geography*. Harrisburg: Commonwealth of Pennsylvania, Bureau of Topographic and Geologic Survey.

Miller, E. W., ed. 1994. *A geography of Pennsylvania*. University Park: The Pennsylvania State University Press.

Myers, R. E. 1972. *Lehigh Valley the unsuspected*. Easton, Pa.: Northampton County Historical and Genealogical Society.

Roberts, H. A., and R. C. Early. 1952. *Mammal survey of southeastern Pennsylvania*. Harrisburg: Pennsylvania Game Commission.

Smith, R. L. 1996. *Ecology and field biology*. 5th ed. New York: Harper Collins College Publishers.

CHAPTER 2

Barnes, J. H., and W. D. Sevon. 1996. *The geological story of Pennsylvania*. Educational Series, no. 4. Harrisburg: Commonwealth of Pennsylvania, Bureau of Topographic and Geologic Survey.

Bennison, A. P. n.d. *Geological map: Northeastern region*. Tulsa, Okla.: American Association of Petroleum Geologists.

Berkheiser, S. W. 1984. Summary of the slate industry in Pennsylvania, 1983. *Pennsylvania Geology* 15, no. 1:10–13.

Berlin, A. 1922. The Bake Oven Knob. *Proceedings of the Lehigh County Historical Society* 6:44–48.

Crowl, G. H., and W. D. Sevon. 1980. *Glacial border deposits of late Wisconsinan age in northeastern Pennsylvania*. General Geology Report, no. 71. Harrisburg: Commonwealth of Pennsylvania, Bureau of Topographic and Geologic Survey.

Geyer, A. R., R. C. Smith, and J. H. Barnes. 1976. *Mineral collecting in Pennsylvania*. General Geology Report, no. 33. Harrisburg: Commonwealth of Pennsylvania, Bureau of Topographic and Geologic Survey.

Geyer, A. R., and W. H. Bolles. 1979. *Outstanding scenic geological features of Pennsylvania*. Environmental Geology Report, no. 7, part 1. Harrisburg: Commonwealth of Pennsylvania, Bureau of Topographic and Geologic Survey.

———. 1987. *Outstanding scenic geological features of Pennsylvania*. Environmental Geology Report, no. 7, part 2. Harrisburg: Commonwealth of Pennsylvania, Bureau of Topographic and Geologic Survey.

Higbee, H. W. [1962.] *Land resource map of Pennsylvania*. University Park: The Pennsylvania State University.

Hoskins, D. M. [1962.] *Common fossils of Pennsylvania.* Educational Series, no. 2. Harrisburg: Commonwealth of Pennsylvania, Bureau of Topographic and Geologic Survey.

Hoskins, D. M., J. D. Inners, and J. A. Harper. 1984. *Fossil collecting in Pennsylvania.* General Geology Report, no. 40. Harrisburg: Commonwealth of Pennsylvania, Bureau of Topographic and Geologic Survey.

Kochanov, W. E. 1987. *Sinkholes and karst related features of Lehigh County, Pennsylvania.* Harrisburg: Pennsylvania Geological Survey.

Levin, H. L. 1999. *The earth through time.* 6th ed. Fort Worth, Tex.: Saunders College Publishing.

McPhee, J. 1983. *In suspect terrain.* New York: Farrar Straus Giroux.

Miller, B. L. 1939. *Northampton County, Pennsylvania: Geology and geography.* Harrisburg: Commonwealth of Pennsylvania, Bureau of Topographic and Geologic Survey.

———. 1941. *Lehigh County, Pennsylvania: Geology and geography.* Harrisburg: Commonwealth of Pennsylvania, Bureau of Topographic and Geologic Survey.

Myers, P. B., and M. Perlow. 1984. Development, occurrence, and triggering mechanisms of sinkholes in the carbonate rocks of the Lehigh Valley. In *Sinkholes: Their geology, engineering, and environmental impact,* edited by B. F. Beck. Boston: Balkema.

Myers, R. E. 1972. *Lehigh Valley the unsuspected.* Easton, Pa.: Northampton County Historical and Genealogical Society.

Parsons, J. 1993. *The Lehigh Water Gap: A documentary history.* Palmerton, Pa.: Lehigh Gap Historical Society.

Potter, N., and J. H. Moss. 1968. Origin of the Blue Rocks block field and adjacent deposits, Berks County, Pennsylvania. *Geological Society of America Bulletin* 79, no. 2:255–62.

Scharnberger, C. K. 1989. *Earthquake hazard in Pennsylvania.* Educational Series, no. 10. Harrisburg: Commonwealth of Pennsylvania, Bureau of Topographic and Geologic Survey.

Schilling, P. 1979. Sinkhole nearly swallows S. Whitehall dump truck. *Allentown (Pa.) Morning Call,* 21 July.

Schultz, C. H., ed. 1999. *The geology of Pennsylvania.* Special Publication, no. 1. Harrisburg: Pennsylvania Geological Survey; Pittsburgh: Pittsburgh Geological Society.

VanDiver, B. 1990. *Roadside geology of Pennsylvania.* Missoula, Mont.: Mountain Press.

Willard, B. 1962. *Pennsylvania geology summarized.* Educational Series, no. 4. Harrisburg: Commonwealth of Pennsylvania, Bureau of Topographic and Geologic Survey.

Wilshusen, J. P. 1983. *Geology of the Appalachian Trail in Pennsylvania.* General Geology Report, no. 74. Harrisburg: Commonwealth of Pennsylvania, Department of Internal Affairs, Bureau of Topographic and Geologic Survey.
————. 1993. Coplay's Cement Kilns. *Pennsylvania Magazine* 16, no. 2:12–14.

CHAPTER 3

Anthony, D. W., and D. G. Roberts. 1990. Recent archaeological discoveries in the Lehigh hills of eastern Pennsylvania. *Proceedings of the Lehigh County Historical Society* 39:296–311.
Colley, D. P. 1976. *A military history.* Vol. 10 of *Two hundred years of life in Northampton County, Pennsylvania,* edited by J. N. Schlegel. Easton, Pa.: Northampton County Bicentennial Commission.
Custer, J. F. 1996. *Prehistoric cultures of eastern Pennsylvania.* Harrisburg: Pennsylvania Historical and Museum Commission.
Glatfelter, C. H. 1990. *The Pennsylvania Germans: A brief account of their influence on Pennsylvania.* Pennsylvania History Studies, no. 20. University Park: The Pennsylvania Historical Association.
Hall, K. L. K., and P. D. Hall. 1982. *The Lehigh Valley: An illustrated history.* Woodland Hills, Calif.: Windsor Publications.
Hobhouse, H. 1989. *Forces of change: Why we are the way we are now.* London: Sidgwick & Jackson.
Hylton, T. 1995. *Save our land, save our towns: A plan for Pennsylvania.* Harrisburg: RB Books.
Illick, J. E. 1976. *Colonial Pennsylvania: A history.* New York: Charles Scribner's Sons.
Joint Planning Commission, Lehigh-Northampton Counties. 1993. *Comprehensive plan for Lehigh and Northampton Counties, Pennsylvania: The Lehigh Valley . . . 2010.* Allentown, Pa.: Joint Planning Commission, Lehigh-Northampton Counties.
Kent, B. C. 1994. *Discovering Pennsylvania's archeological heritage.* Rev. ed. Harrisburg: Pennsylvania Historical and Museum Commission.
Kinsey, W. F., III. 1983. Eastern Pennsylvania prehistory: A review. *Pennsylvania History* 50, no. 2:69–108.
Kraft, H. C. 1986. *The Lenape: Archaeology, history, and ethnography.* Collections of the New Jersey Historical Society, vol. 21. Newark, N.J.: New Jersey Historical Society.
Larson, P. 1987. *Early Bethlehem and the Native Americans.* Bethlehem, Pa.: Oaks Printing.

Lehigh Valley Planning Commission. 1999. *Lehigh Valley profile and trends.* Allentown, Pa.: Lehigh Valley Planning Commission.

Lemon, J. T. 1972. *The best poor man's country: A geographical study of early southeastern Pennsylvania.* Baltimore: Johns Hopkins University Press.

Martin, P. S. 1984. Prehistoric overkill: The global model. In *Quaternary extinctions: A prehistoric revolution,* edited by P. S. Martin and R. G. Klein. Tucson: University of Arizona Press.

Matthews, R. E. 1989. *Lehigh County Pennsylvania in the Civil War: An account.* Lehighton, Pa.: The Times News Printing.

Metz, L. E. 1988. *Cap't Sherman's guide to Hugh Moore Park.* Easton, Pa.: Center for Canal History and Technology, Hugh Moore Historical Park & Museum, Inc.

Morgan, T. 1993. *Wilderness at dawn: The settling of the North American continent.* New York: Simon and Schuster.

Myers, R. E. 1976. Northampton County in the American Revolution. *Publications of the Northampton County Historical and Genealogical Society,* vol. 6. Easton, Pa.: Northampton County Historical Society.

Olmstead, E. P. 1997. *David Zeisberger: A life among the Indians.* Kent: Kent State University Press.

Schmidt, L. G. 1990. The 47th regiment of Pennsylvania veteran volunteers in the Red River Campaign of 1864. *Proceedings of the Lehigh County Historical Society* 39:156–86.

Secor, R., ed. 1976. *Pennsylvania 1776.* University Park: The Pennsylvania State University Press.

Waddell, L. M., and B. D. Bomberger. 1996. *The French and Indian War in Pennsylvania 1753–1763.* Harrisburg: Pennsylvania Historical and Museum Commission.

Wallace, P. A. W. 1993. *Indians in Pennsylvania.* 2d ed. Harrisburg: Pennsylvania Historical and Museum Commission.

Weaver, R. A. 1990. Why did President Adams pardon John Fries? *Proceedings of the Lehigh County Historical Society* 39:227–63.

Weslager, C. A. 1972. *The Delaware Indians: A history.* New Brunswick: Rutgers University Press.

Yates, W. R. 1963. *History of the Lehigh Valley region.* Allentown, Pa.: Joint Planning Commission, Lehigh-Northampton Counties.

CHAPTER 4

Ahrens, C. D. 1991. *Meteorology today: An introduction to weather, climate, and the environment.* 4th ed. St. Paul: West Publishing.

Alu, M. E., and others. 1996. Blizzard of '96 special report. *Allentown (Pa.) Morning Call*, January.

Dovico, W. W. 1985. Classification and prediction of snowstorm severity. *National Weather Digest* 10, no. 2:31–38.

Forbes, G. S., and E. Ostuno. 1998. El Niño impacts on weather. *Pennsylvania Academy of Science Newsletter* 56, no. 1:4–5.

Gelber, B. 1992. *Pocono weather.* Stroudsburg, Pa.: Uriel Publishing.

Glantz, M. H. 1996. *Currents of change: El Niño's impact on climate and society.* New York: Cambridge University Press.

Majumdar, S. K., L. S. Kalkstein, B. M. Yarnal, E. W. Miller, and L. M. Rosenfeld, eds. 1992. *Global climate change: Implications, challenges, and mitigation measures.* Easton, Pa.: Pennsylvania Academy of Science.

Nese, J. M., and G. S. Forbes. 1998. An updated tornado climatology of Pennsylvania: Methodology and uncertainties. *Journal of the Pennsylvania Academy of Science* 71, no. 3:113–24.

U.S. Department of Commerce, National Oceanic and Atmospheric Administration. 1991. *Local climatological data: Annual summary with comparative data.* Asheville, N.C.: National Climatic Data Center.

CHAPTER 5

American Lung Association. n.d. *Sneezeless landscaping* (pamphlet). San Francisco: American Lung Association.

Braun, M. 1948. *Hawks aloft: The story of Hawk Mountain.* Kutztown, Pa.: Kutztown Publishing.

Brett, J. 1986. *The mountain and the migration: A guide to Hawk Mountain.* Kutztown, Pa.: Kutztown Publishing.

Brown, L. 1976. *Weeds in winter.* New York: W. W. Norton.

Chase's calendar of annual events. 1997. Chicago: Contemporary Books.

Germanetti, J., ed. 1997. *Valley guide.* Allentown, Pa.: The Morning Call.

Harris, M. C., and N. Shure. 1969. *All about allergy.* Englewood Cliffs, N.J.: Prentice-Hall.

Hatch, J. M., ed. 1978. *The American book of days.* 3d ed. New York: H. W. Wilson.

Heintzelman, D. S. 1975. *Autumn hawk flights: The migration in eastern North America.* New Brunswick: Rutgers University Press.

Kieran, J. 1959. *A natural history of New York City: A personal report after fifty years of study and enjoyment of wildlife within the boundaries of greater New York.* Boston: Houghton Mifflin.

Lehigh Valley Convention and Visitors Bureau (LVCVB). 1998. *Visitor guide and map: Lehigh Valley.* Lehigh Valley, Pa.: Lehigh Valley Convention and Visitors Bureau.

Levine, C. 1995. *A guide to wildflowers in winter: Herbaceous plants of northeastern North America.* New Haven: Yale University Press.

Morris, B. L., R. E. Wiltraut, and F. H. Brock. 1984. *Birds of the Lehigh Valley area.* Emmaus, Pa.: Lehigh Valley Audubon Society.

Smith, A. 1970. *The seasons: Life and its rhythms.* New York: Harcourt, Brace, Jovanovich.

Smith, N. 1990. *Gone for the day.* Harrisburg: Pennsylvania Game Commission.

Swain, R. B. 1957. *The insect guide: Orders and major families of North American insects.* Garden City, N.Y.: Doubleday.

Teale, E. W. 1951. *North with the spring: A naturalist's record of a 17,000 mile journey with the North American spring.* New York: Dodd and Mead.

Weidensaul, S. 1992. *Seasonal guide to the natural year: A month-by-month guide to natural events: Mid-Atlantic.* Golden, Colo.: Fulcrum Publishing.

Wood, M. 1967. *Birds of Pennsylvania.* University Park: Agricultural Experiment Station, The Pennsylvania State University.

Zegers, D. A., ed. 1994. *At the crossroads: A natural history of southcentral Pennsylvania.* Proceedings of the conference at Millersville University, November 6, 1993. Millersville, Pa.: Millersville University.

CHAPTER 6

Abrams, M. D. 1992. Fire and the development of oak forests. *BioScience* 42:346–53.

Bailey, R. G. 1980. *Description of the ecoregions of the United States.* Ogden, Utah: USDA Forest Service.

Barbour, M. G., and W. D. Billings, eds. 1988. *North American vegetation.* New York: Cambridge University Press.

Bartholomew-Began, S. 1993. The bryoflora of Hawk Mountain Sanctuary, Kempton, Pennsylvania. *Journal of the Pennsylvania Academy of Science* 67, no. 2:55–58.

Bedient, D., and J. Gaylor. 1977. A preliminary study of the woody vegetation on the Walter tract. Thesis, Cedar Crest College.

Betts, T. 1992. Dog days for the dogwood. *Pennsylvania Game News* 63, no. 5:28–31.

Botkin, D. B. 1990. *Discordant harmonies: A new ecology for the twenty-first century.* New York: Oxford University Press.

Braun, E. L. 1972. Reprint. *Deciduous forests of eastern North America.* New York: Hafner Publishing. Original edition, Philadelphia: Blakiston, 1950.

Collins, B. R., and K. H. Anderson. 1994. *Plant communities of New Jersey: A study in landscape diversity.* New Brunswick: Rutgers University Press.

Darwin, C. 1939. *Journal of researches into the geology, and natural history of the various countries visited by H.M.S. Beagle, under the command of Captain Fitzroy, R.N., from 1832–1836.* London: Henry Colburn.

Dzemyan, J. P. 1994. Where have all the flowers gone? *Pennsylvania Game News* 65, no. 5:15–17.

Eyre, F. H., ed. 1980. *Forest cover types of the United States and Canada.* Washington, D.C.: Society of American Foresters.

Fernald, M. L. 1950. *Gray's manual of botany.* 8th ed. New York: American Book.

Gallo, G., K. Pearl, W. Heffner, and J. R. Halma. 1996. Analysis of the woody vegetation and avifauna of the Reimert Bird Haven. *Journal of the Pennsylvania Academy of Science* 70, no. 1:9–14.

Genoways, H. H., and F. J. Brenner, eds. 1985. *Species of special concern in Pennsylvania.* Pittsburgh: Carnegie Museum of Natural History.

Greller, A. M. 1988. Deciduous forest. In *North American terrestrial vegetation,* edited by M. G. Barbour and W. D. Billings. New York: Cambridge University Press.

Halma, J. R., B. Linck, and D. Branch. 1974. A botanical analysis of Greenwich Township, Berks County, Pennsylvania. In *Greenwich Township environmental analysis: A field study 1972–1973,* edited by J. W. Bahorik. Kutztown, Pa.: Kutztown University.

Harrison, R. P. 1992. *Forests: The shadow of civilization.* Chicago: The University of Chicago Press.

Hunter, M. L. 1990. *Wildlife, forests, and forestry: Principles of managing forests for biological diversity.* Englewood Cliffs, N.J.: Prentice-Hall.

Illick, J. S. 1923. *Pennsylvania trees.* 4th ed. Harrisburg: Pennsylvania Department of Forestry.

Keever, C. 1973. Distribution of major forest species in southeastern Pennsylvania. *Ecological Monographs* 43:303–27.

McCormick, J. F., and R. B. Platt. 1980. Recovery of an Appalachian forest following the chestnut blight, or Catherine Keever—you were right! *American Midland Naturalist* 104:264–73.

Monk, C. D., D. W. Imm, R. L. Potter, and G. G. Parker. 1989. A classification system of the deciduous forest of eastern North America. *Vegetatio* 80:167–81.

Niering, W. A. 1953. The past and present vegetation of High Point State Park, New Jersey. *Ecological Monographs* 23:127–48.

Oplinger, C. S. 1977. Environmental analysis of South Mountain park lands. Allentown (Pa.) Urban Observatory. Duplicated.

Orwig, D. A., and M. D. Abrams. 1993. Temperate deciduous forests of the eastern United States. In *Conservation and resource management,* edited by S. K. Majumdar, E. W. Miller, D. E. Baker, E. K. Brown, J. R. Pratt, and R. F. Schmalz. Easton, Pa.: Pennsylvania Academy of Science.

Ostrander, S. J. 1996. *Great natural areas in eastern Pennsylvania.* Mechanicsburg, Pa.: Stackpole Books.

Pretz, H. 1911. Flora of Lehigh County, Pennsylvania. Part 1. *Bulletin of the Torrey Botanical Club* 38, no. 2:45–78.

Pritchard, H. N., and P. T. Bradt. 1984. *Biology of nonvascular plants.* St. Louis: C. V. Mosby.

Pyne, S. J. 1983. Indian fires. *Natural History* 92:6–11.

Rhoads, A. F., and T. A. Block. 2000. *The plants of Pennsylvania: An illustrated manual.* Philadelphia: University of Pennsylvania Press.

Rhoads, A. F., and W. M. Klein, Jr. 1993. *The vascular flora of Pennsylvania: Annotated checklist and atlas.* Memoirs of the American Philosophical Society, vol. 207. Philadelphia: American Philosophical Society.

Russel, E. W. B. 1981. Vegetation of northern New Jersey before European settlement. *American Midland Naturalist* 105:1–12.

Schaeffer, R. L. 1949. *The vascular flora of Northampton County, Pennsylvania.* Ph.D. diss., University of Pennsylvania.

Stephanson, S. L. 1986. Changes in a former chestnut-dominated forest after a half century of succession. *American Midland Naturalist* 116:173–79.

VanKat, J. L. 1990. A classification of the forest types of North America. *Vegetatio* 88:53–66.

Wherry, E. T., J. M. Fogg, and H. A. Wahl. 1979. *Atlas of the flora of Pennsylvania.* Philadelphia: Morris Arboretum of the University of Pennsylvania.

Williams, C. E. 1994. Forests in decline? *Pennsylvania Wildlife* 15, no. 6:15–18.

Yahner, R. H. 1995. *Eastern deciduous forest: Ecology and wildlife conservation.* Minneapolis: University of Minnesota Press.

CHAPTER 7

American Lung Association. n.d. *Sneezeless landscaping* (pamphlet). San Francisco: American Lung Association.

Bormann, F. H., D. Balmori, and G. T. Geballe. 1993. *Redesigning the American lawn: A search for environmental harmony.* New Haven: Yale University Press.

Dorfman, A., and J. Leviton. 1991. Can lawns be justified? *Time* 137, no. 22:63–64.

Duke, J. A. 1992. *Handbook of edible weeds.* Boca Raton, Fla.: CRC Press.

Einsig, B. 1993. Noxious weeds. *Pennsylvania Game News* 64:42–43.

Flint, M. L. 1990. *Pests of the garden and small farm: A grower's guide to using less pesticide.* Oakland, Calif.: Statewide Integrated Pest Management Project, University of California, Division of Agriculture and Natural Resources.

Hartman, H. T., A. M. Kofranek, V. E. Rubatzky, and W. J. Flocker. 1988. *Plant science: Growth, development, and utilization of cultivated plants.* Englewood Cliffs, N.J.: Prentice-Hall.

Jesiolowski, J. 1992. How to handle America's ten least wanted weeds. *Organic Gardening* 39, no. 6:48–53.

Lehigh University Alumni Association. 1990. Robert Rodale '52, 1930–1990 (obituary). *Lehigh University Alumni Bulletin* 77, no. 2: 80.

Lehigh Valley Convention and Visitors Bureau (LVCVB). n.d. *Lehigh Valley wine trail* (pamphlet). Lehigh Valley, Pa.: Lehigh Valley Convention and Visitors Bureau.

Martin, A. C. 1972. *Weeds.* New York: Golden Press.

Medve, R. J. 1990. *Edible wild plants of Pennsylvania and neighboring states.* University Park: The Pennsylvania State University Press.

Miller, E. W. 1991. Spatial evolution of Pennsylvania agriculture. *Journal of the Pennsylvania Academy of Science* 65, no. 2:102–4.

Moll, G., and S. Ebenreck, eds. 1989. *Shading our cities: A resource guide for urban and community forests.* Washington, D.C.: Island Press.

Nuss, J. R. 1995. A guide for selecting shade and flowering trees for Pennsylvania landscapes. University Park: The Pennsylvania State University.

Pennsylvania Department of Agriculture. 1995–1996. *Statistical summary and Pennsylvania Department of Agriculture annual report.* Harrisburg: Pennsylvania Department of Agriculture.

Phillips, L. E. 1993. *Urban trees: A guide for selection, maintenance, and master planning.* New York: McGraw-Hill.

Pimental, D., et. al. 1992. Conserving biological diversity in agricultural/ forestry systems. *BioScience* 42, no. 5:354–62.

Randall, J. M., and J. Marinelli, eds. 1996. *Invasive plants: Weeds of the global garden.* New York: Brooklyn Botanical Garden.

Schery, R. W. 1972. *Plants for man.* 2d ed. Englewood Cliffs, N.J.: Prentice-Hall.

Wasowski, S. 1992. *Requiem for a lawnmower.* Dallas: Taylor Publishing.

Williams, C. E. 1993. Alien invasion. *Pennsylvania Wildlife* 14, no. 5:16–19.

Williams, M. 1989. *Americans and their forests: A historical geography.* New York: Cambridge University Press.

Zimdahl, R. L. 1993. *Weeds and words: The etymology of the scientific names of weeds and crops.* Ames: Iowa State University Press.

CHAPTER 8

Bonta, M. 1992. The urban falcon. *Pennsylvania Wildlife* 13, no. 1:24–27.

Greller, A. M. 1988. Deciduous forest. In *North American terrestrial vegetation,* edited by M. G. Barbour and W. D. Billings. New York: Cambridge University Press.

Harris, L. D. 1984. *The fragmented forest: Island biogeography theory and the preservation of biotic diversity.* Chicago: The University of Chicago Press.

Herkert, J. R., and others. 1993. *Habitat establishment, enhancement, and management for forest and grassland birds in Illinois.* Natural Heritage Technical Publication, no. 1. Springfield, Ill.: Division of Natural Heritage, Illinois Department of Conservation.

Hoover, J. P., M. C. Brittingham, and L. J. Goodrich. 1995. Effects of forest patch size on nesting success of wood thrushes. *The Auk* 112, no. 1:146–55.

Jesiolowski, J. 1992. How to handle America's ten least wanted weeds. *Organic Gardening* 39, no. 6:48–53.

Joint Planning Commission, Lehigh-Northampton Counties. 1993. *Twenty years of land use change in the Lehigh Valley.* Allentown, Pa.: Joint Planning Commission.

Luken, J. O., and J. W. Thieret. 1996. Amur honeysuckle: Its fall from grace. *BioScience* 46, no. 1:18–24.

MacArthur, R. H., and E. O. Wilson. 1967. *The theory of island biogeography.* Princeton: Princeton University Press.

Niemela, P., and W. J. Mattson. 1996. Invasion of North American forests by European phytophagous insects: Legacy of the European crucible? *BioScience* 46, no. 10:741–53.

Robbins, C. S., D. K. Dawson, and B. A. Dowell. 1989. Habitat area requirements of breeding forest birds of the middle Atlantic states. *Wildlife Monographs* 103:1–34.

Robinson, S. K. 1996. Nest gains, nest losses. *Natural History* 105, no. 7:40–47.

———. 1997. The case of the missing songbirds. *Consequences* 3, no. 1:3–15.

Russell, E. W. B. 1983. Indian-set fires in the forests of the northeastern United States. *Ecology* 64, no. 1:78–88.

Rutowski, R. L. 1998. Mating strategies in butterflies. *Scientific American* 279, no. 1:64–69.

Shalaway, S. 1996. Kestrels and meadow voles. *Pennsylvania Wildlife* 17, no. 2:10–11.

Stevens, W. K. 1994. Opportunistic species gain in battle for the backyard. *New York Times,* 1 March.

———. 1997. Something to sing about: Songbirds aren't in decline. *New York Times,* 10 June.

Whitcomb, R. F., and others. 1981. Effects of forest fragmentation on avifauna of the eastern deciduous forest. In *Forest island dynamics in man-dominated landscapes,* edited by R. L. Burgess and D. M. Sharpe. New York: Springer-Verlag.

Wilcove, D. S. 1985. Nest predation in forest tracts and the decline of migratory songbirds. *Ecology* 66, no. 4:1211–14.

Williams, D. G. 1950. Settlement of the Lower Jordan valley. *Proceedings of the Lehigh County Historical Society* 18:53–88.

Worster, D. 1985. *Nature's economy: A history of ecological ideas.* Cambridge: Cambridge University Press.

Yahner, R. H. 1988. Changes in wildlife communities near edges. *Conservation Biology* 2, no. 4:333–39.

CHAPTER 9

Beatty, G. H. 1975. Flora and fauna. In *Pennsylvania 1776,* edited by R. Secor. University Park: The Pennsylvania State University Press.

Brauning, D. W., ed. 1992. *Atlas of breeding birds in Pennsylvania.* Pittsburgh: University of Pittsburgh Press.

Doutt, J. K., C. A. Heppenstall, and J. E. Guilday. 1977. *Mammals of Pennsylvania.* 4th ed. Harrisburg: Pennsylvania Game Commission.

Fergus, C. 2000. *Wildlife of Pennsylvania.* Harrisburg: Stackpole Books.

Frye, B. 1997. On the trail of a Penn's Woods ghost. *Pennsylvania Wildlife* 18, no. 1:17–21.

———. 1997. Pennsylvania's coyote comeback. *Pennsylvania Wildlife* 18, no. 6:17–21.

Hayden, A. H. 1989. The eastern coyote revisited. *Pennsylvania Game News* 60, no. 12:12–15.

Hubbell, S. 1993. *Broadsides from the other orders: A book of bugs.* New York: Random House.

Kosack, J. 1995. *The Pennsylvania Game Commission, 1895–1995: One hundred years of wildlife conservation.* Harrisburg: Pennsylvania Game Commission.

Morris, B. L., R. E. Wiltraut, and F. H. Brock. 1984. *Birds of the Lehigh Valley area.* Emmaus, Pa.: Lehigh Valley Audubon Society.

Roberts, H. A., and R. C. Early. 1952. *Mammal survey of southeastern Pennsylvania.* Harrisburg: Pennsylvania Game Commission.

Smith, N. 1971. *Gone for the day.* Harrisburg: Pennsylvania Game Commission.

Uhrich, W. D., ed. 1997. *A century of bird life in Berks County, Pennsylvania.* Reading, Pa.: Reading Public Museum.

CHAPTER 10

Allen, J. D., and A. S. Flecker. 1993. Biodiversity conservation in running waters. *BioScience* 43, no. 1:32–43.

Bayley, P. B. 1995. Understanding large river-floodplain ecosystems. *BioScience* 45, no. 3:153–58.

Caduto, M. J. 1990. *Pond and brook: A guide to nature in freshwater environments.* Hanover: University Press of New England.

Cooper, E. L. 1983. *Fishes of Pennsylvania and the northeastern United States.* University Park: The Pennsylvania State University Press.

Gilbert, B. 1993. The reptile that stakes its survival on snap decisions. *Smithsonian* 24, no. 1:93–101.

Gregory, S. V., and others. 1991. An ecosystem perspective of riparian zones. *BioScience* 41, no. 8:540–51.

Lipske, M. 1989. Living legacies. *National Wildlife* 27, no. 4:14–16.

Majumdar, S. K., and others, eds. 1989. *Wetlands ecology and conservation: Emphasis in Pennsylvania.* Easton, Pa.: Pennsylvania Academy of Science.

Malecki, R. A., and others. 1993. Biological control of purple loosestrife. *BioScience* 43, no. 10:680–86.

Nature Conservancy. 1999. *A natural areas inventory of Lehigh and Northampton Counties, Pennsylvania.* Allentown, Pa.: Lehigh Valley Planning Commission.

Oplinger, C. S. 1997. Harbinger of spring. *The World & I,* March:164–69.

Pennak, R. W. 1989. *Fresh-water invertebrates of the United States: Protozoa to mollusca.* New York: John Wiley & Sons.

Pollison, D. P., and W. M. Craighead. 1968. *Lehigh River biological investigation.* N.p.: Delaware River Basin Commission, Pennsylvania State Department of Health and the Pennsylvania Fish Commission.

Shaffer, L. L. 1991. *Pennsylvania amphibians & reptiles.* Harrisburg: Pennsylvania Fish and Boat Commission.

Tiner, R. W., Jr. 1987. *Mid-Atlantic wetlands: A disappearing natural treasure.* Newton Corner, Mass.: U.S. Fish and Wildlife Service.

Vance, J. M. 1985. The tortoise and the pair. *Audubon* 87, no. 4:64–69.

Verrell, P. 1982. The sexual behavior of the red-spotted newt, *Notophthalmus viridescens* (Amphibia: Urodela: Salamandridae). *Animal Behaviour* 30:1224–36.

CHAPTER 11

Carson, R. *Silent spring.* Boston: Houghton Mifflin.

Commoner, B. 1971. *The closing circle: Nature, man, and technology.* New York: Alfred A. Knopf.

Ehrlich, P. 1968. *The population bomb.* New York: Ballantine Books.

Gibbons, B. 1981. Aldo Leopold: A durable scale of values. *National Geographic* 160, no. 5:682–708.

Gore, A. 1992. *Earth in the balance: Ecology and the human spirit.* Boston: Houghton Mifflin.

Kline, B. 1997. *First along the river: A brief history of the U. S. environmental movement.* San Francisco: Acada Books.

Leopold, A. 1949. *A Sand County almanac.* Oxford: Oxford University Press.

Sale, K. 1993. *The green revolution: The American environmental movement, 1962–1992.* New York: Hill and Wang.

Taremae, O., and A. R. O'Dell. 1984. Local government responses to solid waste management needs in the Lehigh Valley: A case study. In *Solid and liquid wastes: Management, methods, and socioeconomic considerations,* edited by S. K. Majumdar and E. W. Miller. Easton, Pa.: Pennsylvania Academy of Science.

U.S. Department of the Interior. *America 200: The legacy of our lands.* Conservation Yearbook, no. 11. Special Bicentennial Edition. Washington, D.C.: U.S. Department of the Interior.

White, L., Jr. 1967. The historical roots of our ecological crisis. *Science* 155:1203–7.

CHAPTER 12

Frassinelli, Mike. 1995. Historian says corridor will "leave a big footprint." *Allentown (Pa.) Morning Call,* 9 March.

Hardin, G. 1969. The tragedy of the commons. *Science* 162:1243–48.

Joint Planning Commission, Lehigh-Northampton Counties. 1993. *Comprehensive plan for Lehigh and Northampton Counties, Pennsylvania: The Lehigh Valley . . . 2010.* Allentown, Pa: Joint Planning Commission, Lehigh-Northampton Counties.

Lehigh Valley Planning Commission. 1997. *Lehigh Valley profile and trends.* Allentown, Pa.: Lehigh Valley Planning Commission.

Leopold, A. 1949. *A Sand County almanac.* Oxford: Oxford University Press.

Pennsylvania 21st Century Environment Commission. 1998. *Report of the Pennsylvania Twenty-first Century Environment Commission.* Harrisburg: n.p.

Rivinus, W. M. 1994. *The complete guide to the Delaware and Lehigh National Heritage Corridor.* Bethlehem, Pa.: Lehigh River Foundation.

Index

Scientific names are excluded from the index, but may be found easily in Appendix A. To prevent the index from becoming encyclopedic, specific plants, animals, rocks, and the like are not indexed unless they have received some textual description. Page numbers in italic type refer to illustrations.